The Nation at Sea

The Nation at Sea tells a new story about the federal judiciary, and about the early United States itself. Most accounts of the nation's transformation from infant republic to world power ignore the courts. Their importance, if any, was limited to domestic politics. But the truth is that, in the critical decades following the Constitution's ratification, federal judges decided thousands of maritime cases that profoundly shaped the United States' relations with foreign nations. Judges ruled on the legality of naval captures made by European powers, regulated the conduct of American merchants, and tried pirates and slave traders who sought profit amid the turmoil of transatlantic war. Kevin Arlyck's vivid reconstruction of this forgotten history reveals how, over time, the federal courts helped realize an increasingly bold conception of American sovereignty, one that vindicated the Declaration of Independence's claim to the United States' place "among the powers of the earth."

Kevin Arlyck is Professor of Law at Georgetown University. He is an expert on the history of the federal courts and the early federal government.

See the Studies in Legal History series website at http://studiesinlegalhistory.org/

Studies in Legal History

Other books in the series:

Alastair McClure, *Trials of Sovereignty: Mercy, Violence, and the Making of Criminal Law in British India, 1857–1922*
James Q. Whitman, *From Masters of Slaves to Lords of Lands: The Transformation of Ownership in the Western World*
Marie-Amélie George, *Family Matters: Queer Households and the Half-Century Struggle for Legal Recognition*
Simon Devereaux, *Execution, State and Society in England, 1660–1900*
Giuliana Perrone, *Nothing More than Freedom: The Failure of Abolition in American Law*
Christian G. Fritz, *Monitoring American Federalism: The History of State Legislative Resistance*

(Continued after the Index)

The Nation at Sea

The Federal Courts and American Sovereignty, 1789–1825

KEVIN ARLYCK
Georgetown University

CAMBRIDGE
UNIVERSITY PRESS

CAMBRIDGE
UNIVERSITY PRESS

Shaftesbury Road, Cambridge CB2 8EA, United Kingdom

One Liberty Plaza, 20th Floor, New York, NY 10006, USA

477 Williamstown Road, Port Melbourne, VIC 3207, Australia

314–321, 3rd Floor, Plot 3, Splendor Forum, Jasola District Centre, New Delhi – 110025, India

103 Penang Road, #05–06/07, Visioncrest Commercial, Singapore 238467

Cambridge University Press is part of Cambridge University Press & Assessment, a department of the University of Cambridge.

We share the University's mission to contribute to society through the pursuit of education, learning and research at the highest international levels of excellence.

www.cambridge.org
Information on this title: www.cambridge.org/9781009393065

DOI: 10.1017/9781009393041

When citing this work, please include a reference to the DOI 10.1017/9781009393041

First published 2025

A catalogue record for this publication is available from the British Library

Library of Congress Cataloging-in-Publication Data
NAMES: Arlyck, Kevin, author.
TITLE: The nation at sea : the federal courts and American sovereignty, 1789–1825 / Kevin Arlyck, Georgetown University, Washington DC.
DESCRIPTION: Cambridge, United Kingdom ; New York, NY : Cambridge University Press, 2025. | Includes index.
IDENTIFIERS: LCCN 2025000102 | ISBN 9781009393065 (hardback) | ISBN 9781009393058 (paperback) | ISBN 9781009393041 (ebook)
SUBJECTS: LCSH: Courts – United States – History. | Constitutional history – United States. | Maritime law – United States – History. | Sovereignty.
CLASSIFICATION: LCC KF8719 .A77 2025 | DDC 347.73/209034–dc23/eng/20250114
LC record available at https://lccn.loc.gov/2025000102

ISBN 978-1-009-39306-5 Hardback

In memory of Robert A. Katzmann – an exemplary federal judge, and an exemplary human being

Contents

Figures

Acknowledgments

Like any book, this one has benefited from help from too many people to mention. But here are a few.

I am indebted to the librarians and archivists at many institutions, including the Baker Library at the Harvard Business School, the Bostonian Society, the Hagley Museum and Library, the Historical Society of Pennsylvania, the Library of Congress, the Library of Virginia, the Maryland Center for History and Culture, the Massachusetts Historical Society, the Virginia Historical Society, and multiple locations of the National Archives and Records Administration (Atlanta, Boston, College Park, New York, Philadelphia, and Washington). Special thanks to the foreign archivists who patiently answered my many questions at the National Archives of the United Kingdom (Kew) and the Archives du Ministère des Affaires Étrangères in France (Nantes and La Courneuve).

I have also benefited from the talents of librarians at the several institutions I have called home since this project began: Bobst Library at New York University (NYU), Diamond Law Library at Columbia Law School, and the Library of the Supreme Court of the United States. I am especially indebted to the staff at the Williams Library at Georgetown University Law Center, including Hannah Kim and the tireless folks in the Special Collections and Research Services departments, interlibrary loan wizard Erie Taniuchi, and Lauren Burroughs and Lydia Morgan in Digital Initiatives. Special thanks to my gifted and dedicated research assistants, Luke Wills and Alyce Petit, who took on many unenviable tasks with nary a grumble.

Engaging in such research requires financial support, and I am the grateful for the largesse of several institutions: the Gilder-Lehrman Institute of American History, Harvard University, NYU, the Society for Historians of American Foreign Relations, the Virginia Historical Society, and the William Nelson Cromwell Foundation.

All the money and support in the world is of little use without guidance from mentors, and I have been spoiled rotten. This book has its origins in my PhD dissertation at NYU, which I completed under the tutelage of a three-headed monster of scholarly wisdom and learning. I first got to know Dan Hulsebosch when he tried his best to teach me the law of property in my first year, but it was his sharp insights into the nature of law and politics in the revolutionary Atlantic that helped shape this book. Dan always asks me the most incisive questions about my work, and it is significantly better for it. There is a small army of legal historians who owe a debt of gratitude to Bill Nelson, but perhaps none more than me. Bill encouraged my academic aspirations from the moment I arrived at NYU and was exceedingly generous with his time and counsel – not to mention his unparalleled knowledge of law and courts in early America. And I could not have asked for a finer dissertation advisor than Laurie Benton. Her pathbreaking scholarship on law and empire in the early modern world has been deeply influential (even if our different orientations sometimes put us at intellectual odds). And though she has always been unfailingly encouraging, her willingness to crack the whip (gently) when needed has been invaluable for a young scholar who could easily have lost his way.

Special thanks go to two of my mentors in law. It was as Barry Friedman's research assistant that I first engaged deeply with the political history of the early federal courts. And it is no exaggeration to say that, without his direction and support, I would not be a law professor today. The same is true of Sonia Sotomayor, Associate Justice of the Supreme Court of the United States. As her law clerk, I saw how it was possible for a judge on the most important court in the land to decide cases insightfully, fairly, and always with a deep understanding of the human consequences that would result.

There is a long list of other teachers and colleagues who have helped shape this work, including Rachel Barkow, David Golove, Karen Kupperman, and John Shovlin at NYU; Kate Andrias,

Pam Bookman, Jessica Bulman-Pozen, Henry Monaghan, Trevor Morrison, David Pozen, Dan Richman, and Matt Waxman at Columbia; and Dan Ernst, Brad Snyder, and Bill Treanor at Georgetown. This book has also benefited from commentary and insight from hundreds of members of the broader legal history community, including Greg Ablavsky, Mary Bilder, Mary Dudziak, Sam Erman, Jonathan Gienapp, Eliga Gould, Dirk Hartog, Andrew Kent, Sophia Lee, Tom Lee, Maeva Marcus, Julian Mortenson, Bill Novak, Nick Parrillo, Jim Pfander, Reuel Schiller, Rebecca Scott, Jed Shugerman, Karen Tani, Barbara Welke, and Ted White. Special thanks to Hannah Farber, Jane Manners, John Mikhail, and Gautham Rao, who read the entire manuscript and offered generous and insightful feedback. Pamela Haag and Betsy Kuhn also read the whole thing, and their editorial suggestions improved the writing a great deal.

Finally, this book would not have been possible without Sally Gordon's tireless efforts as editor. Despite her many other obligations, Sally devoted countless hours to reading draft after draft, always pushing me to dig deeper and figure out what I thought was really important in the history I had uncovered. If I have succeeded, it is thanks to her.

Two people who are no longer with us deserve particular mention. Anne Fleming was my co-panelist the first time I presented my work at the American Society for Legal History. We were both graduate students, and little did I know that we would later be colleagues. When I joined the Georgetown faculty, Anne was a font of advice and support, both scholarly and professional. Like many in the field, I miss her deeply. And then there is Robert Katzmann, the former Chief Judge of the United States Court of Appeals for the Second Circuit, to whom this book is dedicated. To my mind, Judge Katzmann epitomized what a federal judge should be. He was brilliant and deeply learned, but humble and selfless to a fault. He lived to serve and to do good in the world. We lost him too soon.

I owe special thanks to my parents. Their encouragement throughout the research and writing process has been priceless, and their genuine curiosity about its progress has helped me see this through.

I started this project at the same time that I met Leigh Davis, an artist with little interest in legal history. When we first started dating, she said she wanted to read some of my work. After more than a decade of marriage, she never has. But she has supported me in innumerable other ways and has opened me to new ways of being in the world. We are raising two delightful kids together, and she is the love of my life. Who cares if she doesn't want to read about pirates?

Abbreviations

Archival Sources

AMAE-AC	France, Archives du Ministère des Affaires Étrangères, Archives Consulaires (Nantes)
AMAE-CC	France, Archives du Ministère des Affaires Étrangères, Correspondance Consulaire et Commerciale, États-Unis (La Courneuve)
AMAE-CP	France, Archives du Ministère des Affaires Étrangères, Correspondance Politique, États-Unis (La Courneuve)
AMAE-MD	France, Archives du Ministère des Affaires Étrangères, Mémoires et Documents, États-Unis (La Courneuve)
JSP	Harvard Business School, Baker Library, Juan Stoughton Papers, Letter Books, Vol. 4
NAFO 5	United Kingdom National Archives, Foreign Office, Political and Other Departments, General Correspondence before 1906, United States of America, Series II
NAFO 116	United Kingdom National Archives, Foreign Office, Consulates, United States of America, Letter Books
NARA	National Archives and Records Administration
NARA-AG	National Archives and Records Administration, Records of the Office of the Attorney General

NARA-NL	National Archives and Records Administration, Miscellaneous Letters Sent by the Secretary of the Navy, 1798–1886, microfilm M209
NARA-PL	National Archives and Records Administration, Notes From the Portuguese Legation in the United States to the Department of State, microfilm M57
NARA-PP	National Archives and Records Administration, Records of the Secretary of State, Petitions for Pardons, 1789–1860
NARA-SL	National Archives and Records Administration, Notes From the Spanish Legation in the United States to the Department of State, microfilm M59
PSC	Virginia Historical Society, Papers of the Spanish Consulate in Norfolk, Virginia, 1795–1846
PSDP	Historical Society of Pennsylvania, Peter Stephen Du Ponceau Papers, Letter Books
USCC-MA	National Archives and Records Administration, United States Circuit Court for Massachusetts, Final Record Books (Waltham)
USDC-MA	National Archives and Records Administration, United States District Court for Massachusetts, Final Record Books (Waltham)
USDC-NY	National Archives and Records Administration, Prize and Related Records for the War of 1812 of the US District Court for the Southern District of New York, 1812–1816, microfilm M928
USDC-PA	National Archives and Records Administration, Admiralty Case Files of the US District Court for the Eastern District of Pennsylvania, 1789–1840, microfilm M988
USDC-SC	National Archives and Records Administration, Admiralty Final Record Books and Minutes for the District Court, District of South Carolina, 1790–1857, microfilm 1182, roll 2
VDP	Hagley Museum and Library, Papers of Victor Dupont, Series A, Correspondence of Victor Dupont

Published Sources

Annals	*Annals of Congress* (Washington, DC: Gales and Seaton, 1834)
ASPFR	*American State Papers, Foreign Relations* (Washington, DC: Gales and Seaton, 1833)
ASPNA	*American State Papers, Naval Affairs* (Washington, DC: Gales and Seaton, 1834)
CFM	Frederick J. Turner, ed., *Correspondence of the French Ministers to the United States, 1791–1797* (Washington, DC: Government Printing Office, 1904)
DCUS	William R. Manning, ed., *Diplomatic Correspondence of the United States Concerning the Independence of the Latin-American Nations* (New York: Oxford University Press, 1925)
DHRC	John P. Kaminski, et al., eds., *Documentary History of the Ratification of the Constitution* (Charlottesville: University of Virginia Press, 2009)
DHSC	Maeva Marcus, ed., *Documentary History of the Supreme Court of the United States* (New York: Columbia University Press, 1985)
FO	Founders Online, National Archives, https://founders.archives.gov
JCC	*Journals of the Continental Congress* (Washington, DC: Government Printing Office, 1908)
LLJS	William W. Story, ed., *Life and Letters of Joseph Story* (Boston: Little and Brown, 1851)
MJQA	*Memoirs of John Quincy Adams, Comprising Portions of His Diary from 1795 to 1848* (Philadelphia: J.B. Lippincott & Co., 1874)
MWJS	William W. Story, ed., *The Miscellaneous Writings of Joseph Story* (Boston: Little, Brown and Company, 1852)
NDAR	*Naval Documents of the American Revolution* (Washington, DC: Department of the Navy, 1964)
PAH	Harold C. Syrett and Jacob E. Cooke, eds., *The Papers of Alexander Hamilton* (New York: Columbia University Press, 1961)

PGWPS	W. W Abbot, et al., eds., *The Papers of George Washington, Presidential Series* (Charlottesville: University Press of Virginia, 1987)
PJM	Charles T. Cullen, et al., eds., *The Papers of John Marshall* (Chapel Hill: University of North Carolina Press, 2006)
PJMPS	Robert A. Rutland, et al., eds., *The Papers of James Madison, Presidential Series* (Charlottesville: University of Virginia Press, 1984)
PJMRS	David B. Mattern, et al., eds., *The Papers of James Madison, Retirement Series* (Charlottesville: University of Virginia Press, 2009)
PTJ	Julian P. Boyd, et al., eds., *The Papers of Thomas Jefferson* (Princeton: Princeton University Press, 1992)
PTJRS	J. Jefferson Looney, et al., eds., *The Papers of Thomas Jefferson, Retirement Series* (Princeton: Princeton University Press, 2004)
RDCUS	Francis Wharton, ed., *The Revolutionary Diplomatic Correspondence of the United States* (Washington, DC: Government Printing Office, 1888)
RFC	Max Farrand, ed., *The Records of the Federal Convention of 1787* (New Haven: Yale University Press, 1911)
WJM	Stanislaus Murray Hamilton, ed., *The Writings of James Monroe* (New York: G. P. Putnam's Sons, 1898)
WJQA	Worthington Chauncey Ford, ed., *The Writings of John Quincy Adams* (New York: Macmillan, 1913)

Introduction

John Marshall was famously far-seeing, but a prediction he made on a hot June day in 1788 proved more prescient – and more important – than even he could have known. The future Chief Justice of the Supreme Court was a delegate to the Virginia convention debating whether to ratify the new Constitution. His task, appropriately enough, was to defend its creation of a national judiciary. The Constitution's critics, known as Anti-Federalists, were alarmed. They claimed that Article III's broad description of "the judicial power" would "annihilate" state autonomy, and they vowed to exert their "whole force" against the institution that would define Marshall's legacy. If they succeeded, the entire project of creating a more perfect union among the fractious states threatened to collapse.[1]

Marshall tried to soothe the Anti-Federalist fears by offering now-familiar explanations of how the federal courts would help ensure the survival of the American republican experiment. The judges' independence, enshrined in the Constitution's text, would allow them to decide contentious cases with "fairness and impartiality." Their authoritative interpretations of the Constitution and statutes would ensure the "orderly" enforcement of federal law. And their decisions in cases between citizens of different states would "preserve the peace of the Union."[2]

Marshall's most prophetic claim was almost an afterthought. The new federal courts, he added, would also be "the means of preventing disputes with foreign nations." He was only half-right.

The Constitution assigned contentious lawsuits involving foreign diplomats to the Supreme Court, but such cases proved exceedingly rare, as did potentially explosive controversies between American states and foreign governments. Even the courts' jurisdiction over suits by foreign subjects against American citizens – a feature of Article III that Anti-Federalists deeply reviled – did not end the diplomatic conflicts it was meant to resolve.[3]

It was instead by adjudicating cases arising from war at sea that the courts secured the United States' place in the world. Marshall could not have known it in 1788, but the global conflicts of empire and rebellion triggered by the French Revolution meant that, for over thirty years, international disputes over persons, ships, and goods caught up in maritime war repeatedly washed onto American shores. Federal judges decided the legality of captures made by warring powers, regulated the conduct of merchants and privateers, and criminally tried those who sought to benefit from the chaos of transatlantic warfare. Many of the Age of Revolution's most consequential battles were fought in the courts.

The courts' decisions were essential to the United States' emergence as a sovereign and independent nation. The Constitution's framers understood that maintaining good relations with empires at war promised peace and prosperity, while failure to do so risked political and economic subjugation and even destruction of the union itself. But the compromises the framers' made to create a viable national government left the first generation of state-builders with limited means to control the behavior of Americans (and others) who threatened to embroil the nation in international conflict. The legal relief the judiciary offered to injured foreigners remedied these deficiencies. It forestalled reprisals by powerful European nations and demonstrated that the fledgling republic had a government worthy of respect.

The courts did more, however, than simply burnish the United States' reputation abroad. Their rulings on the fate of the people, ships, and goods circulating in the revolutionary Atlantic set forth an increasingly bold vision of American sovereignty vis-à-vis other nations. This progression was not linear. Judges feared the consequences that might arise from judicial intervention in the affairs of state, and they often hesitated before accepting responsibility for adjudicating disputes stemming from maritime war. Over time, however, the courts' growing willingness to assert judicial authority over the sea vindicated the Declaration of Independence's claim to an "equal station" for the United States "among the powers of the earth."[4]

This saltwater story of the courts' role in American state-building has been forgotten. Preoccupation with Marshall's famous constitutional rulings has obscured the fact that the early judiciary's most consequential cases arose on the ocean. And while we have grown accustomed to the modern idea that "foreign affairs" are the domain of the legislative and executive branches, the political leaders who first tried to solve the puzzle of constitutional governance did not hew to such rigid notions of institutional responsibility. In fact, Congress and successive presidents repeatedly delegated momentous questions of wartime rights to the courts. By insisting that federal judges alone could resolve legal disputes arising from international conflict, they offered a broad understanding of judicial power that was only implicit in the Constitution's text. If the foundation of the federal courts' authority was their power "to say what the law is," as Marshall explained in *Marbury v. Madison*, the first place that authority was realized was at sea.[5]

* * *

When the federal courts came into being, war was a constant threat to the young republic's hard-won independence. On land, Britain and Spain claimed dominion over vast swaths of North American territory and supported Native people who resisted encroachment by white settlers with force. On the water, armed vessels prowled sea lanes in the Atlantic and the Caribbean in search of merchant ships laden with the mineral and agricultural riches of the Americas. Entanglement in these conflicts would leave the United States vulnerable to invasion, military domination, and economic subservience. As Secretary of State Edmund Randolph put it to James Monroe in 1795, "an infant country" like the United States could have "no greater curse in store for her than war."[6]

At the same time, war also offered political and economic opportunities. Farmers from Virginia and Pennsylvania sold wheat to armies on the battlefields at Austerlitz and Waterloo, which was carried across the Atlantic by ships sailing from Baltimore and Philadelphia. Weakened European empires were willing to cede territory in

North America (most dramatically in the Louisiana Purchase), and their declining potency left Native people vulnerable to the violence of land-hungry Americans. Plus, the disintegration of imperial authority in the Atlantic world opened new markets free from the mercantilist strictures of European colonialism. "The great harvest" for "profits," Thomas Jefferson reminded George Washington in 1793, "is when other nations are at war."[7]

War's most significant opportunity was that it gave Americans the chance to earn international respect. The early United States was in what Randolph called a "state of probation." Many foreign observers doubted that the republic would remain intact for long, let alone that it was a legitimate sovereign. Its inability to fulfill its obligations under treaties and international law drove political elites to create a new government in 1787, one that could be trusted to keep its promises. The war-torn Atlantic of the late eighteenth and early nineteenth centuries would be the Constitution's proving ground (Figure I.1).[8]

But did the Constitution actually create a government that could meet war's challenges? The answer was uncertain. Americans of the founding generation had just rebelled against a distant and oppressive authority. Many were unsure whether they wanted to replace it with a central government that had significant coercive power. The subsequent Federalist-Republican divide that emerged in the 1790s ensured that every exercise of federal authority was subject to partisan scrutiny and resistance.[9]

The result was that, in the early years, there was not much of a federal government at all. Congress could theoretically raise an army and build a navy, but it hardly did so. It had a broad power to tax, but confined itself to charging duties on imported goods. Law enforcement was a particular problem. In the early 1790s, the military was small and widely scattered, the Treasury Department had only 500 officers to police a thousand miles of coastline, and there were fewer than twenty federal legal officers (all part-time employees). Even as the government grew in the nineteenth century, it was still, in one historian's memorable phrase, "a midget institution in a giant land."[10]

The national government did get some things done. It built roads, established banks, delivered mail, and regulated foreign and interstate commerce. It acquired and distributed land, expelled Native people from it, and enabled a system of enslaved labor to exploit it.[11] At

FIGURE I.1 In the late eighteenth and early nineteenth centuries, the federal courts' orientation was primarily toward the sea. Detail from *The World on Mercator's Projection* (London: Sherwood, Neely & Jones, 1810), courtesy of the Library of Congress.

times federal officers even punished those who broke the law. On the whole, however, the early federal government was better at giving Americans what they wanted – land, subsidies, pensions, mail – than preventing them from doing as they wished.[12]

Americans' distrust of national authority put the republic at risk. In the Age of Revolution, the United States was a magnet for entrepreneurs eager to turn the chaos of armed conflict to their personal advantage. Men of commerce looking to increase their profits could rely on high demand for their goods and innumerable opportunities to smuggle them across porous and ill-defined borders. Ex-soldiers found ready employment in the mercenary armies that fought in the period's sprawling conflicts. And North America was an attractive base of operations for the grandiose visionaries who sought to establish independent fiefdoms amid the collapse of European imperial control.[13]

The most troublesome of these adventurers were armed seafarers who sailed from American ports to prowl sea lanes in the Atlantic and Caribbean. Privateers – merchants and sailors who received commissions from governments at war authorizing them to seize enemy vessels and goods – had long been a fixture of early modern warfare. But their tendency to push the bounds of legality triggered diplomatic protests and invited retaliation by aggrieved nations. The Age of Revolution's explosive politics only made their transgressions more perilous. These swashbucklers may have been clever and daring, but they made the world a dangerous place.[14]

Amid the challenges that war posed, defense of American independence fell to the courts. Article III of the Constitution made a national judiciary a possibility, and the First Congress made it a reality by establishing a system of lower federal courts for the entire country. On land, the courts' authority was local and limited. But their primacy on the water was unchallenged. The misadventure of having state tribunals decide questions arising from war at sea during the American Revolution persuaded the constitutional framers to give the federal courts "all cases of admiralty and maritime jurisdiction."[15]

The court's admiralty jurisdiction drew them into international conflict almost as soon as they came into existence. Foreign diplomats stationed in the United States filed suits to recover captured ships and cargoes, and demanded that the government criminally prosecute those who engaged in maritime violence. They collected evidence, hired lawyers, and pressured executive branch officials to intervene in important cases. Judicial proceedings were a theater of international contestation, and law was the weapon of choice.

Federal judges exercised their maritime authority the way judges typically do – they resolved discrete legal disputes with material consequences for individual litigants. Judges decided who was entitled to property that had been captured at sea. They distributed the profits derived from its sale among the many claimants who came before the court. And they imposed monetary penalties and criminal sentences on those who violated the rules of maritime warfare.[16]

Judicial decisions over the fruits of war also enhanced the United States' sovereign legitimacy. Many Americans – especially the elites who framed the Constitution – believed that securing respect abroad required adherence to the United States' obligations under treaty and international law. Judgments the courts made about ships and goods taken at sea signaled that the United States would fulfill those duties. With Congress and the executive branch unable, or unwilling, to regulate maritime violence, judicial resolution of wartime disputes demonstrated the young republic's fitness for admission into the community of "civilized" (that is, European) nations.[17]

This judicial articulation of American sovereignty grew more assertive over time. Modern conceptions of sovereignty are often framed territorially, with nation-states seeking to establish exclusive claims to authority over the people and resources within their boundaries. But if we understand sovereignty instead as a "continuing manifestation of power" not defined by formal borders, it includes the increasingly broad claims to authority the courts made over people, ships, and goods across the Atlantic world. In the 1790s, the courts contravened treaties and international law to assume jurisdiction over captures made by French privateers. In the War of 1812, judges abandoned the defensive neutrality that had long shaped American statecraft to assert the United States' prerogative to wage war on equal terms with European empires. And, in the post-war period, the courts' willingness to punish criminally all those who perpetrated violence in the name of republican liberty foreshadowed the emergence of a new, imperial vision of the United States' sovereign rights both on land and on the water.[18]

In the end, the courts' increasingly confident declarations of maritime authority reflected a profound shift in how Americans understood their place in the world. The founding generation created a federal judiciary to help ensure the vulnerable republic's survival. But, over the next several decades, the courts crafted a theory and practice of American sovereignty that rivaled the pretensions of the most powerful nations on earth.

* * *

This history of judicial sovereignty-making is largely unknown. Existing accounts of the United States' transformation from infant republic to nascent empire tell a story of taxation, territorial acquisition, and economic development, all backed by the force of arms wielded primarily against North America's native inhabitants. On this telling, even when federal officers struggled to assert their authority over the diverse peoples of the Americas, the national government's domestic resources – fiscal, military, economic, and legal – are what enabled thirteen quarrelsome former British colonies to establish their dominion over the continent. Despite Stephen Skowronek's famous description of the early American governance as being conducted by "courts and parties," the federal judiciary barely figures in narratives of early American state-building.[19]

The essential role the courts played in establishing American sovereignty abroad has also been obscured by the stories we tell about the early judiciary at home. One popular tale credits the Supreme Court under John Marshall with laying the constitutional foundation for American nationhood. Marshall, the story goes, first established the courts' supremacy in matters of constitutional interpretation in *Marbury*. He then used that power to inculcate a nationalist vision of the Constitution that promoted the federal government's supremacy over the states. Marshall's rulings, according to one common plaudit, "knit the American people into an indivisible nation," and established the "more perfect Union" that the Constitution promised (Figure I.2).[20]

A second account of the early courts is more skeptical of their importance. Compared to the state and local tribunals whose decisions most profoundly shaped Americans' daily lives, the federal judiciary was small and remote. It was also institutionally weak and politically embattled. Early presidents had difficulty persuading eminent lawyers and politicians to accept judicial office, and some – notably Thomas Jefferson – attacked them when they did. Even the Supreme Court's supposedly "great" nationalist decisions of the 1820s had little impact in the face of Andrew Jackson's political ascendancy. Marshall's talent for rendering decisions that promoted judicial power while avoiding direct clashes with dangerous rivals only demonstrated the courts' vulnerability. The authority "to say what the law is" meant little if no one was listening.[21]

Both of these stories miss an important truth: The federal judiciary *did* profoundly shape the trajectory of early American sovereignty, but through cases that asserted its power – and the nation's – at sea. Even as political partisans sought to strip the courts of jurisdiction and remove judges from office, litigants from around the world packed the federal dockets with high-stakes disputes arising from maritime

FIGURE I.2 By the time John Adams appointed John Marshall as Chief Justice of the Supreme Court (at age thirty-five), he had already served as a Revolutionary War officer, delegate to the Virginia ratifying convention, member of Congress, envoy to France, and Secretary of State. Portrait by Cephas Thompson (1809–10), courtesy of the National Portrait Gallery, Washington, DC.

commerce and war. By the time the Marshall Court began issuing its famous rulings about the federal government's domestic power, the courts had spent nearly thirty years deciding crucial cases about the scope of the United States' international authority.[22]

The obscurity of the courts' maritime role in establishing American sovereignty is perhaps understandable. For modern lawyers, admiralty law is a specialized backwater. It addresses disputes over seamen's wages, shipboard injuries, and marine insurance, questions that sound in the private law of tort and contract, not in public international and constitutional law. But in the early republic, the courts' most important cases arose from captures made by private armed vessels, an archaic form of warfare whose political significance is largely unintelligible to us now.[23]

To tell a new and more potent story about the courts, we have to shift our attention away from the familiar narratives of judicial history and the usual methods of writing it. The well-known early controversies over advisory opinions, circuit-riding, judicial review, and impeachment all appear here. But they are in the background, as context and counterpoint. Formerly obscure Supreme Court opinions, written in an unfamiliar legal grammar, take on new importance. So do the overlooked records of early admiralty proceedings and the reams of correspondence between the government officials, foreign diplomats, lawyers, merchants, and privateers who brought their wartime disputes to the federal courts. Taken together, these sources reveal the courts' essential role in establishing the United States' place in the world.[24]

The courts' international prominence was not preordained. Foreign officials resented having to litigate the status of captures at sea, and they demanded that the executive and legislative branches act to protect their nation's rights. Private parties also resisted the courts' authority, and at times defied judicial orders. Even some political leaders had doubts. Alexander Hamilton was a staunch advocate of federal judicial power, but in 1793 he argued that disputes between sovereigns arising at sea had to be settled "by reasons of state, not rules of law."[25]

Judges also had misgivings. Histories of the federal judiciary often assume that early jurists (especially John Marshall) were eager to expand their power, even if they had to do so quietly and indirectly. In truth, many federal judges did not want to take on the hundreds of admiralty disputes that the Age of Revolution brought into their courts. They worried that their rulings would provoke diplomatic controversy, rather than resolve it, and it would diminish the courts' standing in the process. And like any government bureaucrat, many resented the extra work that was involved.[26]

Surprisingly, the most insistent declarations of judicial authority over international controversies came from the other branches of government. The Constitution gave Congress broad power in war and foreign affairs, but cautious legislators relied on the courts to develop the rules governing maritime conflict. The executive branch had equally strong claims to constitutional authority abroad, but was even more willing to defer to the courts. Cabinet officers rebuffed foreign demands for executive resolution of disputes over ships and goods captured at sea, directing claimants to seek redress in the courts instead. Even Thomas Jefferson, the federal courts' most virulent nineteenth-century critic, declared that disputes arising from maritime war belonged "to the Judiciary alone."[27]

Such statements of judicial supremacy in foreign affairs are almost incomprehensible to modern ears. The conventional wisdom, including among judges themselves, is that their lack of expertise demands submissiveness to Congress and the President. Even commentators who argue that the courts *should* be more assertive in international matters, especially in remedying human rights abuses, rarely dispute the reality that, in practice, judges are deeply deferential.[28]

Yet giving judges responsibility for resolving critical questions of international law and politics made perfect sense to early American policymakers. As Jefferson explained in 1793, any decision the executive branch made about the fate of ships, goods, and people claimed by powerful foreign empires was bound to "give dissatisfaction to both parties, and produce complaints from both." Referring international controversies to the judiciary divided big diplomatic problems into smaller legal disputes, and spared political actors from having to choose sides.[29]

Elected officials also turned to the courts because they had no other choice. A distracted and divided national legislature had no appetite for establishing rules governing maritime conflict. The executive branch, in turn, lacked the tools it needed to enforce what law there was. By routing maritime disputes to the courts, Congress and successive presidents sought to enlist a coordinate branch of government to resolve controversies they had neither the will nor the means to handle on their own.

Repeated insistence that only the courts could resolve important wartime controversies eventually produced a rough consensus about the legitimacy of judicial intervention in the affairs of state. Foreign officials discovered that filing suit in federal court enabled them to combat their enemies with law rather than arms. Judges, too, ultimately embraced a robust conception of judicial power in foreign affairs. Justice Joseph Story made this clear in one of the Supreme Court's last privateering cases in 1822. The federal courts' fitness for resolving international legal disputes had long been contested, Story conceded. But the practice of the previous three decades was for the judiciary to answer such questions, and it was now "too late to disturb it."[30]

Thirty-four years earlier, John Marshall had to justify the federal courts' existence without the benefit of history and hindsight. The young lawyer who defended the idea of a national judiciary to skeptical Virginians in 1788 could not have known that, decades later, he would lead that institution as it confronted the United States' gravest foreign affairs crises. But Marshall's mild prediction that the courts would "prevent [] disputes with foreign nations" proved more accurate than he realized. If his legacy is the establishment of both judicial and national authority, this book shows that he and his contemporaries did so, first and foremost, at sea.

1

From Confederation to Constitution

Alexander Hamilton was undoubtedly tired of defending the Constitution. He had been writing nonstop for more than six months, in a frantic effort to persuade his fellow New Yorkers to accept the new charter of national government he had helped draft. By late May 1788, Hamilton had churned out nearly fifty essays of *The Federalist*, scribbling them down in every moment he could spare from his thriving law practice (including while sailing on the Hudson River with his wife). The prodigious output was partly tactical; Hamilton's opponents complained that the sheer volume of his words "would jade the brains of any poor sinner." But he would not relent. Eight states had ratified the Constitution, leaving supporters one short of the total needed. Conventions would soon convene in New York and Virginia, and in both states the Anti-Federalist opposition was vociferous and powerful. If the opponents prevailed, it might well doom the effort to construct the national government that Hamilton – and many others – believed was needed to save the young republic from collapse.[1]

Hamilton's final assignment was perhaps the most urgent and the most challenging: defending the Constitution's creation of a national judiciary. The courts had received relatively little attention at the Constitutional Convention (at least according to James Madison's notes), and Article III of the final document did little more than outline the contours of judicial power. But for Hamilton and his fellow travelers, the federal courts were critical. Without them, the national government had no way to ensure that the United States would fulfill its obligations under treaty and international law, to the detriment of the United States' standing abroad.[2]

Hamilton knew how difficult it would be to convince Americans of the need for a robust national judiciary. That aspect of the constitutional plan, sympathizers acknowledged, had provoked "more objections ... than all the other parts." Anti-Federalists dreaded the despotic tendencies of a supreme tribunal vested with the power to strike down democratically enacted legislation, and they worried that the Constitution's failure to guarantee jury trials in civil cases, combined with federal judges' life tenure, left the courts "subject to no control." Hamilton tried to assuage these fears in his final *Federalist* essays. Judges would have "neither force nor will" to infringe on the people's rights, and they would exercise the power of judicial review only to vindicate the popular sovereignty expressed in the Constitution itself.[3]

There was one aspect of the federal courts' power that Hamilton saw no need to justify: their jurisdiction over cases arising at sea. Even the "most bigotted idolizers of state authority," Hamilton wrote in *The Federalist*, conceded that the national judiciary should have "cognizance of maritime causes." His Pennsylvania ally, James Wilson, also presumed that the Constitution's critics would offer "little objection" to such a "proper and unexceptionable" authority. Hamilton and Wilson were skilled rhetoricians, always attuned to how they could use their opponents' words against them. But the consensus they invoked was not an exaggeration. Indeed, George Mason of Virginia, one of the leading Anti-Federalists, allowed that he would "cheerfully" support the new government if federal jurisdiction were limited to cases arising at sea. The courts' potentially vast powers may have caused deep consternation, but not because of their maritime jurisdiction.[4]

This agreement was born of bitter experience. During the Revolutionary War, fealty to principles of state sovereignty and local control had prompted the Confederation Congress to embark on an "experiment" of allowing state-court juries to decide the legality of captures made by American armed vessels. The results were disastrous. Juries upheld the unlawful seizure of vessels and goods owned by neutrals, allies, and even other Americans, infuriating foreign governments whose support was essential to the struggle for independence. The Revolution's unpleasant lessons were not lost on the delegates who drafted and debated the Constitution nor on the members of Congress who first framed the national judiciary. "[M]aritime causes" necessarily belonged to it, Hamilton wrote in *The Federalist*, because they "so commonly affect the rights of foreigners."[5]

Recovering the federal courts' beginnings in war at sea helps us make sense of an otherwise puzzling constitutional origin story. How could an institution that held neither the "purse" nor the "sword," as Hamilton famously put it, ever be a coequal branch of government? According to one of the early courts' leading chroniclers, the judiciary received only an "honorable mention" in the Constitution, when compared to the attention the document paid to the executive and legislative branches. And even that rough sketch was subject to fierce critique, as debates over jury trials, judicial review, and the federal courts' encroachment on state authority roiled the nation for years to come. But the generation that framed and debated a new government in the late 1780s understood the importance of giving the courts authority over maritime cases. If Americans truly wanted a government that could fulfill the nation's international obligations and maintain harmony with other sovereigns, they needed a judiciary with the power to resolve disputes arising at sea.[6]

* * *

By the late 1780s, Americans were intimately familiar with the challenge of controlling maritime violence through law. Though the term "privateer" did not come into regular use until the seventeenth century, the practice of licensing private vessels to make war dated back several centuries earlier. In the late middle ages, European monarchs began issuing "letters of marque" or "letters of reprisal" that authorized their subjects to raid and seize foreign property at sea. These ventures were privately funded, though the crown generally shared in the spoils, and often the raids were conducted under some form of royal direction or instruction (like Francis Drake's expeditions against Spanish possessions in the late sixteenth century). In 1708, however, the British Parliament renounced any governmental claim to a share of prize proceeds, to give privateers greater incentive to destroy enemy commerce. Privateering flourished in the eighteenth century, despite the growth of public navies, as commerce raiding formed an integral part of the European imperial powers' struggle for military and mercantile supremacy.[7]

Colonial North Americans were no strangers to the maritime dimensions of imperial rivalry. British and American privateers sailed in the War of the Spanish Succession (1701–1714), the War of Jenkins' Ear (1739–1748), and the nine years of conflict between Britain and France from 1754 to 1763. The colonies were well supplied with sailing vessels that could be converted to warlike purposes, as well as the officers and sailors needed to man them. The continent provided timber and other naval stores needed to build and maintain a private armed fleet, and the North American coast offered harbors and anchorages from which privateers could launch their raids. Proximity to transatlantic sea lanes also gave Americans easy access to merchant ships and the valuable trade goods they ferried between the New World and the Old. As Benjamin Franklin acknowledged in 1785, the coincidence of geography, economy, and opportunity rendered Americans "better situated than any ... to make profit by Privateering."[8]

North Americans' aptitude for private war was most apparent when it came to their struggle for independence. At the start of hostilities in 1775, neither the states nor the Continental Congress had any armed vessels to deploy against British ships patrolling the eastern seaboard, and building a navy would take time. Yet within weeks of the shots fired at Lexington and Concord, small boats fitted out under the authority of Massachusetts officials were harassing British vessels near Martha's Vineyard. By that summer, private armed ships were engaging British cruisers. At first, state governments took the lead in licensing privateers. But in March 1776 – months before declaring formal independence – the Continental Congress began issuing privateering commissions.[9]

While some historians assert that these privateers were "little more than licensed pirates" who "contributed little to the American cause," a more sober assessment reveals their importance. By the war's end, the Continental Navy had fewer than seventy public vessels, but Congress and the states combined to license more than 2,000 privateers. They seized thousands of British merchant ships, taking many millions of dollars' worth of cargo. In addition, their raiding diverted British naval forces from offensive operations, strained the Crown's supply lines, and drove up insurance rates for embattled British merchants.[10]

Privateers also made a psychological impact, as they were the only force able to take the war to Britain itself. The appearance of privateer squadrons in the eastern Atlantic reportedly inspired "universal Terror" in seaports on Britain's western coast. At the same time, privateer exploits emboldened the American rebels, demonstrating to the world both "our strength" and "the weakness of our enemies," as John Adams put it. His wife Abigail agreed. "[T]he Rage for privateering is as great here as anywhere," she reported from Massachusetts not long after her husband signed the Declaration of Independence, "and I believe the success has been as great."[11]

For some revolutionary Americans, however, privateering was more a curse than a blessing. Benjamin Franklin was the greatest skeptic. He was a free trader at heart and he believed that allowing commerce to go unmolested, even in wartime, operated to everyone's benefit. Plus, privateers' financial incentives were not always aligned with the government's war priorities. Privateers' higher wages and the share of profits they offered tempted men away from the Continental armed forces – a problem so severe that state governments imposed temporary embargos on privateer enlistments during the war. In 1775, Congress hesitated before authorizing initial raids on British supply ships, for fear that American seamen would focus only on plunder.[12]

No one embodied Americans' conflicted feelings about privateering more than Robert Morris. A native of England who made his fortune through overseas trade, Morris was a member of Congress, a leading Philadelphia merchant, and reputedly the wealthiest man in the United States. In September 1776, Morris declared that the practice of forcibly taking the maritime property of fellow merchants "does not square with my Principles." But Morris was also the financier of the Revolution who bankrolled the American war effort, and he knew that patriotism and profit could go hand in hand. A few months later, he sent an associate in the Caribbean confidential instructions to fit out a "Stout Privateer" on his account. Morris swore his agent to secrecy, for fear of sullying his professional reputation. But having lost several vessels to British cruisers, Morris considered himself perfectly justified – "in the Eyes of God or Man" – to seek retribution for his injuries (the ship was aptly named *Retaliation*). By the following spring, Morris's scruples about privateering were "all done away." The "Rapine, Plunder, & Destruction" by British forces convinced him of his duty to "oppose and distress so Merciless an Ennemy in every Shape we can."[13]

As Franklin and Morris knew, the difficulty with privateers was ensuring that they stayed within legal bounds. In theory, neutral ships and goods were generally not subject to capture by belligerents under the laws of war. In practice, eighteenth-century armed vessels routinely seized maritime property belonging to the citizens and subjects of nations not formally at war. At times, these seizures were justified. Enemy goods found in neutral ships were fair game – they were "good prize" – which gave privateers a reason to stop and search all sorts of vessels. In addition, merchants from belligerent nations routinely disguised their cargoes as neutral property to avoid enemy capture, and a discerning privateer could make a handsome profit if his suspicions about a prize's true identity proved accurate. But many privateers were not very discerning, and seized neutral ships on the slightest pretext. They knew that goods illegally taken from neutrals might be smuggled and sold in far-flung markets, with few questions asked. And if the property did end up in court, they knew that a sympathetic judge might not pay close attention to the evidence.[14]

Privateers' willingness to push the boundaries of legality at sea had long been a challenge for the sovereigns who licensed them. As the web of global mercantile connections thickened in the seventeenth century, statesmen, jurists, and political thinkers increasingly came to see unconstrained attacks on maritime commerce not just as an injury to the individual victim, but also a threat to the economic well-being of all nations. Unlawful seizures of merchant vessels could trigger severe consequences, including abrogated trade agreements, broken alliances, and even war. Perhaps the most famous example was Henry Every's 1695 capture of a valuable Indian merchant ship, which incurred the wrath of the Mughal Emperor and threatened England's lucrative trade privileges, spurring royal authorities to launch an unsuccessful global manhunt to bring Every to justice. The Crown had more success in later years pursuing William Kidd and other "pirates" who transgressed the limits of their commissions, but privateering's diplomatic hazards persisted well into the eighteenth century.[15]

FIGURE 1.1 Unlawful privateer seizures in the American Revolution complicated efforts by American diplomats like Benjamin Franklin (depicted here at the court of France in 1778) to secure support from European sovereigns. Painting by Anton Hohenstein (c. 1868), courtesy of the Library of Congress.

American statesmen knew that privateers' proclivity for evading the rules of war was a serious obstacle to independence. Unlike Great Britain, the United States could hardly afford to anger neutral nations. Unlawful privateer raids jeopardized Congress's efforts to secure funds, diplomatic recognition, and military aid from France, Spain, and the Dutch Republic, and American diplomats abroad regularly had to apologize for such acts (Figure 1.1).[16] Morris complained in early 1777 (without a trace of irony) that privateers' "irregular Conduct" and "Arbitrary Thieving" was a "palpable Insult" to the nations the United States needed to placate. Franklin agreed; given the difficulty of keeping American privateers "within bounds," he recommended Congress prohibit them from cruising off the French and Spanish coasts entirely. Failure to restrain American armed vessels, Franklin later cautioned, would only "produce ill blood."[17]

Privateering was all the more problematic in light of the United States' commitment to free trade and neutral rights. One of the Americans' chief complaints in seeking independence was that their mercantile subjugation to the British metropole, enforced through restrictive trade regulations, drew them into imperial conflicts against their will. Inspired by Enlightenment political economy and European writings on law of nations, Americans looked to a future in which they would be able to trade freely and peaceably with all nations. These sentiments found expression in a model treaty prepared by Franklin and others in 1776 to serve as a basis for commercial agreements the United States hoped to sign with Britain's rivals. It endorsed the proposition that "free ships make free goods" – that is, neutral nations were entitled to trade freely in time of war, even when carrying enemy cargo. But it was hard for American political leaders to demand that European sovereigns protect neutral rights when the nation's armed vessels were infringing that very principle.[18]

The Continental Congress struggled to prevent privateers from undermining relations with foreign sovereigns. In a 1778 proclamation, it noted that "unjustifiable and piratical acts" perpetrated against neutral nations "reflect dishonour upon the national character." It ordered privateers to pay a "sacred regard" to neutral rights and to the customs of "civilized nations," and warned that the government would not defend Americans who violated them. In 1781, Congress issued a revised set of privateer instructions, which included several articles specifically prohibiting the seizure of neutral property (something it had not deemed necessary to specify in the original 1776 version). Congress also centralized the commissioning of privateers in 1780, so that individual states would no longer license them. Yet complaints from neutrals continued to roll in throughout the war. It was therefore of "utmost consequence," Franklin advised Congress in 1777, that it develop a means of providing "speedy justice" for the victims of unlawful captures.[19]

* * *

For George Washington, the key to controlling privateering's excesses was not the proclamations of a legislative body, but rather the rulings of a judicial one. Six months into the war, Washington was in command of patriot forces laying siege to Boston. Among his concerns was what to do about British vessels captured in and around Massachusetts Bay. The United Colonies – as they were then known – did not yet have a navy, but Washington had commissioned several armed vessels to cut off British supplies coming from the sea. The seizures helped the war effort, but now Washington had to decide what to do with the captured ships and goods. He awarded the officers and sailors a third of the value of the cargoes as "Encouragement" to continue their efforts, and he restore private property taken from loyalist Americans. But Washington did not want responsibility for assessing the "legallity of Seizures," a task that necessarily involved "inextricable difficulties." He asked John Hancock, Congress's president: "Should not a Court be established ... to take Cognizance of Prizes?"[20]

Washington's suggestion was not an innovation, as admiralty tribunals had long been maritime nations' chief instrument for regulating private war. The principle was simple: A captor was not entitled to the ships and goods he seized at sea unless they were deemed lawfully captured by a prize court. The origins of this procedure are somewhat mysterious. According to Sir Edward Coke, the English admiral's power to resolve legal disputes arising at sea existed from a "time out of mind." But the first true admiralty tribunals arose in England in the fourteenth century, to hear claims related to piracy and illegal capture that had typically been addressed ad hoc by common law courts, seigneurial boards, local councils, or special arbitral bodies. These institutions proved unequal to the task of ensuring the lawfulness of maritime captures, and admiralty courts eventually received broad powers to resolve such disputes. They also assumed responsibility for taking bonds guaranteeing the good behavior of Englishmen granted letters of marque and reprisal by the king. Similar institutions arose among other European powers around the same time.[21]

At their core, admiralty courts were an expression of sovereign power. Creating tribunals to resolve maritime disputes that would otherwise be adjudicated by other political actors was a way for ambitious European monarchs to assert supreme juridical authority over the domains they claimed to rule. In this sense, the establishment of admiralty courts with exclusive jurisdiction to judge the legality of maritime conflict was one aspect of the broader "monopolization of violence" that characterized the rise of the modern state. Admiralty courts also projected sovereign authority externally. Monarchs unable to prevent their subjects from unlawfully seizing foreigners' property might be obligated to provide victims with redress. Uncompensated victims had a right to reprisal, and small disputes over captured ships and goods threatened to spawn larger conflicts if left unresolved. By restoring illegally seized ships and goods to their rightful owners, admiralty courts demonstrated to those outside the realm that a sovereign had both the *ability* and the *authority* to police his own polity, helping to disrupt the cycles of violence at sea.[22]

Admiralty courts had two attributes that helped establish sovereign control over maritime violence. First was exclusive jurisdiction over prizes captured by the sovereign's commissioned vessels. In the Elizabethan period, when privateers shared their spoils with the crown, adjudication in English admiralty courts helped ensure that captors paid over amounts due to the royal fisc. By the eighteenth century, however, a more theoretical explanation for this exclusive jurisdiction arose, grounded in theories of state responsibility and sovereign equality. Under the law of nations, a sovereign was ultimately responsible to his fellow sovereigns for the conduct of his subjects in war. At the same time, no sovereign could be called to account in the tribunals of another. As the Supreme Court of the United States explained in 1816, "every sovereign [was] the acknowledged arbiter of his own justice," and he had both the authority and the obligation to verify the legality of captures made under his commissions.[23]

This exclusive authority was largely undisputed. In Elizabethan England, the common law courts undermined the admiralty courts' jurisdiction over maritime-related disputes that did not literally arise at sea, such as those involving seaman's wages or shipping contracts. But prize cases, which *did* arise on the water, were a separate and largely protected species.[24] Similarly, colonial Americans deeply resented what they saw as unfair adjudications by British vice-admiralty courts in revenue and piracy cases. But the vice-admiralty courts' rulings in matters of prize elicited little complaint. By the time Washington made his suggestion to Hancock, there was little question that disputes over the capture of vessels and goods in wartime would be resolved by admiralty courts.[25]

The second way in which admiralty courts enhanced sovereign authority was through their mutual legibility. Over time, maritime captures across the European zone of influence were adjudicated under a body of law – the law of prize – that was substantially the same. Its sources were various, a mix of ancient codes of maritime law, treaty provisions, municipal regulations, prior judicial decisions, and the accumulated practice of centuries. By the late eighteenth century, the synthesizing efforts of leading law of nations "publicists" resulted in a number of widely read treatises expounding the legal principles governing the seizure of enemy ships in wartime. As the British jurist Lord Mansfield put it in 1782, prize courts the world over were "governed by one and the same law, equally known to each other." As a result, foreign litigants could have confidence that their claims to ships and goods would receive a fair hearing.[26]

In reality, admiralty courts were not always the dispensers of equal justice they purported to be. The supposedly universal principles of prize law were intricate and often susceptible to multiple interpretations when applied to complex facts. Complaints about judicial bias in favor of captors were common and often justified. In theory, however, prize law's universality rendered admiralty rulings internationally acceptable and legitimate.[27]

The Confederation Congress heeded Washington's recommendation to establish prize courts. But it did so with accommodations for American revolutionary ideology that political leaders would later come to regret. In November 1775, Congress issued a resolve declaring that any supplies intended for British forces were lawful prize to American public and private armed vessels. Recognizing that seizures made in the confused state of civil war might cause innocents to suffer, the resolve also provided for tribunals "to determine the propriety of captures." But they would not be Congress's own courts. Instead, the resolve urged individual colonies to confer prize jurisdiction on existing courts or establish new courts to hear prize cases. The only transcolonial legal authority was a right to appeal unfavorable decisions to Congress itself. Curiously, Congress also recommended that all prize cases in colonial courts be decided not by an admiralty judge, but by a jury.[28]

The unusual form of the nation's first prize courts reflected a deeper uncertainty about the nature and future of a polity that was not yet a nation at all. In late 1775, the "United Colonies" were barely united and still very much colonies. Many Americans – including some who took up arms against the British – harbored hopes of reconciliation. Even those who rejected both royal and parliamentary rule were unsure about what should replace it. Leaving individual colonial governments with responsibility for adjudicating prize cases made a great deal of sense, as they had the greatest claim to authority and legitimacy. In addition, by the time Washington suggested that Congress act, Massachusetts was already setting up its own prize courts, so there was little point in reinventing the wheel. The provision allowing for appeals to Congress ensured that any mistaken judgments by colonial courts would be swiftly corrected, at least in theory.

The provision for jury trials similarly derived from fealty to republican principles. It was an unusual decision; as Adams later acknowledged, empowering lay jurors to decide prize cases was an "innovation" that ran contrary to "the practice of the world." But it was a deliberate choice, one inspired, according to Charles Cotesworth Pinckney, by the colonists' "attachment to a trial by jury." This attachment had deep roots. Criminal juries had long been considered an essential protection against arbitrary rule in the Anglo-American tradition. By 1768, William Blackstone could confidently assert that the criminal jury was the "surest guardian[] of public justice" – indeed, it was the very "glory of English law."[29]

The American veneration of *civil* juries was more directly a product of the colonial experience. Juries in colonial common law courts were a site of resistance to parliamentary acts regulating imperial trade. Colonial governors complained that their revenue officers had "no chance with a jury," which was invariably composed of an illicit trader's "well-wishers." The crown's response was to bypass juries altogether. In 1696, it established vice-admiralty courts, presided over by a judge alone, with jurisdiction over trade and revenue cases brought by crown officials. This rankled colonial merchants, who resisted by political and legal means (and occasionally with violence). Yet the metropole only doubled down. Beginning in the 1760s, Parliament passed a series of infamous acts designed to extract greater revenue from the colonies to pay off debts from the Seven Years' War, and simultaneously expanded the vice-admiralty courts' jurisdiction.[30]

For many Americans, protection of the civil jury became synonymous with the struggle for independence itself. In 1768, John Adams defended John Hancock against smuggling charges by describing a vice-admiralty court's power to try trade and revenue cases without a jury as "a Brand of Infamy, Degradation and Disgrace" that placed every American "below the Rank of an Englishman." When Hancock became the first signatory of the Declaration of Independence eight years later, he was no doubt pleased that it included among King George's offenses deprivation of the "Benefits of trial by Jury."[31] To drive the point home, nearly every state included a civil jury right in its post-independence constitution. George Mason captured the revolutionary understanding in Virginia's 1776 Declaration of Rights: In civil cases, "the ancient trial by jury" was "held sacred."[32]

The republican influence on the United States' first prize courts proved deeply problematic for its relations with foreign sovereigns during the American Revolution. Juries in seafaring communities tended to decide prize cases in favor of American captors, even when the facts and the law dictated otherwise. According to Adams, jurors understood neither "the nature nor the law of foreign transactions." The result, Pinckney asserted, was that they "condemned indiscriminately" the property of friendly nations seized by American privateers. Adams and Pinckney likely exaggerated the problem; the extant records suggest that juries regularly ruled in favor of neutral owners, and instances of blatant captor favoritism seem to have been rare, even if Congress did have to reverse a number of jury verdicts on appeal. Yet the alarm among American political leaders over juries was real. In 1779, a congressional committee appointed to reconsider prize procedure concluded that jury trials in prize cases undermined "Just and uniform Execution of the Law of Nations," and prevented Congress from "giving Satisfaction to foreign Nations." According to Adams, within a few years "all the world" grew "weary" of this innovation.[33]

The perils of jury bias were compounded by the fact that Congress was ill-equipped to supervise how state courts adjudicated prize cases. A number of congressional delegates were lawyers with admiralty experience, but reliable sources of legal authority were scarce. This deficiency in expertise was exacerbated by Congress's decision to refer appeals from state courts to ad hoc committees formed for reviewing individual cases, which impeded the development of institutional knowledge and undermined decisional uniformity. Congress eventually created a standing Committee of Appeals, but its revolving membership meant that consistency was still elusive. Plus, Congress was overwhelmed by the task of managing a war on behalf of thirteen separate sovereigns and a bitterly divided populace, resulting in lengthy delays that frustrated captors and claimants alike. A petition from prominent Philadelphians – including James Wilson and Robert Morris – emphasized that the privateering trade depended on the captors receiving "the rewards of their Success and Bravery" as soon as possible, so delay in adjudication was "uncommonly destructive."[34]

Most troubling was Congress's lack of coercive power. During the Revolution, the states were no more eager to relinquish control over maritime captures than they were to cede authority over taxation or raising troops. Massachusetts and New Hampshire initially only allowed appeals to Congress over captures made by vessels fitted out at Congress's own expense (a very small number). Virginia's statute – drafted by Thomas Jefferson – only permitted appeals for captures of enemy property (not neutral or friendly). Even when a federal appeal was possible, litigants generally retained the option to appeal in the state courts instead. As a result, Congress heard only sixty-four cases from 1776 to 1780, a small percentage of the hundreds of prize cases likely tried in state courts. Nor could Congress oblige states to abide by the appellate judgments it did render. Outright resistance was rare, but in one high-profile dispute Pennsylvania judges and elected officials doggedly refused to enforce the Committee of Appeals' reversal of a state court judgment. The dispute was not resolved until three decades later, when the Supreme Court ruled that a state legislature could not annul the judgments of a federal tribunal.[35]

Congress recognized the diplomatic problems that state prize courts caused. A 1779 committee report on state intransigence stressed the importance of central government "controul" over prize cases. Otherwise, "a jury in any one State [might] involve the United States in hostilities." As complaints from foreign representatives mounted, Congress considered establishing national appellate courts that would sit without juries and have the power to hold in contempt state officers who refused to enforce their decrees. The proposed reforms also required that states conduct admiralty proceedings "according to the usage of nations" – that is, "not by jury."[36]

A divided Congress could not muster the political will to ensure national authority over prize proceedings. It did create a single appellate tribunal, the Court of Appeals in Cases of Capture, staffed with three judges. In the place of the contempt power, however, Congress merely "recommended" that states pass laws to ensure speedy execution of the Court's judgments. And the proposed command to abolish jury trials similarly shrank to a suggestion that states allow their courts to sit without juries, given that such proceedings had proven to be "inconvenient." There was doubt as to whether even such diluted measures were within Congress's authority. Article IX of the Articles of Confederation gave Congress the "sole and exclusive power" to establish an appellate prize court, but the states did not fully ratify the Articles until 1781.[37]

The Continental Congress was never able to solve the puzzle of prize courts. In November 1782, an American privateer seized the Spanish brig *San Antonio* for allegedly carrying British contraband under cover of false papers. Spanish and French officials warned that such an attack on neutral rights threatened the "good harmony" between their nations and the United States. Congress asked Massachusetts Governor John Hancock to help the Spanish claimants. Such an "unprovoked violation of the law of nations," wrote Elias Boudinot, "call[ed] loudly for the interference of Government."[38] But Hancock took no action, and soon after a jury decided in favor of the captors. The federal Court of Appeals ultimately reversed, but the captors refused to satisfy the judgment against them, and other foreign claimants experienced similar difficulties in collecting on appellate rulings in their favor. As the leading account of Congress's fitful efforts puts it, ultimately the national government's authority over maritime captures "extended only as far as the states tolerated."[39]

There was a profound irony in the diplomatic troubles caused by jury rulings in prize cases. Before the Revolution, Americans lauded the jury's localist orientation as a bulwark against oppression by distant imperial authority. Now jury parochialism threatened to undermine colonial Americans' struggle to be free of that authority.

Surprisingly, the mounting evidence that American prize courts would not provide justice to foreign claimants did not seem to shake political leaders' confidence in them. Benjamin Franklin, who was stationed in Paris until 1785, was fully aware of the problems that biased decisions created. He also knew that it was possible to adjudicate the legality of maritime captures without favoritism. As minister to France, Franklin was responsible for judging seizures made by American privateers operating from French ports. Franklin did not enjoy the task, but he took seriously his obligation to ensure a meticulous respect for neutral rights, and he refused to condemn captured vessels without strong "Proofs" of their enemy character.[40]

Even though prize courts in the United States seemingly did not share Franklin's scruples, he praised them nonetheless. He assured the foreign ministers who badgered him with complaints that American tribunals would punish violations of neutral rights and provide injured parties with redress. Officials in the United States echoed this view. When a Massachusetts court condemned cargo seized from a Portuguese vessel, Secretary of Foreign Affairs Robert Livingston affirmed that there was nothing to do but wait for review by the Court of Appeals: "You know so much of our constitution," he wrote to Franklin in 1783, "to see that it is impossible to interfere farther in these matters." This became the government's official position. When Spanish officials complained about the *San Antonio* capture, Congress responded with a resolve stating that the "proper mode" of obtaining redress was "prosecution in due course of law."[41]

This unwarranted confidence in domestic courts' ability to resolve international legal disputes was largely a function of necessity. Because the Continental Congress had neither the will nor the means to ensure just outcomes in privateering cases, political leaders had no choice but to refer claimants to the nation's nascent judiciary. A similar dynamic soon emerged under the new federal government, and the principle of judicial primacy in maritime war articulated by men like Franklin and Livingston strengthened in the coming decades. The revolutionary experience suggested that courts were not always able to vindicate the rights of foreign sovereigns and their subjects. At the same time, they were often the only institution of government that could do so. If the republic was going to acquire the sovereign legitimacy its leaders craved, it needed tribunals that could act at sea.

* * *

The Revolution's lessons about the need for a national judiciary were not lost on the men who gathered in Philadelphia in the summer of 1787. For the Constitution's framers, the diplomatic problems that prize cases provoked were but one manifestation of the broader crisis of legitimacy that drove them to reconstitute the national government. They knew that securing the favorable "opinions of mankind," as the Declaration of Independence put it, had been crucial to the success of their struggle for independence. Their early military victories in the war, for example, had persuaded France to provide financial support and enter into a formal alliance. Yet they understood that the republic's reputational gains were tenuous. In the 1780s, foreign opinion about the condition of American government was anything but positive. European observers – including allies – derided the Confederation as an unsteady collection of republics undeserving of trust and unfit for acceptance into the community of nations.[42]

The central problem the United States faced after the war was that it seemed unable to keep its promises. Under the Articles of Confederation, Congress did not have the power to tax Americans to pay back the substantial European loans it had taken out to fund the war. It could only ask that the state governments do so, but they were disinclined to demand greater contributions from citizens who had just fought a bloody conflict, in large part, to be free from financial levies imposed by distant authority. This recalcitrance was potentially disastrous for a government that needed further loans to stay afloat. "[T]he nation who eludes the payment of debts," John Jay explained, "ceases to be worthy of further credit."[43]

Of equal concern was Americans' unwillingness to satisfy their treaty obligations. Articles 5 and 6 of the 1783 Treaty of Paris, for example, called for the restoration of property confiscated from loyalists during the war and a prohibition on future takings. But many Americans had little interest in returning property taken from British subjects and sympathizers, and most of the laws authorizing such seizures were upheld when contested in state courts.[44] British subjects also found it nearly impossible to collect debts owed by Americans, especially southern farmers whose pre-war livelihood depended on credit extended by British merchants. Though Article 4 of the treaty provided that creditors on both sides would "meet with no lawful Impediment" to debt recovery, a number of states allowed them to be paid in depreciated paper money, authorized juries to deduct interest accrued during the war, and even closed their courts to British creditors entirely.[45]

For Americans suffering economic hardship, discrimination against the former enemy was simply justice. States defended their actions as legitimate retaliation for British atrocities during the war, which included the alleged "carrying off" of enslaved persons that the law recognized as chattel property. Some Americans took resistance to extremes. Violent mobs intimidated lawyers pursuing claims on behalf of foreign creditors, and disgruntled farmers used force to close courthouses, even burning some to the ground. Compliance with the treaty was so spotty that Jay complained to Adams in 1786 that there had not been "a single Day ... on which it has not been violated in America."[46]

The international consequences of the states' refusal to adhere to the United States' commitments alarmed many elites. British merchants and property holders complained loudly and vociferously about their ill-treatment, and British politicians saw the debt and confiscation issues as justification for punitive measures. A British Order-in-Council of 1783 excluding American ships from the West Indies crippled efforts to revive the lucrative carrying trade that had been one of the cornerstones of the pre-war American economy. Britain also refused to withdraw its soldiers from a number of forts in the western territories, as called for by Article 7 of the 1783 treaty, leaving those areas vulnerable to attack by Native peoples resisting the encroachment of white settlers. Spain's refusal to allow unfettered American navigation of the Mississippi only exacerbated the feeling that the nation was deeply vulnerable. By 1787, men like Alexander Hamilton believed that Americans' refusal to keep their promises had led the United States to "the last stage of national humiliation," and put "[t]he faith, the reputation, [and] the peace of the whole Union" at risk.[47]

For the delegates to the Constitutional Convention of 1787, the remedy for the United States' degraded standing abroad was creating a national government with real power to act internationally. The new Constitution reduced the national government's reliance on states by giving Congress a host of war-related powers, as well as the authority to tax the people directly "for the common Defense." The Constitution also gave Congress authority over commerce with foreign nations, to strengthen the federal government's hand in negotiating commercial treaties with European powers and reduce the violence between white settlers and Native peoples. At the same time, the new charter expressly denied such powers to the states. They would still have collective influence over the conduct of foreign affairs, especially through the Senate, which had the power to approve treaties. But, on the whole, the Constitution sought to allow the national government to operate abroad with a relatively free hand.[48]

A national government with independent authority over foreign affairs also needed a mechanism for making its new powers effectual. What good was the ability to make treaties or to pass laws regulating foreign commerce if states and their citizens could simply ignore federal commands? The Constitution gave the president the power – the duty, in fact – to ensure that "the laws be faithfully executed," but not necessarily the means to do so. In theory, he was commander in chief of the nation's armed forces, but there was little appetite for using federal military force as a means of coercing recalcitrant states or their citizens. Thomas Jefferson might have wished in 1786 that the Continental Congress had a way to "shew[] its teeth" to the states, but a year later he – like the delegates in Philadelphia – hoped instead to find "some peaceable means ... to enforce compliance."[49] The Convention also rejected Madison's proposal to allow Congress to "negative" state laws that ran afoul of the federal constitution. But these decisions left the fundamental question unanswered: "To what expedient can congress resort," Edmund Randolph asked his fellow delegates, "to compel delinquent States to do what is right?"[50]

The solution to the problem of state intransigence was "an authority in the federal courts," as Hamilton put it in *The Federalist*. The judiciary received comparatively little attention at the Convention, but there was general agreement that an effective federal government required a judicial power that could uphold the nation's legal obligations. The lack of such an institution, according to Hamilton, was the shortcoming that "crown[ed] the defects of the Confederation." Without federal courts, federal law was "a dead letter," because state courts, Madison argued, were untrustworthy "guardians of the National authority and interests." Randolph concurred: "[T]he Courts of the States cannot be trusted with the administration of the National laws." Even the Constitution's critics agreed, to a point. George Mason complained in the Virginia ratifying convention that federal courts would "destroy the State Governments," but he conceded the need for jurisdiction over cases involving ambassadors, treaties, and maritime matters.[51]

Accordingly, Article III of the Constitution sketched the contours of a national judiciary that could bolster the United States' international legitimacy. It established a Supreme Court with original jurisdiction over cases involving foreign ambassadors, ministers, and consuls. Given the implications such cases had for "the public peace," Hamilton believed that only "the highest judicatory of the nation" should hear them. In fact, Article III granted the federal courts jurisdiction over nearly all legal disputes that might affect the interests of foreigners. This included authority over cases arising under federal law, which expressly encompassed treaties and implicitly comprehended the law of nations, as well as jurisdiction over all disputes between Americans and foreign states, citizens, or subjects – which would include, for example, suits by British creditors against American debtors currently languishing in state courts. For the framers, these measures were critical to the nation's prosperity and security. "The denial or perversion of justice," Hamilton explained in *The Federalist*, was "among the just causes of war." Giving the federal courts jurisdiction over all cases involving foreigners was essential to both "public faith" and "public tranquility."[52]

What the Constitution left largely unsaid was precisely *how* the national judiciary would ensure that the United States upheld its international commitments. Part of the answer was the Supreme Court's appellate authority, which would allow it to review state court decisions on questions of national importance. The Supremacy Clause declared that the Constitution, federal statutes, and treaties were the "supreme law of the land." The operating assumption seems to have been that both state and federal judges would engage in what we now call judicial review – the invalidation of state laws that conflicted with federal law.[53] This was not entirely an innovation. There was a long tradition in the British Empire of centralized review of colonial legislation "repugnant" to the laws of England, and a handful of state courts in the 1780s had struck down or refused to apply laws that conflicted with higher legal authority (including treaties). But it was far from clear how a general principle of judicial review would apply in the new environment of constitutional federalism.[54]

Article III offered another mechanism for ensuring adherence to federal law: creating a nationwide system of federal courts to bypass the state courts entirely. The more nationalist delegates to the Convention doubted that a single appellate court would be able to superintend state judiciaries effectively. With only the power to review decisions already made, even a watchful tribunal would struggle to remedy what Madison called "the biased directions of a dependent Judge" or "the local prejudices of an undirected jury." But delegates who were suspicious of federal power distrusted the idea of lower courts and expressed confidence that a right of appeal to the Supreme Court was sufficient to "secure the national rights." In the end, the delegates reached a compromise – typically credited to Madison – that deferred the issue: Article III gave Congress the power to establish "inferior courts," but not the obligation to do so. As with virtually everything else in the Constitution, questions about how the federal judiciary would help the new nation keep its legal promises would be answered through trial and error.[55]

The prospect of a national judiciary with a broad mandate to ensure that Americans hewed to their legal obligations provoked fear and outrage among the Constitution's critics. Their complaints ran the gamut. Some were specific and pragmatic. A supreme tribunal with the power to superintend all manner of state-court cases would be a monstrous inconvenience for citizens forced to defend appeals hundreds of miles from home. But lower federal courts implanted throughout the nation were no more palatable. They were a needless expense, given the already-existing state courts, and represented an "unnecessary encroachment" that would engender a "revolt" by disgruntled citizens.[56]

The Anti-Federalists' principal fear was less coherent, but no less potent: The Constitution made the federal courts – and, by extension, the federal government – too powerful. Taken together, the several categories of jurisdiction Article III conferred on the federal judiciary formed a "boundless ocean" with no "defined limits." They included not only cases arising under treaties and federal law (already a field of "stupendous magnitude"), but also many disputes governed entirely by state law. It would take little ingenuity for federal judges to extend their power "to every conceivable case."[57]

Anti-Federalists had no doubt that the federal courts would accept the Constitution's invitation to assume power. They thought that judges were naturally inclined to "enlarge[] the sphere of the[ir] jurisdiction" whenever possible, as demonstrated by the grasping machinations of both the chancery and common law courts in England. Moreover, judges would do so imperceptibly. "A bad law immediately excites a general alarm," explained the anonymous Federal Farmer. But an abuse of judicial power, "though not less pernicious," happens largely out of public view. This silent invasion would do more than simply "annihilate" the state courts, Patrick Henry predicted. It would lead to nothing less than a wholesale "consolidation" of the states themselves "under one government."[58]

The threat lay not only in the courts' broad jurisdiction, but also in their ability to expand federal power beyond the Constitution's text. Article III, they pointed out, extended federal jurisdiction to cases "in Law" and "in Equity." Equity's historical purpose was to fill in gaps in the common law, to offer redress to injured parties as a matter of justice and natural right. But in the hands of federal judges, such unguided interpretive power was dangerous. Judges charged with defining the scope of Congress's legislative authority under the Constitution, Brutus argued, would not be confined by the charter's "words or letter," or controlled by any "fixed or established rules." Instead, they would be empowered to construe the Constitution "according to what appears to them, [its] reason and spirit."[59]

For many Anti-Federalists, empowering federal judges to define the government's authority according to the Constitution's "spirit" portended disaster. They were already concerned that a theory of implied constitutional powers – one advanced by James Wilson, among others – would give Congress the authority to pass legislation on just about any subject that had previously been within the province of state governments. In particular, implied powers might allow Congress to abolish slavery. Allowing federal judges to interpret the Constitution equitably only magnified this concern. George Mason made the connection clear when he complained that extending federal jurisdiction "to all cases in law and equity" meant it would go to "every object of private property."[60]

Anti-Federalists thought the danger the courts posed to state autonomy was all the greater because there was no countervailing power to restrain them. The President was to appoint federal judges with the "Advice and Consent" of the Senate, but the executive and legislative branches had little formal control over judges once they were in office. Article III gave them life tenure as long as they maintained "good behavior," which meant that neither the president nor Congress could remove them without cause (and only by impeachment). Congress was also prohibited from reducing a judge's salary.[61]

The Constitution's protections for judicial office had deep roots. Americans of the revolutionary generation resented the fact that colonial judges generally served at the King's pleasure. Those concerns resurfaced in the face of perceived state legislative tyranny in the 1780s. Judges could only resist the "oppressions of the representative body," Hamilton argued in *The Federalist*, if they did not have to rely on the legislature's goodwill for their offices. Thomas Jefferson agreed: In *Notes on the State of Virginia*, he complained that legislative control over judges' compensation and tenure rendered them unlikely to challenge the lawmakers' "despotic" assumption of power.[62]

Despite this tradition, Anti-Federalists worried about the consequences of freeing the new federal courts from all control. In England, Parliament could correct erroneous judicial rulings. But with no superior tribunal above the Supreme Court, there was no body under the Constitution that could correct misguided decisions made by unelected, unaccountable magistrates (Figure 1.2). "Men placed in this situation," the writer Brutus warned, "will generally soon feel themselves independent of heaven itself."[63]

For the Constitution's critics, the threat of uncontrollable courts was especially grave because of what the document did *not* include – the guarantee of a jury trial in civil cases. There was consensus at the Convention that the Constitution would guarantee a jury trial in *criminal* cases, but the question of a civil jury right did not arise until late in the drafting process. Every state provided for one by constitution or statute, so perhaps advocates simply assumed the same would be true at the federal level. But when George Mason argued that a civil jury guarantee would "give great quiet to the people," his proposal was voted down. Once Congress made the Constitution's draft public, critics immediately excoriated the Convention for failing to protect the civil jury. The attacks were so vehement – and so

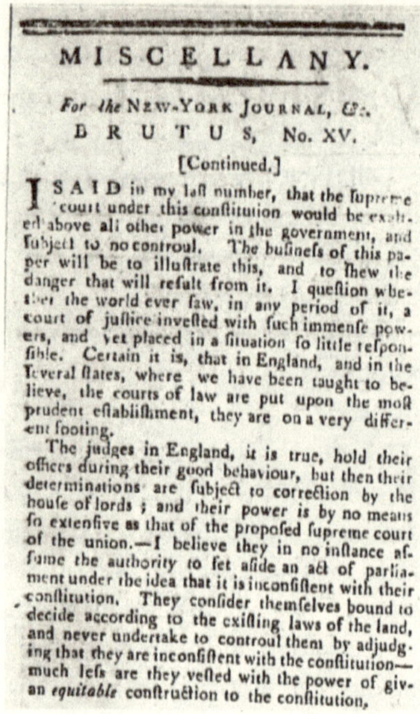

MISCELLANY.

For the NEW-YORK JOURNAL, &c.

BRUTUS, No. XV.

[Continued.]

I SAID in my laſt number, that the ſupreme court under this conſtitution would be exalted above all other power in the government, and ſubject to no controul. The buſineſs of this paper will be to illuſtrate this, and to ſhew the danger that will reſult from it. I queſtion whether the world ever ſaw, in any period of it, a court of juſtice inveſted with ſuch immenſe powers, and yet placed in a ſituation ſo little reſponſible. Certain it is, that in England, and in the ſeveral ſtates, where we have been taught to believe, the courts of law are put upon the moſt prudent eſtabliſhment, they are on a very different footing.

The judges in England, it is true, hold their offices during their good behaviour, but then their determinations are ſubject to correction by the houſe of lords; and their power is by no means ſo extenſive as that of the propoſed ſupreme court of the union.—I believe they in no inſtance aſſume the authority to ſet aſide an act of parliament under the idea that it is inconſiſtent with their conſtitution. They conſider themſelves bound to decide according to the exiſting laws of the land, and never undertake to controul them by adjudging that they are inconſiſtent with the conſtitution—much leſs are they veſted with the power of givan *equitable* conſtruction to the conſtitution,

FIGURE 1.2 Anti-Federalists like the pseudonymous Brutus feared the Constitution's creation of a federal judiciary "subject to no controul." "Brutus, No. XV," *New-York Journal and Patriotic Register* (Mar. 20, 1788).

effective – that Hamilton devoted an entire essay of *The Federalist* to explaining and defending the omission.[64]

The jury's importance lay in its ability to resist judicial enforcement of unjust and oppressive laws. In both England and the colonies, the jury was long understood to have both fact-finding *and* law-finding power. That notion still held true in late eighteenth-century America, despite an increasing belief that judges held particular legal expertise. As John Jay explained to a federal jury in 1794, questions of both fact and law were within its "power of decision." This was precisely the power that enabled colonial juries to check oppressive parliamentary legislation and allowed post-independence state juries to rule in favor of debtors. If a jury did not like the outcome the law prescribed, it could choose another. Anti-Federalists extolled this idea. They conceded that jurors were not "minutely skilled in the laws." But they had something more precious – a "common sense" understanding of justice.[65]

For Anti-Federalists, the jury's popular notions of legality were a bulwark against the federal courts' potential despotism. Judges, drawn from the political and professional elite, were always "much better friends to government than to the people." The jury, in contrast, came from the citizenry itself (or at least from its white, male, and propertied portion). It was the mechanism by which the people exerted their "just and rightful controul in the judicial department," the "check of the democratic branch" made manifest in the courts. Without such protection, asked the Democratic Federalist, "[w]hat refuge shall we then have to shelter us from the iron hand of arbitrary power?"[66]

For the Constitution's supporters, however, allowing populist sympathies to intrude in legal proceedings was a recipe for international disaster. Hamilton acknowledged that civil juries were a "valuable safeguard to liberty," and nothing in the Constitution prevented Congress from providing for them by statute. But a blanket guarantee was dangerous, especially in cases where jurors would be tempted to rule in favor of their neighbors against foreigners. This was most apparent in suits over debts Americans owed to British creditors. Even when the laws were in the creditors' favor, John Marshall later recalled, the debts simply "could not be recovered" in the state courts. Farmers sued by foreign creditors could count on a sympathetic jury infected with what Madison termed "local prejudices."[67] Such obstructionism appalled the many delegates concerned about the nation's reputation abroad. The United States would be unable to restore its "public or private credit," warned James Wilson, if it could not offer debtholders a "just and impartial tribunal."[68]

Hamilton homed in on the foreign relations problem of jury incapacity in *The Federalist*. "I feel a deep and deliberate conviction" he wrote, "that there are many cases in which the trial by jury is an ineligible one." Chief among them were those implicating "the public peace with foreign nations." Such disputes often turned on questions of international law that ordinary jurors were ill-equipped to understand. Moreover, Hamilton suggested delicately, juries were susceptible to "impressions" that distracted them from the "considerations of public policy" which ought to guide their deliberations. He was more explicit in private correspondence: "When the deliberative or judicial powers are vested wholly or partly in the collective body of the people," he confided to Gouverneur Morris, "you must expect error, confusion and instability."[69]

Despite Hamilton's best efforts, his opponents prevailed, at least in part. Article III underwent no revisions, leaving in place the several categories of jurisdiction and the equitable authority that worried Anti-Federalists, and the states ratified the Constitution without a civil jury right. But enactment of the Seventh Amendment two years later ensured that a jury trial right would "be preserved" in most civil cases. For better or for worse, many of the legal disputes that shaped the nation's relationships with foreign sovereigns – like suits over British-held debts – would be decided by the people.[70]

* * *

For all the arguments Article III provoked, there was one point on which everyone agreed: Federal judges would be exclusively responsible for resolving disputes that arose at sea. Though this uncontested jurisdiction was only theoretical at ratification, it would prove to be the most important source of judicial authority in the courts' early years.

The unanimity on this point was striking. According to the Constitution's supporters (like James Wilson), admiralty jurisdiction "ought to be given wholly to the national Government." Madison echoed the point in the Virginia ratifying convention; the federal judiciary needed "exclusive jurisdiction" over maritime cases. Even the Constitution's critics agreed. The Virginia ratifying convention, for example, issued a report recommending the creation of only a single supreme court, and abolishing the judiciary's power to hear cases arising under federal law and those between citizens of different states. But it allowed for the establishment of "courts of admiralty," vested with the power to hear all cases of "maritime jurisdiction." The same was true in New York, where Anti-Federalists conceded that lower federal courts could try admiralty and piracy cases. In fact, none of the 200-plus constitutional amendments submitted to the First Congress recommended stripping the courts of their admiralty jurisdiction.[71]

The consensus in favor of the judiciary's maritime authority held when it came time for the First Congress to create a functioning system of federal courts. This was the "most important business" the legislature confronted in its first session, according to one member, and it was not easy. As a Virginia commentator put it, Article III only "crayoned in the outlines" of a new national judiciary, so Congress had to "fill up and colour the canvas."[72] In particular, the Convention had left it to Congress to decide the most controversial issues, such as the establishment of lower federal courts and whether the federal courts would have all the jurisdiction that Article III allowed. When Congress first established a quorum in April 1789, it had an entire government to create, so responsibility for fleshing out the details of federal judicial power fell to a Senate committee headed by Oliver Ellsworth, a Connecticut lawyer and judge. It took the committee more than two months to report a bill, and final passage required another three months of debate and revision.[73]

The legislation that Congress eventually approved represented a compromise on federal judicial power. The Judiciary Act of 1789 established a judicial presence across the nation. It created a Supreme Court that sat twice a year, and provided for a district court, manned by a single judge, in each of the eleven states that had ratified the Constitution (plus Maine and Kentucky). Without these lower courts, advocates argued, the new government would not have "the power necessary to carry its laws into execution." More controversially, the Act also created three circuit courts presided over by one district court judge and two Supreme Court justices. The circuit courts did not create new federal offices – an important point for critics of an expansive federal apparatus. But they did have jurisdiction over a broad range of cases, including most federal crimes, disputes involving foreigners or between citizens of different states (known as diversity jurisdiction), and high-value suits by the government.[74]

The Judiciary Act also included significant concessions to those who remained fearful of federal judicial authority. Most notably, the Act did not grant the courts general jurisdiction over cases "arising under" federal law, which meant that state courts would be the primary forum for adjudicating cases implicating important federal rights and interests. In addition, the circuit courts' diversity jurisdiction was limited to cases worth more than $500 – a meaningful restriction, given the low dollar amount of most debt suits. The result was that many cases that Congress *could* have allocated to the federal judiciary would remain in the state courts. In addition, the Act anticipated the Seventh Amendment by stipulating that a jury would decide questions of fact, and it prohibited appellate judges from revisiting such determinations. With these limitations, proponents of federal authority sought to reassure critics that their worst fears about a judicial assault on state autonomy would not come true.[75]

When it came to judicial power over the seas, however, no compromise was needed. In essence, the district courts were the federal admiralty tribunals that even the Constitution's fiercest critics conceded were a "necessity." Most of the courts alternated their sessions between multiple locations within their districts, and almost all were in seaboard towns. The Judiciary Act gave them jurisdiction over some land-based cases, including minor federal crimes and small-dollar suits brought by the government. But the "real meat" of their jurisdiction, as Julius Goebel evocatively put it, was their authority over "all civil causes of admiralty and maritime jurisdiction." In addition, the circuit courts had appellate jurisdiction in all admiralty suits worth more than $300, ensuring that the Supreme Court justices would have the opportunity to review important matters arising at sea.[76]

The Judiciary Act also contained two provisions inspired by the bitter experience of having state courts decide prize cases during the Revolutionary War. First, the district courts' admiralty jurisdiction was "exclusive" – meaning, "exclusive[] of the courts of the several States." This was one of the few aspects of the district courts' jurisdiction they did not share with state courts, confirming that even the greatest skeptics of federal power no longer believed that the states had a role in resolving waterborne conflicts.[77]

Second, the Act stipulated that the trial of factual issues in both district and circuit courts would be by jury in all cases, *except* those "of admiralty and maritime jurisdiction." In fact, by its terms, the Act also excluded juries from customs and revenue cases – a surprising decision, given the pre-Revolutionary outrage over juryless proceedings in vice-admiralty courts in cases involving violations of colonial trade and navigation laws. But as Justice Samuel Chase would explain two decades later, Congress's reason for placing revenue cases under the courts' admiralty jurisdiction was because such disputes – like matters involving captures at sea – were too important to be "left to the caprice of juries." Going forward, responsibility for adjudicating maritime controversies would belong to federal judges.[78]

The legislators who passed the Judiciary Act knew that it was only a beginning. Madison admitted to a friend that the legislation was "pregnant with difficulties." Not simply because it fleshed out an aspect of federal power which had been "most criticized" in the ratification debates, but also because the Act itself created a system that was "peculiarly complicated & embarrassing." The support the Act received in Congress also belied the disgust it provoked among its critics. William Maclay, who kept a diary of Senate proceedings, faithfully recorded his persistent opposition to the "vile bill" Ellsworth had brought forth.[79]

Less than a year after the Act's passage, Congress decided to take a second look. It asked Edmund Randolph, whom George Washington had appointed as Attorney General, to prepare a report on all matters of federal justice "as may require to be remedied." Randolph was a sensible choice to identify defects in Congress's effort to create a judiciary that would be palatable to all. He was an able lawyer and experienced politician, having served in multiple state and federal government positions. He was a proponent of the new national government, but was critical of the Constitution he had helped shape, believing that certain of its aspects formed "the foetus of a monarchy." He also had an unfailing instinct for taking middle-of-the-road positions, often to the frustration of his contemporaries.[80]

Randolph's report to Congress in December 1790 reflected his concern that the Judiciary Act's compromise between federal and state authority would undermine national harmony. His solution was to distinguish their respective domains more clearly, in ways that simultaneously expanded and contracted federal judicial power. One recommendation was to give the federal courts exclusive authority over certain matters implicating national interests, such as federal crimes and suits against the United States. He also proposed an express grant of jurisdiction over cases arising under federal law, which was conspicuously missing from the Judiciary Act. At the same time, he recommended removing the federal courts' authority to issue "all writs" not otherwise provided for by statute – a capacious grant of power that had already sparked controversy. Most notably, he proposed eliminating Section 25 of the Act, which gave the Supreme Court broad authority to review state court decisions on questions of federal law. Randolph predicted – correctly – that the Court's appellate power over state tribunals would cause strife and resentment, and his solution was to provide litigants an alternative path to federal court that would not trench on state autonomy.[81]

Like his contemporaries, one aspect of the Judiciary Act that Randolph thought needed little modification was its exclusive grant of federal jurisdiction over admiralty and maritime matters. He identified it as the "first" among the categories of federal judicial power that, under the "vital principles of the Union," necessarily "shut[] out the jurisdiction of the State courts." Recognizing that even minor maritime disputes could have significant consequences if not handled fairly and expeditiously, Randolph proposed to exempt admiralty cases from the minimum value requirement he applied to all other lawsuits filed in the federal courts, and to allow district courts to hold special sessions only in admiralty matters. Not every water-related incident needed to be in federal court; state tribunals could handle suits over seamen's wages, for example. But any case with greater stakes, such as "piracies and felonies on the high seas" or "prizes in time of war," was exclusively federal.[82]

In his report, Randolph took pains to explain *why* giving the federal courts plenary authority over maritime cases was a matter of national importance. Most proponents, like Hamilton, Wilson, and Madison, rarely bothered to justify this position, perhaps because they believed the explanation was too obvious. But Randolph thought it crucial to remind his readers *why* admiralty jurisdiction had to be exclusively federal. The first reason was pragmatic and deeply familiar. As the revolutionary experience demonstrated, allowing state courts to adjudicate cases implicating the rights of foreigners might cause international conflict, obliging the United States to provide "reparation of some injury" or perhaps even "involv[ing] the confederacy in war."[83]

The second reason for exclusive federal authority over the waters was more abstract, but no less critical. Admiralty jurisdiction, Randolph explained, was an expression of sovereign authority. The oceans were the "great highway of mankind," shared by all nations, and each had the authority to resolve disputes over seagoing ships, goods, and people. As a result, asserting and exercising the power to adjudicate cases arising on the water was universally considered one of the principal "attributes of independence." If the United States wanted to act like a sovereign nation, and be treated like one, it was essential that its courts have "prerogative" over maritime matters.[84]

In the end, Randolph's plan to put the federal judiciary on firmer footing went nowhere. His exaltation of admiralty jurisdiction aroused no apparent comment, but his proposal to eliminate Supreme Court review of state court rulings appalled those who believed that it would give free reign to "local interests" that sought to "obstruct the ... administration of justice." For Randolph's critics, the whole point of creating a federal judiciary was to ensure that state parochialism did not undermine national interests. Whatever the merits of Randolph's other proposed reforms – and there were many – his report was essentially doomed from the start.[85]

The swift demise of Randolph's proposals meant that responsibility for defining the bounds of federal judicial power would fall largely on the judges themselves. For Madison, the Judiciary Act was only a "first essay." He hoped the Act would "undergo a reconsideration under the auspices of the Judges," for they alone could "set it to rights."[86] It would not be easy. As John Jay predicted shortly after becoming Chief Justice, the "difficulties" that inhered in the compromise system the First Congress created meant that judges would "often find themselves embarrassed." Even the courts' largely unquestioned authority over admiralty and maritime matters would require elaboration and specification. The "minute detail" of the courts' jurisdiction and procedure, Randolph believed, "ought to be consigned to the judges," for "time and practice can alone mature the judicial system." The first generation of federal judges would soon have that opportunity, whether they wanted it or not.[87]

PART I

THE STRUGGLE FOR NEUTRALITY, 1793–1797

2

War Comes to America

In early May 1793, Gideon Henfield piloted the British merchant ship *William* into Philadelphia harbor, and was promptly thrown in jail. Henfield was a Revolutionary War veteran from Massachusetts, and the *William* was his prize of war. But it was not an American capture. The *William* had been seized off the Delaware coast by the *Citoyen Genet*, a French-commissioned privateer whose name reflected the revolutionary enthusiasm and outsized ambition of the new French minister plenipotentiary to the United States, Edmond-Charles Genet. Genet had recently landed in Charleston, and had immediately set about licensing privateers to attack British merchant ships in the western Atlantic. Henfield enlisted in the French cause, along with other Americans motivated by dreams of republican brotherhood and the allure of lucrative prizes. After the *William*'s capture, Henfield sailed her to Philadelphia, to be condemned and sold by French officials.[1]

Henfield's rude reception was not what Genet anticipated. A few weeks earlier, thousands of cheering Philadelphians had greeted the arrival of the French naval frigate *Embuscade*, and Charlestonians had welcomed Genet with similar exuberance. Genet protested Henfield's arrest to Secretary of State Thomas Jefferson. Henfield had done no wrong in defending "the glorious and common cause of liberty," Genet argued, and he demanded the seaman's immediate release.[2]

Jefferson politely declined to intervene in the judicial proceedings against Henfield. The executive branch, he explained to Genet, had no authority over the officers who had taken Henfield into custody. "In our country," Jefferson later elaborated, "the Judiciary is sovereign in its department, and can neither be controuled nor opposed by the Executive." Jefferson nonetheless promised that Henfield would be afforded every opportunity to defend his conduct before a jury of his co-citizens, supervised by federal judges of "learning and integrity."[3]

Jefferson's defense of judicial autonomy sounded in constitutional principle, but it was inspired by international politics. He and his colleagues in George Washington's cabinet *wanted* the federal courts to decide Henfield's fate. Many Americans – including Jefferson himself – supported revolutionary France's struggle against the allied monarchies of Europe. But the Washington administration was desperate to keep the United States out of the war. Entanglement threatened the United States with economic and military devastation, while remaining neutral would show the world that the fledgling republic could fulfill its legal obligations to other nations. Steering clear of the expanding conflict, however, was an enormous challenge, both politically and legally.

Faced with an existential crisis it could not manage on its own, the Washington administration turned to the newly established federal courts for help. It asked the justices of the Supreme Court to endorse its neutrality policy, it sought criminal convictions against adventurers like Henfield, and it encouraged British officials to file civil suits to recover ships seized by privateers. The Washington administration's view, Attorney General Edmund Randolph told a federal judge, was that the judiciary was "combined with the Executive" in preserving American neutrality.[4]

The Neutrality Crisis, as this episode came to be known, marked the emergence of a new role for the federal courts in establishing national sovereignty. The diplomatic travails of the 1770s and 1780s convinced political leaders in the United States to create a national judiciary that would uphold the nation's obligations under treaty and international law (see Chapter 1). But the global struggle that erupted in 1793 presented a different challenge. The United States was caught between the competing demands of powerful foreign empires, and it was not clear what the nation's duties even were. By giving the courts responsibility for resolving difficult and highly consequential legal disputes, the Washington administration sought to avoid taking sides in a contest with existential implications both at home and abroad.

The administration's acts were also born of desperation. The annals of Washington's presidency have long provided fodder for scholarly debates over whether the constitutional framers meant to give Congress or the president greater authority in war and foreign affairs. In reality, deep tensions over the scope of federal power meant that the executive and legislative branches of government had limited ability to prevent maritime adventurers from dragging the United States into conflict. If the nation was going to steer a neutral path through the conflagration consuming the Atlantic world, the courts would have to take the lead.[5]

Federal judges, however, had deep doubts about the role assigned to them. Washington's appointees to the bench wanted to help the executive branch navigate the Neutrality Crisis, but they were not the acquiescent handmaidens in foreign affairs that modern commentators imagine. They balked at violating longstanding principles of international law, and they were wary of compromising the judiciary's own institutional integrity by intervening in the affairs of state. In the midst of an international conflict of unprecedented scope, the framers' earlier confidence that the federal courts would unerringly champion the nation's interests looked premature. The Neutrality Crisis was the first test of the new federal government's ability to defend American sovereignty, and it was very possible that it would fail.

* * *

The challenge the French Revolution posed for American political leaders was evident from the moment Genet arrived. Only thirty years old, he was a rising star in French republican circles. He entered the royal diplomatic service as a teenager, and in 1788 he was named secretary of the French legation in Russia. Catherine the Great eventually expelled him, for publicly advocating revolutionary principles in "a much higher Tone" than was deemed proper. But the Girondins who came to power in France after abolition of the monarchy were delighted to find an ardent republican in the diplomatic corps. Soon after Genet returned to Paris in 1792, he was appointed minister to the United States (Figure 2.1).[6]

Genet's mission to solicit American help was crucial to the "worldwide risings" that his revolutionary supervisors envisioned. They

FIGURE 2.1 Edmond-Charles Genet's defiance of the Washington administration's neutrality policy nearly dragged the nation into war. Portrait by Adolf Ulrich Wertmüller (1784), oil on canvas, courtesy of the Albany Institute of History & Art, bequest of Nancy Fuller Genet, 1978.6.1

recognized that the United States was too weak to assist on the battlefield. But Americans could make advanced payments on the United States' outstanding Revolutionary War debt, send shipments of grain to feed a starving French populace, and enter into a new commercial treaty that would benefit France (and disadvantage Great Britain). Brimming with optimism, French idealists assumed that their fellow-republicans across the Atlantic would come to France's aid. When Genet left France in early 1793, the ship he sailed on bore a message of revolutionary solidarity on its sails: "Freemen, we are your brothers and friends."[7]

There was also a more aggressive dimension to Genet's mission. His instructions from Paris directed him to undermine British and Spanish power in North America by incubating "revolutionary principles" among its residents. One prong of this strategy involved building a military force to seize Spanish possessions along the Mississippi. Genet's second and far more consequential assignment was to use the United States as a base for maritime raids on British commerce. When he left France, he carried with him hundreds of blank privateering licenses, to be delivered to American merchants and ship captains willing to fight the Republic's enemies.[8]

Genet's privateering plans were a critical component of the French war effort. The British Navy was the world's most powerful, while the Revolution's social upheavals had caused disarray in the French naval service. In addition, political instability and slave rebellion had disrupted French control of its Caribbean territories, leaving its maritime forces few safe harbors in the Western hemisphere. Meanwhile, American port cities teemed with fast vessels and experienced sailors, many of whom had been privateers during the American Revolution. With American support, French-commissioned ships could wreak havoc on British trade.[9]

Genet's initial reception in the United States promised great success. Charleston's decidedly pro-French population greeted him with banquets, speeches, and friendly audiences with the city's social and economic elite. On his way north to Philadelphia, he was cheered by adoring crowds and entertained by southern grandees, living, as he put it, "in the midst of perpetual fetes." James Monroe reported to Thomas Jefferson that in Virginia one could "scarcely find a man unfriendly to the French revolution." When Genet finally reached the capital, a delegation of leading citizens paraded him into town before an assembly of thousands. For the next several days, Genet attended public dinners featuring liberty caps, rounds of toasts, and roaring renditions of "La Marseillaise." For Genet, this rapturous reception was proof of Americans' eagerness to aid their brothers across the Atlantic.[10]

This public enthusiasm prompted Genet to ignore the Paris government's warning not to antagonize American officials, and he embraced his self-assigned role as the Revolution's advance sentinel. He had no trouble finding takers for his privateering commissions. There were French people "full of zeal for their country" in every American seaport, he reported. But U.S. citizens also joined the effort, inspired by a mixture of republican ardor, a desire for adventure, and the possibility of sudden riches.[11] Genet was eager to capitalize on the excitement. He distributed commissions to French consuls located in other port cities, with instructions to set up ad hoc prize tribunals that would transform seized vessels and cargo into cash for the captors. Soon, French-commissioned privateers were prowling the eastern seaboard from Boston to Savannah, hunting for unsuspecting British and Spanish ships.[12]

George Washington was much less enthralled with Genet's mission. The president set out for Philadelphia from his home at Mount Vernon as soon as he got wind of privateers fitting out in American ports. But first he quickly scribbled letters to both Jefferson and Secretary of the Treasury Alexander Hamilton. Washington thought it crucial that the United States maintain "strict neutrality" in the war between France and Great Britain, and wanted his cabinet to come up with a plan for "proper & effectual" action as soon as possible. His urgency bore fruit. On April 22, 1793 – only two weeks after Genet's arrival – the president issued a short statement declaring that the United States' "duty" and its "interest" demanded that it act impartially toward the European powers at war. Any American citizen who engaged in hostile acts would receive no protection from the government. Indeed, the administration would pursue criminal prosecutions in federal court against those who violated the law of nations.[13]

The Neutrality Proclamation, as it came to be known, belied the fact that Americans were anything but impartial when it came to the French Revolution. Many bore longstanding and bitter resentment against Great Britain, and were eager to see it humbled by stout fellow-republicans.[14] But the support for France had a deeper wellspring than simple revenge. Many Americans believed that republicanism itself was under threat, both abroad and at home. The divisions in the American body politic exposed by the debates over the Constitution's ratification were growing more prominent. In particular, the delicate consensus among political elites that produced and defended the Constitution – exemplified by Hamilton's collaboration with James Madison in *The Federalist* – was beginning to fray. The unraveling originated in divergent ideas about the national government's role in finance and the economy. By 1793, however, Jefferson and his adherents feared a broader "monocratic" conspiracy to introduce British institutions into the United States, concentrate authority under a quasi-king, and even reestablish subservience to the English crown.[15]

For the partisans who came to be known as Republicans, Europe's future would decide America's. Many Jeffersonians feared that, if the allied monarchies defeated France, the "craving appetite of despotism" would accept "nothing less than American vassalage," as one newspaper put it. Genet's arrival gave worried Americans hope that constitutionalism, republicanism, and popular sovereignty would triumph over the forces of monarchy and tyranny. Even when events in France took a more violent turn – such as the execution of Louis XVI – Americans wore cockades and the *tricolor*, renamed streets to promote republican values, and celebrated every French victory on European battlefields.[16]

In contrast, Federalists feared the radical displays of popular sovereignty in Europe as much as Jeffersonians celebrated them. For men like John Adams and Alexander Hamilton, the French Revolution had devolved from a "struggle for liberty" into "crimes and extravagancies." If French radicals prevailed over the forces of stability and established government, the disorder would inevitably spread across the Atlantic.[17]

Domestic developments amplified the Federalists' apocalyptic concerns. France's declaration of war against Great Britain inspired Americans across the country to form "democratic societies" devoted to the promotion of civil liberty. Federalists were convinced that these associations were conduits through which the evils of absolute democracy would flow from France into the United States, and – according to George Washington – "poison the minds of the people."[18] They did not have to look far to see their worst fears being realized. The spread of revolutionary principles around the Atlantic had already helped inspire a massive rebellion by black enslaved persons in the French colony of Saint Domingue. The tales of violence and death reported by white refugees especially horrified southern slaveholders. If the forces of radical republicanism prevailed in Europe, arch-Federalist Harrison Gray Otis predicted, Americans would need to prepare to be "good and dutiful subjects to the French" (Figure 2.2).[19]

Divergent views of the French Revolution stoked conflict in Washington's cabinet, as well. Hamilton saw the political instability in France as reason to ignore Genet, and even repudiate the existing treaties between France and the United States. Jefferson opposed this idea as legally unjustified and deeply offensive to France. Their growing political rivalry entangled the Neutrality Proclamation itself. Jefferson argued that a declaration of neutrality was equivalent to a declaration of war, which the Constitution said only Congress could make. Hamilton published a series of essays defending the Proclamation and articulating an expansive view of executive power in war and foreign affairs. Jefferson was appalled by Hamilton's

FIGURE 2.2 Political cartoons expressed federalist fears that the French revolution would inspire anarchy in the United States. Here, a man presumed to be Thomas Jefferson pledges to "knock[] down a government," joined by an unsavory character invoking the French revolutionary anthem "Ca ira" and a person of African descent asserting it would be "our turn nex[t]." "A Peep into the Antifederal Club" (New York, 1793), courtesy of the Library Company of Philadelphia

"heresies," and he urged Madison to respond and "cut [Hamilton] to peices in the face of the public." Though Hamilton prevailed on issuance of the Neutrality Proclamation, bigger fights over the constitutional allocation of power were soon to come.[20]

Amid their deepening differences, the members of Washington's cabinet agreed on one basic principle – the United States should stay out of the war. It was a simple question of costs and benefits. Joining the conflict would be of little help to France. The United States was bereft of both soldiers and money, so a declaration of war would simply saddle France with a junior partner requiring more in protection than it could provide in aid. And the dangers of war were potentially enormous. Territorially, the United States was surrounded by British, Spanish, and potentially hostile Indian forces, and any belligerent conduct in France's favor risked retaliation that the United States was unprepared to resist. Plus, the national economy depended on maritime commerce, both in exporting American-grown food to European colonies in the Caribbean and in carrying products from those colonies to markets in Europe. Formal entry into the confrontation would allow British warships to decimate American shipping.[21]

Neutrality also offered the United States the chance to profit from others' misery. Jefferson recognized that war in Europe would increase demand for American products, especially food. Indeed, one of Genet's assignments was to buy American grain, and he promised the Washington administration that he would use any advanced debt payments to purchase war material and other supplies. Neutrality also gave American merchants a competitive edge. While the vessels of belligerent nations were subject to capture by their enemies, neutrals were free to trade with each other and with belligerents – at least in theory. More ambitiously, European powers preoccupied by conflict across the Atlantic might be cajoled into making concessions over North American territory they could no longer manage (as France later did with the Louisiana Purchase).[22]

Neutrality's strategic advantages appealed to Hamiltonians and Jeffersonians alike. Hamilton's vision for an American economic powerhouse depended on the tax revenue that flowed from robust commerce with Europe. The growth in foreign trade that would result from staying neutral could swell government coffers, while wartime disruptions threatened the new nation's fiscal well-being.[23] Jeffersonians were more ambivalent; they feared commerce's corrupting influence on individual morals, and the foreign entanglements that came with overseas trade. In his more fanciful moments, Jefferson envisioned the United States as a self-sufficient republic that would "abandon the ocean altogether." But he also had a realist side, and he recognized that the virtuous agrarian polity he dreamed of could not thrive without foreign markets for its produce. If nothing else, Jefferson proclaimed with his characteristic combination of eloquence and avarice, war between European powers meant that "the new world will fatten on the follies of the old."[24]

For Jefferson, maintaining neutrality also demonstrated the United States' moral superiority. He understood war to be fundamentally incompatible with republican government, and with the American character. "No country," he declared soon after Genet's arrival, "was ever so thoroughly disposed against war, as ours." He understood it to be a necessary evil at times, whether to throw off the yoke of oppression (as in the American Revolution) or to retaliate against the supposed barbarities of less-civilized polities (like Native nations or the Barbary States). But war was expensive, resulting in high taxes and debt. And it reeked of despotism, as it invariably empowered the executive branch – a particular concern of those, like him, who saw "monarchical" tendencies among Washington's supporters. The struggle between France and the allied powers offered the United States a chance to prove that differences between sovereigns could be resolved without resort to violence – "by appeals to their interests," he explained to James Madison, rather than "by appeals to arms." A free and neutral republic, standing apart from the bloody conflict ravaging Europe, would be a "precious example to the world."[25]

* * *

Neutrality, it turned out, was easier to declare than it was to achieve. Within days of Washington's proclamation, French prizes arrived in Philadelphia, to the delight of crowds that assembled to greet them. Even before Genet arrived, the government in London alerted its minister in Philadelphia, George Hammond, about the French mission to advance the "dangerous and delusive Principles of Liberty and Equality." Permitting French sympathizers to violate American neutrality, the British warned, was "disgraceful to the character of a Sovereign Neutral Power," and would be "most injurious to [its] interests." Once Genet's plans began to bear fruit, Hammond bombarded Jefferson with complaints, warning that the United States' toleration of such activities would have "dangerous consequences."[26]

Genet and his subordinates had no intention of relenting. The French minister acceded in the administration's request that he restore a vessel seized by a French warship in Delaware Bay, but French consuls condemned and sold a number of other prizes with Genet's blessing. In mid-May 1793, Jefferson warned Genet that the United States would not allow continued privateering, and in early June the administration ordered that French privateers armed in the United States depart from American waters. But Genet showed little inclination to cooperate. Soon after the administration's directive, Hammond complained to Jefferson that French privateers were still fitting out in U.S. ports.[27]

The problem was that Genet and the Washington administration had divergent understandings of what it meant to be neutral. The cabinet came to agreement that the United States had to maintain "strict" neutrality, which meant equal treatment of both sides. Administration officials – Jefferson in particular – found support for this position in the writings of the law of nations publicists. According to Emmerich de Vattel, neutral nations were to remain "strictly impartial towards the belligerents ... without favoring either side." Luminaries such as Grotius, van Bynkershoek, and Wolff agreed; neutrals had to abjure "favouritism toward or prejudice against either belligerent." For the Washington administration, this meant that neither the British nor the French could use the United States as a base for launching attacks on the other. Permitting one side to do so, Jefferson explained (paraphrasing Vattel), would be a "fraudulent neutrality, of which no nation would be the dupe."[28]

Neutrality meant something very different to Genet. France did not want the United States to formally join the war, but it expected preferential treatment. Writers on the law of nations promoted "strict" neutrality in theory, but, in practice, nations commonly engaged in "benevolent" neutrality, which involved unacknowledged but sometimes quite obvious favoritism. A neutral nation might allow one of the belligerents to raise troops in its territory, or it might provide financial assistance to one side. This was precisely what France did early in the American Revolution. It maintained a formally neutral stance while providing Americans with loans, military equipment, and vessels of war. In fact, France allowed American privateers to use French ports as bases for preying on British shipping, in violation of France's treaty with Britain. Genet therefore had every reason to believe that American impartiality could – and should – shade in France's favor.[29]

There was also the matter of treaties. As Vattel acknowledged, a sovereign who wanted to stay out of a war could maintain "strict neutrality" yet still "fulfill his obligation" under a treaty. Indeed, the law of nations *required* that a neutral nation honor its agreements. In Genet's view, the treaties the United States made to secure France's support for the American Revolution now authorized him to launch privateering raids from American ports. In particular, Article 17 of the 1778 Treaty of Amity and Commerce between France and the United States permitted each nation's armed ships to bring their captures into the ports of the other, and forbade government officers from arresting such prizes or "mak[ing] examination concerning the[ir] lawfulness." Article 22, in turn, prohibited any nation at war with one of the signatories (i.e., Great Britain) from fitting out their ships in the other's ports, or from selling their prizes there.[30]

Genet understood these treaty provisions to give him carte blanche to arm and equip privateers in American ports, while denying the same right to Great Britain. He also believed that French consuls in the United States had exclusive authority to condemn and sell ships and cargo seized by French privateers. And Genet thought American participation in privateering was entirely permissible, because nothing in the treaties or in federal statutory law forbade it. Even Edmund Randolph admitted that these provisions created "great perplexities" for the United States, for they seemed to give France legal rights that were denied to Great Britain.[31]

In response, the Washington administration pushed the principle of strict neutrality to its limit. It would deviate from equal treatment only when a treaty expressly gave France a particular right. Article 22, for example, *denied* Great Britain the right to arm its ships in U.S. ports, but nowhere did the treaties expressly *grant* that right to France. So strict neutrality obliged the United States to deny permission to both. Likewise, the law of nations only allowed a foreign representative to assume jurisdiction over maritime captures when expressly permitted by the host nation. Article 17 precluded U.S. officers from assessing the "lawfulness" of French prizes, but it did not confer authority on French consuls to do so.[32] Nor could Americans participate in French privateering. The law of nations required that a neutral nation prevent its citizens from injuring foreign subjects, and nothing in the treaties gave Americans the right to join the French war effort. In short, there was nothing in the French treaties that explicitly overcame the United States' legal obligation to treat both sides the same.[33]

The administration framed its rigid approach to neutrality as a legal imperative, but it was as much a political choice. Historical examples of ostensibly neutral nations providing aid to a belligerent – like France in the American Revolution – suggested that "strict" neutrality existed more in theory than in fact in the late eighteenth century, regardless of what Vattel and others wrote. And even if the administration understood the law of nations to impose a binding obligation of strict neutrality, it interpreted the United States' treaty obligations as narrowly as possible, to reach the conclusion that France had no right to arm privateers in the U.S. ports. When faced with legal questions susceptible of multiple answers, the administration chose those that would help it stay out of the war.[34]

The Washington administration's interpretive decisions underscored the challenge it faced in turning the Constitution's promise of national sovereignty into a reality. As we saw in Chapter 1, the new charter was intended to enable the United States to fulfill its responsibilities under treaty and international law. If the republic wanted to be treated as sovereign, it needed to act like one. But what if its legal duties were unclear, and subject to dispute? What if the United States found itself caught between powerful European empires with conflicting views of what the United States owed them? It was all well and good to design a government in 1787 that, in theory, had the capacity to uphold the nation's commitments to foreign sovereigns. But amid the global realities of 1793, the government first had to figure out what those duties were, and convince others to agree.

Getting everyone on board with the administration's understanding of neutrality proved impossible. In late June, the administration learned that Genet was converting a recently captured British merchant vessel into a privateer, right in plain view in Philadelphia. Shocked by Genet's audacity, Jefferson asked him to keep the ship in port until President Washington could decide how to proceed. Genet flew into a rage, and railed that the administration's neutrality policy violated the 1778 treaty. After calming down, he made vague assurances that the vessel would stay put, but then ordered it to set sail anyway. Making matters worse, the administration learned that Genet, believing the American people supported him more than the president, also threatened to appeal his neutrality policy "to the people." For Washington, these acts bordered on sedition. "Is the Minister of the French Republic," Washington fumed, "to set the Acts of this Government at defiance—*with impunity*?"[35]

Genet's disobedience prompted the Washington administration to turn to federal judges to justify its understanding of neutrality. Shortly after Genet allowed the controverted privateer to depart, Jefferson prepared a list of questions for the Supreme Court justices addressing the key issues that Genet and the administration were disputing. For example: Could France arm privateers in U.S. ports? If it was unlawful to fit out privateers entirely, could French ships still augment their force in the United States? Could French consuls in the United States condemn prizes? If not, could privateers sell their prizes in the United States before they had been condemned by a French admiralty tribunal? Answers to these questions, Jefferson explained to the justices, would help the government avoid "errors dangerous to the peace of the United States."[36]

In truth, the administration did not really need the justices' legal guidance. Jefferson claimed that the questions were of "considerable difficulty," and that the administration would benefit from the justices' "knolege of the subject." But the cabinet was largely in agreement on the most important issues. It had already decided that French-commissioned ships could not arm in U.S. ports, and Washington had ordered Genet's privateers to leave. The administration likewise agreed that French consuls could not convene prize tribunals in U.S. territory, and Jefferson threatened those who conducted such proceedings with revocation of their consular status in the United States. In fact, before even receiving the justices' response, the administration issued a set of privateering rules that addressed nearly every issue in Jefferson's questions.

What the administration needed help with was getting *others* to come around to its views. Genet was no more likely to defer to the Supreme Court than he was to President Washington. But the headstrong minister was not the only audience. Judicial endorsement of the administration's legal position might help persuade the French government in Paris that Genet had gone too far (in fact, the cabinet was considering requesting his recall). More important, the justices' views might have an impact domestically. As Jefferson explained to a friend, Americans' "predilection" for France was the reason that that French-commissioned ships were still arming in U.S. ports and enlisting American seamen.[37] The cabinet hoped that an opinion from the Supreme Court would persuade everyone involved to adhere to the administration's strict neutrality policy. The justices' "authority" in matters of domestic and international law, Jefferson told them, would "ensure the respect of all parties," as well as the "public."[38]

The administration had every reason to believe that the Supreme Court would endorse its understanding of neutrality. Washington had populated the early judiciary with like-minded political elites, steadfast supporters of the new Constitution and federal government. James Wilson, for instance, was one of the most influential members of the Constitutional Convention and an ardent defender of the Constitution in ratification debates in Pennsylvania. William Paterson, from New Jersey, was also an important Convention delegate, having played a key role in ensuring equal representation for small states in the Senate. Even Supreme Court nominees chosen primarily to ensure geographic balance, like James Iredell of North Carolina, could be trusted to defend federal authority. And one justice had already publicly demonstrated his support. In a grand jury charge delivered in Virginia in May 1793, Chief Justice John Jay declared that, under the law of nations, a neutral nation had to observe "a strict impartiality" toward both sides in war. As Iredell later reported to Edmund Randolph, the justices were eager to use their position to affirm "the duties of Individuals in [support] of the Government."[39]

The administration also had every reason to expect that the justices would answer its questions. Advisory opinions – legal opinions from judges outside the context of a litigated case – were common in the English tradition, and in the justices' own early practice. Plus, cabinet members and justices regularly consulted on legal and political matters during Washington's presidency. Jay was particularly close to both Washington and Hamilton, and he even wrote the first draft of the Neutrality Proclamation.[40]

Despite this tradition of advice-giving, the justices declined to answer the administration's questions. They recognized the urgency of Jefferson's request, but in their view it would be improper to decide important legal issues "extrajudicially." Such conduct would blur the "Lines of Separation" the Constitution drew between the three branches of government. The justices were fully prepared to help the president in any way "consistent with their official duties," but they were also confident that he was capable of preserving the nation's "Rights, Peace, and Dignity" on his own.[41]

The justices' refusal has long puzzled historians and legal scholars. Traditional accounts of this episode credit them with adhering to a self-evident prohibition against "advisory opinions" grounded in Article III's extension of the judicial power only to "Cases" or "Controversies."[42] The justices' reference to "Lines of Separation" between the branches lends credence to this interpretation, but virtually all modern commentators agree that early separation of powers principles were not well formed enough to preclude advisory opinions.[43] A related theory suggests that the justices "drew sharp lines" between themselves and the executive branch to enhance the credibility of rulings supporting the administration's position they knew they would eventually make in litigated cases. But it is unclear why the justices believed that the Washington administration would benefit from their refusal to give answers it clearly wanted.[44]

The justices' caution makes more sense when viewed in light of how federal judges responded to the Neutrality Crisis as a whole. For the next several years, they hesitated before embracing the prominent role that the Washington administration asked them to play in defusing a major foreign affairs crisis. One can understand why. The explosive domestic politics that surrounded the French Revolution ensured that any decisions judges made would be subject to intense criticism. In fact, the administration's request sparked complaints in the Republican press that the proper interpreter of the nation's international legal obligations was not "a bench of judges," but "the voice of America." The justices may also have been worried about committing themselves to particular legal positions at a moment of great political and legal uncertainty. They may well have thought that a cautious approach to adjudicating the rights of foreign sovereigns, in the context of actual cases, was the more prudent approach.[45]

The justices were already familiar with the perils of making unpopular decisions. Their refusal in 1792 to adjudicate pension claims from Revolutionary War veterans had stirred resentment in Congress and calls for impeachment in the newspapers. For the next two years, the justices studiously avoided ruling on the constitutionality of the statute that assigned them those duties, in the hopes that Congress would solve the problem (which it did).[46] Their February 1793 decision in *Chisholm v. Georgia* – that states could be sued by citizens of other states in federal court – provoked widespread outrage, and led to an eventual reversal by constitutional amendment. And just as the administration was preparing its neutrality questions, Jay came under personal attack for his circuit court ruling that the 1783 Treaty of Peace invalidated Virginia state laws protecting its citizens from the collection of British debts. So the justices had every reason to avoid stepping into yet another political dispute, especially one inflaming partisans on both sides of the Atlantic.[47]

The justices' refusal may also have been motivated by more mundane concerns. Answering the administration's questions would require serious research and thought, and the justices were already displeased with their workload. As they put it in a plaintive 1792 letter to Congress, their circuit riding duties required them to travel the country for months at a time, at their own expense, "to pass the greater part of their days on the road, and at Inns, and at a distance from their families." The conditions were often miserable; they traveled roads that alternated between impassable mud and choking dust, crossed frozen rivers, and had to "sleep in a room with five People and a bed fellow of the wrong sort." As Gouverneur Morris memorably put it, serving as a Supreme Court justice required "less the learning of a judge than the agility of a post boy."[48]

Most of the justices were eager to be rid of circuit riding. Throughout the 1790s, they tried to persuade Congress to eliminate or at least lessen their obligations, and they even volunteered to give up a large part of their salaries in return. To be sure, circuit riding was not all bad. At times, the justices enjoyed the company of friends and local dignitaries, and their travels allowed them to make valuable political and social connections. James Wilson even met his second wife – thirty-two years his junior – while presiding at court in Boston. But for most the burdens outweighed the pleasures.[49] Thomas Johnson retired in 1793 specifically due to circuit riding, and Jay's continued displeasure prompted him to run twice for the more sedentary position of governor of New York (the second time successfully). The justices' bitterness may explain why, in their letter declining to opine on the Neutrality Crisis, they noted that the president's constitutional power to demand opinions from government officers was "expressly limited to *executive* Departments." This would not be the last time the justices resisted the Washington administration's effort to saddle them with the work of steering the nation through international controversy.[50]

* * *

The Washington administration did have another way of getting federal judges to weigh in on the legality of French privateering. Seeking to make good on Washington's threat in the Neutrality Proclamation, cabinet officials instructed federal district attorneys to identify illegal privateering conduct anywhere in the country and "bring the culprits to condign punishment." Gideon Henfield, the American mariner who landed in jail after sailing the *William* into Philadelphia, was the first of several privateers to be hauled before a federal court.[51]

From the administration's perspective, criminal prosecutions enabled judges to help preserve American neutrality in two ways. First, they gave the justices of the Supreme Court another opportunity to "try the question" of the United States' legal obligations, as Jefferson put it, but now in the context of an actual case. The circuit courts had original jurisdiction over most federal crimes. They were composed of a justice of the Supreme Court and the judge of the local federal district court, and they met twice annually, in spring and fall. When the court convened, a grand jury – a body of "discreet and respectable" citizens – decided whether evidence of criminal conduct was sufficient to allow prosecutions to go forward (if so, they were tried before a "petit" jury). Crucially, grand jurors made their decisions under judicial guidance. The presiding judge – usually the Supreme Court justice – informed the jury of the law governing an indictment.[52]

Grand jury charges were more than a set of legal instructions. They were an opportunity for the nation's "republican schoolmasters," as one historian described the judges, to educate jurors and the public about the responsibilities of citizenship in a constitutional republic. As future justice William Paterson put it when debating the Judiciary Act in Congress, the circuit courts would edify the people by "carry[ing] Law to their Homes." The justices may have resented their circuit riding duties, but their arrival was a major event in local communities. Newspapers reprinted their jury charges, and the grand jurors themselves often published formal responses, giving rising to a legal and political dialogue between the government's most prominent jurists and the citizenry (or at least the "respectable" members selected for jury service).[53]

The judges' pedagogical platform gave them the opportunity to promote the administration's position on neutrality both at home and abroad. Jefferson anticipated that federal judges presiding over grand jury proceedings would "study and define" the law of neutrality for an untutored American audience, as Chief Justice Jay did in Virginia in May 1793. His lengthy discourse was reprinted in several newspapers, ensuring a wide audience for judicial condemnation of acts that endangered the nation. Jefferson forwarded copies to American representatives in Paris and London. Judicial pronouncements about the nation's rights and duties under law, he argued, were proof of the United States' "bona fide intentions to preserve neutrality."[54]

The second benefit of criminal prosecutions was that they would "satisfy the complaint" made by British officials about French privateering, as Jefferson put it. He promised British minister George Hammond that the United States would use "all the means in our power, to protect and defend [British] vessels and effects." Meting out criminal penalties to men like Henfield was one way to fulfill that obligation. Jay said so in his May 1793 grand jury charge: A neutral nation's obligation to maintain "exact Impartiality between the parties at war" made it the jurors' duty to "prosecute and punish" anyone who threatened it.[55]

In truth, the law of nations did not clearly require the United States to assume responsibility for suppressing French privateering entirely. As a general principle, a sovereign nation that permitted its citizens to injure foreigners effectively caused the injury itself, and was responsible for providing a remedy – for example, by punishing the offender. Failure to do so justified reprisals by the injured nation, and could lead to war. But the duty to prevent injuries extended only to cases in which it was actually within the sovereign's power to do so. As Vattel explained, even "the best governed State" could not always command "exact obedience" from its citizens. In addition, a nation's obligations to remedy injuries caused by its *own* citizens did not necessarily translate into a duty to control the behavior of *foreign* citizens within its borders (for example, French citizens who enlisted on French-commissioned privateers).[56]

Assuming a duty that international law did not mandate, however, gave the United States an opportunity to demonstrate that it was truly sovereign. If the law of nations required a neutral state to prevent violations by persons over whom it exercised authority, it was essential that the United States show the world that it had could actually exercise control over those within its territory. Hamilton, in particular, balked at admitting to any deficiency in federal power. A legitimate sovereign was presumed to have "a competent police" to prevent infractions of its duties toward foreign nations. A government that sought to excuse its failures by pointing to its own weakness was one that would never be worthy of international esteem. This was not a new position for Hamilton; he made the same point five years earlier in *The Federalist*. "The rights of neutrality will only be respected," he exhorted his audience, "when they are defended by an adequate power."[57]

The problem for the Washington administration was that the federal government did not have "adequate power" to deal with the French privateering crisis. In fact, in 1793 there was barely a government at all. The State Department – created by Congress to handle matters respecting foreign affairs – had fewer than ten employees in the United States. The Treasury Department was better staffed, with more than 500 workers, most of whom were responsible for customs collections along the east coast of the United States. But they rarely left the ports in which they were stationed, which left it to thirty-odd officers in revenue cutters to patrol 1,000 miles of coastline. Finally, there were only sixteen federal district attorneys – one for each judicial district – and these were only part-time government officers.[58]

It was also unclear who was in charge of this skeletal federal administration. In early May 1793, William Vans Murray, a member of the House of Representatives from Maryland, wrote to Hamilton for advice about what local federal officers should do about a captured British ship that had just arrived in Chesapeake Bay. Murray thought it his duty, as a citizen, to uphold Washington's Neutrality Proclamation, but he needed guidance from the executive branch, "some *leading impression*." He even reached out to the federal district court judge for Maryland, looking for someone – anyone – who could instruct him. In the meantime, the British consul at Norfolk contacted the state governor, and local merchants simply wrote to Washington directly.[59]

This confusion over the structure of federal governance was understandable. Congress in 1789 had provided little direction as to the responsibilities of the three primary executive departments – Treasury, War, and State – so "the line of partition" between them, Edmund Randolph complained, was "not always obvious." Nor was it clear what kind of problem French privateering posed. Was it a diplomatic matter for the Department of State, or a military issue under the purview of the Department of War?[60]

In practice, the Washington administration made its decisions collectively. The cabinet met more times in 1793 than in all the other years of Washington's presidency combined. This approach had advantages; it helped ensure that the administration's policy was measured and subject to scrutiny from political leaders with different priorities. But internal wrangling over details made quick and decisive action difficult.[61]

The deeper challenges the Washington administration faced were political partisanship and personal rivalry. Anti-Federalist fears of centralized government power had not disappeared after ratification. In some ways, they had grown stronger, by being focused on the person of Alexander Hamilton. As Treasury Secretary, Hamilton was the head of the department whose reach extended to every corner of the republic. Republicans were convinced – with some justification – that Hamilton was using his office to enhance the federal government's fiscal authority and aggrandize executive power. He was more successful with the former than the latter, but Jefferson spoke for many when he described Hamilton as the Federalists' "colossus," a "host within himself."[62]

Hamilton's influence with Washington meant that Jefferson was perpetually on alert for any action by the Treasury Secretary to consolidate his authority. So Jefferson recoiled when Hamilton proposed that the government interdict French privateering by having customs officers report suspicious activity to him directly. Jefferson considered incidents affecting foreign nations to be in his bailiwick. Plus, Hamilton's proposal evoked bitter memories of the abuses perpetrated by British customs officers prior to the Revolution. Jefferson argued that Hamilton's plan would transform the customs collectors into a "corps of spies or informers" and augment a department that already enjoyed much "business, patronage, and influence."[63]

The result of the cabinet standoff was an awkward compromise that once again tried to leverage judicial power to preserve American neutrality. Jefferson argued that the job of detecting infractions should be left to grand juries, the "constitutional inquisitors and informers of the country," who were "scattered everywhere [and] see everything." But Randolph thought it would be self-defeating for the administration not to take advantage of customs officers' ability to gather information, and proposed that they report suspected neutrality violations to the local federal district attorney, who would set in motion "the grand jury, judges, and rest of the judicial apparatus." Hamilton eventually agreed, but did not issue instructions to the customs collectors for several months. In the meantime, Randolph instructed the district attorneys to seek information from customs collectors and bring charges against offenders, but how the system was to work in practice was not clear.[64]

The administration's difficulties were most apparent in its relations with state governors. As Randolph explained, the nation's sheer size made it necessary to "substitute[e] the agency of the Governors in the place of an instantaneous action in the Federal Executive." The federal military had only a few thousand soldiers, most of whom were tasked with fighting Native people in the western territories. Congress passed a statute in 1792 empowering the president to call out a state militia when the laws were violated by "combinations too powerful to be suppressed by the ordinary course of judicial proceedings." But Washington had yet to exercise that authority, and there is no indication the administration considered it.[65] Instead, Secretary of War Henry Knox circulated the administration's neutrality rules to the state governors, asking them to "suppress all practices" tending to violate those regulations, and Jefferson instructed federal district attorneys to convene arbitral panels that would advise governors on what to do with seized vessels.[66]

State officials proved to be unreliable guarantors of American neutrality. A few governors took the responsibility seriously, and at times complaints by British officials triggered restoration of captured property through gubernatorial intervention.[67] But even diligent state officials let suspected privateers go free, deterred by the political and financial consequences of detaining vessels without specific instructions from the executive branch. Some governors were downright recalcitrant. Massachusetts Governor John Hancock allegedly acted slowly against French privateers because he was "obviously in favour of the French Claims," and British officials claimed that most state governors, especially in the south, were so hostile to Great Britain that they would "readily connive" in French schemes.[68]

The greatest problem for the Washington administration was that it had no constitutional authority to compel state governments into action. South Carolina Governor William Moultrie was a Revolutionary War veteran and an admirer of Washington. But, like many South Carolinians, Moultrie supported the French Revolution, and he encouraged Genet's privateering plans even as the French minister's provocative conduct led others to turn against him. When the administration asked state governors to restore French prizes seized in violation of American neutrality, Moultrie politely demurred. He had sworn an oath to uphold the federal Constitution, and it stipulated that treaties with foreign nations were the supreme law of the land. In Moultrie's view, Article 17 of the 1778 Treaty precluded American officials – including state officers – from scrutinizing the "lawfulness" of French prizes. He recognized that the Washington administration interpreted the treaty differently, but his constitutional duty to "exercise [his] own judgment" obliged him to refuse the president's request for aid. Treaties might be supreme law, Moultrie seemed to say, but nothing in the Constitution gave the president supreme authority to decide what they required of American officials.[69]

Despite the law enforcement challenges the Washington administration faced, Gideon Henfield's prosecution in July 1793 started off well enough. The presiding judge, Justice James Wilson, was a staunch proponent of federal power generally, and his experience as a lawyer and legislator under the Articles of Confederation had convinced him of the need for national judicial authority that would enforce the United States obligations under treaty and international law (Figure 2.3). Wilson was also a renowned legal theorist, and he regaled the Henfield jurors with a learned (if meandering) disquisition

FIGURE 2.3 Justice James Wilson's erudite support of the Washington administration's legal position was not enough to persuade jurors to criminally convict Americans who enlisted on French privateers. Portrait by Jean Pierre Henri Elouis (c. 1792), courtesy of the Smithsonian American Art Museum

on the law of nature, the law of nations, and the common law. But his central point was clear enough. Because the wayward actions of a single individual could drag the entire country into a conflict, conduct that compromised American neutrality – like Henfield's enlistment on a French privateer – was criminally punishable in federal court.[70]

As he lectured his audience, Wilson paused to acknowledge the difficulty public authorities faced in attempting to control the behavior of adventurers like Henfield. Noting with regret that "disorderly citizens" were found in every polity, Wilson asserted that even "the best regulated state" could not be expected to "superintend the whole Behaviour of all the Citizens." Accordingly, it would be unjust to hold a sovereign responsible for every instance of individual misconduct.[71]

Wilson's preemptive apology might have seemed out of place in admonishing a jury to act decisively against those who threatened the nation' security. But he knew there were flaws in the government's case. There was no statute or treaty that expressly forbade Americans from participating in French privateering (as Genet delighted in pointing out). Neither Wilson nor anyone in the cabinet thought this was a serious problem. In their view, Henfield's conduct violated both the general law of nations and the guarantee of peace between Great Britain and the United States in the 1783 Treaty of Paris, both of which were "the laws of the United States."[72] But not everyone was sure the federal courts had authority to punish crimes that were not specified by statute. There was precedent in English and state practice, but the idea triggered fears of unrestrained federal power, which would come to a head later in the decade. Indeed, Jefferson himself would ultimately deny that the federal courts had jurisdiction over so-called "common law" crimes.[73]

The more fundamental problem for the Washington administration was that Henfield's jury might simply decide for itself what the law of neutrality required. As we have seen, Americans venerated the jury because of its authority to determine both the facts and the law free from judicial control (see Chapter 1). The government's prosecutor, District Attorney William Rawle, tried to circumvent the jury's possible obstinacy by appealing to its sense of international duty. The federal executive, he explained, was incapable of the "unusual exertions of power" needed to satisfy its neutral obligations. But the executive's weakness could be remedied by the courts. Judges and jurors were empowered to apply the law of nations, and could ensure that disputes between sovereigns over the rights and duties of neutrality would be resolved by resort to "the scales of justice," not "the sword of war."[74]

The Henfield jurors rejected Rawle's appeals to law and duty, and in doing so they severely undermined the Washington administration's effort to preserve American neutrality. The jury acquitted Henfield after several adjournments, despite Wilson's closing admonition that they were bound by the law and could not decide the case "as they pleased." It is unclear precisely why the prosecution failed. Henfield's attorneys argued that he became a French citizen prior to enlisting, and therefore his actions were neither attributable to the United States nor punishable by it. Some – like Alexander Hamilton – suspected that the acquittal stemmed from pro-French sympathies among the jury and the broader public. It is also possible that the jury simply found Henfield's conduct innocent, given that he had enlisted before news of Washington's Neutrality Proclamation had reached Charleston.[75]

Whatever its logic, the Henfield verdict was a nightmare come true for those of the founding generation who doubted whether juries could be trusted to act in the national interest. Just like in the Revolution and under the Confederation, an unaccountable jury reached a decision that prevented the United States from keeping faith with its international legal obligations. The Washington administration tried to mitigate the damage, stressing to both domestic and international audiences that the verdict did not technically mean that Henfield's conduct was legal. Jefferson sent copies of Wilson's grand jury charge to Paris and London, and Randolph penned an anonymous newspaper note emphasizing that the judges, "with whom the law rests," had declared Henfield's actions to be criminally punishable.[76]

For others, however, the Henfield jury had simply performed its constitutional duty of letting the people decide what the law required. The result in Philadelphia was soon replicated elsewhere. In Georgia, several men indicted for serving on a French privateer were, like Henfield, acquitted "contrary to the opinion of the judges" but, according to a sympathetic commentator, in keeping with "the rights of man." Four men arrested in Boston on charges of "piratically" capturing the vessels of friendly nations were ultimately indicted only for a misdemeanor offense, and apparently never tried. Criminal prosecution ended in failure even when the French consul in Boston forcibly resisted a federal marshal's attempted arrest of a British prize. The federal district attorney had proven the facts, but the grand jury "doubted of the law," and on that question it "did not chuse to consult the court."[77]

French sympathizers hailed these exonerations as confirmation that Americans had the right to join the war effort. Republicans in Boston toasted the "virtuous and independent" Henfield jurors, and a Philadelphia writer declared that a citizen of the United States could now "lawfully" serve on board a French privateer without fear of prosecution. Genet was ecstatic, and he published newspaper advertisements inviting all "Friends of Liberty" to enlist in the republican cause. Even Henfield himself reenlisted in the French service. As John Marshall later recalled, the verdict may have "bereaved" the Washington administration of the judicial support it was hoping for in maintaining American neutrality, but many in the United States celebrated the result with "extravagant marks of joy and exultation."[78]

* * *

Jefferson may have been frustrated by the result in *Henfield*, but he was undeterred. In fact, he was already pursuing an alternate strategy for enlisting the courts' help in preserving American neutrality, one that did not rely on executive power or juries. By June 1793, the cabinet was embroiled in a debate over what the executive branch should do about British ships seized by the first wave of French privateers. Hamilton warned that failure to provide restitution for all captures made in violation of American neutrality would make the United States "an accomplice in the hostility" and give Great Britain grounds for retaliation. But Jefferson argued that restoring prizes taken before the administration had formally prohibited privateering would be an aggression against France.[79]

Jefferson also knew there was another institution of government that could decide what to do with ships and goods captured in wartime. He advised Hammond that lawsuits by private parties over seizures that violated American neutrality would be "cognisable in our Courts of Admiralty." Any victim of French privateering who sought recovery of their property, Jefferson advised, should therefore "take measures as in ordinary civil cases for the support of their rights judicially."[80]

Steering disputes over French prizes into the courts made a lot of sense to cabinet officers caught between the Scylla and Charybdis of warring European powers. As Jefferson admitted, even "rigorous justice" from the executive branch regarding property captured in violation of American neutrality would "give dissatisfaction" to both France and Britain and "produce complaints from both." Requiring the owners to seek restitution by lawsuit relieved the administration of making such diplomatically fraught decisions. In addition, a civil suit gave the federal courts another opportunity to articulate the law of American neutrality to both domestic and foreign audiences – but this time without the interference of a jury. By apprising those involved in French privateering of "what they might or might not do," as Jefferson put it, judges could give the administration the legal support they were unable (or unwilling) to provide in other contexts.[81]

The problem with Jefferson's scheme was that no one else thought the federal courts had such a role to play in resolving the Neutrality Crisis. When Genet got wind of lawsuits over French prizes, he protested that French consuls had exclusive jurisdiction to adjudicate the legality of captures made by French armed ships. Any alleged violations of American neutrality could only be addressed by negotiation between governments, for no court had the power to "interpose itself between two nations." Hamilton agreed with Genet (for perhaps the only time in his life). The Treasury Secretary believed in federal judicial authority, but he believed in executive power even more. Controversies over the redress owed to victims of French privateering, he argued to Washington, were "an affair between ... Governments," to be settled "by reasons of state, not rules of law."[82] British officials in the United States concurred. They were already displeased with how the federal courts were handling debt cases, and thought Jefferson's plan for privateer litigation to be "perfectly inexpedient." In their view, intervention by the executive branch was the "only medium" through which restoration of captured ships could be effectuated.[83]

Jefferson persisted, however, and some skeptics began to come around. As the Neutrality Crisis worsened, Hamilton recognized that failure to provide recourse to the victims of privateer seizures would leave "a great *chasm* in the law." British officials also opened up to the possibility of going to court. Hammond continued to demand that the executive branch restore British ships, but he recognized that contesting the validity of French captures through multiple avenues might lead to better outcomes. He persuaded the owners of the *William* – the prize that Gideon Henfield had sailed into Philadelphia – to file suit in federal court, setting the stage for another confrontation over the judiciary's power to enforce American neutrality.[84]

The difficulties posed by Jefferson's strategy were evident from the start. William Rawle, the federal district attorney in Pennsylvania, represented the *William*'s owners (in his capacity as a private attorney). The district court, following standard admiralty procedure, issued a writ of attachment against the vessel. The French consul condemned the *William* as good prize anyway, and ordered that it be sold. When the deputy marshal of the district court tried to break up the French auction, Genet demanded that the *William*'s captors be compensated for their lost profits, and warned Jefferson against future judicial meddling. Yet the French captors also recognized the need to defend their seizure in court. They hired a prominent attorney of their own, French émigré Peter Stephen DuPonceau, who had also defended Henfield in his criminal prosecution.[85]

DuPonceau was a talented lawyer, and he immediately identified the weak spot in Jefferson's plan: It was doubtful whether international law allowed American courts to take jurisdiction over suits challenging French captures. First, DuPonceau argued that the Treaty of Amity's prohibition on American officers examining the "lawfulness" of French prizes extended to federal judges. Second, he contended that jurisdiction was prohibited by the law of nations rule that only the courts of the capturing nation could judge a prize's validity. A sovereign, DuPonceau explained to the court, was solely responsible for the conduct of his subjects in war. If a French-commissioned privateer unlawfully injured the citizens or subjects of another nation, France alone was responsible for righting the wrong. A neutral court's assumption of jurisdiction would infringe on French sovereignty. The way to redress neutrality violations was through the executive – "the only organ of government by which we communicate with foreign nations."[86]

In response, Rawle dodged DuPonceau's legal points, and instead extolled the virtues of judicial decision-making in a republican government. He conceded that disputes over privateer violations of American neutrality *could* be settled by diplomatic negotiation. But adjudication in court was the better option. Executive branch decisions would be unduly influenced by "motives of policy," while judges would adjudicate cases on their merits, according to established principles of international law. Indeed, Rawle argued, in a republic the courts were the only institution upon which an injured party could depend. While "despotic sovereignties" could restore captured vessels by fiat, in a "government of laws" the judiciary alone could redress wrongs.[87]

Richard Peters, a leading jurist and experienced admiralty judge, was not convinced by Rawle's paean to judicial authority. Peters was a reliable Federalist and entirely sympathetic to the Washington administration's position. He began his opinion in the *William* by acknowledging that cases arising from French privateering implicated the United States' "national dignity." And he had no doubt that, under the law of nations, neutrality violations required restitution to the victims. But neither the illegality of the *William*'s capture nor the necessity of remedying the injury answered the central question: "*Who* is to enquire into the matter, and either give or attempt the redress?"[88]

For Peters, remedying the deficiencies of American sovereignty was not the judiciary's responsibility. He carefully reviewed all the international legal authorities the parties cited, and agreed with DuPonceau. The courts of a neutral nation had no business adjudicating the validity of a prize of war. In fact, Rawle had not cited a single case or treatise suggesting that such jurisdiction was permissible. The logical conclusion was that the federal courts had no power to resolve legal disputes arising from "contests between belligerent powers."[89]

Peters's decision was yet another blow to the Washington administration's effort to secure judicial assistance in extricating the United States from calamity. Cabinet members expressed hope that Peters would reconsider his position, or that one of his colleagues would form a "contrary Opinion." But Peters soon dismissed another French capture case, and other district court judges followed suit. Like Peters, James Duane in New York believed that the United States had a "duty" to restore British property. But international law did not allow courts to do the political branches' dirty work. Where "the sovereignty of nations is concerned," Duane concluded, the "intervention of a neutral court" was too "exceptionable" to be considered. William Paca in Maryland agreed: All the authorities he read persuaded him that "exclusive power" over maritime captures rested with the courts of the capturing nation. In South Carolina, Thomas Bee simply noted that any complaint about a privateer's illegal conduct "must be made to the executive."[90]

Whether the district courts' denial of jurisdiction over French privateer captures was a constitutional success or failure depends one's perspective. The Constitution's framers created the federal judiciary, in significant part, to ensure compliance with the nation's obligations under treaty and the law of nations, especially in matters arising at sea. For the Washington administration, that meant the courts could enforce the nation's legal duty to observe strict neutrality between the warring parties. But for the district judges, a different responsibility took precedence – the command not to intrude on France's exclusive jurisdiction over its prizes. In choosing between conflicting legal principles, federal judges chose the one that limited their own power.

The rulings also reflected the judges' ongoing caution about intervening too directly, given the tensions of international politics and the uncertainties of domestic constitutionalism. The nation's "constitution and laws," they noted, did not "point[] out the channel" through which the United States should respond to neutrality violations. In fact, the "existing arrangement of our government" was not aimed at resolving "contests between other nations." And because judicial power should only be assumed "on a solid basis," they would confirm their decisions to the "usage of nations."[91]

For the judges, hewing to established international practice was the only prudent course. The United States was caught between jealous belligerents sensitive to any favoritism toward their rivals, a predicament Peters could not resist describing through maritime analogy: "[W]hile we are endeavouring to avoid one rock, we may split on another." The best way to demonstrate the United States' evenhandedness toward the warring parties was to adhere to "the customs of other nations" and decline jurisdiction. Peters admitted that his decision left him "anxious for the peace and dignity of my country." But to his mind, "political convenience" did not justify judicial intervention in the affairs of state.[92]

* * *

The Washington administration's repeated failures in court emboldened French officials. As the summer of 1793 wore on, French-commissioned privateers continued operating from American ports, despite the administration's repeated declarations that such conduct was illegal. Genet refused to allow a federal marshal in New York to take possession of a ship seized by a French privateer, on the ground that a decision on the capture's legality was exclusively his to make. The French vice consul in Boston went a step further, placing an armed guard on a French prize to stop a federal marshal from seizing it. Privateer crews evaded federal authority by deception and even threats of violence.[93]

The administration's inability to suppress French privateering infuriated Washington. Shortly after Gideon Henfield's acquittal, a cartoon circulated in Philadelphia depicting the president and Justice Wilson hauled before a guillotine. The president's head poked through the lunette, Hamilton and British Minister Hammond looked on mournfully. Washington exploded in anger when Knox mentioned the cartoon in a cabinet meeting. The president railed about the personal abuse he constantly received, despite the "purest motives" that guided his every decision. Working himself into one of his famous rages, Washington declared (according to Jefferson) that he would "rather be in his grave than in his present situation."[94]

Exasperated, Washington and his cabinet agreed to seek Genet's recall. Even Jefferson, who had initially been charmed by the French minister, now conceded that even the "most furious Jacobin" would find his conduct "indefensible." Jefferson was worried – correctly – that Genet's behavior risked undermining public support for France, and for the emerging Republican party Jefferson hoped to lead. With the cabinet's approval, he prepared a long letter to the American minister in Paris detailing Genet's misconduct – in particular, the arming of privateers and the assertion of exclusive jurisdiction over prizes. Above all, Genet had "insulted and set at defiance" the duly constituted government of the United States.[95]

The cabinet recognized, however, that Genet's ouster would not solve its problems. Even if the French government agreed to replace him, a response would take months to arrive. In the meantime, French officials could continue to make war from the United States without consequence. "What must the world think of such conduct," Washington plaintively asked Jefferson, "and of the Government of the U. States in submitting to it?"[96]

In truth, the Washington administration knew full well what the federal government's impotence looked like abroad. Hammond groused to his superiors in London that the administration was afraid to anger both France and the "French faction" in the United States, and therefore resorted to "half-measures and empty assertions of authority" that "would disgrace the miserable republic of San Marino." But British officials thought the problem went deeper, for the federal government seemed to lack the "energy" needed to enforce the law. Indeed, the diffuse American constitutional order itself was to blame. "In so relaxed a system of Government," the British consul at Philadelphia complained, "little reliance is to be placed upon the Protection of Laws."[97]

In desperation, the Washington administration turned to Congress. This was not a new idea. Jefferson had suggested calling the legislature into early session in the summer of 1793, but his cabinet colleagues were hesitant to give Genet another forum for challenging the president's authority (and Hamilton likely wanted to give the executive a free hand to deal with the crisis). By late 1793, however, the situation had become dire. When Congress met in regular session in December, Washington asked for legislation strengthening American neutrality. He had already declared, multiple times over, that it was unlawful to arm privateers in American ports, but the penalties for violations of the law of nations were either "inadequate" or "indistinctly marked." What the government needed was positive law delineating the bounds of permissible conduct.[98]

Getting neutrality-strengthening legislation through a divided Congress was a difficult task. Attorney General Randolph drafted a bill criminalizing participation in French privateering, but after a brief debate it was referred to committee, and did not reemerge until March 1794. When it did, it contained a new, highly controversial provision: A ban on the sale of prizes captured by any of the warring powers, irrespective of whether the capturing vessel had violated American neutrality. French sympathizers in Congress were irked by this transparently pro-British provision. Because of British dominance at sea, French privateers needed continued access to markets in the United States to make their ventures worthwhile, while British armed ships did not. The bill squeaked through the Senate, but in the House the pro-French faction – led by James Madison – managed to table it for several more months.[99]

The delay in the neutrality legislation could not have come at a worse time. Relations between Britain and the United States had long been rocky, and much of the disharmony had roots dating back to the American Revolution. Americans resented the ongoing British occupation of western forts, while the British complained about the continued obstacles British creditors faced in recovering their debts. Other difficulties were of a more recent vintage, such as British impressment of American seamen, Britain's alleged role in encouraging attacks in the Mediterranean by vessels from the Barbary states, and what many Republicans thought were unreasonable British restrictions on American trade.[100]

Tensions reached fever pitch in early 1794, as British warships began seizing hundreds of American merchant vessels trading with

French-controlled ports in Europe and the Caribbean. The House of Representatives passed resolutions calling for the sequestration of debts owed to British creditors to compensate for the seizures, and Madison led a successful effort to enact a temporary embargo on foreign trade, aimed at injuring Britain. Out in the streets, angry citizens took measures of their own. A Boston mob attacked the captain of a former American vessel that had been seized by British cruisers and sold in Barbados, and Hammond recalled the British consul in Baltimore to Philadelphia out of fears for his personal safety.[101]

Many in the United States thought war with Britain was imminent. The British consul at Philadelphia opined to his superiors that the United States, "tho' but an infant," was undoubtedly "the avowed Rival of Great Britain." To stave off the disaster of open conflict with the world's most powerful empire, in May 1794 Washington sent Chief Justice Jay to Britain to negotiate a treaty addressing the myriad difficulties between the two nations. As Jay left on his mission, the future of American neutrality looked precarious.[102]

Not all hope was lost, however. Genet continued to challenge the president's authority, even promising his superiors in December 1793 that he would "attack Washington himself in the Federal Court." Little did Genet know, however, that the new Jacobin regime in Paris had already agreed to his recall. The French government was disappointed by what it saw as Washington's favoritism toward Great Britain, but it had no desire to alienate the United States. So a new, more conciliatory minister arrived in Philadelphia in February 1794. Genet, however, did not return to France. The Jacobins had tried and executed many of his Girondin allies, and Genet feared that the guillotine awaited him back home. He married the daughter of New York Governor George Clinton, and lived the rest of his days in the United States as a gentleman farmer.[103]

Genet's exit from the political stage came just as a new possibility for judicial resolution of the Neutrality Crisis was emerging. This hardly seemed likely in early 1794. The judicial system the framers designed to uphold the republic's international commitments had failed to punish privateers who undermined its security or restore the vessels and goods they seized. The judges even failed to definitively declare that French privateering was a violation of the United States' neutral duty. And, in January of that year, Judge Duane of the New York federal district court joined his colleagues in refusing to take jurisdiction over privateer captures.[104]

Duane noted, however, that whether the federal judiciary could adjudicate cases implicating American neutrality was a question of "novelty and importance." As such, he believed that an answer was needed from "a much higher tribunal" than a district court. Duane did not specify the body to which he was referring. But in light of the Washington administration's repeated efforts to secure help from the justices of the Supreme Court, the answer was perhaps obvious.[105]

3

The Courts as Compromise

By the spring of 1796, Benjamin Moodie was tired of losing in federal court. He had arrived in Charleston two years earlier, in the midst of the Neutrality Crisis, full of enthusiasm for his duties as Great Britain's consul in Georgia and the Carolinas. But recovering ships and cargo seized by French-commissioned privateers was more frustrating work than Moodie anticipated. When he first assumed his post, Moodie expected that disputes over privateer captures would be "speedily removed by the Executive." But it soon became clear that the Washington administration wanted judges to decide what to do about British property seized in alleged violation of American neutrality. So Moodie filed dozens of lawsuits to recover captured ships and cargo. He succeeded in entangling a number of French prizes in litigation. But privateer subterfuge and judicial solicitude for France's treaty rights resulted in the dismissal of many of his cases.[1]

Then Moodie caught a break. Oliver Ellsworth, the newly appointed Chief Justice of the Supreme Court, happened to be riding the southern circuit through Charleston in May 1796. Ellsworth did not really want to be there. He was from Connecticut, and he had anticipated being assigned to ride the relatively benign eastern circuit. But as he explained in a plaintive note to his wife and young children, a "different arrangement" among his colleagues meant that "Daddy [wa]s going about a thousand miles further off, where the oranges grow."[2]

Ellsworth's appearance in Charleston may have been a personal misfortune, but it was a boon for the British – and for those in the

United States who wanted to stay out of Great Britain's expanding war with France. A recently concluded Anglo-American treaty, negotiated by John Jay, banned the sale of French prizes in the United States. The Jay Treaty (as it came to be known) was deeply divisive at home, and Moodie could not persuade state and federal officers in Charleston to enforce it. But Ellsworth had no such qualms. He was a staunch Washington administration ally, and had led the treaty's defense in the Senate. With a bit of legal ingenuity, the Chief Justice granted Moodie's request for an injunction prohibiting the auction of a recently arrived French prize, and soon federal courts around the country began issuing similar orders. The problem of French privateering soon faded away, and the peace Jay secured with Great Britain was preserved.[3]

Ellsworth's "lucky interposition," as British officials described it, underscored how the international political dynamics of maritime war in the 1790s reshaped the federal courts' place in the American constitutional order. As we have seen, the framing generation envisioned the judiciary as a vital institution for keeping faith with the United States' obligations under treaty and the law of nations (see Chapter 1). But the Washington administration in 1793 wanted the courts to do more – to take responsibility for adjudicating disputes between powerful foreign empires that threatened the nation's peace and security. The judges initially resisted, reluctant to transgress foundational limits on their own powers and expose themselves to the opprobrium that might result (see Chapter 2).

Over the next several years, however, federal judges gradually exerted greater authority to define the boundaries of American neutrality. In early 1794, the Supreme Court suddenly – and somewhat inexplicably – decided that federal judges *could* police the wartime conduct of belligerent nations. British officials like Moodie responded to the Court's invitation by launching a proxy war against French privateers in federal court. They did not always prevail, but the courts' ability to provide redress that the executive branch could not – or would not – helped keep the United States at peace. By 1796, Ellsworth's willingness to enforce a deeply controversial international agreement against the interests of a foreign sovereign confirmed the courts' more assertive role.

A tale of judicial ascendancy in the 1790s might seem at odds with our usual understanding of the courts as the weakest branch of the early federal government. But the truth is that the Washington administration deliberately sought to make the courts supreme, at least at sea. Faced with a diplomatic crisis that it could not manage on its own, the executive branch insisted that the judiciary was the proper institution of American government for resolving disputes over the legal rights of foreign nations. Executive branch officials rejected French demands that they intervene to stop suits over French prizes brought by British consuls, and echoed Jefferson's assertion that the federal judiciary that was "liable neither to controul nor opposition from any other branch of the Government."[4]

Like any other constitutional evolution, the rise of judicial authority in the Neutrality Crisis was neither linear nor inevitable. To justify the courts' primacy, cabinet officers recast inchoate and disputed ideas about judicial autonomy as foundational principles of American constitutionalism. British officials were skeptical of the courts' ability to enforce the United States' treaty obligations, and their French counterparts never accepted the legitimacy of judicial decision-making on questions of sovereign right. Judges themselves – including Ellsworth – harbored doubts of their own. They were troubled by the consequences of ignoring the limits that international law placed in their own jurisdiction, and worried about the burdens that privateering cases imposed on an institution that was still struggling to find its feet. Yet they eventually came to accept that judicial resolution of disputes arising at sea was necessary to keeping the United States out of the war. In the end, Jefferson's vision of a robust judicial role in promoting American sovereignty prevailed.[5]

* * *

Thomas Jefferson resigned from Washington's cabinet in December 1793, but it was largely thanks to him that a judicial role in resolving the Neutrality Crisis remained possible. The claimants in the first French privateering case in federal court – involving the *William* – chose not to appeal the Pennsylvania district court's ruling that it lacked jurisdiction over the matter (see Chapter 2). But Jefferson was determined to bring the question before a higher authority, and the June 1793 capture of the Swedish sloop *Betsey* by the same French privateer – the *Citoyen Genet* – offered another opportunity. The *Betsey*'s owners initially asked the captor's namesake, French minister

Edmond-Charles Genet, to return the vessel. But he refused, and the French consul at Baltimore decreed the ship a valid prize.[6]

Fearing the loss of their property, the *Betsey*'s owners asked Jefferson to intervene and restore the vessel. He did not respond (or at least there is no record of a response), so the owners went to court. When federal district court judge William Paca dismissed their suit in August 1793, they again sought Jefferson's help, and he referred their request to Secretary of War Henry Knox. Knox concluded that the *Betsey* did not qualify for restoration by the executive branch under the Washington administration's rules. An appeal to the circuit court, he advised, was the only way forward.[7]

Jefferson knew what he was doing in steering the *Betsey*'s owners toward a higher tribunal. Knox was apparently wrong that the vessel did not qualify for restoration by the executive branch, but Jefferson evidently made no effort to correct the mistake.[8] The day after the district court dismissed the case, Jefferson wrote to Gouverneur Morris, the American minister in Paris. Jefferson acknowledged that the federal district courts had declined to take jurisdiction over privateering captures. But the question of which branch of government would resolve such disputes was "not yet perfectly settled," and he expressed confidence that the justices of the Supreme Court would "decide it finally." So when the circuit court affirmed the district court's denial of jurisdiction, Jefferson again declined the owner's request that the executive intervene. A "remedy in the courts of justice," Jefferson explained, was "the only one" available to them.[9]

Jefferson's obstinacy reflected just how essential judicial resolution of privateering disputes had become. The Washington administration took the position that the law of nations obliged the United States, as a neutral, to do everything in its power to prevent France from using the country as a staging ground for attacks on British subjects. One way to fulfill this duty – securing criminal prosecutions against suspected privateers – had proven impossible (see Chapter 2). So in response to continued British demands for action, the administration pledged that it would either restore British ships seized in violation of American neutrality or pay compensation.[10]

The Washington administration's pledge to restore property seized in violation of American neutrality, like its stringent understanding of what neutrality generally entailed, sounded as much in politics as in law. Jefferson admitted that no treaty imposed such a requirement. At Washington's request, Attorney General Edmund Randolph probed mercantile opinion in Philadelphia on the question, but he could find no indication that restoration of seized property by neutrals was a practice known in Europe. But assuming responsibility for ships and goods captured by French privateers would appease the British. And it would demonstrate that the United States could remedy injuries resulting from the behavior of those within its borders.[11]

The problem was that restoring ships and cargo seized by French privateers proved just as difficult as restraining them in the first place, for many of the same reasons. Initially, the administration tried to decide restoration questions by itself. But coordinating with state and federal officers in far-flung locales proved cumbersome, and Washington's deliberative style made decisive action even more difficult. As Jefferson admitted to British minister George Hammond, the cabinet's "functions" were "not analogous to the questions of law and fact produced by these cases." Nor were French officials inclined to cooperate. Despite Jefferson's threat of revoking consuls' permission to stay in the United States, they continued to facilitate the sale of prizes. On occasion, privateers resisted with force efforts by state and federal officers to take back captured property. If the courts did not intervene, it seemed, the administration's promise to repair the injuries caused by privateers would be an empty one.[12]

The significance of the test case that Jefferson manufactured was not lost on anyone. *Glass v. Sloop Betsey* was a "case of consequence," wrote Justice William Cushing shortly after the Supreme Court argument in February 1794, one of "utmost importance to us as a nation," according to Congressman Uriah Tracy. The attorneys who argued *Glass* also emphasized the stakes. Peter DuPonceau, representing the captors, warned that the federal courts' assumption of jurisdiction would give France "a just and honorable cause of war." The claimants' lawyers – leading Philadelphia lawyer Edward Tilghman and former federal judge William Lewis – agreed as to the case's importance, but for the opposite reason. The courts' failure to take jurisdiction would represent a rejection of the nation's neutral duty to Great Britain, for even foreigners were entitled to have their property protected by law.[13]

The parties' legal arguments covered familiar ground. DuPonceau and his co-counsel leaned heavily on the law of nations rule giving courts of the capturing nation exclusive jurisdiction over prizes, as well as the prohibition in Article 17 of the Treaty of Amity on American "examination" of French prizes. Lewis and Tilghman argued in response that captures made at sea came under admiralty and maritime jurisdiction, which both the Constitution and the Judiciary Act granted to the federal courts. And they noted that Article 17 only prohibited the "examination" of prizes France took from its "Enemies," which seemingly excluded seizures of neutral property like the Swedish-owned *Betsey*.[14]

Lewis and Tilghman buttressed their position by repurposing arguments Jefferson had made to Genet for why the courts had the authority to adjudicate lawsuits over French captures. Such proceedings, Jefferson suggested, were not really prize cases at all. They did not inquire into the lawfulness of a seizure in the way a prize court typically would – for example, by asking whether the French privateer had a valid commission, or whether the seized vessel and cargo were truly British property. Instead, the suits in federal court asked only whether the captors had violated American neutrality. And *that* was a question the U.S. government could answer without infringing on France's right to adjudicate the lawfulness of its prizes.

What is more, the sovereign people of the United States could assign questions about neutrality violations to whichever branch of government they chose. In fact, according to Jefferson, judicial resolution of cases involving privateer captures was constitutionally obligatory. At bottom, these were disputes between individuals over private property. Under the American scheme of government, Jefferson had explained to Genet, such matters were "ascribed to the Judiciary alone."[15]

Lewis and Tilghman knew it would not be easy to get the Supreme Court to accept Jefferson's property-rights conception of jurisdiction. The notion that lawsuits over French captures were merely disputes over property between private parties – though perhaps formally correct – was almost laughable. Indeed, only a month earlier, New York district court judge James Duane had refused jurisdiction in part because privateer violations of neutrality were an "affront to the state," not a "private injury."[16]

To make Jefferson's theory more palatable, the attorneys invoked the particular virtues of republican government. European monarchies, they reminded the justices, despotically commingled judicial and executive authority "by force, or fraud, or both." The people of the United States, in contrast, wisely agreed to divide the nation's sovereign powers among the branches of government, and put "determinations upon property" in judicial hands. Preventing the courts from exercising their lawful jurisdiction, they argued, risked aggrandizing the executive beyond constitutional bounds and threatened individual liberty itself. It would leave the rights of foreign claimants, they noted unironically, dependent upon nothing more than "the will of a secretary of state."[17]

It is difficult to know whether lawyerly appeals to the unique genius of American constitutionalism are what persuaded the justices to accept jurisdiction over French prizes. Despite four days of argument in the case, the Court's three-paragraph opinion in *Glass v. Sloop Betsey* said little, and remains one of the great mysteries of its early years. The Court declared that the federal district courts possessed "all the powers of a Court of admiralty," and therefore the Maryland district court had jurisdiction to decide whether the *Betsey*'s restitution was warranted under domestic and international law. The decision was apparently unanimous, despite the fact that it was contrary to the decisions of the lower courts and the consensus of international authority.[18]

The Court's ruling in *Glass* was undoubtedly motivated by the justices' support for the Washington administration's foreign policy. Justices such as Jay and Wilson had already demonstrated their eagerness to help in criminal cases, and allowing a judicial venue for recovery of property seized by French privateers could similarly help soothe tensions with Great Britain.[19] In fact, the Court even went out of its way to answer a question that was not addressed by the attorneys or the courts below: whether French consuls could convene prize tribunals in the United States. The Court declared that question to be of "great public importance," and it held that foreign nations could only establish prize tribunals in the United States by special agreement. In so ruling, the Court affirmed the Washington administration's longstanding position on that issue – and the French government in Paris took note.[20]

The justices' embrace of judicial authority in *Glass* was more equivocal, however, than is generally recognized. The Court's statement that the federal courts enjoyed full admiralty jurisdiction only begged the key question: Did that jurisdiction include maritime seizures made by the ships of a foreign nation? It did in the present case, but the Court's opinion offered no reasoning in support, leaving contemporaries unsure about its broader implications. British minister Hammond, for example, believed that the Court had decided only that American admiralty courts could hear cases involving captures made within U.S. territorial waters. And because the *Betsey* was a neutral vessel, it was still possible that Article 17 of the Treaty of Amity prevented the courts from hearing cases involving British ships (as DuPonceau would argue in the Court's next case). Plus, the French government in Paris had already repudiated Genet's assertion of consular jurisdiction over prizes, so the Court's ruling on that issue was largely moot. In the end, the only thing the Court definitively resolved was that the lawsuit by the *Betsey*'s owners could go forward.[21]

The Court's opaque ruling evinced the caution that had characterized the judicial encounter with French privateering from the beginning. In important cases, the justices often issued separate, lengthy opinions explaining their individual reasoning. But in *Glass* the explanation was brief and unsigned. Perhaps the justices believed that unanimity would strengthen the ruling's authority (a tactic the Court would later adopt under John Marshall). But it seems just as likely that the ruling's anonymity was driven by the justices' desire to avoid being individually associated with a controversial decision of questionable legality. They did not want to foreclose entirely Jefferson's scheme for providing redress through the courts. But, as in the advisory opinion episode, they also did not want to assume full responsibility for resolving the many difficult legal and political issues that French privateering raised (see Chapter 2). Whatever the reason, the Court's restraint meant that the precise bounds of judicial authority to resolve disputes over maritime war would be worked out case-by-case.[22]

* * *

Any hope federal judges harbored of avoiding entanglement in the Neutrality Crisis were soon dashed. In 1794, France began to reestablish control over its colonial possessions in the Caribbean, and French political and military authorities willingly gave privateering commissions to ships from the United States. Charleston quickly became the center of what Alexander Hamilton described as "very alarming" French privateering activity. The city had long been the subject of British complaints, given its close proximity to French-held islands and its significant population of French expatriates and sympathizers.[23] At the French consul's urging, Charleston merchants and ship captains pooled their resources to purchase seaworthy vessels and refit them for commerce raiding. The Paris government ordered French officials to stop conducting formal condemnation proceedings, to avoid offending the Washington administration. But in practice consuls still facilitated sales of captured ships and goods, and the city's harbor swarmed with prizes. The spike in privateering activity was so dramatic that one student of the period has described Charleston as "a French palatinate in South Carolina."[24]

The British described the situation less charitably. Charleston, in Hammond's words, was a "sink of villainy." What most frustrated British officials was how easily French privateers violated American neutrality. They outfitted ships as innocent merchant vessels, and then brought arms aboard after clearing port, or they arranged for pretended sales to French purchasers in the Caribbean. Even French officials admitted (at least to their superiors) that their privateers regularly armed themselves in the United States.[25]

The British blamed American officials for the surge in French privateering. Hammond thought it was pointless to seek help from the federal executive. Part of the problem was consistency; the administration's policies shifted so frequently, Hammond complained, that he found it impossible even to guess at the government's future conduct. British officials also suspected American bad faith. In their view, complaints about privateer captures were too often referred to state governors sympathetic to the French cause, who simply looked the other way.[26] Even the Washington administration itself could not be trusted. In mid-1794, Hammond brought up the government's earlier promise that it would compensate British subjects if their ships were not restored. Edmund Randolph (who succeeded Jefferson as

Secretary of State) replied that the executive could make no payments without an appropriation from Congress. For Hammond, this was nothing more than evasion of the United States' responsibilities, and it confirmed that no help would be forthcoming.[27]

Hammond's pessimism was justified, for the Washington administration made it clear that it wanted the courts – and only the courts – to resolve disputes over captured property. Randolph encouraged Hammond to pursue appeals in failed cases, "to maintain court protection over the property." He also asked state governors to refrain from intervening in any case that fell within the courts' jurisdiction – which, after the Supreme Court's ruling in *Glass*, might include any capture arguably made in violation of American neutrality. According to Randolph, judicial resolution of privateering disputes would avoid the "vexation" that accompanied executive intervention. And it would leave questions about the limits of privateering to the institution that was best suited to expound the law. Allowing the judiciary to take the lead would best ensure that the United States' legal obligations were "preserved from violation."[28]

With diplomacy leading to dead ends, British officials resigned themselves to battling French privateers in the courts. According to the consul at Philadelphia, this approach was "the only medium thro' which Justice is to be obtained." The British were reluctant converts. They felt that the federal courts had already proven themselves inadequate to the task of recovering debts owed to British creditors, so they had serious doubts about the judiciary's capacity to protect their compatriots' interests. Hammond promised British merchants that he would continue to seek restitution from the executive for captured ships, as the judiciary was an "experiment[]" that was "in many respects defective and incomplete."[29]

Despite their skepticism, British officials came to appreciate the benefits of going to court. In theory, having the President as the sole head of the executive branch meant that he could act quickly in an emergency – with "[d]ecision, activity, secrecy, [and] dispatch," as Hamilton put it in *The Federalist*.[30] In the Neutrality Crisis, however, executive action was far more belabored than Hamilton predicted. Every allegation of illegal privateering directed to a state or federal officer required a judgment call about whether to act. State governors referred privateering questions to the executive for advice, and

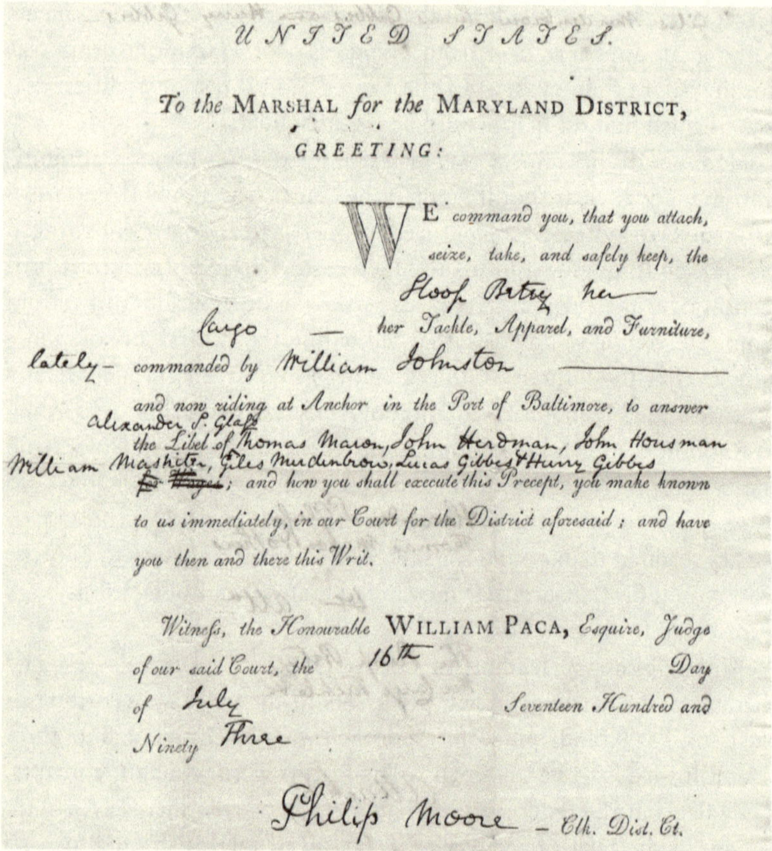

UNITED STATES.

To the MARSHAL for the MARYLAND DISTRICT,

GREETING:

WE command you, that you attach, seize, take, and safely keep, the Sloop Betsey her Cargo — her Tackle, Apparel, and Furniture, lately— commanded by William Johnston ——— and now riding at Anchor in the Port of Baltimore, to answer the Libel of Alexander S. Glass Thomas Mason, John Herdman, John Housman William Mashiter, Giles Murdenbrow, Lucas Gibbes & Henry Gibbes; and how you shall execute this Precept, you make known to us immediately, in our Court for the District aforesaid; and have you then and there this Writ.

Witness, the Honourable WILLIAM PACA, Esquire, Judge of our said Court, the 16th Day of July Seventeen Hundred and Ninety Three

Philip Moore — Clk. Dist. Ct.

FIGURE 3.1 Attachment orders from federal district court judges (as in *Glass v. Sloop Betsey*, shown here) prohibited French privateers from selling their prizes until the legal proceedings were finished. Courtesy of the National Archives and Records Administration

Washington's deliberative style seemed agonizingly slow to British merchants desperate to recover their property.[31] A judge, in contrast, did not have to consult with other officials to issue a writ of attachment and prohibit the sale or departure of a captured vessel (Figure 3.1). And attachment of disputed property was essentially automatic upon filing suit, rendering litigation "the most probable and speedy mode of effecting restitution," according to Hammond.[32]

Most important, filing suit in federal court bought time. Admiralty proceedings were generally quick, but a decision in a disputed prize case could take months, and appeals could drag a case out longer still. As Hammond explained to a frustrated claimant, such delays were actually beneficial. They ensured that the property remained intact while he pursued diplomatic channels, and it deprived the captors of any profits in the meantime.[33]

Benjamin Moodie was the British government's greatest litigation enthusiast. Realizing that "fair words and threats" would do little to deter Charlestonians from joining the French war effort, he went to court. The earliest British lawsuits required that British officials persuade the owners of captured ships to assume the expense and inconvenience of litigation. Now Moodie regularly filed complaints himself, on the owners' behalf. He was an aggressive litigator, suing over half of the British vessels brought into Charleston as prizes in 1794.[34] He engaged the ablest lawyers he could find to argue his cases (including an attempt to enlist Alexander Hamilton after his resignation from the cabinet in January 1795). Moodie paid informants to procure information and, according to his opponents, even bribed witnesses and suborned perjury.[35] Moodie recognized the risks of an aggressive approach, and declined taking action when a vessel was not worth much, or the evidence offered little hope of victory. Moodie also worried whether the British government would repay his expenses when he lost.[36]

Moodie's superiors supported his efforts, despite the difficulties that litigation posed. They understood that unless consuls sued to recover British-owned property, there was "no chance of so much as a discussion of the legality of the capture." Judicial proceedings offered the "only Hope of redress" for French seizures. The way to combat French privateering, British officials decided, was in the courts.[37]

The greatest challenge British officials faced was not financial or political – it was legal. The Supreme Court's decision in *Glass* allowed the possibility of federal court jurisdiction over French captures, but subsequent district court rulings were not promising. Judge Richard Peters in Pennsylvania seemed unwilling to extend *Glass* beyond its facts; the federal courts could take jurisdiction over cases involving American and neutral-owned property, he suggested, but not British. As before, both legal and diplomatic considerations shaped Peters' decision. "[N]o neutral sovereign or state," he opined in April 1795, "has the right to examine into questions concerning prizes." Plus, meddling in privateering cases risked angering belligerents and could subject American commerce to reprisal.[38] Thomas Bee in South Carolina was also hesitant, though for a different reason. The Constitution "wisely separated" the judicial and executive branches, and federal court adjudication of privateering disputes threatened to "infringe the barriers."[39]

Over time, however, the British litigation campaign pushed federal judges toward a more expansive view of their authority. This evolution was most evident in Judge Bee's decisions in South Carolina. He recognized that there were limits on the courts' jurisdiction over French captures. At minimum, Article 17's prohibition on the "examination" of prizes by American officers had to mean something. Accordingly, Bee thought federal courts could not entertain complaints that a French seizure was invalid under the general law of prize – for example, because the captors did not have a valid commission, or the captured property did not belong to an enemy of France. In other words, American courts did not have free-ranging authority to judge the lawfulness of French prizes.[40]

But Bee came around to the notion that the courts nevertheless had a role to play in promoting the United States' sovereign authority at sea. The key was his implicit acceptance of Jefferson's theory that neither treaty nor the law of nations precluded the courts from hearing credible allegations of neutrality violations.[41] In Bee's Charleston courtroom, captures made by privateers owned or manned by American citizens, or by privateers armed and equipped in the United States, became legitimate grounds for suit. Bee never explained his reasoning in detail, but the key point was clear enough: Those who endangered the United States' peace and security would not get a free pass from the federal judiciary.[42]

With neutrality violations as the key to the courts' jurisdiction, the legislation that had been languishing in Congress became much more important. The administration's supporters finally managed to push the law through in June 1794, thanks to Washington's plea to enact "stronger and more vigorous" laws "to keep America in peace." The final product, known as the Neutrality Act, was not everything the administration hoped for. Notably, it did not resolve questions about the courts' jurisdiction over French captures. Edmund Randolph's initial draft gave them authority to hear "all complaints" made by Americans and neutrals, but the enacted version only gave explicit jurisdiction over captures made within U.S. territorial waters (which French officials had long since conceded were unlawful). As a result, the full scope of judicial authority over privateering would still have to be decided by judges.[43]

The Act did proscribe specific conduct that violated American neutrality, including acceptance of privateering commissions and enlistment on ships. It also forbade anyone from fitting out or augmenting the force of any ship in U.S. ports with the intent of privateering. These prohibitions were substantively no different than those the Washington administration had announced more than a year earlier. But by enshrining them in statute, Congress mooted the question that had haunted criminal prosecutions – whether the President's directives had the force of law. And the Act's specificity about what conduct violated American neutrality was a boon for British consuls trying to persuade federal judges that their adversaries had broken the law.[44]

Armed with this new statute, Moodie's effort to attack French privateers in the courts gained momentum. The question of whether a privateer had been armed in the United States was highly fact-intensive, often necessitating documents and testimony from far-flung witnesses. So, in Bee's courtroom, the threshold issue of jurisdiction was only resolvable after the very sort of invasive judicial investigation that French officials thought were prohibited by Article 17.[45] And because a proven neutrality violation was, in Bee's view, also grounds for judicial restoration of a captured vessel, "jurisdiction" and "merits" merged into one query. In later cases, Bee ignored the jurisdictional question altogether, and simply determined whether the capturing privateer had augmented its force in the United States. As a result, British suits were no longer dismissed at the outset for lack of jurisdiction. Now every case required minute examination of the facts surrounding a privateer's armament and voyage. The disputed vessels and cargo remained under the court's control in the meantime, so privateers could not sell their prizes and reap the profits.[46]

Judge Bee's willingness to scrutinize French captures was a godsend for the British litigation campaign. Indeed, in a moment of puffery, Moodie boasted to a British vice-admiral that his legal efforts had done more to protect British property at sea "than even the success of his Majesty's Cruizers."[47] Of course, Moodie did not win every case. Bee dismissed libels when there was insufficient evidence that the privateer had been armed in the United States.[48] Even when they had, Bee ruled that the subsequent alleged sale of a privateer to a French purchaser effectively cleared the vessel of any neutrality violation.[49] In fact, it appears that Moodie lost at least as many cases as he won, and he doubted his chances of success when appealing unfavorable rulings. Yet he was undeterred. Litigation's importance for the war effort, he explained to his superiors, meant that he had "gone too far to stop now."[50]

* * *

French officials never fully accepted that their nation's sovereign rights could be defined by American courts. Their position moderated somewhat after Genet's removal. The government in Paris recognized that his combative style had done more harm than good, and his successor, Joseph Fauchet, was more conciliatory. In particular, by mid-1795 Fauchet conceded to Secretary of State Randolph that the courts could take jurisdiction over *some* suits – notably, those involving privateers who violated American neutrality. In so doing, Fauchet seemed to accept Jefferson's basic premise: Americans could decide for themselves which institution of government was responsible for adjudicating controversies between foreign sovereigns, and questions involving maritime property were the province of the judiciary.[51]

The catalyst for the French shift in tone was the lawyerly pragmatism of their primary attorney on privateering matters, Peter DuPonceau. He was only thirty-two years old when the Neutrality Crisis began, but he was an obvious choice to serve as "Counsel of the French Republic" in the United States. A Frenchman by birth, DuPonceau declared to Fauchet his "attachment to the Cause and to the principles of the french Republic." But DuPonceau was also highly attuned to American sensibilities. He had emigrated to the United States as a teenager during the American Revolution, and served in the Continental Army as an interpreter. After the war, he studied with noted attorney William Lewis, and became one of Philadelphia's leading practitioners, with special expertise in international and maritime law. He was also an astute observer of American politics and government – especially when it came to the judiciary – and was well positioned to give his clients advice on how best to defend French interests both in and out of court.[52]

DuPonceau recognized the futility of resisting the idea that privateering disputes could be resolved judicially. After the Supreme Court ruled in *Glass* that the federal courts could take jurisdiction over a French capture, one attorney in the French camp proposed challenging the decision as legally infirm and motivated by "political expediency." DuPonceau acknowledged that the courts' jurisdictional boundaries were shaped as much by "the political opinions of the day" as they were by law. But he saw no profit in attacking *Glass* directly, which would result only in "expense" for the litigants who tried to overturn such a recent precedent and "ridicule" for the attorneys hired to do so. In DuPonceau's view, it was better to emphasize *Glass*'s limited holding and distinguish new cases on their facts – which he often did successfully. In short, he was willing to oppose France's enemies with every legal and factual argument at his disposal, but he accepted *Glass*'s basic premise: Such battles would be fought in the courts.[53]

French officials gradually came around to DuPonceau's views. With his guidance, consuls from Boston to Charleston became active participants in federal court proceedings. They hired lawyers, paid fees, collected depositions, secured witnesses, and shared strategic advice. Fauchet explained the situation to his superiors in Paris in late 1794. He would continue to advocate France's treaty rights to the Washington administration "with warmth." But when French-commissioned privateers violated American neutrality, he could defend them "only with lawyers."[54]

Acceptance of the courts' authority in theory, however, only made French officials more resentful of how their British opponents took advantage of it. Consuls like Benjamin Moodie, the French complained, "launch[ed] their birds of prey" as soon as a captured vessel came into port. They bribed witnesses to make false accusations, and used legal proceedings to "discourage and fatigue the captors." Privateers based in Charleston were so outraged by Moodie's tactics that they sent an agent directly to the government in Paris to demand diplomatic intervention.[55]

The French anger over American litigation was more than diplomatic jousting. It comported with a deep suspicion of the judiciary that ran through the politics of the French Revolution. Under the *ancien regime*, courts in France – especially the regional *parlements* – were strongholds of aristocratic privilege, reviled for exercising quasi-legislative powers and interfering with the administration of justice. Cabining judicial authority became a central tenet of revolutionary reforms. The French constitutions of 1791 and 1795, for example, forbade judges from interfering with either the legislature or the executive branch. Courts were not the only problem; litigation itself interfered with citizens' enjoyment of their rights. One member of the Constituent Assembly summarized the revolutionary perspective in stark terms: "Rendering justice is only the second obligation of society. Preventing lawsuits is the first."[56]

French officials saw the British success in court as reflection of a fundamental defect in the American political character. The French Revolution had decimated the ranks of attorneys in France (at least temporarily), but the post-revolutionary United States was a nation "peopled by lawyers." The American enthusiasm for legalism made it easy for British officials to inundate the courts with meritless lawsuits. Worse yet, many federal judges were British partisans – "Tor[ies] by any other name" – who willfully ignored British dirty tricks. Sworn to uphold treaties between France and the United States, judges had instead proven themselves to be "unfaithful guardians of the alliances between nations." Seeing no hope for justice through litigation, the French government gave its consuls one general directive: whenever possible, "avoid contestations with American courts."[57]

The Washington administration's response to French complaints was to insist on the courts' primacy ever more forcefully. Genet's successor, Fauchet, proposed two solutions to the problem of frivolous British lawsuits. First, he asked that plaintiffs be required to post security when they filed suit, to cover costs and damages they would owe to the captors if the case was dismissed. Such a measure, Fauchet averred, would render Moodie and his colleagues "less ingenious in their proceedings." Second, Fauchet suggested that the executive branch pre-screen British cases to see if there were sufficient grounds to proceed. His proposal was short on details, but the goal was clear. If it was too easy for British litigants to harass French privateers in court, the solution was for the executive branch to prevent suits from getting there in the first place.[58]

Randolph rejected Fauchet's proposals outright, on the ground that they would violate the judiciary's constitutional independence. He agreed with his French counterpart that privateers should not be "wantonly vexed" by British litigation. But the Washington administration's hands were tied. Under "the constitution and the law," the courts were "entirely independent of Executive mandates." This was precisely what Jefferson had earlier argued to Genet: Once a litigant submits his claims to a court, "there is no power in this country which can take them out."[59] The administration's approach was not entirely hands-off. In late 1795, for example, the federal district attorney for Pennsylvania filed a "suggestion" with the district court urging dismissal of a suit against a French naval warship, on the basis of sovereign immunity. Yet when the plaintiffs simply refiled their case in another court, Randolph's successor as Secretary of State, Timothy Pickering, responded to French outrage by repeating the administration's long-held position: "[A]s long as the question is in the hands of the courts," he asserted, "the Executive cannot withdraw it."[60]

At times, cabinet officers' pronouncements shaded into declarations of judicial supremacy. Jefferson, in fact, said exactly that to Genet: The federal courts exercise "the sovereignty of this country in judiciary matters," and "are supreme in these." Whenever the courts could "give a remedy" – that is, by restoring a ship seized in violation of American neutrality – "the Executive do not intermeddle." The courts, in other words, were not simply an institution of government that *could* provide redress to those injured by neutrality violations. Any relief the government provided, Jefferson indicated, *had* to come from the courts. Pickering made the same point three years later, when British officials demanded return of a British prize subsequently retaken by its crew and sailed to New York. There was "no constitutional power in the Executive branch" to restore the ship, Pickering explained, "without the intervention of the Judiciary."[61]

As Jefferson and his successors knew, these proclamations of judicial authority and autonomy extended core principles of American constitutionalism in new and controversial directions. Many of the Constitution's framers believed that an independent judiciary was an essential feature of republican government, especially to protect private property from democracy run amok. The Revolutionary generation's experience with state prize courts persuaded them that the federal judiciary had a particularly important role in vindicating the legal interests of foreigners in their *maritime* property (see Chapter 1). As Jefferson pointed out, that is what privateering cases ultimately were about.[62]

But the notion that *only* the courts could resolve disputes over French privateer captures was entirely fictitious. Under the law of nations, it was doubtful whether neutral courts could adjudicate the legality of maritime captures at all. Everyone from Edmond-Charles Genet to Alexander Hamilton agreed with Judge Peters of the Pennsylvania district court that, as a general matter, such disputes had to be "settled by sovereignties alone" (see Chapter 2). Nor was the judiciary's supposed supremacy in matters of maritime war inherent in Article III's design. The evil a national judiciary was meant to remedy was discrimination perpetrated by state legislatures, judges, and juries. No one in 1787 or 1788 suggested that the Constitution disabled the executive branch of the federal government from providing foreigners with redress. Indeed, the Washington administration's first response to the Neutrality Crisis was to have the executive branch of government – both federal and state – decide whether particular seizures violated American neutrality. So even the government's own policies undermined Jefferson's claim that the Constitution required that privateering cases be resolved "by the Judiciary alone."[63]

The cabinet officers who rebuffed French demands for intervention never admitted that they were inventing an American tradition of judicial supremacy in disputes over maritime property. Nor did they explain what motivated them to do so. But the answer seems evident. Little more than five years after the Constitution's ratification, giving the courts exclusive responsibility for resolving privateering disputes looked like the surest means of making good on the promise of a national government that could preserve American independence.[64]

* * *

The justices of the Supreme Court were not sure they wanted responsibility for ensuring the nation's peace and security. The British litigation campaign produced a flood of cases that worked their way up the appellate ladder. In 1796 and 1797, the Court heard twenty-one privateering cases, which represented nearly three quarters of its entire docket in those two years, and was more than the total number of cases it heard the previous five years combined. Eleven of the cases were originally filed by Benjamin Moodie, the British consul in Charleston. Suddenly, an institution that had barely appeared on the national stage (except when it did something controversial) was now responsible for keeping the United States out of a war that threatened the nation's very existence.[65]

The Court seemed to embrace an expanded judicial role in suppressing French privateering at first. *Talbot v. Jansen* – its first case after *Glass v. Sloop Betsey* – involved the capture of a Dutch ship by two French-commissioned privateers fitted out in the United States and captained by Americans. It was a devilishly complicated case, requiring ten days of argument and resulting in four separate opinions. But the justices were unanimous in ruling that the federal courts could restore vessels and cargo captured by French privateers manned by American citizens. The Court rejected Peter DuPonceau's argument that, under *Glass*, the courts had jurisdiction only over captures of American or neutral vessels (France and Holland were at war). In fact, the justices largely ignored the jurisdictional question and focused instead on the wrongfulness of the privateers' conduct.[66]

What united the Court was what seemed to motivate their earlier decision in *Glass* – the existential necessity of providing judicial remedies for violations of American neutrality. The privateer captains in *Talbot* had openly colluded to evade the Neutrality Act's restrictions, but criminal prosecutions against them had failed. Allowing such conduct to go entirely unaddressed, the justices warned, would condone a "fraudulent neutrality," and "war might [be] the consequence." The Court continued this approach the following year, issuing two rulings of questionable legality to ensure that privateers who broke the law would be obligated to compensate their victims.[67]

As more cases crowded the Court's docket, however, the justices began questioning whether providing judicial redress for alleged neutrality violations was consistent with the United States' international obligations. In a 1796 opinion, Chief Justice Oliver Ellsworth reminded his audience that the 1778 Treaty of Amity with France "must have its effect." For example, the Neutrality Act prohibited the arming of ships to make war, but the Court ruled that some alterations were permissible, in light of the Treaty's provision allowing French privateers to visit American ports for repairs. The Court also ruled that, even when a vessel violated the Neutrality Act, subsequent sale to a French purchaser cleansed it of the stain of American involvement and put it outside the court's power. Justice Iredell even questioned whether the federal courts could restore captured property at all. The Neutrality Act did not expressly give them that authority, and he doubted whether the law of nations did either.[68]

The Court was not swayed by arguments that a constrained understanding of the Neutrality Act – and of the judiciary's own powers – compromised the United States' security. The justices may have agreed with the Washington administration that observing perfect impartiality between the warring powers was the safest path to pursue through the crisis. But the importance of keeping faith with the nation's treaty commitments trumped such considerations. Ellsworth made the point explicit in response to the suggestion from an attorney representing British claimants that it was politically dangerous to allow French privateers to equip in United States ports. "Suggestions of policy and conveniency," the Chief Justice retorted, "cannot be considered in the judicial determination of a question of right."[69]

The justices' concern for protecting France's sovereign rights was decisive in the Court's decisions. The captors prevailed in nearly every case the Court decided in 1796 and 1797; Benjamin Moodie, the British consul in Charleston, lost every one of his. These raw numbers overstate the scope of the French victory, as privateers often did not appeal when they lost in the lower courts. Moodie, on other hand, often pursued cases he lost in the district court as a delaying tactic, so in most of the matters before the Court the facts were against him. Nevertheless, the captors' repeated victories signaled the justices' belief that the diplomatic imperatives underlying the Washington administration's strict neutrality policy could not overcome the limits on judicial authority imposed by treaty and the law of nations.[70]

The justices also had a less lofty reason for not fully accepting the role the Washington administration envisioned for the courts. Adjudicating privateering cases was hard work. District court judges had to sift through reams of evidence in order to determine whether a privateer had been built, armed, manned, sold, or commissioned in the United States. The same was true for appellate judges, including the justices of the Supreme Court. In early cases, they followed the traditional admiralty practice of reviewing cases on "appeal," which transferred an entire proceeding to a superior tribunal for full rehearing (and sometimes a new trial). It was not clear that this was correct procedure under the Constitution and the Judiciary Act of 1789, but the justices reflexively conformed to British and pre-Ratification state practice. As a result, privateering cases consumed the Court's attention. In the midst of the ten-day argument in *Talbot*, Justice Iredell complained to his wife that he was trapped in Philadelphia because the attorneys were "so scandalously long in arguing" the facts of the case.[71]

The justices did not appreciate the increased demands of their burgeoning maritime docket. They were paid a fixed salary, so additional work was effectively uncompensated. And they were already aggrieved by Congress's repeated refusal to relieve them of their circuit-riding duties.[72] Justice Iredell was the most vociferous in his complaints. In his first years on the Court, he was tasked with the lengthy southern circuit, which required travel of close to 2,000 miles in unforgiving conditions. His colleagues recognized the inequity, and privately agreed to each pay a portion of their own salaries to whichever colleague was saddled with that responsibility. But even after Congress mandated rotation of assignments (something Iredell's colleagues had refused to do voluntarily), Iredell was still unhappy. Before setting off on the relatively easy middle circuit in March 1796, he wrote to his wife Hannah that it was "impossible [to] lead this life much longer."[73]

For Iredell and his colleagues, the privateering cases exacerbated an already bad situation. The Neutrality Act's specification of what privateer conduct was punishable under federal law created what Iredell termed "an inexhaustible fund of dispute" that enterprising litigants like Benjamin Moodie could use to invoke the federal courts' jurisdiction. The justices of the Supreme Court bore the brunt as much as their district court colleagues. They first had to hear appeals on circuit, where their factual and legal complexity prolonged the courts' sessions in places the justices did not want to be. And then they often had to rehear the cases, in their entirety, at the Supreme Court. Such "petty inquiries," Iredell griped in a 1796 draft opinion, were not a fit undertaking for "a Court of Justice."[74]

The solution the justices came up with reflected their ongoing ambivalence about what role they should play in resolving disputes arising from maritime war. Section 19 of the Judiciary Act of 1789 required circuit courts to specify the facts in the record upon which they based their judgments, usually in a statement by the presiding judge. In the midst of the privateering appeals, the justices ruled that such a statement was conclusive in the Supreme Court when the appellate record did not include the evidence presented in the court below (such as copies of depositions and exhibits). This meant that the parties could not present their evidence anew to the Court, which would prevent the kind of interminable arguments that so frustrated Iredell. The Court then went a step further, and ruled that a circuit court's statement of facts was conclusive even when the record *did* contain other evidence. In other words, the justices could not independently review the record evidence in an admiralty case. And in a subsequent decision, the Court extended this principle to its logical conclusion: The Court could not investigate the facts in an admiralty case even when the record included *no* statement from the court below. In short, the scope of the Court's review was limited to questions of law.[75]

As the justices knew, questions about the Supreme Court's power to revisit the decisions of lower courts were deeply contentious. During the ratification debates, critics of the Constitution like Patrick Henry asserted that Article III's grant of appellate jurisdiction to the Supreme Court "both as to Law and Fact" would "destroy the trial by jury," by displacing the latter as the arbiter of fact. For the Constitution's proponents, this was precisely the point, at least in cases that implicated foreign relations. Lay juries, argued Alexander Hamilton in *The Federalist*, were ill-suited to decide issues that implicated "the rights of other nations." James Wilson agreed; given the bitter experience with juries in prize cases during the Revolutionary War, it was "essentially necessary" that superior courts be able to "reconsider and set aside the verdict of those juries."[76]

Nearly a decade later, Wilson still had deep concerns about limiting the Supreme Court's appellate authority. The fact that he could compose a rigorous and thoughtful opinion on the subject in August 1796 is remarkable enough, given that his personal finances were collapsing and about to land him in jail. But Wilson felt strongly about the need for plenary review. Juries were no longer the issue, since admiralty cases did not have them. But Wilson was nevertheless worried that restricting the Court's review to questions of law compromised its ability to uphold the nation's legal obligations. Wilson served on the committee in the Continental Congress that heard appeals in state court prize cases, and had witnessed firsthand the diplomatic damage wrought by uncontrollable lower courts. And admiralty cases implicated the rights of foreign nations now more than ever. It was essential to the United States' "security and dignity," Wilson argued, that its highest tribunal scrutinize a lower court's conclusions as to both law *and* fact. Justice Paterson agreed; forbidding the Court from reconsidering the evidence presented to a lower court "shut[] the door against light and truth," and left "too much to the discretion and judgment of a single Judge."[77]

For Wilson and Paterson's colleagues, however, the anxieties that inspired the federal judiciary's original design were no longer present. Chief Justice Ellsworth had served on the same Continental Congress appeals committee as Wilson, and even drafted the ordinance that created the national appeals court that was meant to supervise wayward state prize tribunals. But Ellsworth apparently drew a different lesson from that trying experience. Centralized review of factual determinations by state juries may have been a diplomatic necessity during the American Revolution. But the same was not true in juryless admiralty proceedings in the new federal courts.[78]

Ellsworth's confidence in the lower federal courts was perhaps not surprising. He had taken the lead role in their creation under the Judiciary Act, and understood that their principal purpose was to ensure that responsibility for the enforcement of federal law did not fall on the Supreme Court alone. Ellsworth fully recognized the international implications of limiting the Court's review, but he echoed the assurances the Washington administration gave French and British officials throughout the Neutrality Crisis: Even without the Supreme Court's involvement, the facts of each case would be evaluated by "an impartial and enlightened tribunal" in which the parties could have full trust.[79]

The timing of the Court's rulings underscored just how complicated and potentially vexing the judiciary's role had become. By mid-1796, the Jay Treaty's ban on the sale of French prizes in the United States gave the justices reason to think that litigation over French privateering would soon come to an end. But the crush of cases they confronted offered them a glimpse of an unappealing future. In an era of perpetual maritime war, plenary review of all admiralty cases meant that the burdens of federal judicial office would only increase in the years to come. The Court's response was to refuse responsibility for ensuring a correct outcome in every case that landed on American shores. Instead, in Ellsworth's words, the Court's function was only to "preserve unity of principle" and ensure "the administration of justice."[80]

* * *

Despite the Supreme Court's rejection of many of Benjamin Moodie's lawsuits, British hopes for judicial intervention were not lost. Moodie initially lamented that federal judges had "entirely set aside" both the Neutrality Act and the law of nations. He expected privateers to redouble their operations, emboldened by favorable rulings and flush with funds from the sale of the prizes. But the Senate's 1795 ratification of the Jay Treaty – and its ban on the sale of French prizes – offered Moodie new reason to think that the courts would intercede in his favor. This was the same prohibition that James Madison had successfully excised from the Neutrality Act, to the disappointment of both British officials and Federalists in government. They considered a ban on prize sales crucial for suppressing French privateering, and Washington had specifically authorized Jay to include such a prohibition in any agreement he reached.[81]

Moodie was eager to make use of this new legal tool, but he was unsure how. When a valuable French prize named the *Amity* arrived in Charleston in April 1796, Moodie asked state officials to prevent its impending sale by the French consul. Moodie knew that enforcement of the Jay Treaty's terms by state officials was not guaranteed. The Washington administration had kept the agreement secret for months, and the Senate only ratified it on a party-line vote. That approval sparked fierce opposition, and a heated debate over whether the treaty could take effect without congressional action inflamed the House of Representatives in the spring of 1796.[82]

The ongoing controversy over Jay's agreement made vigorous treaty enforcement unlikely, especially in a town like Charleston that retained sympathy toward France. The state attorney general and the

FIGURE 3.2 Under Oliver Ellsworth's leadership, the justices of the Supreme Court sought to reconcile the Washington administration's neutrality policy with France's rights under treaty and international law and their concern for the courts' own institutional integrity. Courtesy of the Library of Congress

federal district attorney each declined to opine on Article 24's legal effect, no doubt wary of inviting controversy. And the commander of the local militia responded to Moodie's request for intervention with a familiar refrain: "[T]he Courts of the United States are open to all the subjects of his Britannic Majesty," the colonel averred, and they would provide "every degree of Justice." But Judge Bee of the federal district court was not inclined to help either. He recognized that the Jay Treaty banned the sale of prizes. But he stuck to his view that Article 17 of the 1778 treaty with France prohibited the courts from interfering with French captures unless they violated American neutrality (and in this case there was no allegation that the *Amity*'s captor had done so).[83]

Then Chief Justice Ellsworth arrived in town, and issued an order enjoining the *Amity*'s sale under the Jay Treaty (Figure 3.2). The legality of this move was uncertain. Ellsworth entertained Moodie's application "at his chambers" – that is, not in the regularly constituted circuit court (which would have included Judge Bee). It was also doubtful whether admiralty courts had the power to grant injunctive relief. So Ellsworth apparently relied on an obscure provision in an obscure statute. The Judiciary Act of 1793 – which Ellsworth had helped draft – gave individual justices the power to issue injunctions in cases where the circuit court or Supreme Court might do the same. After hearing argument from both sides, Ellsworth enjoined the sale until the opening of the circuit court session three days later, where he and Bee apparently confirmed the order.[84]

Despite its irregularity, Ellsworth's intervention was less surprising than it might have seemed. In privateering cases before the Supreme Court, he was protective of France's sovereign rights under the Treaty of Amity. But he was also a steadfast Federalist and Washington administration supporter. Just before his arrival in Charleston, he delivered a grand jury charge exhorting the citizens of Georgia (many of whom were involved in privateering) to give the executive branch their "unceasing co-operation." "Institutions without respect," he explained, "perpetually hazard the national peace," and sow "the seeds of death."[85]

The Jay Treaty's ratification allowed Ellsworth to square his political and legal commitments in Moodie's favor. France's privateers had certain privileges under the 1778 agreements, but the Jay Treaty created a countervailing and definitive British right prohibiting its enemies from selling prizes in the United States. Even the raging controversy over whether the treaty could go into effect without congressional legislation did not deter Ellsworth. Despite Republican opposition, the consensus among the nation's political leaders was that treaties were self-executing. In fact, the Supreme Court said just that at its spring 1796 term, in *Ware v. Hylton*. Though Ellsworth joined the Court too late to participate in that decision, he surely agreed with it.[86]

Finally, enforcing the treaty also seemed to align with the justices' self-interest. A ban on prize sales would discourage privateers from bringing their prizes to the United States, and deplete the "inexhaustible fund of dispute" that so frustrated Ellsworth and his colleagues. Less litigation over privateer captures would mean less time traveling the southern circuit, whose afflictions the Chief Justice was just beginning to appreciate. Upholding the treaty, in fact, might get the courts out of the privateering business altogether.[87]

British officials used Ellsworth's ruling to spur the Washington administration into action. By this time, both Jefferson and Randolph had resigned from Washington's cabinet, and it was dominated by

Anglophile Federalists eager to act aggressively against French privateers. Secretary of State Pickering asked Ellsworth to circulate his opinion to all federal judges "for their information and guidance," and Secretary of the Treasury Oliver Wolcott ordered customs collectors to prevent French privateers from unloading cargo from British captures. To top off the British successes, Federalists in the House of Representatives overcame Republican opposition and voted to implement the Jay Treaty. A British official happily reported to his superiors that, by the summer of 1796, the agreement was taking effect "even at Charleston."[88]

French officials were much less pleased with Ellsworth's intervention. In their view, Jay's treaty concessions were a crass betrayal that privileged American self-interest over the binding commitments the nation had made to France in the United States' hour of need two decades earlier. The French consul in Baltimore quipped to his superiors that by agreeing to the "Treaty of Amity and Commerce" with Great Britain – as the Jay Treaty was officially named – Americans had "prostituted their friendship to save their commerce." The French minister in the United States, Pierre-Auguste Adet, was so alarmed that he tried to sink the agreement by publicizing it when the administration was keeping it secret.[89]

Ellsworth's order was the cruelest blow. The ban on prize sales deprived French privateers of their most lucrative market for captured vessels and goods. As the Charleston consul described the fallout to Adet, judicial enforcement of the ban "entirely change[d] our political situation in this country." Adet briefly considered appealing Ellsworth's ruling, but was apparently persuaded by DuPonceau that such an attempt would be legally futile. Conceding the impossibility of his situation, Adet ordered French consuls to cease facilitating prize sales until he received further instructions from Paris. Though he continued to press his case in correspondence with cabinet officers, he and his subordinates understood their reality all too well. Under the 1778 Treaty of Amity, one consul wrote, France was ostensibly in a "privileged" relationship with the United States. "[B]ut today our privileges are so imperceptible that it becomes ridiculous to even use the term."[90]

The French complaints went beyond the Jay Treaty. In March 1796, Charles Delacroix, the French minister of foreign affairs in Paris, presented James Monroe with a summary of conduct that, in France's view, demonstrated the United States' favoritism toward Great Britain in the war. It included American acceptance of expansive British definitions of contraband of war, tolerance of armed British ships calling in American ports, and the failure to pursue French deserters.[91]

The French government's primary grievance was against the courts. Their assumption of jurisdiction over prizes taken by French privateers, Delacroix wrote, was contrary to the express stipulations of the 1778 Treaty of Amity between the two nations. And despite good faith French efforts to develop alternative arrangements for resolving disputes over captured ships and cargo, the Washington administration had failed to prevent the court's "usurpation" of France's authority to judge the legality of its own captures. As Adet expressed it to Pickering, the United States had "abandoned French privateers to its courts of justice."[92]

Monroe was an unlikely candidate to defend the administration's position that the courts could take jurisdiction over captures made by French privateers. Like Jefferson, he was strongly pro-French, and was distrusted by Anglophiles in the cabinet. In fact, Washington recalled him from Paris soon after his exchange with Delacroix.[93]

On the privateering question, however, Monroe – like Jefferson – was a faithful agent. He agreed with Delacroix that, in the abstract, American courts could not judge the validity of French captures. But when a privateer violated American neutrality, the United States was bound to uphold its own sovereign rights, just as France would in the same situation. Whether vindication came via "tribunals" or "some other branch of our Government" was not the business of other nations. What mattered was that the United States acted as a neutral party in the war.[94]

The French government was no more satisfied with Monroe's explanations than Genet had been with Jefferson's three years earlier. French privateers in the Caribbean soon began seizing American merchant vessels on flimsy pretexts, in response to what France perceived to be the United States' repeated breaches of faith. These aggressions prompted a series of recriminations between the two nations that would soon lead to an undeclared maritime conflict, known as the Quasi-War. Though the federal courts' assumption of jurisdiction over French prizes was only one item on the list of

French grievances, it was a significant one – in Delacroix's words, it was France's "first complaint."[95]

The fact that hostilities broke out between the former allies in 1798 does not mean that the Washington administration failed the country by turning to the courts in 1793. Judicial intervention in the Neutrality Crisis may have helped precipitate armed conflict with France, but it also helped prevent the greater evil of war with Great Britain. Litigation in federal court was never British officials' first choice in combatting French privateering, but they recognized that even a sympathetic executive branch lacked the "energy" required to enforce compliance with the obligations of neutrality. And they came to appreciate that resort to the judiciary could help further their political and military goals.[96]

Confirmation of the wisdom of the Washington administration's approach came after the Neutrality Crisis ended. One of the Jay Treaty's provisions called for a bilateral commission to adjudicate British and American claims arising from maritime captures. American claimants were to receive compensation from Britain for seizures that violated American neutral rights, and British claimants were to receive compensation for seizures made by French privateers armed in American ports. The commission began its work in October 1796. By the time it finished in 1804, it had awarded more than $11.5 million to American claimants for unlawful British depredations. In contrast, the commission awarded British claimants less than $150,000.[97]

The huge discrepancy between the two awards was vindication of Jefferson's strategy for delegating privateering cases to the federal courts. Under the Jay Treaty's terms, American claimants were to receive compensation for British seizures whenever they could not secure it "in the ordinary course of Justice" – i.e., when they were unsuccessful in seeking restoration of unlawfully seized property in British admiralty courts. And there Americans faced numerous obstacles. British tribunals in the Caribbean were often predisposed to rule in favor of the captors, regardless of the facts of the case. Indeed, some American claims arose from adjudications by an illegal prize court established by British military forces for the express purpose of condemning captured ships. Making matters worse, American claimants had very little time in which to appeal unfavorable rulings, and then had to suffer endless delays before their appeals were heard. In light of the blatant discrimination and mistreatment of British courts, the Jay Treaty commission awarded compensation to hundreds of American claimants.[98]

The same was not true for British claimants. The standard for granting them compensation by the United States did not refer to the federal courts directly. They were to receive payment if the United States had failed to use "all the means in [its] Power to protect and defend [British] Vessels and Effects" from French privateering. This language was not in the Jay Treaty itself. It came from the 1793 letter from Jefferson to British minister Hammond in which the Washington administration pledged it would do everything possible to suppress French privateering in the United States. Of course, the administration's attempt to restrain French privateers through executive branch action failed, quite miserably. Yet the Jay Treaty commission only awarded British claimants compensation in a small handful of cases.[99]

The reason the commission decided that the United States owed the British almost nothing was because, unlike British vice-admiralty courts, the federal judiciary had provided claimants with meaningful redress for injuries resulting from French privateering. The commission repeatedly noted in its rulings that the courts had been open to lawsuits for violations of American neutrality. The commission discussed the Supreme Court's decision in *Glass v. Sloop Betsey* at length, and remarked that, after that ruling, "justice was speedily and impartially administered" in courts across the nation, "even in Charleston." As a result, the United States was under no obligation to use force to compel restoration of captured ships and cargo, or provide any other mode of redress. Moreover, the commission deemed it irrelevant whether British litigants had actually prevailed in court and secured compensation for their losses (and many had not). According to the commission, all the United States owed claimants was an adequate *process* for pressing claims. And that is precisely what the federal courts provided.[100]

The claims commission's ratification of Jefferson's theory underscored the degree to which the challenges of maritime war had stretched the boundaries of a judicial role in foreign affairs. The Constitution's framers intended the federal courts to be the guarantors of the nation's international legal obligations, but when the Neutrality Crisis began many observers doubted whether that constitutional mandate gave the courts the authority to adjudicate wartime disputes arising between foreign nations. Even as the protagonists came to accept litigation's legitimacy, some – including the justices of the Supreme Court – did not think it was the best mode of dealing with a major foreign affairs controversy. Yet, within a few years of the Crisis' conclusion, there was Anglo-American agreement that the judiciary not only *could* resolve such disagreements, but that it had done so fairly. Indeed, in the commission's eyes, American courts had proven themselves to be far more capable than British tribunals of providing justice to foreigners.

To understand the distance the courts traveled in the 1790s, consider the results of a different commission established under the Jay Treaty. It was established to decide the compensation the United States owed to British creditors who had been denied recovery on their debts, as guaranteed by the 1783 Treaty of Peace. Upholding British creditors' legal rights had been one of the primary reasons for creating the federal courts in the first place (see Chapter 1). The Jay Treaty's provision was tacit acknowledgment that the courts had failed to provide complete justice. The debt commission never finished its work, but in 1802 the United States agreed to pay British creditors over $2.5 million to settle their claims. Compared with the paltry sum the United States owed for privateering-related claims, one thing seems clear: When it came to resolving international disputes that threatened to undermine the United States' international standing, the federal courts were most effective at sea.[101]

The end of the Neutrality Crisis did not signal the end of the federal courts' role in foreign affairs. In the fall of 1799, Chief Justice Ellsworth had the good fortune of being assigned to ride circuit in his home state of Connecticut, where he presided over a criminal trial. The defendant, Isaac Williams, was accused of having accepted a French privateering commission to commit acts of violence against Great Britain, in violation of the Jay Treaty (which forbade Americans and Britons from engaging in hostilities against the other). Williams – a "noted privateersman" – argued that this prohibition did not apply to him, because he had become a French citizen in the early 1790s.

Ellsworth rejected that argument, even though French privateering against British merchants was no longer a significant diplomatic problem and the nation's attention was consumed by the vituperative domestic politics surrounding the Alien and Sedition Acts. For Ellsworth, the ongoing threat of becoming ensnared in armed conflict meant the federal government had to be "vigilant in restraining our own citizens," even those who claimed to no longer owe allegiance to the United States.[102]

Ellsworth justified his decision by recalling the difficulty of remaining neutral in the contest between France and Great Britain earlier in the decade. "We wished to have nothing to do with the war," the Chief Justice explained, "but the war would have something to do with us." Ellsworth's "we" meant the nation as a whole, but he could just as easily have been referring to his colleagues on the federal bench. The vicissitudes of maritime conflict had forced them to become the arbiters of the rights of sovereign nations, sometimes against their better judgment.[103]

As Ellsworth recognized, the danger of international entanglement remained. At the time he wrote, American naval vessels were protecting merchant ships from French privateers and naval vessels operating in the Caribbean. In Europe, Napoleon Bonaparte was on the verge of consolidating power and expanding the war against Great Britain. From the vantage point of 1799, it seemed doubtful that the United States would be able to avoid involvement in the global conflicts of the future. The same would prove true for the courts.[104]

PART II

THE JUDICIARY AT WAR, 1812–1816

4

The Problems of Prize

In November 1812, the merchants of Baltimore were angry – with Congress, with federal officers, and especially with the courts. The United States had declared war against the world's greatest maritime power several months earlier, and the nation's maritime entrepreneurs had immediately poured their resources – at "heavy charge and cost" – into arming fast vessels well suited for raiding the British merchant fleet. These financiers knew their service was essential. As in the American Revolution, the United States in 1812 barely had a navy. But privateers, Thomas Jefferson memorably claimed, would wreak havoc on enemy trade and make the British "squeal, & cry out for peace."[1]

The problem, according to the privateers, was that the federal courts were undermining their ability to challenge British dominance at sea. In keeping with the framers' vision for the judiciary, Congress in 1812 gave the courts responsibility for deciding whether captures made by American armed ships were lawful. This meant that the captors would not see a cent until a judge condemned and sold a prize. But neither Congress nor the executive branch had prescribed any rules for how the federal courts should dispose of such cases. With proceedings "left entirely open to the discretion of the judges," the merchants complained, prize proceeds were tied up in the courts, exposing them to "certain loss." Judicial control over the spoils of maritime war, in their view, was making it difficult for the United States to fight one.[2]

The Baltimore petitioners were not the only people dissatisfied with the judiciary's supervision of the war effort. The courts' laxity in handling the government's share of money that flowed from privateer captures exasperated harried cabinet officers managing a conflict the nation was unprepared to wage. Foreign diplomats registered far fewer complaints than their predecessors had in the 1790s, but they were still unhappy with what they saw as the courts' failure to prevent American privateers' worst abuses. Even newly minted Supreme Court Justice Joseph Story – the early nineteenth century's most fervent proponent of federal judicial power – was unsparing in his critique. In his view, the judiciary was supposed to be the "guardian of the public interest" in maritime war. But the "great irregularities" that characterized judicial proceedings in the War of 1812 made it impossible for the courts to fulfill that role.[3]

Despite all the complaints, no one in government seriously contemplated limiting the courts' authority in wartime. Congress refused to give privateers the control they sought over the disposition of prizes, and largely left it to the judiciary to devise and apply the rules that would regulate the nation's "private navy." Executive branch officials responded to foreign and domestic critiques of the courts' performance by insisting, as they had in the 1790s, that only the judiciary could resolve sensitive questions over the capture of maritime property. Even Justice Story believed that the remedy for the courts' wartime deficiencies was not restrictions on their power, but expansion of it. When it came to adjudicating disputes arising at sea, the federal courts still reigned supreme.

Judicial authority on the water was now more important than ever. The War of 1812 has long been the nation's "forgotten conflict," but it was a transformational moment for the United States. It did not precipitate a fundamental change in American government and society, unlike the Revolutionary and Civil Wars. It did not even have a clear winner, militarily or diplomatically. But it marked the death of the Federalist Party as a political force on the domestic front, and ushered in a brief but potent period of national unity and economic development. Internationally, many Americans understood 1812 as a "second War of Independence" from Great Britain, and from European hegemony more generally. Or, as a congressional committee headed by a young John Calhoun described it, the war was "a contest for [our] sovereignty."[4]

To affirm its sovereignty and independence through war, the United States needed its courts. Historians who study the fiscal and administrative apparatuses that enabled early modern nation-states to engage in armed conflict have largely ignored the judicial role in warmaking. But, as the revolutionary generation learned, the courts' responsibility for ensuring that private armed vessels hewed to the laws of war was critical to maintaining the nation's international credibility. The equally important judicial task in 1812 – and the more difficult one – was keeping the nation's maritime war machine running. The courts' stewardship of prize proceeds married government authority to private enterprise, making it possible for the United States to defend its claim to political equality with European empires. If the judiciary's role in the 1790s was to keep the nation out of a conflict that threatened its sovereignty and independence, its job in 1812 was to enable the nation to fight a war that vindicated those principles.[5]

The courts not only helped the United States make war in 1812. The war also helped make the courts. The fifteen years leading up to the conflict had not been kind to the federal judiciary. Whatever goodwill judges had developed in the Neutrality Crisis of the 1790s evaporated in the face of domestic political controversy. Jeffersonians fearful of the courts' supposed partisan and antidemocratic tendencies engaged in a frontal assault on judicial power in the first decade of the nineteenth century. Yet, as in earlier decades, elected officials continued to extoll the judiciary's ability to resolve the myriad disputes that arose from maritime conflict. The one place where the courts' authority remained secure was at sea.

* * *

As with most armed conflicts, there is no single explanation for why the United States went to war in 1812. At bottom, the decision stemmed from a desire to reassert the nation's political and economic independence – from Europe generally and from Great Britain specifically. Economically, the first years of the nineteenth century were good ones for the United States. With much of Europe ravaged by the Napoleonic Wars, the foreign demand for American agricultural produce and raw materials was insatiable. In addition, the protection that the laws of war offered to the ships of neutral nations, though always fragile and contingent, meant that American vessels became a favored form of transport for merchants around the Atlantic world. With imports and exports climbing, customs revenues grew to unprecedented levels, enabling the Jefferson administration to pay off substantial portions of the federal debt, even as it cut taxes and bought the Louisiana Territory.[6]

As the European struggle intensified in the first decade of the nineteenth century, the United States began to suffer. France and Great Britain became increasingly hostile to any trade that benefited their enemies. Through a series of restrictive decrees, each belligerent effectively prohibited trade with the enemy – not only by their subjects and allies, but also by neutrals. The result was that American vessels trading with almost any port in Europe were subject to capture as prize of war by one side or the other. Britain's control of the seas meant that its warships and privateers posed the greatest threat to American commerce, and British armed ships captured hundreds of American vessels a year. In addition, by 1810 France began to relax its restrictions – at least in theory – leading many Americans to see Britain as the nation's chief antagonist. These abuses were particularly offensive, according to President James Madison, because the oceans were where all "independent nations" had "equal and common rights." If Americans did not respond with force, he warned, they would prove themselves "not an independent people, but colonists and vassals."[7]

The British seized not only American ships, but also American sailors. Britain's maritime dominance depended on manpower that the island kingdom itself could not provide. So the Royal Navy increasingly resorted to impressment – forcing mariners that it found on board foreign vessels into royal service (Figure 4.1). Technically, only British subjects who owed allegiance to the King could be impressed. But the press-gangs that roamed docks and clambered aboard merchant ships had an expansive understanding of subjecthood. Any seaman with an English-sounding name was fair game, including naturalized and even native-born Americans. Despite sailors' protestations of U.S. citizenship, many spent months or years in the British service, working for low pay in dangerous and degrading conditions. British impressment practices inflamed the American public, and it was the centerpiece of the Madison administration's explanation for going to war.[8]

FIGURE 4.1 The British Navy's impressment practices, depicted here in a 1779 etching, were a source of longstanding complaint among American seafarers and one of the principal causes of the War of 1812. "The Liberty of the Subject," by James Gillray (1779), courtesy of the National Portrait Gallery, London

Impressment galled Americans because it was more than a theft of bodies and labor. It was an affront to American autonomy, both individually and collectively. Americans who assumed the legitimacy of bonded labor for people of African descent could not tolerate Britain's "enslavement" of white sailors. And the British claim that English-born seamen were forever the King's subjects denied the very legitimacy of American independence itself. If natives of British dominions (including Irishmen and others) had no individual ability to switch their allegiance from one sovereign to another, then what justified the choice North American colonists made in the 1770s to abandon their fealty to the British Crown? As one historian argues, every act of impressment felt like a reenactment of the Revolution, only this time with the British winning. For many Americans, anything less than a declaration of war would be, as one pamphlet declared, a "SURRENDER OF THEIR SOVEREIGNTY."[9]

The threat that impressment posed to American self-determination mirrored the broader threat that British hostility posed to independence itself. France's transformation from revolutionary democracy to rapacious empire mean that many Americans saw themselves as the sole independent republic left in the world. (Few had room in their political imaginations for a Haitian republic founded and led by former enslaved persons.) Jeffersonians who had spent the previous two decades warning about the danger of domestic monarchism posed by the Federalists could now point to the danger posed by a real and all-too-familiar king. For Americans who had spent the previous three decades trying to figure out how to be English no longer, fears of renewed subservience to the British Crown loomed large.[10]

The prospect of achieving true liberation from British domination also fired Americans' imperial imagination. The continued British and Spanish presence in North America had been a sore point for decades. White settlers seeking to dispossess indigenous people of lands in the western interior chafed at the support British and Spanish authorities gave to Native nations resisting such incursions (however inconstant that support was). Southerners also resented that Florida often provided a haven for enslaved persons fleeing bondage, and saw Spanish territory as fertile ground for extending the nation's growing slave economy. Expelling European powers from North America would make possible the continental hegemony of which many Americans – at least white ones – dreamed. The eye for territory also roamed north, into Canada. Its timber and naval stores helped fuel British maritime power, and provided Britain an important commercial hub. As with Florida, control over Canada would help cement the United States' continental dominance.[11]

Though few Americans in 1812 identified territorial expansion as their chief war aim, few disclaimed it either. Congressman Richard Johnson of Kentucky asserted that Americans wanted nothing more than "the quiet enjoyment of independence." But in light of Britain's "continued hostility," Johnson hoped to see her driven from North America, "and her territories incorporated with the United States." Secretary of State James Monroe made the same point to British diplomats, albeit more mildly. Land acquisition was not the Madison administration's objective in pushing the nation to war, but its political leaders did not have final say. A republican government, directed by popular will, would find it "difficult to relinquish Territory which had been conquered."[12]

If the War of 1812 began with lofty ambitions, the military reality was more sobering. The army had little more than 5,000 men, while the British military had over 200,000. Yet with British forces locked in an interminable land war in Europe, many American politicians were confident – too confident – that troop recruitment and mobilization of state militias would give the United States an advantage on the ground. The bigger problem was at sea. In 1812, the Royal Navy was as large as the rest of the world's navies combined. It had nearly 1,000 warships; the United States had twenty (including some in serious disrepair). The United States never faced the Royal Navy's full might during the war, occupied as it was by the ongoing conflict with Napoleonic France. But just a fraction of British naval power overmatched what the United States could put forward. Even those who supported the war fretted over the disparity. "Our navy is so Lilliputian," John Adams wrote on the war's eve, "that Gulliver might bury it in the deep by making water on it."[13]

The navy's puniness was not an accident; the United States had almost no maritime force because most Americans did not want one. For centuries, European sovereigns had steadily built governance structures that allowed them to make war on others. Early modern states built fiscal and administrative capacities that facilitated organized violence in order to acquire territory, subjugate hostile populations, extract resources, and even bring "civilization" to supposedly benighted corners of the globe. In theory, the Constitution likewise gave the federal government many of the powers it needed to fight wars. Congress could raise armies and navies, and the president was charged with directing them. The government also had the financial tools required for modern warmaking – namely, a robust source of revenue (from customs duties) and the ability to finance war-related expenses by incurring debt.[14]

In practice, the federal government's martial capacity at sea was virtually nonexistent. The Continental Congress disbanded its small fleet after the American Revolution, and the new federal Congress only revived it briefly in the 1790s to repel attacks on American commerce by the Barbary States and France. After his election in 1800, Thomas Jefferson halved the navy's budget, dismissed scores of officers, and considered doing away with the fleet entirely. Throughout his presidency, the Republican-controlled Congress repeatedly rejected proposals to build new ships.[15]

The Jeffersonian retrenchment had deep ideological roots, for Republicans viewed military establishments as an unnecessary evil under free government. Many – including Jefferson himself – were willing to perpetuate violence when they thought it justified, especially when the targets were non-European. But an expansive and permanent military provoked fears of executive aggrandizement. This was Madison's particular concern. Even as president, he worried that militarism inevitably strengthened executive power. It was also costly, leading to the Republican anathema of increased public debt and higher taxes.[16] In addition, large armies and navies threatened the creation of a quasi-aristocratic officer class. Most troubling, a permanent navy threatened to enmesh the United States in European power politics and undermine American self-determination. "Show me a nation possessed of a large navy," a Republican congressman told his colleagues in early 1812, "and I will show you a nation always at war."[17]

Jeffersonians also believed that there were peaceful means of resisting European aggression on the water – namely, by refusing to trade. Beginning in 1806, the Republican-controlled Congress passed a series of increasingly severe embargos on American engagement in foreign commerce. In theory, cutting France and Britain off from valuable American goods and markets would coerce the belligerents into ceasing their assault on American merchants. As it turned out, European nations proved less dependent on trade with the United States than expected, and many Americans continued to engage in foreign commerce anyway. In the end, the embargos' most significant results were to depress the American economy and forestall any possibility of a military buildup.[18]

Even on the war's eve, Republican skepticism of military expenditures scuttled any chance of meeting the challenge of maritime conflict. Madison formally alerted Congress in November 1811 that war seemed likely, but he only suggested that the legislature consider "adaptations" to the nation's naval force. This moderate proposal nevertheless met resistance; the House halved the Navy Secretary's proposal for a $7 million naval construction program before it even reached the floor, and ultimately rejected it. Secretary of the Treasury Albert Gallatin worried that military spending would raise interest rates on the loans the government needed to fight the war, and opposed any discussion of naval appropriations at all. Besides, constructing new ships took time, and many in the United States expected that the war would be short. As Thomas Jefferson famously predicted, conquering Canada would be a "mere matter of marching."[19]

Yet as the war shifted from republican (and Republican) fantasy into military reality, its maritime dimensions assumed greater importance than expected. The invasion of Canada was troubled before it started, due to lack of preparedness, poor military leadership, and widespread reluctance by the states to mobilize their militias. The Madison administration also realized that allowing the Royal Navy free rein to attack American merchant vessels would be an economic disaster, especially for a government that depended on import duties for revenue. With a protracted and costly conflict looking increasingly likely, the administration changed its views. A week before Congress declared war against Great Britain in June 1812, Madison wrote to Gallatin that the United States should focus its efforts on the "maritime war only."[20]

For many Republicans, the way to fight a war without an established military was obvious – by "putting our seamen on board privateers, and covering the sea with them," as Gallatin had earlier put it. Most naval histories of the War of 1812 pay little attention to private armed vessels. The regular navy was small, but its heroic exploits, especially in single-ship actions against British men of war, buoyed patriot spirits disheartened by ignominious defeats on land, and allowed Americans to believe that the war might still be won. Political leaders in Washington, however, recognized that the navy alone could not prevail at sea. In its formal declaration of war, Congress empowered President Madison to issue commissions to the "private armed vessels of the United States," authorizing them to seize all British "vessels, goods, and effects." A week later, Congress passed legislation outlining the requirements for securing such licenses. Thomas Jefferson spoke for many when, on Independence Day in 1812, he urged that "every possible encouragement should be given to privateering."[21]

Using privateers to prosecute the war against Great Britain made military and political sense. The United States' goal was not to confront the Royal Navy directly; even the most heavily armed privateer avoided confrontation with British cruisers (Figure 4.2). Instead, the

FIGURE 4.2 American privateers avoided direct engagement with British armed vessels, but not always successfully. Here the privateer *General Armstrong* repulses a boarding attempt by Royal Navy officers and sailors. "American privateer 'General Armstrong' Capt. Sam Reid" (N. Currier, 1838–1856), courtesy of the Library of Congress

objective was to raid British commerce. Seizing merchant vessels and cargo imposed financial losses on the enemy directly (through a reduction on import duties, for example) and indirectly (by raising insurance rates). In addition, commerce raiding forced the Royal Navy to devote resources to escorting and protecting British merchant ships, leaving fewer naval vessels for blockades or other operations against the United States. Plus, privateers could prey on British commerce as effectively as the U.S. navy could, and more cheaply. In the war's early days, Jefferson wrote to a friend that the British fleet would likely "annihilate" the U.S. navy. "[B]ut our privateers," he predicted, "will eat out the vitals of their commerce."[22]

A temporary fighting force was also the perfect antidote to the threat that standing military forces posed to domestic liberty. Americans had long lauded the militia on land as a pillar of republican government, and privateers were the maritime equivalent. They could be called forth from the people in times of crisis, as patriotic (and profit-seeking) merchants in port towns would add sailors and guns to their fastest ships to cruise against enemy commerce. Like the militia, the privateersmen would then "melt back into civil society" when the conflict ended, leaving no perpetual military establishment that might lead to despotism. Indeed, privateering success would prove that a freedom-loving republic could wage war without the oppressive, war-mongering apparatus erected by tyrannical European nations. By licensing private armed vessels, Jefferson gushed, "the whole naval force of the nation is truly brought to bear on the foe."[23]

Americans were also particularly suited for privateering. By the early 1800s, Americans had almost two centuries of experience with commerce raiding. Privateers operating from the British colonies in North America played a significant role in the imperial conflicts of the seventeenth and eighteenth centuries, and the federal and state governments commissioned hundreds of privateers to plunder British merchants during the American Revolution (see Chapter 1). If anything, the United States in 1812 was even better prepared to wage private war than before. Two decades of experience evading French and British warships gave the nation a love for small, fast-sailing vessels that could easily be converted into privateers, as well as the seasoned officers and seamen needed to man them.[24]

American merchants and seafarers needed little encouragement to join the war effort. They had suffered a decade's worth of British indignities, and they relished the opportunity to extract some revenge – and hopefully handsome profits, too. Within weeks of Congress's declaration of war, scores of "well-appointed sea-dogs" had already "spread the[ir] canvas to the breeze," according to one newspaper, bearing commissions authorizing them to seize British ships and cargo. By war's end, the government still only had a handful of naval vessels at its command, but it had issued over 500 privateering licenses. In fact, private enthusiasm for the war outran public capacity to manage it. By July 1812, several customs collectors notified cabinet officers that they had run out of privateering commissions and the local citizenry was "anxiously awaiting" the arrival of more.[25]

Privateering might have solved the dilemma of how to fight a republican war, but it created international problems of its own. Arming and equipping a vessel of war was expensive, and privateers' sole source of compensation was the proceeds from the sale of captured ships and cargo. This worked out fine for some. A leading Baltimore merchant, Henry Didier, Jr., lamented at the war's end that, had the conflict lasted two more years, he would have made enough money to retire. But profits were by no means guaranteed. British merchant ships carried guns and traveled in convoys with naval vessels. Prizes were lost or recaptured when sailed back to the United States for condemnation. For every successful cruise, there were dozens of sorties that resulted in little or no gain. Privateer owners managed this risk by engaging in multiple ventures and sharing the costs via partnerships that could include dozens of individual investors. But their hopes were often disappointed. According to one recent study of War of 1812 privateering, almost three-quarters of the vessels commissioned in its first six months failed to turn a profit; fewer than half of all privateers captured any ships at all.[26]

The difficulty of finding legitimate prizes inevitably tempted privateers to push the bounds of legality. Sometimes their unlawful seizures were justifiable. A privateer officer peering at a ship's papers in the dim light of a cramped cabin often found it impossible to determine whether vessels or cargo were good prize under the laws of war. The wisest choice was often to seize first, and answer questions later.[27] At other times, however, privateers knew that their conduct was suspect. They seized ships and cargo belonging to non-belligerents on flimsy pretexts, hoping that a friendly or inattentive prize court would ratify their conduct. Or they simply stopped neutral vessels and plundered everything of value. Hard currency was the most welcome find, as it was easy to transport and liquidate. But privateers eager for booty would take anything they could sell or consume – including, in one case, pigs, parrots, oranges, tobacco, and rum.[28]

Privateers committed their most egregious acts out of desperation. Privateering was financially risky for owners and investors, but for the crew it could be a matter of life or death. This was obviously true in the bodily sense; seafaring was always dangerous, even without encountering an armed merchant ship willing to resist capture (to say nothing of a British cruiser bristling with cannon). But privateering could also be economically catastrophic. The only compensation crew members received was a share of the proceeds, so no prizes meant no pay. The very name of the document memorializing a seaman's entitlement to hypothetical profits – the "prize ticket" – evoked privateering's lottery-like characteristics.[29] Desperate sailors did not always wish to observe the niceties of international law when prizes were scarce. They might disparage a captain who decided not to board a passing vessel as an "old woman" or "no man to sail with." Or they might take matters into their own hands. The disappointed crew of the privateer *Anaconda* made their priorities clear when their captain released a "noble prize" they had seized. While pointing one of the ship's guns at him, they reminded him that they had not come on the voyage simply "for pleasure."[30]

Mutiny and plunder were no surprise to privateering's critics. According to German jurist Georg Friedrich von Martens, who wrote in the 1790s, naval officers were inspired by "glory and duty" to put the needs of their sovereign first. Privateers, in contrast, were "indifferent to the fate of the war, and often of [their] country." Their only feeling was "the love of gain." Americans shared these concerns. Benjamin Franklin was opposed to war generally, but he held privateering in special contempt. It was nothing more than a "mischievous kind of gaming," he wrote in 1783, one for which his compatriots had developed "too strong a relish." Supreme Court Justice William Paterson was similarly disparaging more than a decade later. Having witnessed first-hand the cupidity and lawlessness among French-commissioned privateers during the Neutrality Crisis of the 1790s, Paterson condemned the practice as nothing more than "licensed depredation ... [a]ctivated by a predatory spirit."[31]

Privateering's detractors were realistic about the prospects for its immediate abandonment. Paterson "wished" to abolish privateering entirely, but knew that the United States' naval inferiority made that unlikely. The same was true even for Horatio Nelson, the legendary admiral who secured British maritime dominance at the Battle of Trafalgar (and lost his life for it). Befitting the views of an unabashed naval chauvinist, Nelson declared in 1801 that privateering was a "disgrace to the country which tolerates [it]." Like Paterson, he hoped it would be banned outright – but only "after this war."[32]

As John Marshall himself acknowledged, what sovereigns at war needed was a way to keep privateers in line. The "temptation" that neutral vessels presented to men of "unprincipled avarice," he wrote as

Secretary of State in 1800, demanded "strong & efficient restraints." His colleagues on the Supreme Court later agreed. "It has been the great object of every maritime nation," Justice Story declared in one of the Court's first War of 1812 opinions, to "regulate the conduct of its privateers." Their "irregularities of conduct" threatened to involve their sponsoring government in disputes with both neutrals and allies. "If a power did not exist to restrain their operations," Story warned, "the public faith might be violated ... and endless embarrassments arise."[33]

* * *

Responsibility for supervising the United States' private navy fell to the federal courts almost by default. This was not an innovation; as we have seen, admiralty courts had been a favored instrument for controlling maritime violence for centuries (see Chapter 1), and the early nineteenth century was no exception. The maritime powers of the Napoleonic Era relied on an extensive network of prize tribunals to judge the legality of captures and distribute proceeds. And their work was essential. Marshall, like many Americans, thought that the "unjust decisions" of British vice-admiralty courts encouraged British privateers and naval vessels to prey on neutral commerce. Yet, as he declared shortly before becoming Chief Justice, he remained convinced that the "most effectual restraint" against such misconduct was "an upright judiciary."[34]

The notion that the federal courts would be the solution to a major problem of American governance would have seemed improbable in 1812. The Washington administration extolled judicial authority in matters of international conflict during the existential predicament of the Neutrality Crisis, but the subsequent decade and a half had been difficult for federal judges. The courts still suffered from the lack of respect that dogged their early years. Congress briefly relieved the Supreme Court justices of their tiresome circuit riding duties in 1801, but Republicans soon reinstated them. Not coincidentally, the Court's composition turned over almost completely between Jefferson's election in 1800 and the War of 1812. Successive Presidents had difficulty persuading their nominees to accept a position on the bench. John Jay was unsparing in explaining his rejection of John Adams's invitation to return as Chief Justice in 1801: "[T]he Efforts repeatedly made to place the judicial Departmt. on a proper Footing, have proved fruitless."[35]

Perhaps the most telling symbol of the judiciary's early ignominy was architectural. While the government was spending millions to house Congress and the President in Washington's two grandest buildings, the Court occupied what the government's chief architect admitted in 1809 was a "half-finished," "meanly furnished," and "very inconvenient" committee room in the Capitol. When ongoing construction work forced the Court into the drafty library, the justices decamped to a local tavern to hear cases.[36]

The justices' physical indignities paled in comparison to the political attacks they suffered in the years before the war. Federalist judges' willingness to use the 1798 Alien and Sedition Acts to stifle criticism of the Adams administration enraged Republicans. Public anger over those laws helped bring the Republicans to power in 1800, and Federalists tried to pack the federal judiciary with their partisans on their way out. A few weeks before President John Adams's term ended, Congress created sixteen new circuit judgeships and more than forty justices of the peace, and Adams filled them with as many reliable Federalists as he could. Adams also nominated Marshall as Chief Justice.[37]

Republicans castigated the Federalists for using the judiciary as a "strong hold" from which they could resist the Revolution of 1800. James Monroe echoed the military analogy when he complained that federal judges' life tenure and guaranteed salaries meant that they could not be "starved out." The Republicans' metaphors may have been overwrought, but their fears were justified. Federalist leaders were unapologetic about their tactics, and deployed dramatic imagery of their own. They were about to face "a heavy gale," Gouverneur Morris predicted in 1801, so they could not be faulted for using the courts as "anchors to hold their ship through the storm."[38]

Jefferson may have viewed federal judges as valuable partners during the 1790s, but Republicans spent much of his presidency trying to cow them into submission. They first repealed the so-called "Midnight Judges Act" and eliminated the new offices it created. Soon after, Jefferson instigated impeachment proceedings against Federalist judges, including Justice Samuel Chase; many observers expected that Republicans would next move against Marshall, for whom Jefferson had particular scorn. Chase and Marshall ultimately kept their offices, but the threat of impeachment hung over the courts for the next several years. Even Republican-appointed judges were subject to Jefferson's public ire when their rulings undermined his policy goals. In fact, many Jeffersonians questioned whether the courts had any special status at all. In their view, each branch of government had equal authority to interpret the Constitution.[39]

The Jeffersonian threat obliged the Supreme Court to tread lightly. Marshall's tenure as Chief Justice is usually remembered as a time when the federal judiciary assumed a leading role in shaping American constitutional law, but his first decade on the bench was largely a struggle for political survival. Under his leadership, the Court upheld Congress's repeal of the Midnight Judges Act, despite Federalist complaints that the elimination of judgeships violated the Constitution's guarantee of life tenure. Even the early Court's most famous assertion of power, in *Marbury v. Madison*, did not challenge Jefferson directly.[40]

The Court largely managed to stay out of Republican sights during Madison's first term in office, but state governments began to challenge the federal judiciary more openly. Pennsylvania's defiance reached its apogee in 1809, when its decades-long refusal to abide by federal court judgments in a Revolutionary-era prize case resulted in an armed standoff in Philadelphia between federal officers and state militiamen.[41] Madison's mild intervention obliged Pennsylvania to back down, but Republican hostility to the courts increasingly found expression in state court insubordination. The Virginia Supreme Court's rejection of an 1813 Supreme Court ruling, on the ground that the Court had no constitutional power to review state court decisions on questions of federal law, augured the challenges ahead.[42]

For all their travails, the federal courts of the early nineteenth century still had one source of authority that few meaningfully questioned: their jurisdiction over admiralty and maritime cases. It was enshrined in the Constitution and granted exclusively to the federal courts under the Judiciary Act of 1789 (see Chapter 1). It was also the most important power the early courts exercised. Congress did not permanently grant the courts general jurisdiction over cases arising under federal law until the late nineteenth century, and their authority over state law matters was limited to high-value cases involving citizens of different states. But the courts had no shortage of admiralty matters. They heard disputes involving torts and injuries at sea, contracts over seaman's wages and commercial loans, and claims to maritime salvage.[43]

Admiralty was also a potentially expansive power. In a series of early cases, the Supreme Court ruled that it included disputes involving arms exportation, the slave trade, and – most significantly – customs and revenue matters. When an enterprising and ambitious young lawyer named Joseph Story joined the Court on the war's eve, he declared his ambition to expand the definition of admiralty to include virtually any case that touched upon the water.[44]

The Jeffersonian Revolution did not disturb the courts' maritime primacy. Shortly after Jefferson took office in 1801, Secretary of State James Madison responded to a letter from the Danish minister seeking compensation for three Danish ships seized by U.S. naval vessels during the undeclared Quasi-War with France. The minister had already sought help a year earlier from John Marshall, who was Secretary of State under John Adams. But Marshall had declined, in language that echoed Jefferson's rejoinder to French Minister Edmond-Charles Genet several years earlier. One of the captures was already subject to litigation, and the executive branch "could not take upon itself to interfere with the proceedings of the Judiciary." Despite the Jeffersonians' deep distrust of the federal courts, Madison's response to the Danish minister was much the same. Before importuning Congress or the president, redress for illegal seizures in wartime "should be first prosecuted judicially."[45]

This bipartisan faith in the courts' ability to resolve diplomatically sensitive disputes persisted even in moments of tension. Later in 1801, a federal circuit court's decision not to restore a French ship captured by an American naval vessel during the Quasi-War infuriated Jefferson. Marshall, newly installed as Chief Justice, was well aware of the judiciary's delicate predicament, and avoided a direct conflict with the president by creatively interpreting the relevant treaty in a way that required the ship's restoration. Seemingly satisfied, Attorney General Levi Lincoln reaffirmed the courts' influence in maritime matters. Lincoln thought Marshall's legal reasoning, however congenial, was wrong, and advised Jefferson that he could decide for himself whether or not to restore French ships in future cases. But Lincoln also echoed the respect for judicial decision-making that Jefferson himself had articulated during the Neutrality Crisis. The Court's decision was "binding" in this case, Lincoln declared, and going forward it would behoove the executive to "pay[] a great deference" to the Court's opinions on legal questions governing the seizure of ships at sea.[46]

Congress confirmed the federal judiciary's responsibility for regulating conflict at sea as soon as the War of 1812 began. Eight days after Congress's formal declaration of war, it granted the courts exclusive jurisdiction over all prizes that naval vessels and privateers brought into the United States. If the court concluded that a capture was unlawful – i.e., that the vessel or cargo was not a valid prize – it was to restore the property to the rightful owners. In addition, if the court found that the captors acted without probable cause, or behaved "otherwise unreasonably," it could order the privateer's owners and commanders to pay damages to the injured party. Even when a capture was lawful, the courts could deny shares of the prize to anyone who engaged in "gross misconduct."[47]

The courts' leading role in keeping American privateers in check was also confirmed by what Congress and the Madison administration did *not* do. The Prize Act of 1812 imposed only two requirements for obtaining a privateering commission. The applicant had to provide basic information about the vessel (including the ship's name, tonnage, weaponry, and general description), along with the names of the owners and the intended crew size. The owners also had to post a bond, to ensure good behavior. The statute offered privateers a few financial inducements, such as bounties for destroying enemy vessels and exemption from laws enacted before the war prohibiting the importation of foreign goods. But neither the 1812 act nor an additional law passed in January 1813 prescribed any rules regarding what ships and goods privateers could – and could not – seize.[48]

The Madison administration matched Congress's regulatory silence. The Prize Act gave the president the authority to issue instructions governing privateer conduct, but Madison hardly used it. Following the Act's passage, he issued a short set of orders that simply exhorted privateers to respect the rights of neutral vessels and treat the enemy with "justice and humanity." Two months later, in August 1812, Madison instructed privateers not to interfere with

American-owned vessels that had sailed from Britain before the start of the war, but that was the extent of his guidance.[49]

The executive branch also made little use of the enforcement tools at its disposal. There is no indication that federal customs collectors rejected applications for privateering commissions in any significant number, and they issued most licenses within a day or two. And while the Prize Act gave the president authority to revoke privateering commissions "at pleasure," it appears that Madison almost never exercised that power. And criminal prosecutions of privateers for piracy were almost unheard of. Perhaps for good reason: As the Washington administration had learned in the 1790s, it was nearly impossible to persuade a lay jury to punish privateers criminally for their violent acts (see Chapter 2).[50]

This deferral of authority to the courts was a striking departure from both British and earlier American practice. At least as far back as the late seventeenth century, the British Parliament passed highly elaborated statutes regulating the conduct of naval ships and privateers. It repeatedly tinkered with this legal regime during the Seven Years' War, hoping to prevent depredations that angered neutral nations, a trend that only increased during the global conflict that erupted between Britain and France in the 1790s. Similarly, the Continental Congress issued detailed rules governing privateering during the American Revolution, which included specific instructions about whether particular ships and goods were liable to seizure. Yet neither Congress or the Madison administration took similar action in the War of 1812.[51]

Even the archetypal mode of regulating military conduct at sea proved unavailing. The Prize Act of 1812 stipulated that any privateer accused of a serious offense was punishable by naval court martial. This had long been the practice in Britain, where the Royal Navy's vast reach allowed it to convene a tribunal of naval officers almost anywhere in the world. But the U.S. Navy had only a handful of vessels and a few hundred officers, none of whom could easily be spared for court martial duty. Plus, such proceedings usually addressed issues of shipboard discipline, and many American naval officers thought that trying privateersmen for disobeying orders was beneath their dignity.[52] Officials in the Madison administration recognized these deficiencies, but were not able to get Congress to devise a different means of handling privateer offenses. In the end, only five of the hundreds of court martial proceedings held during the war were against privateers, and only two involved conduct that violated the rights of neutrals.[53]

Why the political branches of government left it to the federal courts to regulate the nation's private maritime war is a harder question to answer, but some familiar explanations present themselves. Much like the Washington administration in the 1790s, the Madison administration simply lacked the capacity to take stronger measures. Discord and mismanagement plagued the American war effort from the start. Military preparations were almost nonexistent, and the government executed the plans it did make with shocking incompetence. Political divisions only made matters worse, as war-related legislation repeatedly bogged down in endless congressional debate. This ineptitude was most apparent in the area of finance. Republicans were reluctant to impose politically unpopular new taxes, and they moved slowly on rechartering the Bank of the United States. As a result, by 1814 the federal government was essentially broke. In this context, neither Congress nor the executive branch had the wherewithal to regulate privateers.[54]

Elected officials struggling to manage the war may also have believed that the courts would be able to ensure that privateers hewed to governing legal norms. In the absence of substantive rules from the executive or the legislature regarding the seizure of ships and goods, federal judges could simply apply the highly articulated body of legal precepts articulated by European jurists governing war at sea. To be sure, in 1812 the courts had little experience directly applying the international law of prize. The controversies of the 1790s had turned primarily on questions of neutrality under treaty and statute (see Chapter 3), and the courts heard few true prize cases arising from the Quasi-War with France. But, at a broader level, the courts had two decades of experience resolving a range of challenging legal disputes arising from maritime conflict.[55]

Crucially, federal judges would decide the lawfulness of maritime seizures without juries. This was typical of admiralty proceedings generally, at least when the suit was brought *in rem*, against the disputed property itself (as were all prize cases). And, as we have seen, the Continental Congress's "experiment" with having state juries decide prize cases during the American Revolution threatened the United States' relationship with much-needed allies (Chapter 1). Indeed, one of the chief reasons for creating lower federal courts – and the only one everyone could agree on – was to ensure that judges would decide prize cases free from the parochialism that supposedly infected juries.[56]

In fact, prize's juryless nature might explain why neither Congress nor the President made much effort to regulate privateers in the War of 1812. Extensive rules governing maritime captures may have been a necessity in the American Revolution, when state courts repeatedly failed to uphold the international laws of war. But the experience of the 1790s, when judges helped steer the federal government through a foreign affairs crisis with existential implications, suggested that the courts could be trusted to preserve the nation's peace and security in 1812. More than two decades after the courts' creation, the United States' formal entry into a renewed war for independence meant they could fulfill their original purpose.

* * *

The challenges the courts faced in regulating American privateers began almost as soon as the war itself. In August 1812, the British schooner *Perseverance* arrived in Charleston, prize to the armed vessel *Nonsuch*, the first privateer commissioned in Baltimore. Obidiah Dill, the prize master who steered the *Perseverance* to the United States, presented the ship's papers to the federal district court. The judge immediately ordered the translation of Spanish documents found among the papers, and appointed local merchants as commissioners to interview the *Perseverance*'s crew. The commissioners' job was to ask a series of standard interrogatories regarding the ship's voyage, the circumstances of the capture, and the ownership of the ship and cargo. Two days later, Dill's attorney formally filed a complaint – known as a libel – asking the court to condemn the *Perseverance* as a lawful prize.[57]

Prize proceedings usually moved rapidly, especially in Charleston. Three days after Dill filed his libel, the marshal of the court published a newspaper notice admonishing anyone with an interest in the *Perseverance* or her cargo to present themselves in court the following day. This speed was typical. District court judge John Drayton had only assumed office in early 1812, but he was an experienced lawyer and politician, having already served two terms as the state's governor. Drayton deftly presided over prize cases, and condemned most prizes within a week of their arrival in court.[58] The judge understood how important it was that the court decide such matters quickly. When he had to leave town unexpectedly in October 1812, he ordered court officers to continue conducting any business that did not require his presence, to avoid any "inconvenience" to litigants in pending cases.[59]

Prize cases proved more difficult to adjudicate when privateer misconduct was potentially at issue. As it turned out, the *Perseverance* was not a British schooner. It was a Spanish-owned ship, also known as the *Barbaretta*. Because Spain and the United States were not at war, the ship was not a good prize, and Judge Drayton ordered her restoration to her captain. Then there was the question of damages owed to the owner for losses resulting from the seizure. Given that the *Barbaretta*'s neutral status only became clear after four days of courtroom testimony and argument, Judge Drayton concluded that the captors had probable cause for seizing her, which was typically a defense against damages. But Drayton nonetheless awarded the claimants more than $500 for spoiled cargo, and ordered the captors to pay an additional $150 to the ship's captain for some doubloons taken by the privateer crew.[60]

If anything, Drayton may have been too lenient. A few weeks later, the same privateer, the *Nonsuch*, seized an American vessel sailing close to the British island of St. Thomas, on suspicion of trading with the enemy. The privateers put the merchant crew in irons and detained the vessel overnight, before sending her to Cuba, where she ran aground. On appeal to the Supreme Court, Chief Justice Marshall acknowledged that the initial seizure was justified. He also recognized that privateers provided "meritorious" service to the nation. But the *Nonsuch* had acted with a "culpable disregard to the rights of others," and the privateer's owner had to pay compensation for the losses they inflicted.[61]

In general, federal judges were careful to balance privateer accountability against the nation's need for sea power. In an early circuit court case, Justice Story denied a claim for lost profits and spoliation of cargo from a merchant who anticipated selling his wrongly seized goods for much more than he had originally paid. The captors had unreasonably detained the ship, so damages were permissible. But Story was reluctant to punish the captors too harshly. The seizure had taken place barely a month after the war began, and all parties could be forgiven for imperfectly understanding "their relative rights and duties." Plus, Story sympathized with privateers who had to figure out on the spot whether a ship they stopped on the high seas was a lawful prize, and he worried that punishing them for every unforeseen consequence of their captures would be a "discouragement upon the public service."[62]

Moreover, the ubiquity of commerce raiding in early modern warfare meant that losses due to wrongful captures were inevitable. Merchants were often insured against seizures at sea (whether lawful or unlawful), and lost profits were simply a cost of doing business in wartime. Story recognized this as well as anyone. Congress and the President had authorized privateers to make war on British trade, and it was not for the courts to judge the "policy or impolicy" of that decision. Nor was it their job to "punish every irregularity," for too-stringent vigilance would effectively amount to "a prohibition of captures." The courts' only function, Story maintained, was to "guard the citizen from unjustifiable seizures."[63]

In truth, federal judges did not often have to decide whether privateer misconduct warranted punishment, because it seems that they largely behaved themselves during the war. There were cases where privateers seized ships and cargo that a court later restored to the owners because they turned out not to be lawful prizes. But unjustified seizures and outright plunder were seemingly rare. A comprehensive study of Baltimore privateering found only three instances of serious misconduct, and other sources agree with the conclusion that "quasi-piratical behavior" was an anomaly.[64]

The surviving federal government records tell the same story. Of the hundreds of cases the district courts adjudicated during the war, judges required the captors to pay damages on only a handful of occasions. Similarly, diplomatic correspondence from the period points to just a few instances of privateer misconduct that were sufficiently serious to trigger foreign objections. This relative silence is striking when compared with the continual remonstrations by British officials in the 1790s over American involvement in French privateering (see Chapter 2), and similar protests by Spanish and Portuguese representatives after the War of 1812 (see Chapter 6). And it is doubtful that the courts were unusually lenient, or that significant privateer misconduct simply went unnoticed or unaddressed. Throughout this period, foreign officials stationed in the United States diligently monitored comings and goings on the waterfront, and were quick to sound the alarm whenever their compatriots suffered injuries at sea.[65]

The likeliest explanation for American privateers' apparent probity was the courts themselves. One of prize law's fundamental rules was that ships and goods seized at sea did not become the captors' legal property until a competent tribunal declared the capture lawful. Sea raiders sometimes sold prizes without judicial approval, as demonstrated by French privateers during the Neutrality Crisis. But doing so lowered the sales price, so captors had a strong incentive to bring their prizes before a court, at least when they stood a reasonable chance of prevailing. Plus, sending a dubious prize to the United States for adjudication was risky. Manning a prize depleted the privateer crew, and it might be recaptured by enemy cruisers on route. Seeking condemnation cost money, in the form of fees to attorneys and court officers, not to mention the possibility of a damages award if the court ruled the prize to be no good. So privateers had strong incentive to only seize vessels and goods that were likely to be judged lawful. Judicial control over prizes, in other words, encouraged men motivated by profit to stay on the straight and narrow path.[66]

The more daunting task the courts faced during war – and the more consequential one – was ensuring that the United States' war machine stayed afloat. The proceeds from court-ordered prize sales were the only compensation privateer owners, officers, and crew received, and they were a significant share of compensation for naval officers and seamen, too. So judicial decisions about how to dispose of maritime captures were an essential part of the incentive structure that undergirded the republic's maritime war effort. But the courts' rulings also impacted the attorneys and agents who managed privateer ventures, not to mention the carpenters, sailmakers, and other tradespeople whose livelihood depended on finding clients who could pay for their services. In short, the health of the private navy that sailed from the docks of the eastern seaboard depended on judicial stewardship.[67]

In theory, once a court determined that a prize was valid, its responsibility for dividing war's financial rewards was largely ministerial. Court officers auctioned the captured property, deducted court fees and other charges from the proceeds, and distributed the amounts remaining according to a written agreement among investors, officers, and crew. In some cases, allocating the monies from a prize was a simple matter of arithmetic. But it could be difficult to determine who should partake of the spoils. Many seamen who served on privateers could not afford to wait for weeks or months before the alchemy of prize law transformed captured enemy property into cash. Sailors exchanged their prize shares for advances from the privateer's owners or agents, or from the shopkeepers and publicans who supplied the necessities of life on the waterfront. Sometimes sailors bartered too actively, like the seaman who, "being very much intoxicated," sold his prize ticket twice, leaving it to the district court to figure to whom the shares rightfully belonged.[68]

Untangling the skein of privateering's financial obligations involved more than apportioning prize money. Judicial control over sales proceeds encouraged anyone involved with a privateer to seek payment for their services from the court. Seamen filed suits seeking prize shares wrongly withheld, or extra payment for injuries suffered.[69] Privateer captains argued for additional compensation because their officers and crew already owed them more than their shares were worth.[70] Prize agents, who represented the investors and crew in prize proceedings, petitioned the court for a greater share of the earnings, citing their "labor and attention" in ensuring that auctioned goods fetched the highest return possible.[71] Attorneys who could not collect their fees from clients asked the court to award them instead.[72]

Like their predecessors in the 1790s, federal judges in the War of 1812 had decidedly mixed feelings about assuming the burden of resolving the many disputes that arose from maritime conflict. Some embraced the responsibility of properly distributing prize proceeds. In one of New York district judge William Van Ness's earliest cases, he issued a rule requiring the court clerk to prepare a report in each case detailing the value of every individual share in the prize, which could include over a hundred entries (Figure 4.3).[73] In South Carolina, Judge Drayton's instructions to court officers respecting the sale of

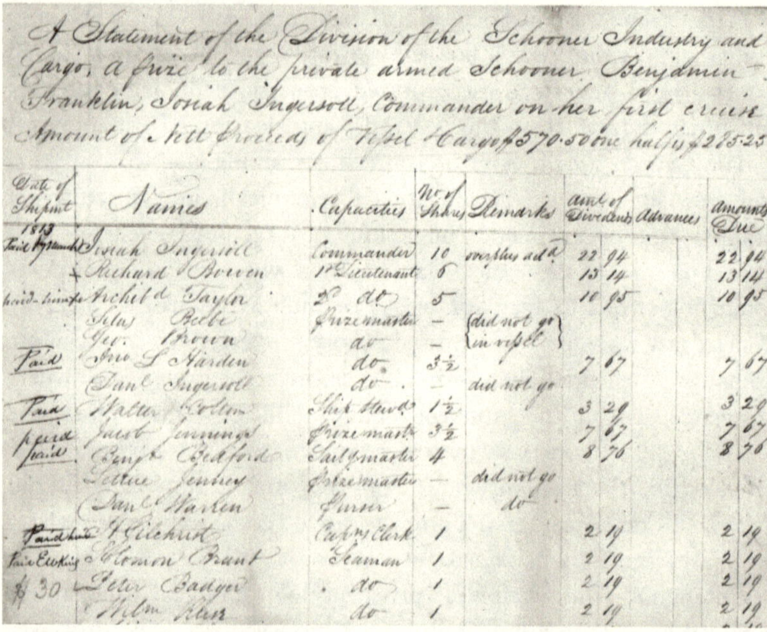

A Statement of the Division of the Schooner Industry and Cargo, a Prize to the private armed Schooner Benjamin Franklin, Josiah Ingersoll, Commander on her first cruise
Amount of Nett Proceeds of Vessel & Cargo $570.50 one half is $285.25

Date of Shipment 1813	Names	Capacities	No. of Shares	Remarks	Amt of Dividends	Advances	Amounts Due
Paid [illegible]	Josiah Ingersoll	Commander	10	[illegible]	22 94		22 94
	Richard Bowen	1st Lieutenant	6		13 14		13 14
[illegible]	Archibald Taylor	2d do	5		10 95		10 95
	Silas Beebe	Prizemaster	—	did not go in vessel			
	Geo. Brown	do	—				
Paid	Jno L Harden	do	3½		7 67		7 67
	Danl Ingersoll	do	—	did not go			
Paid	Walter [illegible]	Ship Steward	1½		3 29		3 29
Paid	Jacob Jennings	Prizemaster	3½		7 67		7 67
Paid	Benjn Bedford	Sailmaster	4		8 76		8 76
	[illegible]	Prizemaster	—	did not go			
	Danl Warden	Gunner	—	do			
Paid	[illegible] Gilchrist	Captns Clerk	1		2 19		2 19
Paid [illegible]	Solomon Brant	Seaman	1		2 19		2 19
$30	Peter Badger	do	1		2 19		2 19
	Wilm [illegible]	do	1		2 19		2 19

FIGURE 4.3 Judicial control over the proceeds derived from prize sales meant that judges and court personnel played a critical role in sustaining the United States' "private navy." Courtesy of the National Archives and Records Administration

a prize and the distribution of proceeds were more detailed than his initial ruling regarding the prize's validity.[74]

Other judges were less enthusiastic about fulfilling their supervisory duties. The judge of the Louisiana district court was content to allow the captors to distribute prize proceeds themselves.[75] And it appears that even Judge Van Ness in New York lost his passion for administrative detail. His clerk complained that it was "impossible" to determine accurately which crew members were entitled to shares in complex cases, and the inevitable mistakes required significant time (and judicial intervention) to sort out. By war's end, the court abandoned the practice of minutely apportioning prize monies. As before, judicial willingness to support the political branches' efforts to defend American sovereignty only went so far.[76]

Judges were not the only ones who questioned whether the courts should be responsible for managing the nation's maritime war effort.

Throughout the conflict, privateers fighting the war and executive branch officials directing it critiqued the judiciary's authority. As was often the case in disputes over prizes, the disputes were ultimately about money.

The privateers' complaint was simple: The courts were making it too hard for them to get their hard-earned financial rewards. According to the Baltimore merchants who petitioned Congress in late 1812, prize cases moved quickly in certain courts but "vexatious delays" were common in others, even when the condemnation went unopposed. A group of New York investors wryly contrasted the difficulty of navigating the judicial system with the challenge of evading British cruisers: It was easier "to get the prizes into port" than it was "to get the money out of court." This judicial delay undermined the war effort. It withheld funds owners needed for further expeditions, and was unjust to the "hardy seaman" who risked his life in the national defense.[77]

Worse yet, aside from "a few words" in the Prize Act of 1812, neither Congress nor the Supreme Court had prescribed rules governing prize proceedings in the fourteen different federal district courts where captured ships might end up. The petitioners contrasted this procedural morass with the situation in Great Britain, where numerous parliamentary acts ensured captors speedy and certain access to their profits. The privateers found it inconceivable that Congress would subject the rights of Americans serving their country to the vagaries of judicial whim.[78]

The privateers had reason to complain. Complex prize cases could take months (or even years) to resolve, and even straightforward decisions might be followed by a lengthy process for allocating the proceeds. What is more, prize procedure did vary among the district courts. In some ways, this diversity was a feature of the federal system, not a bug. In 1789, Anti-Federalist fears about the new judiciary's consolidationist tendencies led the First Congress to decide that the federal courts would apply state procedural rules in common law cases. Three years later, Congress exhorted the courts to follow traditional "principles, rules and usages" in admiralty matters, but allowed individual courts to make whatever "alterations and additions [they] deem expedient." And while Congress also gave the Supreme Court authority to prescribe general rules for such cases, the Court never exercised that power, no doubt mindful of perpetual Jeffersonian suspicions of centralized government. As a result, each district court had latitude to operate, as the Baltimore petitioners complained, in a manner "peculiar to itself."[79]

What privateer investors really wanted, more than speed or uniformity, was control. They resented that they had to wait for a court to dispose of their captures, while in Britain the captors could usually sell prizes themselves after judicial condemnation. The courts' involvement also reduced privateers' profits. The marshal of the court received a commission of up to six percent for managing prize auctions. Cutting out this middleman could increase the return on a valuable prize by hundreds or even thousands of dollars. Control over proceeds would also give investors leverage over officers and crew members in the inevitable disputes over amounts owed.[80] On occasion, privateers frustrated by the courts' ponderous oversight defied judicial orders and tried to auction their captures directly. Sometimes they ignored the courts entirely, and simply divided the cargo amongst themselves.[81]

Executive branch officials also criticized the courts' handling of the profits of war, but for different reasons. By law, a percentage of prize proceeds was set aside to pay pensions for disabled seamen, both privateer and naval. These funds had deep symbolic importance, even though only a fraction of the thousands of men who served on privateers received compensation. The pensions were the result of a broad and increasingly successful effort by military veterans and their spouses, dating back to the American Revolution, to persuade Congress that the nation owed a debt of gratitude to those who were injured in its defense. Early pension programs were limited to officers, but in the War of 1812 Congress extended benefits to all service members, regardless of rank. It was therefore fitting that privateers were the first class of combatants to whom Congress offered universal coverage. If privateers were truly a "militia moving upon the water," arising organically from the populace to protect the United States from external threats, then it was only right that *all* citizen-sailors be rewarded for their sacrifices.[82]

The courts, however, repeatedly failed to secure the prize proceeds needed to support those who shed blood in the republic's defense. Court officers responsible for handling prize monies often did not deposit them in a bank, and almost never filed accounts of their receipts with the Navy Department.[83] At times, the dereliction of duty was more serious. In South Carolina, Judge Drayton repeatedly issued orders obliging the marshal to account for proceeds he had failed to pay over, and the federal district attorney eventually filed suit against him. Apparently unable to account for the missing money, the marshal was eventually arrested and thrown into jail.[84]

Executive branch officials had little success cajoling court officers into fulfilling their fiscal obligations to the nation's protectors. They chastised recalcitrant clerks and marshals for the "loose manner" in which they performed their legal duties, and threatened to adopt "rigorous measures" to secure their compliance.[85] But court personnel continued to resist. They quibbled with navy officials over the exact nature of their responsibilities, denied having received proper instructions, and disclaimed any responsibility for – or even knowledge of – alleged mismanagement.[86] The problems continued even after the Secretary of the Navy Benjamin Crowninshield persuaded Congress to pass legislation specifying court officers' duties and imposing heavy fines for failure to fulfill them.[87]

Compounding matters, federal judges seemed to have little appetite for supervising their subordinates. Judge Van Ness in New York may have initially taken seriously his responsibility to disburse prize proceeds, but he did not appreciate the executive branch's intrusion into his domain. Fed up with Crowninshield's increasingly agitated letters berating the clerk and marshal of his court for their errors, Van Ness insisted that those officers owed the Navy Secretary "no obedience." Indeed, they "obey[ed] the orders of the court, and none other."[88]

Van Ness may have wished he had been more accepting of executive branch oversight. He was an able lawyer and experienced political operative who had schemed to deliver the contested 1800 presidential election to Aaron Burr (and served as Burr's second in the fatal 1804 duel with Alexander Hamilton). But Van Ness apparently did not relish the less glamorous duties of judicial office. Upon ascending to the bench in early 1812, he decided to lighten his workload by rescinding his predecessor's rule that any bank withdrawals by the court clerk required the judge's signature. (Van Ness apparently liked to retire to his mansion in upstate New York when court was not in session, and did not want to be bothered there with court business.) The clerk repaid the judge's trust by absconding with more than $100,000. A congressional committee concluded that Van Ness did not actively participate in the embezzlement. But the report made clear that his lax supervision was nothing like the "constant vigilance" Congress expected the courts to exercise in safeguarding the government's wartime finances.[89]

* * *

Despite all the frustration with the courts' wartime performance, nobody in government wanted to limit their power to regulate the nation's private navy. If anything, the exigencies of administering the war at sea bolstered the courts' authority. In 1813, Congress responded to privateer complaints about the lack of procedural uniformity with more detailed regulations that only confirmed the judiciary's importance. Vessels and goods condemned in federal court were to be sold at public auction "by the marshal of the district," not anyone else. The marshal was also responsible for distributing the proceeds according to the agreement between the owners, officers, and crew. As Justice Story put it in a subsequent circuit decision, privateer seizures were "still subject to the control and regulation of the prize court," and it was the judge's duty "to ascertain the proper parties entitled to share."[90]

At first glance, Congress's decision to leave control over prizes in the courts' hands is a bit perplexing. Elected officials were fully responsive to privateers' others complaints. Congress reduced the import duties the Treasury Department collected on prize goods, and relinquished entirely the government's claim to vessels and cargo that privateers had seized in the war's early months for violations of the Non-Importation Act. Congress also capped at one percent the commission federal marshals received for auctioning prizes, and offered privateers greater bounties for taking prisoners and destroying enemy ships. Plus, given the doubts judges and others had about their fitness for managing the war at sea, it would have been easier simply to follow the British model, and allow the captors to dispose of prizes themselves.[91]

What likely motivated Congress's decision to reaffirm judicial authority over prizes was a belief that this was the only way to ensure the proper functioning of the nation's maritime war machine. Judicial control of prize proceeds discouraged privateers from violating the laws of war, and it ensured – at least in theory – that lawful seizures resulted in just rewards for everyone involved. Not just officers and crew, but the government as well, in the form of import duties owed on prize goods and the percentages due to the pension fund. William Jones, Benjamin Crowninshield's predecessor as Secretary of the Navy, repeatedly underscored the courts' importance. They were not just a convenient forum for resolving claims to captured maritime property that captors could bypass when they chose. Failure to maintain judicial control over prizes, Jones wrote, left "great room for fraud." The result would not only be injury to the public fisc, but possibly "derangement" of the American war effort itself. The courts, Jones declared, were "the only Guardians of the Public interest" in wartime.[92]

Cabinet officers defended judicial authority even more forcefully when speaking to foreign governments. In March 1813, the Portuguese minister to the United States complained to Secretary of State James Monroe about the alleged plunder of several Portuguese vessels by American privateers. This "unprincipled" conduct toward a neutral, the minister argued, violated the law of nations, and he demanded return of the stolen property and punishment for the offenders. Such grievances were relatively rare, but other foreign officials also complained to Monroe about unlawful seizures and outright robberies committed by American armed ships.[93]

Monroe responded that the judiciary, not the executive branch, was responsible for remedying privateer violations of other nations' sovereign rights. President Madison had already enjoined privateers from seizing neutral property, and any party alleging injury by American privateers had "a suitable remedy ... in our courts of law." In fact, according to Secretary of the Treasury Alexander Dallas, claimants *had* to make their arguments to a federal court, because it was "the only Tribunal" that could provide relief. In so holding, Monroe and Dallas repeated nearly verbatim the arguments the Washington administration made to French officials in the Neutrality Crisis two decades earlier: The executive branch could not intervene in judicial proceedings, even in wartime, for the courts were not "under the controul of any other branch of the Government."[94]

At times, the Madison administration's insistence on judicial resolution of wartime disputes led it to take extreme positions. In 1813, the Swedish minister warned that failure to restore Swedish-owned property wrongfully seized by naval officers near Georgia would compromise relations with a "friendly power." Monroe promised he would do what he could to ensure that the dispute was speedily resolved, but warned that he was powerless to intervene in judicial proceedings. This was dubious, as Monroe could have instructed the federal district attorney to abandon his effort to have the property condemned. Even the Swedish owner's American lawyer was confident the property would be "given up." But the Madison administration apparently did not want to take sides in a dispute between naval officers eager for a valuable prize and a neutral government wanting it back. So Monroe reprised Thomas Jefferson's line. "According to the principles of our Constitution," he declared, "a judicial tribunal takes cognizance of all such questions."[95]

Monroe's insistence on the sanctity of judicial decision-making in wartime was downright disingenuous at times. Shortly after the war ended, he responded to the British minister's complaint about the seizure of a British vessel with the familiar refrain: Once a court was "judicially possessed of [a] case," there was no ground upon which the executive could "interfere." Yet only three months earlier, he had asked the same minister to intervene in ongoing proceedings in a British prize court to restore an American ship captured by a British naval vessel. Monroe, in other words, was perfectly comfortable with the idea that foreign governments might interfere with their *own* prize tribunals to protect the rights of other nations. But in the United States such a suggestion bordered on sacrilege.[96]

Monroe's apparent inconsistency was perhaps the point. For more than twenty years, he and his predecessors had repeatedly insisted that the executive branch had no power over the courts when it came to matters of maritime war. European kings and emperors might enjoy that prerogative, thanks to their exercise of commingled judicial and executive authority. But in a republican government predicated on separation of powers, the executive could not intrude on the judiciary's nautical domain. Of course, the text of the Constitution itself said no such thing (at least not directly). And in 1793 such pronouncements had been met with British skepticism and howls of derision from self-proclaimed "real republicans" like Edmond-Charles Genet. But thanks to more than two decades of repetition, Article III's promise of judicial responsibility for "all cases of admiralty and maritime jurisdiction" had become a reality. On the water, the judiciary was supreme.[97]

Even the courts' fiercest wartime critic – Justice Story – turned out to be a staunch champion of judicial authority at sea. Story was only thirty-two years old when he joined the Supreme Court, but he was the perfect man for the moment. He was raised and educated in coastal Massachusetts, and was already an experienced politician and admiralty lawyer when he ascended to the bench. That did not stop him from "most industriously reading Prize Law," as he put it, as soon as war broke out. Befitting his pedagogical tendencies (later realized as a professor at Harvard), Story pursued a course of study that included the writings of the leading law of nations publicists as well as treaties and municipal statutes governing prize among European nations. The central works on Story's reading list, however, were recent reports of judicial decisions in prize cases in England and the United States, as well as a collection of standard writs, forms, and orders used in British admiralty proceedings. Taken together, these works revealed prize to be "a beautiful science."[98]

What troubled Story was that few in the American legal profession seemed to share his dedication to mastering the intricacies of prize law, especially those on the bench. He had many criticisms. Judges assessing damages resulting from unlawful seizures heard evidence ex parte, without notice to the other party. They neglected to specify the reasons for awarding the amounts they recommended. They allowed witnesses to give incomplete and evasive answers about the circumstances of captures. The greatest offenders were courts in southern states, whose permissive approach fostered what Story saw as "mischievous irregularity." But his critique was not sectional. Even John Davis, his Massachusetts district court colleague, did not escape censure. Story professed deep respect for his colleagues (most of them, anyway), but he could not stay quiet while they made mistakes that undermined prize law's proper functioning.[99]

For Story, the courts' cardinal sin was importing cumbersome "common law notions" into prize cases. In his view, prize procedure's beauty, and its utility, stemmed from its simplicity. All the court usually required in order to decide whether a seized vessel and its cargo were enemy property was the ship's papers and the answers its crew gave to the standard interrogatories. This parsimony meant that prize cases could be disposed of quickly, to the benefit of both captors and owners. Plus, Story believed that efficiency promoted just outcomes. Extrinsic sources of evidence, like affidavits from third parties or oral testimony in court, might enhance truth-seeking in proceedings under the common law. But allowing the parties to support their claims with later-adduced evidence gave crafty litigants opportunities for obfuscation, and "derange[d] the simplicity of prize." Given the courts' duty to "guard as much as possible against frauds," adhering to particular rules was not a "mere matter of practice or form." It was the "very essence" of prize procedure.[100]

Story recognized that American courts were not entirely to blame for their shortcomings. British tribunals had adjudicated the legality of maritime captures for centuries, and could rely on an extensive body of statutory law and judicial precedent. In contrast, legislative and executive neglect in the United States had left the federal courts with only "the general regulations of admiralty proceedings" for guidance. And judicial comprehension of that shared corpus of international law was woefully inadequate. The United States was no stranger to maritime war, but the last time its legal community had any significant experience with actual prize cases was during the American Revolution. Making matters worse, the commercial restrictions of the Napoleonic period meant that few European treatises on prize were available in the United States. As a result, prize law and practice in the United States, in Story's words, were "so little methodized, and so little known."[101]

But Story's patience with his colleagues' "shameful ignorance" had its limits. He had overcome the same obstacles through diligence and hard work. The nation's lack of familiarity with prize may have explained the lamentable state of practice at the war's outset, but by its end "that apology no longer exist[ed]."[102]

For all Story's criticisms, however, he believed that reform – not restriction – was the key to remedying the defective judicial administration of war. And he appointed himself reformer-in-chief. He packed his wartime opinions with extensive discourses on the legal procedure of maritime captures, as much to educate lawyers and judges as to resolve the cases before him. He arranged to have his decisions reported and published (partly at his own expense), and sought out ways to get them before the public. And, shortly after the war ended, Story distilled his extensive learning into two "notes" on prize law – totaling nearly 100 pages – that he anonymously appended to his protégé Henry Wheaton's reports of Supreme Court decisions. His express hope was that, by sharing his expertise, he would spare future prize proceedings the "embarrassment" of continued ignorance.[103]

Story did not simply want to improve the courts' performance; he also wanted to extend their authority over wartime disputes as far as he could. This was entirely keeping with his expansive understanding of the courts' waterborne domain generally. A few years after joining the Court, Story wrote a treatise-like opinion that explored "the whole jurisdiction of the admiralty" in order to reach the conclusion that, under Article III, the federal courts could adjudicate all manner of commercial disputes connected to the water (such as those involving contracts for marine insurance). Story was so enamored with the federal courts' admiralty power, the legend went, that he would take jurisdiction over a "corn cob floating in a bucket" if someone brought it into his courtroom.[104]

Little surprise that, in Story's hands, the federal courts' prize jurisdiction encompassed any legal dispute that bore the slightest connection to a maritime capture. "[O]nce the prize court has acquired jurisdiction over the principal cause," he wrote, "it will exert its authority over all the incidents." This power included distributing prize money, awarding damages to persons injured in connection with a seizure, and resolving contractual disputes over the disposition of proceeds. In fact, Story did not think a capture even needed to be on the water for the courts to take jurisdiction. As long as a dispute involved the seizure of sea-going vessels (or the goods that traveled in them), the federal courts could hear it.[105]

In Story's view, the national interest also demanded an *exclusive* judicial authority in matters of war. This was especially true when it came to control over the proceeds from prize sales. It went almost without saying that "court[s] of common law" – i.e., state courts – could have no role in distributing the monies that were so essential to maintaining the nation's war effort. And while Story typically viewed British prize law as the model for the United States to follow, he disagreed with the British practice of letting captors sell prizes.

Relinquishing judicial control made it difficult for the court to ensure "proper responsibility" or quash any "attempt of fraud." For the "most obvious reasons of public policy," Story declared, decisions about who was to profit from the nation's war at sea belonged "exclusively to the prize court."[106]

Ultimately, Story's belief in the federal courts' central role in defending American sovereignty outweighed his doubts about their fitness for the task. A few years after the War of 1812 ended, he sent published reports of his circuit court decisions to Sir William Scott, who was the judge of the British High Court of Admiralty from 1798 to 1828. Story admired Scott deeply (as we will see in Chapter 5). He deemed the British jurist's opinions in admiralty cases to be without equal for their "learning and sagacity." Perhaps feeling self-conscious about the length of his opinions in prize cases, Story apologized for their "minute discussions" of procedural points. But it could not be helped. At the war's outset, he explained, prize law was a "new system" in the United States, and Americans had only "feeble and indistinct lights" to guide their way. In the absence of direction from the political branches, federal judges had been obliged to figure out for themselves how to superintend the nation's private navy, and many had struggled to do so.[107]

Story's letter nevertheless voiced optimism about the judiciary's future, especially at sea. Congress and the Madison administration had repeatedly affirmed that responsibility for administering the laws of war fell exclusively to the judiciary, despite critiques of the courts leveled by foreign diplomats, executive branch officials, and privateers themselves. Perhaps that is why he expressed his confidence to Scott that "a foundation had been laid" on which future generations could establish principles and doctrines that would bolster both judicial and national authority. As Story knew full well, that movement was already well under way, and he was a central figure in its progress.[108]

5

A Belligerent Court

In May 1815, Joseph Story picked up his pen to write his friend Nathaniel Williams again about what Story had described, three years earlier, as the "beautiful science" of prize law. While his earlier letter had been enthusiastic about the opportunity the War of 1812 offered to shape the laws of maritime conflict, now Story was far more melancholy. His youngest daughter – only eleven months old – had just died, one of the five Story children who did not live to see adulthood.[1]

To assuage his "unspeakable sorrow," Story threw himself into writing a dissenting opinion in the *Nereide*, a War of 1812 case involving an American privateer's capture of an armed British merchant vessel carrying Spanish-owned cargo. Chief Justice John Marshall wrote the majority opinion ruling that the cargo was not lawful prize. Spain and the United States were not at war, and Marshall did not think that conveyance in an armed British ship transformed neutral goods into enemy property eligible for capture. Story was appalled. "[N]ever in my whole life," he told Williams, "was I more entirely satisfied that the Court were wrong in their judgment."[2]

Story usually did not air his disagreement with the Court's decisions. Under Marshall's leadership, the justices typically presented a united front, and Story agreed that public dissent "weaken[ed] the authority of the Court." But in the *Nereide* he could not hold his tongue. He was convinced that Marshall's opinion would embolden unscrupulous merchants who claimed the protection of neutral rights while tacitly aiding the British war effort. By shipping his goods in a British ship, Story argued, the Spanish claimant had created "a perfect identity of interests and of objects" between himself and the United States' enemy. This "false and hollow neutrality," Story warned, was "infinitely more injurious than the most active warfare."[3]

Story lost in the *Nereide*, but he largely prevailed in a broader struggle among the justices over the laws of war. In prize cases arising from the War of 1812, the justices repeatedly advanced doctrines that validated the seizure of ships and goods on the high seas rather than those that protected maritime commerce from such depredations. In many instances, the Court maintained the surface unanimity that characterized much of its prior jurisprudence. But the war also exposed unprecedented divisions among the justices, and between Story and Marshall in particular. While the Chief Justice continued to advocate for the legal protections for merchants that he had championed for over a decade, his influence waned in the face of Story's determination to favor the rights of nations at war.

Understanding the belligerent trajectory of the Supreme Court's War of 1812 cases challenges long-held assumptions about the federal courts, the law of war, and the path to American sovereignty and independence. Scholars who study the ways in which the early United States used organized violence to expand territory and subjugate people have exploded the myth of the fledgling republic as an inherently pacific entity. But there persists a belief that the early Supreme Court – and the nation's political leaders more generally – were firmly committed to protecting non-belligerents from the effects of armed conflict. This is correct, up to a point. Promoting neutral rights was a staple of early American legal and political discourse, and in Marshall's first decade the Court fashioned a jurisprudence that was more protective of commerce than the harsh doctrines imposed by France and Britain during the Napoleonic Wars. Indeed, the nation went to war in 1812 in significant part to vindicate the principle that war should not impinge on the rights of neutrals to trade.[4]

What the traditional stories fail to recognize is how the Court's War of 1812 rulings heralded a more aggressive judicial approach to promoting American sovereignty in time of war. For Story, anyone who aided the enemy while sheltering under the banner of free trade was legitimately subject to the courts' authority, and the nation's. Indeed, Story reserved his greatest ire not for neutrals, but for Americans who put their personal interests ahead of national ones, by trading with the enemy. Doctrinally, Story's pro-belligerent decisions did not prompt a fundamental change in the international law of maritime war. If anything, skepticism about the legitimacy of maritime commerce raiding increased in the post-Napoleonic period. But Story's opinions marked a significant attitudinal shift. They signaled that federal judges were increasingly willing to exercise judicial power against all those who threatened American peace and security at sea.

The disagreement between Marshall and Story also reflected a generational divide over how to defend, and extend, American independence. Marshall – who had fought in the Revolutionary War and witnessed first-hand the challenges of the 1780s – seemingly never abandoned the belief that a vulnerable nation, dependent on international commerce, benefited most from legal protections for maritime trade. Story, who came of age during Washington's presidency, saw a different future for the United States, in which a robust military establishment directed by a strong central government would best enable the United States to establish itself as truly sovereign. To facilitate this evolution, federal courts had to abandon the defensive role they played in the 1790s, when their goal was to keep the United States out of war. Instead, the nation needed courts that would not only superintend the war effort (as we saw in Chapter 4), but that would also advance legal doctrines that enabled the nation to meet the challenges it faced.[5]

Recognizing the jurisprudential shift the War of 1812 inspired also changes our understanding of the early Supreme Court's institutional dynamics. Historians and lawyers have long marveled at the lack of public disagreement among the justices during Marshall's tenure. But the War of 1812 produced visible cracks in the façade of uniformity that Marshall worked so hard to build, something a handful of scholars have noticed but have been unable to explain. The simple answer is war. Though the War of 1812 is commonly viewed as a minor conflict, Americans were deeply split over its meaning and how to fight it. Those divisions found expression in the justices' clashing views of how to balance the interests of commerce against the prerogatives of combatants. The War of 1812 may have affirmed the judiciary's primacy at sea, but it also undermined the Supreme Court's decisional cohesion. War, it turns out, shaped the early courts in more ways than one.[6]

* * *

The Supreme Court in the first decade of the nineteenth century was a harmonious place, perhaps because the justices were not actually together for much of the year. The Court held only two sessions annually, in February and August; for the rest of the year they rode circuit or resided in their home communities. They had good reason to stay away from the nation's capital, for at the start of Marshall's tenure it barely existed. Aside from the prosperous enclave of Georgetown, the grand metropolis imagined by Pierre Charles L'Enfant a decade earlier consisted largely of a handful of half-finished government buildings surrounded by shabby wooden houses (Figure 5.1). The Court's

FIGURE 5.1 Washington, D.C.'s half-finished state in the early nineteenth century meant that the justices of the Supreme Court spent a great deal of time together when court was in session. "A view of the Capitol of Washington before it was burnt down by the British," by William Russell Birch (c. 1800), courtesy of the Library of Congress

accommodations were little better (see Chapter 4). The committee room at the Capitol where justices heard cases had "a certain cellarlike aspect," according to one observer. After the British burned Washington in 1814, the Court met for two years at private homes in the city.[7]

Ironically, the Court's meager and peripatetic existence helped build collegiality. Without a building or staff of their own, the locus of the Court's working life was the boardinghouse where the justices stayed when hearing cases. It was by no means a monkish existence. Story claimed to a friend that he scarcely went to "places of pleasure or fashion," but the evidence suggests the justices had active social lives. It was their communal living environment, however, that defined their time in Washington. They ate together most evenings, where they discussed the day's arguments "with freedom," according to Story. The arrangement was no accident. Marshall, in particular, was keen to ensure that the justices remained in close quarters. According to Story, the "unaffected intimacy" that developed among the justices – enlivened by "gay and frank conversation" and Marshall's willingness to pair sober legal analysis with a glass or two of madeira – allowed them to decide cases quickly and amicably. Within a few weeks of joining the Court in 1812, Story was pleased to report to a friend that the justices were "all united as one."[8]

The harmony that Story encountered was evident in the Court's opinions, which were nearly always unanimous. In the 1790s, the Court's general practice had been for the justices to issue individual "seriatim" opinions, though that began to change when Oliver Ellsworth became Chief Justice. When Marshall assumed the seat, he embraced Ellsworth's practice of issuing "opinions of the Court," through which the justices spoke collectively, rather than as individuals. More often than not, Marshall wrote and delivered the Court's opinion himself. Separate writings were exceptionally rare; the justices issued none in Marshall's first few years on the bench, and averaged only one per year from 1804 to 1807.[9]

There was greater disagreement among the justices than their rulings indicated. At times, the Court's opinion indicated that it spoke for a "majority" of the justices, rather than for all of them, and occasionally an earlier, hidden disagreement would emerge in a later case. But Marshall's self-described "custom" was to suppress any difference of opinion and "acquiesce silently." Bushrod Washington agreed; whenever he had the "misfortune" to differ from his colleagues, his "habit" was to say nothing.[10]

Even William Johnson fell in line. Thomas Jefferson appointed Johnson to the Court in 1804 to challenge its Federalist leanings. He did, to a certain extent. He persuaded his colleagues to rotate responsibility for delivering the Court's opinion, rather than leave the honor solely to Marshall. He also authored nearly half of the dissents and concurrences the justices issued during Marshall's tenure, a record of independence that earned him the moniker "The First Dissenter." But ultimately Johnson came around. As he later explained to Jefferson, the "lectures" his colleagues gave him about the "indecency" of critiquing his colleagues persuaded him to "ben[d] to the current."[11]

The justices' united front stemmed from more than collegial bonhomie, for speaking with a single voice enhanced the Court's authority. It was well and good for Marshall to declare in *Marbury v. Madison* that the federal courts had the power "to say what the law is," but federal judges had little ability to command adherence to their judgments. Decisions emanating from the Court as a whole, rather than a single justice, located their authority in a coequal branch of government. The Marshall Court's collective opinions, James Thayer observed over a century ago, gave it "a unity like that of the executive." And *unanimous* opinions enhanced the Court's authority even more. The men of "high & respectable character" who sat on the Court, Marshall claimed while defending the controversial decision in *McCulloch v. Maryland*, would never "sit by in silence" while legal principles they disagreed with were "advanced in their name." Factually, this was not true – the justices often dissented silently. But Marshall understood that the *appearance* of agreement enhanced the Court's legitimacy.[12]

Marshall's critics also understood how unanimity heightened the Court's standing, and they resented it. James Madison noted wistfully in critiquing *McCulloch* that seriatim opinions, rather than Marshall's single oeuvre, might have "impaired the force of [the] precedent" by revealing "discordance" among the justices. Thomas Jefferson was the greatest skeptic of the Marshall Court's practices. He had always been suspicious of collective opinions, but his personal and bitter rivalry with the Chief Justice deepened Jefferson's anxieties. In the years after he left the presidency, the man who had so forcefully defended the federal courts to foreign interlocutors in the 1790s became convinced that, under Marshall's leadership, the judiciary was the chief threat to states' rights and republican government – a "subtle corps of sappers & miners constantly working under ground to undermine the foundations of our confederated fabric."[13]

Jefferson believed that single opinions, "cook[ed] up in conclave," only enhanced the Court's destructive capabilities. They made it impossible to hold individual justices accountable for decisions that contravened the popular will. Worse yet, the Court's practice allowed a "crafty Chief judge" – abetted by "lazy or timid associates" – to "sophisticate[] the law to his mind by the turn of his own reasoning." Even in his final years, Jefferson continued to rail against a practice that, in his view, undeservedly inflated the Court's prestige, and Marshall's in particular.[14]

Marshall's dedication to ensuring amity among his brethren paralleled his commitment to promoting peace on the high seas. In his first opinion as Chief Justice, Marshall signaled that the Court would privilege neutral rights over the prerogatives of nations at war, even when doing so contravened American interests and Congress's will. In *Talbot v. Seeman*, the Court confronted a federal statute that seemed to oblige the owners of a neutral Hamburgian ship to pay American naval officers half the ship's value for having rescued it from capture by French cruisers during the Quasi-War. But the general laws of war did not require neutrals to pay that much for protection, and Marshall was not willing to interpret a congressional enactment in a way that would "infract the common principles and usages of nations." With an artful bit of statutory interpretation, Marshall concluded that the statute did not apply, and he awarded the seamen only one-sixth of the ship's value. To give them more, Marshall seemed to believe, would favor the interests of belligerent nations – including, in this case, the United States – over those who wanted to engage in peaceable commerce.[15]

Marshall's concern over the predicament neutrals faced in time of war did not break new ground, for him or the nation. He argued in favor of free trade as an envoy to France in the 1790s. And support for neutral rights was a staple of American foreign policy since the republic's beginnings (see Chapter 1). The stance was partly pragmatic. It made sense for a militarily weak nation like the United States to promote protections for its merchants that it could not provide by force of arms. This was not a uniquely American position. It was no coincidence that the European nations who formed the 1780 League of Armed Neutrality were all second-rate military powers.[16]

American advocacy of neutral rights also stemmed from a more ideological belief in the benefits of unfettered international commerce. This ethic had roots as far back as the early seventeenth century, when the Dutch jurist Hugo Grotius declared in his *Mare Liberum* ("the free sea") that the oceans should be open to all. But it was the *philosophes* of the Enlightenment who persuaded North Americans in the late eighteenth century that free trade between nations promised the greatest good for humankind. It promoted economic growth more effectively than the mercantilist approaches favored by most European sovereigns. It also fostered peace and sociability, as extensive commercial relationships produced greater cross-cultural understanding and made war between nations self-defeating. The "unbounded extension of Commerce," George Washington explained to Americans when he resigned as commander of the Continental Army in 1783, was a "meliorating influence on mankind."[17]

Even Americans who were economically and morally distrustful of international trade recognized that the young United States benefited from its protection. Republicans of the Jeffersonian persuasion, believing that commerce bred corruption and undermined virtue, were congenitally suspicious of the mercantile class both at home and abroad. But they recognized that yeoman American farmers could not thrive without foreign markets for their crops. What Jefferson most wanted was American economic independence, and free trade in time of war would help secure it. As he explained in protesting British seizures of neutral vessels in 1793, it was his view that every nation should enjoy its "natural right" to buy and sell in time of war with "all nations, belligerent or neutral."[18]

The global conflict triggered by the French Revolution tested Americans' commitment to free trade. British and French armed vessels seized hundreds – if not thousands – of American merchant ships in the Atlantic and Caribbean. The precise legal theories supporting such captures differed, but they boiled down to the principle that neutral ships engaged in commerce with an enemy could lawfully be captured. Most notoriously, in 1793 the British revived the "Rule of 1756," a regulation from the Seven Years' War that essentially barred neutrals from trading with French possessions. The rule's rationale was that, by doing so, neutral nations effectively took France's side in the war, by supplying its colonies and relieving it of the burden of protecting its own merchants from British capture. As the revolutionary struggle of the 1790s morphed into an imperial contest in the early nineteenth century, France and Great Britain imposed more stringent restrictions. In a series of escalating measures and counter-measures, the two warring empires largely prohibited any trade by neutrals with enemy territory. Under these harsh rules, many American ships were fair game for both French and British cruisers.[19]

Under John Marshall's leadership, the Supreme Court responded to these pressures by articulating legal doctrines protective of transatlantic merchants. The justices rarely had an opportunity to opine directly on the French and British restrictions, since they were applied in French and British prize courts. But the justices did what they could to mitigate the new legal regime's most pernicious effects. For example, in the 1808 case of *Rose v. Himely*, Marshall sought to limit the reach of French trade restrictions by characterizing the bloody civil war in the former French colony of Haiti as a mere domestic disturbance, not a conflict between sovereign powers. American policymakers would come to regret this precedent about sovereignty and revolution a decade later (see Chapter 6). But in the midst of the Napoleonic Wars, the ruling denied France the wartime prerogative of seizing American merchant ships trading with that island.[20]

As demonstrated by the *Talbot* decision, the Court's concern for merchants' rights even extended to ships and goods seized by American armed vessels. Somewhat improbably, two early cases involved the same Connecticut-born merchant, Jared Shattuck, who had moved to the Danish-held island of St. Thomas as a child. In 1800, United States naval vessels seized two of Shattuck's ships on suspicion of violating a 1798 statute that restricted American trade with French possessions (which Congress passed in response to French seizures of American vessels in the Quasi-War). Despite doubts about whether Shattuck was truly a Danish subject, Marshall treated him as one, and therefore exempted his property from seizure.

Marshall even ruled that the commanding officers of the capturing American vessels were personally liable to Shattuck for costs and damages. The decisions' import was clear: Whenever it could, the Court would shield both American and foreign commerce from the devastations of maritime war.[21]

* * *

As the United States' engagement in the armed struggles of the Napoleonic Era intensified, the Court's collegiality and its commitment to neutral rights both began to fray. Not on a personal level; the justices still lived and dined companionably, and the lack of turnover on the Court fostered camaraderie and a shared sense of purpose. But starting in 1808 – the year that Jefferson tried to institute a general embargo on American trade with foreign nations at war – the justices began diverging in ways they never had before. Marshall's second decade on the Court saw a pronounced spike in concurrences and dissents (especially during the war years). From 1812 to 1816, Justices Johnson and Story each wrote separately eight times, Brockholst Livingston six times, and Gabriel Duvall twice. Marshall himself dissented four times in 1814 and 1815 alone, which comprised nearly half of the nine total dissents he issued in his thirty-five years on the bench.[22]

The wedge that drove the justices apart was disagreement over the law of maritime conflict. Even before the War of 1812 began, cases involving the interpretation of embargo legislation, the deference given to the judgments of foreign admiralty courts, and the power of belligerent nations to seize neutral ships for alleged trading violations pushed the justices to express contrary views they earlier might have suppressed. Notably, all of Marshall's dissents during the war years came in cases where the Court ruled against a merchant seeking compensation for injuries resulting from armed conflict.[23]

The change in the Court's jurisprudential dynamics seemed to catch Marshall off guard. He publicly noted his dissent for the first time in an 1810 case involving neutral rights. Two years earlier, in the *Rose* case, he had written the "opinion of the court" that limited the reach of a French ordinance restricting foreign trade with Haiti. But now his colleagues ruled that France had a sovereign right to prevent foreigners from trading with the so-called rebels in the former French colony, and could exercise that right against neutral merchants on the high seas. Marshall was taken aback. He thought his earlier opinion in *Rose* had carried a majority of his colleagues, but, he noted ruefully, "in this [I] was mistaken."[24]

Marshall was still generally reluctant to air his jurisprudential disagreements publicly, but his colleagues' growing proclivity for announcing their contrary views put him in a quandary. As he explained in a three-sentence separate opinion in an 1815 embargo case, he normally would have kept his disagreement on one point quiet. But because Johnson had dissented, Marshall worried that keeping silent "might [be] construed into an assent" to rulings that he thought were mistaken. Publicizing disagreement among the justices, it seems, was now the norm rather than the exception.[25]

Two events in 1812 exacerbated the growing judicial tensions over war and maritime commerce. One, predictably, was the United States' initiation of formal hostilities against Great Britain, which triggered a flood of complicated and difficult cases into federal court. Two, and more unexpectedly, was Joseph Story's appointment as justice of the Supreme Court several months earlier (Figure 5.2).

Story was only James Madison's fourth choice for the position, but from the moment he joined the bench he made it his mission

FIGURE 5.2 Joseph Story was only thirty-three years old when James Madison appointed him to the Supreme Court, but he had an outsized influence in the Court's maritime cases. Engraving by George Parker (1834), courtesy of the University of Michgan, William L. Clements Library

to promote the legal principles he thought necessary to vindicate the United States' sovereign rights in wartime. The Court heard no War of 1812 cases in Story's first year, so it was on the circuit court that he first articulated his views. The backlog of cases left him by his predecessor would have daunted most novice judges. For Story, however, they were the proving ground for his legal theories. Many of the hold-over cases stemmed from the Jeffersonian embargo, and the circuit court's jurisdiction over the coastal communities of Massachusetts, Rhode Island, and Maine ensured a steady diet of maritime cases going forward. Once Congress declared war in June 1812, prize cases also began streaming into Story's court.[26]

Unlike many of his colleagues, Story loved riding circuit. Formally, he was only one member of a two-judge court; the circuit courts were composed of a traveling Supreme Court justice and a local district court judge. In practice, however, the New England circuit was Story's domain. He wrote all of the court's opinions, and consulted with district court judges to ensure that cases came up on appeal in a posture that would allow him to address the issues he thought important. Story also made sure that his opinions had a wide audience. One of his first acts upon appointment was to arrange for their publication by his former student, John Gallison. This was an innovative practice; few circuit court cases were reported and published, and none as comprehensively as Story's. When Congress later considered a bill to abolish circuit riding, he urged his friend Daniel Webster to kill it. "I am sure," he told Webster, "that I am a better Judge for my circuit labors."[27]

The circuit court also gave Story a platform for influencing his Supreme Court colleagues. His favorite tool was the "certificate of division," a mechanism Congress created in 1802 that allowed circuit court judges to send difficult legal questions to the Supreme Court for resolution. In theory, the mechanism was meant for cases in which the two circuit court judges disagreed on the law. In practice, the "division" between them was often a fiction that enabled the Supreme Court to bypass constraints on its appellate jurisdiction and issue comprehensive opinions on pressing legal issues. The justices regularly communicated about lower court cases that were promising candidates for certification, and they collaborated with attorneys and district court judges to ensure proper presentation of the questions involved. Story was a certification enthusiast. He invented disagreements to ensure that important questions came before the full Court, and monitored other dockets with what he termed "a jealous eye," in order to spot cases that offered opportunities to promote his views.[28]

Story had a decided advantage when maritime cases came before the Court. He had an unrivaled understanding of the bodies of law that touched the water, thanks to his circuit duties and his indefatigable appetite for study. And with the Court's wartime docket "stuffed with all sorts of complicated questions, particularly of Prize Law," Story's brethren were happy to defer to him on the difficult issues that maritime war raised. Marshall was especially reliant. He was admittedly "not versed in admiralty proceedings," and repeatedly sought Story's counsel in such cases. Legend has it that once he had drafted an opinion, the Chief Justice would turn to his junior colleague and say: "There, Story; that is the law of this case; now go and find the authorities."[29]

Still, Story knew that persuading his colleagues to accept his more controversial views on law and war posed a challenge. So he tried to overwhelm them. His circuit opinions were long and erudite, packed with extensive discussions of English and continental authorities on the rules of maritime conflict. Story recognized that, no matter how deeply he researched and how carefully he elaborated his opinions, his colleagues could easily "overrule" him by simple majority vote. But at least he could force them to confront his reasoning. As he explained to a friend in 1815, opposing the legal arguments he developed on circuit would require that his fellow justices engage in "a very laborious examination of authorities, to understand the whole stress of the points."[30]

The case of the *Nereide* exemplified the challenge Story faced in convincing his colleagues to abandon their longstanding sympathy for transatlantic merchants in wartime. The central question in the case was one of neutral rights. Manuel Pinto, a Spanish merchant, arranged to ship goods from London to Buenos Aires in an armed British convoy, to protect them from French and South American privateers. Spain was allied with Britain against France, but it was not at war with the United States. Could an American privateer nevertheless seize Pinto's goods from the British vessel? Marshall thought not, and a majority of the Court agreed.

In Marshall's view, neutral property was exempt from capture as long as the owner's conduct did not directly injure one of the belligerents. The simple act of putting goods on board a British armed ship did not transform a neutral into an enemy. Justice Johnson concurred, finding it entirely reasonable for a Spanish subject to put his property under armed protection. In a world "darkened by the horrors of war," Johnson asserted, the Court could not ignore "the desponding claims of man engaged in the peaceful pursuits of life."[31]

Story thought his colleagues' compassion for neutrals who aligned themselves with the enemy was deluded, and potentially dangerous for American peace and security. In a bristling dissent, he argued that the hazards of transatlantic commerce did not give Spanish subjects the right to claim neutrality while effectively taking sides against the United States. He admitted that, under the laws of war, neutral goods found aboard enemy ships were usually not subject to seizure. But convoying was an effective way Britain used its naval superiority to protect its merchant ships from attack. In Story's view, Pinto's willing sponsorship of this collective defense effort made him no different than a neutral who spied for a belligerent or carried its dispatches. Such conduct, Story declared, was "the most odious hostility," not "the good faith of a friend."[32]

Story lost in the *Nereide*, but his skepticism about neutral rights gained traction on the Court. In the *Commercen*, Story persuaded his colleagues to rule in favor of an American privateer who stopped a neutral Swedish ship carrying British-owned grain to the British army in Spain. As in the *Nereide*, Marshall thought the Swedish ship owner had visited no wrong on the United States. British troops in Spain were not fighting American forces, and any support a Swedish subject offered the British in a separate conflict did not justify aggression against him by the United States. Story again disagreed, and this time he carried the Court. It did not matter that the Swedish shipment to Spain did not directly support British hostilities against the United States. In his view, almost any assistance a neutral provided to the enemy was justification for a seizure.[33]

Story's hostility toward neutrals who sought to profit from the chaos of war spread to his colleagues. Justice Johnson sided with Marshall in the *Commercen*, because he agreed that the Swedish shipper had not injured the United States. But in a later case Johnson concluded that a neutral merchant who attempted to disguise British goods was worthy only of contempt. Such people, Johnson raged, lacked all "national character or feeling," for "their consciences are in the market." Their duplicity made the ship's entire cargo a lawful prize to the American captors, even goods that were not involved in the attempted concealment. Johnson admitted that this rule was "highly penal." It had the merit, however, of deterring neutrals from "attempting frauds upon belligerent rights."[34]

The wartime divide between Story and Marshall over neutral and belligerent rights was surprising in many respects. The two men were close, both personally and jurisprudentially. Story's admiration for Marshall was evident from the moment he joined the Court, and the feeling was mutual. It helped that the two men largely agreed on most questions that came before the Court. They were not ideological twins; at times, Story's aggressive nationalism went too far even for the Chief Justice (for example, on the question of common law criminal jurisdiction). But they shared a belief that the republic's future depended on the strength of its national institutions – especially the courts.[35]

Story also shared Marshall's belief in the virtues of free trade, at least in the abstract. The junior justice came from the seafaring community of coastal Massachusetts, and built his professional career by representing the interests of merchants and businessmen. Story was nominally a Republican, but he did not share Jeffersonian fears about commerce's corrupting effects, and he was a strong proponent of free trade before the war. For example, a poem he composed for his graduation from Harvard in 1798 excoriated France for its attacks on "our nation's neutral trade," and eight years later he authored a memorial to Congress lambasting the British government for similar infringements. Like many of his contemporaries, Story believed that international commerce was a powerful source for good. It not only improved material comforts, but also "foster[ed] the best interests of humanity."[36]

The deeper the United States plunged into transatlantic conflict, however, the more Story and Marshall diverged. For Story, market imperatives had to give way to martial ones. The initial catalyst was the Jeffersonian Embargo. Story generally viewed Jefferson's draconian restrictions on trade as legitimate exercises of legislative and executive authority, and he had little patience with Americans who undermined the embargo's enforcement. But he doubted whether prohibiting American commerce with the world was the best way to coerce Britain and France into respecting American rights. In his view, only an aggressive response to European provocations would guarantee the United States' prerogative to trade with other nations. The problem with Jefferson's embargo, in other words, was not that it went too far in constricting trade (as most critics argued). The problem was it did not go far enough in responding to infringements of American sovereignty.[37]

For Story, the way to resist British oppression was with force. He had long advocated for a significant increase in U.S. naval power, a position he maintained after joining the Court. This was heresy for most Republicans, but Story believed that military might, especially at sea, was essential to protecting the United States' commercial rights. He made the point directly in his 1806 memorial to Congress criticizing British restrictions on neutral trade. Like most Americans, he wished the United States could simply "reap the fruits of a just neutrality." But if the powers of Europe would not let Americans engage in commerce peaceably, then the nation had to be prepared to take up arms for the "necessary protection of our honor."[38]

Marshall was far less enthusiastic about the War of 1812. He was by no means a pacifist. War was "strangely woven" into Marshall's life, as his leading biographer put it, and the Chief Justice believed that the violence that secured American independence from Great Britain three decades earlier had been justified. He also deplored British impressment and harassment of neutral trade in the Napoleonic Wars. But he believed that France posed the greater threat. He shared Federalist misgivings about the French Revolution in the early 1790s, and his experience as an envoy to France later that decade had deepened his distrust. Moreover, he hated Napoleon, and thought the conqueror of Europe had duped Madison and the Republicans into war with Great Britain, "the only power which protects any part of the civilized world." For Marshall, the War of 1812 was "unnecessary, unwise, and unrighteous."[39]

The disagreement between Story and Marshall over how to respond to the British threat to American sovereignty also reflected a generational divide. The Chief Justice had experienced war first-hand.

At the age of nineteen, he enlisted as a lieutenant and served for six years in the American Revolution. He defended Philadelphia in the Battles of Brandywine and Germantown, and he wintered with George Washington at Valley Forge. Marshall knew the satisfaction and even glory that came from fighting in support of a cause one believed was just. When he first reported for duty in Virginia in 1775, he reportedly told the men under his command that they were assembling to "defend their country and their own rights and liberties." When he later wrote about the war in his biography of Washington, he did not share much about his personal experience. But he did extoll his fellow-soldiers for their "virtuous suffering, in danger and in glory." For Marshall, seeing "brave men … risk[] life and everything valuable in a common cause" was a transformative moment that inspired him to consider "America" – not Virginia, or the British Empire – "as my country."[40]

But Marshall had also seen what a fellow-soldier called "the horrors of war in perfection." He personally experienced the misery that armed conflict caused for combatants and civilians, including the appalling scenes of deprivation at Valley Forge and the bloody carnage at the Battle of Great Bridge in Virginia. He knew that war, no matter how noble its inspiration, was filled with "ill-judged measures, of which the consequences are felt long after the motives are forgotten." He also witnessed the cowardice, selfishness, and disloyalty that the conflict engendered among his fellow-citizens, including that of the "sordid traitor" Benedict Arnold. For Marshall, war could be a terrible curse.[41]

Story, on the other hand, had experienced neither the Revolutionary War's triumph nor its tragedy. Born in 1779, he did not even have direct memories of the conflict. Its legacy came only second-hand. As historians have noted, the disappointment of arriving too late to participate in the Revolution haunted the men of Story's cohort. Among them, nineteenth-century concerns over the fate of the American republican experiment mingled with doubts about whether their generation was capable of preserving it.[42]

A renewed conflict with Great Britain presented Story's generation the opportunity – indeed, the obligation – to replicate their forefathers' heroic exploits. "The charter of independence," thundered an 1807 pamphlet denouncing British aggressions, "still cries out for blood of American citizens to seal it." Richard Rush, son of Benjamin

Rush, signer of the Declaration of Independence, embraced the challenge when he urged the nation to war in July 1812. If the United States did not take up arms, Rush asked, "where would be the spirit, where the courage of their slain fathers?" An 1810 newspaper editorial made the same point: "Our sires ... gave their blood for independence.... Are their sons unworthy?"[43]

Men like Story may have been largely ignorant of the realities of armed conflict, but they were eager to embrace its regenerative potential. The careful, measured neutrality of heroes such as Washington, Franklin, and Marshall offered Story and his peers no path to glory, no means of matching their fathers' martial achievements. Story made this clear in an address he gave to the Massachusetts legislature upon accepting his appointment to the Supreme Court in 1812. He noted mournfully that many of the "Revolutionary worthies" he admired were no longer present to offer guidance and support in this time of national peril. But the "memory of their deeds" would inspire their progeny "gloriously to contend for their injured country." Story closed his speech with a remarkable passage evoking war's political and spiritual possibilities:

> I persuade myself that the flame kindled in the Revolution will burn with inextinguishable splendor; that, when the voice of the nation shall call to arms, this hall will witness a heroic firmness, an eloquent patriotism, and a devotion to the public weal, which have not been exceeded in the annals of our country.[44]

* * *

For Story, the United States' rebirth through war demanded legal doctrines that would empower the nation to challenge the world's most powerful empire at sea. Perhaps surprisingly, he found what he was looking for in the opinions of a British admiralty judge.

In the *Nereide*, Marshall grounded his defense of neutral rights on first principles. He briefly cited leading authorities on the law of nations – Bynkershoek and Vattel – for the general proposition that neutral goods shipped aboard an enemy ship were not subject to capture. But those writers did not distinguish between armed and unarmed vessels, so Marshall had to decide for himself – based on logic and common sense – whether traveling in a British convoy stripped the Spanish cargo of its neutral character. As he explained in other wartime opinions, the law of nations was "founded on the great and immutable principles of equity and natural justice." If leading authorities did not directly answer the question in a case (and they almost never did), then judges had no choice but to turn to "reason and justice" to resolve it.[45]

Marshall's opinion in the *Nereide* was reflective of his jurisprudence more generally. He was widely acknowledged to be a brilliant lawyer (even by his enemies), whose opinions were unmatched for clarity and persuasiveness. He was not a legal scholar, however. He spent a few months attending law lectures by George Wythe at William and Mary in his youth, but the "original bias" of Marshall's mind was to "general principles," not to "technical or recondite learning," as Story later explained in eulogizing his colleague. Or as constitutional historian Edward Corwin later put it, Marshall "made more use of his brains than of his bookshelves."[46]

Story deeply respected Marshall's analytical abilities, but he thought the Chief Justice's untutored approach entirely unsatisfactory in deciding cases implicating the rights of nations at war. Story esteemed the erudition of the "learned civilians," and was probably as knowledgeable about the leading treatises on the law of nations as any lawyer in the United States. That familiarity, however, bred a certain degree of contempt. For Story, the general principles the publicists announced were too often of little use in deciding particular cases. He conceded in the *Nereide* that, broadly speaking, neutral goods shipped aboard the vessels of a belligerent nation were not subject to capture. But that simply proved that jurists such as Grotius or Vattel had failed to consider the question in its real-world applications – for example, whether the carrying vessel was armed or unarmed, or was captured with or without resistance. "Elementary writers," Story noted acidly, "rarely explain the principles of public law with the minute distinctions which legal precision requires."[47]

Story believed that the United States needed a law of war that was more scientific, and more suited to the interests of a nation seeking to establish its status as a global power. "Legal science" was a term that many of its proponents (Story included) did not define precisely, but it generally meant law that was organized and systematized. American law in the early nineteenth century was hardly that. Part of the problem was the multiplicity of sources. The United States' imperial heritage meant that the laws of England, the British North American colonies, the post-independence states, and even the new federal government all laid claim to authority – not to mention the possible applicability of French, Spanish, and Native American legal principles in certain matters.[48]

Legal pluralism was not new to the United States, nor unique to it. The deeper problem for Story and his contemporaries was that much of this varied law was not written down, and certainly not in one place. When James Kent, the chancellor of New York's highest court, came onto the bench, he found few comprehensive treatments of American law available, even on particular subjects. Nor was there any systematic reporting of judicial decisions. "We had no law of our own," Kent later lamented, "and nobody knew what it was."[49]

A generation of scientific jurists was just beginning their efforts to impose rationality on American law when the War of 1812 began. In 1803, St. George Tucker, a professor at William and Mary and future federal judge, published an annotated edition of Blackstone's *Commentaries on the Laws of England.* Many American lawyers (including Story) admired Blackstone's lucid exposition of English law. Story himself started dabbling in legal systematization shortly before joining the Court. He began work on a comprehensive "digest" of American law, and the Massachusetts legislature appointed him to a commission charged with consolidating the state's statutes.[50]

Treatise-writing came into full flower in the decades after the war. Kent published the first volume of his celebrated *Commentaries on American Law* in 1826, and Story soon after published the first of nine texts on various legal subjects, including the law of agency, equity jurisprudence, and conflicts of laws. His most well-known work, *Commentaries on the Constitution of the United States*, came out in three volumes in 1833. By the turn of the twentieth century, his treatises had collectively gone through seventy-five editions.[51]

The scientific jurists wanted to do more than simply bring order to chaos. They wanted to adapt the law to the circumstances of American life in the nineteenth century. Tucker's version of Blackstone is a good example. At the time he published it, Blackstone's *Commentaries* was probably the most widely used (or at least widely owned) legal text in the United States, but it was far from perfect. For some, Blackstone was too closely associated with the British monarchy, and a clean break with the imperial past necessitated a rejection of English law. For Tucker, the more fundamental problem was that Blackstone's synthesis was not well adapted to Virginian economy and society, including its dependence on slavery. Tucker therefore not only included commentary pointing out where Virginia law differed from English principles, but also noted how he thought unsettled questions of Virginia law *should* be resolved.[52]

Tucker was a proponent of state power, but for Story and most of his contemporaries "rationalizing" the law meant "nationalizing" it, as one historian describes it. Coherent and uniform legal principles would transcend regional differences and bind the nation's fractious peoples together. The most important task was articulating and disseminating rules promoting economic development. A more rational and consistent body of law – one that protected private property interests above all – would promote predictability in commercial relationships, essential qualities for a growing and increasingly interdependent nation. The scientists disclaimed any intent to reshape the law to serve particular ends. The treatise-writer's "first duty," explained Kent, was "to state the law *as it is*." But Kent admitted that it was also appropriate to "point out its defects," and to "suggest alterations and improvements." Story agreed; the learned lawyer's duty was not only "ministration" of the "noble science of the law," but also its "correction."[53]

In Story's view, the law of war was one field of jurisprudence that cried out for "correction." Throughout the War of 1812, Story repeated the critique he leveled in dissent in the *Nereide*: The abstract doctrines outlined by the "great writers on national law" – the European law of nations publicists – were "imperfect on many maritime questions." What the United States needed was a set of rules governing conflict at sea that remained broadly consistent with longstanding principles of neutral and belligerent rights, yet that was adapted to the realities of war in the nineteenth century.[54]

There was one jurist who elucidated and applied the laws of war with the clarity and rigor Story yearned for – Sir William Scott, the judge of the British High Court of Admiralty during the Napoleonic Wars. Scott's position presiding over the most important admiralty court of the world's foremost maritime power offered him an unparalleled opportunity to shape the international law of maritime conflict. Of course, by Scott's time, the British admiralty courts already had more than two centuries of decisions they could look to for guidance. Scott's skill was less in creation than it was in organization. He distilled layers of accumulated precedent into clear principles, and then applied those principles with careful attention to both the factual context of particular cases and the broader realities of wartime mercantile economy. More important, Scott wrote formal opinions and published them in regular reports. Before his ascension to the bench, reporting of decisions in admiralty cases was virtually nonexistent. The small community of lawyers who practiced before the High Court of Admiralty relied on private notes and personal recollections to establish applicable precedent. Scott's opinions, in contrast, were fully reasoned and authoritative.[55]

Scott's opinions were a godsend for American judges desperate to put the law of maritime war on firmer footing. By the start of the War of 1812, Scott had written more than a decade's worth of decisions applying the laws of war amid the period's turbulent politics. Story's fellow-travelers, like James Kent, extolled the "wisdom and learning" in Scott's opinions, particularly when compared with the "loose dicta of elementary writers." Kent did not simply praise Scott; he also relied on him, citing Scott's opinions 140 times in the section of his *Commentaries* addressing the law of nations.[56]

Story, too, treated Scott's opinions almost as gospel. Shortly after joining the Supreme Court, Story acknowledged that he was already in debt "to that eloquent and able judge." In Story's view, American courts had inherited English prize law even more fully than they had inherited English common law. And while scientific jurisprudence required that the common law be "moulded and fashioned" to respond to the different conditions of life in the United States, the same was not true for the legal principles governing the seas. "[T]he rules of admiralty law," Story asserted, were already "disclosed in English reports."[57]

Story's colleagues on the Supreme Court were not as eager to adopt Scott's jurisprudence. Marshall described the English judge as a "great man." He conceded that English prize law *had* been American prize law, and it largely still was after independence. But Marshall believed that prize had to be "adapted" to American circumstances, just like every other body of law, and Scott's rulings carried no more weight than the decisions of other foreign tribunals. He would treat Scott's doctrines with "respect," but "not as authority." Justice Johnson held the same view: He considered Scott's decisions "for as much as they are worth in principle," and based his rulings on his "own researches."[58]

Marshall and Johnson asserted their jurisprudential independence because they worried that Scott's rulings were insufficiently protective of neutral rights. As Marshall put it, Scott "lean[ed] strongly in favor of the captors," a charge that others in the United States echoed. This was not entirely true. In the Napoleonic conflict's early years, Scott tried to mitigate some of British policy's harshest effects on neutrals. But he was a government man at heart. He served as King's Advocate for ten years before becoming judge, and he consulted with the Privy Council before issuing decisions in certain cases. As the war progressed, he largely acquiesced in his government's hostile treatment of neutral rights. In particular, Scott defended – in both judicial decisions and speeches to Parliament – the hated Orders in Council, which treated nearly all trade with French-held territory as subject to seizure. According to Scott's otherwise-laudatory American biographer, in this instance Scott conducted himself "as more a functionary of the British government than a fair, unbiased judge." Even Scott's contemporary admirers in the United States, like Story's protégé Henry Wheaton, acknowledged that Americans had cause to complain about Scott's "injurious doctrines."[59]

Story did not share his colleagues' qualms about Scott's principles. In case after case, Story cited Scott's decisions as legal authority for upholding seizures of neutral property made by American armed ships. He identified Scott by name, and quoted him at length, relying on Scott's reputation in "Europe and America" while also enhancing it. Unlike Marshall or Wheaton, Story never directly acknowledged the pro-belligerent bent of Scott's jurisprudence, but it was clear that, in Scott's "lofty principles," Story found the jurisprudence of war he thought that the United States needed.[60]

There was a deep irony in Story's veneration of his British colleague. Americans had been one of the chief victims of British hostility to neutral rights – a hostility that Scott abetted from his seat on the admiralty bench. Yet now, Story's adoption of Scott's doctrines was pushing the Supreme Court to espouse the very sorts of belligerent rights that drove the United States into war in the first place.

It is safe to assume, however, that Story saw no irony at all. The United States was no longer neutral. It was in a struggle for its very survival, and it needed legal tools that would allow it to counter what Story termed the "wanton barbarity" of British aggression on land and at sea. The great law of nations publicists were learned and wise, but they wrote their treatises before the Napoleonic age of total conflict, which, as Edmund Burke famously put it, had unleashed the "hell-hounds of war, on all sides." Faced with a form of global warfare that equated neutrality with enmity, Story seemed to believe that federal judges had no choice but to respond in kind.[61]

* * *

The aggressiveness of Story's wartime jurisprudence was most evident in decisions regarding those he saw as the nation's most dangerous enemy – Americans themselves. The War of 1812 is often framed as a two-sided contest between imperial Britain and republican United States. But the reality was far more complex. The "civil war of 1812," as one historian has termed it, challenged formal conceptions of national allegiance by triggering multiple conflicts within and among various groups of North Americans. Legacies of republicanism and loyalism dating to the American Revolution produced varied constituencies on both sides of the porous Canadian border. The war exposed and exacerbated divisions among Native peoples who held divergent views of how to respond to the threat of white encroachment. And when the conflict came to the South, enslaved persons had to decide whether to remain with their masters or pursue the possibility of freedom behind British lines.[62]

For Story – and for many others – the greatest danger the war posed to American union was the treasonous behavior of his fellow New Englanders. The Madison administration's bumbling prosecution of the war gave Federalists hopes of a revival in their political fortunes, and antiwar activism became their badge of honor. They lambasted the conflict as the culmination of a decade's worth of pro-French and anti-commercial Republican policies that compromised the nation's security and ruined its economy. Story's home state of Massachusetts become a hotbed of domestic resistance. Caleb Strong, the Federalist governor, declared a day of fasting to protest Congress's declaration of war in 1812, and he refused to put the state militia under national control (as did a few other states). The state legislature – which Story had urged to display "heroic firmness" in his parting address – called on the people to express their disapproval of the war. Some Federalists in New England spoke openly of seceding from the union.[63]

Republicans responded to Federalist resistance with outrage and violence. A mob in Baltimore attacked the offices of a Federalist newspaper that was critical of the Madison administration's policies, resulting in severe injuries and at least one death. Federalists pointed to such incidents as evidence of their opponents' lawlessness and "Jacobin" inclinations, but Republicans did not back down. With a casualness that belied the violence of his words, Jefferson assured Madison that Federalist obstructionism could be overcome with force. In the southern states, where support for the administration was strong, "a barrel of tar" would "keep all in order." In the north, however, the "rougher drastics" of hangings and confiscation of property might be required. Even Elbridge Gerry, a Massachusetts signer of the Declaration of Independence with a longstanding reputation for nonpartisanship, succumbed to the vituperation. "If we do not kill them," he wrote of the Federalists, "they will kill us."[64]

Story, too, was mortified by New England's subversion of the war effort. He was a Massachusetts native with no attachment to the southern and western states from which the Jeffersonians drew most of their strength. But Story was first and foremost a nationalist. He worried that his neighbors' obstructionism would doom the war effort and perhaps the republic itself. British efforts to drive a wedge between the states only heightened his concern. Coastal communities starved by the conflict made peace with British forces, and the Massachusetts governor sent an emissary to Nova Scotia to secure British military assistance in the event of a break with Washington. When Massachusetts invited the other New England states to a convention in December 1814 to discuss their common grievances, many Republicans believed that, in Story's words, "severance of the Union" would follow.[65]

Story's antidote for the poison weakening the American body politic was greater power for the federal government. Upon his appointment to the bench, he dispatched the backlog of circuit court cases left over from the Jeffersonian Embargo with rulings that affirmed executive branch authority to enforce the law against those who subverted national regulations. Like many of his predecessors, Story also seized upon grand jury charges as a forum for delivering sermons on the duties of citizenship in a constitutional republic. Judges such as James Wilson and John Jay had extolled the virtues of neutrality in the 1790s, but in wartime Story's focus was treason. He defined it broadly; any "combination" that used force to "resist or oppose the execution of any general act or statute of the U.S." was guilty of the crime. No Federalist politician was ever charged with treason in Story's court (or in any other). But rhetorically Story's point was clear: In a time of war, respect for the law was paramount.[66]

The centerpiece of Story's effort to confront the crisis of national authority was expanding the scope of federal criminal law. In his view, the government did not have the legal tools it needed to punish those who undermined it. Story blamed Congress for a federal criminal code he found "grossly and barbarously defective." Federal statutes did not reach numerous acts subversive of public order, leaving enforcement in the unreliable hands of state officials. Story urged his allies in Congress to sponsor legislation giving the federal courts a general power to punish crimes committed against the national government, but those efforts failed, leaving Story bitter. Congressmen, Story complained to a friend, were too concerned with their reelection prospects to give proper attention to "the great concerns of the public."[67]

Despairing of a legislative solution, Story turned to the common law, but with no greater success. He believed the federal courts had inherent authority to punish offenses against the government without express statutory authorization. That was already a controversial position in 1793, when the Washington administration argued it in support of its failed prosecutions of French privateers (see Chapter 2). It was even less tenable in 1812. Most Republicans denounced the idea that appointed judges, rather than democratically elected legislators, could decide what conduct was criminally punishable under federal authority. The Supreme Court agreed, despite Story's best efforts. The same term Story joined the Court, a majority of justices invalidated a nonstatutory federal prosecution for libel. A year later on circuit, Story ruled that federal courts had authority to punish criminal conduct related to a maritime capture in the absence of any positive legislation. But the full Court summarily reversed him, and Story never persuaded his colleagues to reconsider.[68]

Like cabinet officers in the Washington administration, Story found the federal courts' admiralty jurisdiction to be a better tool than criminal law for bringing government power to bear against those who threatened the nation's peace and security. In the 1790s, the targets were French-commissioned privateers who undermined American neutrality by using the United States as a base for attacks on British commerce (see Chapter 3). In the War of 1812, Story's focus was on Americans who supported Britain through trade.

Trading with the enemy was a deeply vexing issue during the war. In some quarters, intercourse between the Americans and British continued as if there was no conflict at all. In the war's first two years, for example, Americans provided more than half of the beef that fed the British army in Canada. According to one army officer, so many cattle crossed the battle lines that they resembled "herds of buffaloes … press[ing] through the forests." Americans also supplied British ships that blockaded the eastern seaboard and launched the invasion of Washington. While Federalist newspapers noted this "brisk business" with quiet satisfaction, Republican outlets excoriated the "unprincipled men" willing to forsake their nation in pursuit of profit. By 1814, enemy trade was enough of a "public scandal" that Congress asked Secretary of the Treasury Alexander Dallas to report on "the best mode of correcting the evil."[69]

Enemy trading angered Republicans, but did not surprise them. Great Britain had been the United States' most important commercial partner for decades, and Americans had longstanding social, familial, and economic ties with British subjects on both sides of the Atlantic. Cutting off all intercourse threatened privation and financial ruin, while finding ways to keep trading amid war's scarcity promised hefty profits. In addition, Americans of the early nineteenth century were deeply experienced in the subterfuges that allowed commerce to continue in wartime. Their ancestors had trafficked with the enemy in the colonial period and during the American Revolution, and, by 1812, they had more than two decades of experience evading the federal government's efforts to regulate maritime commerce.[70]

The difficulties that had long dogged government efforts to quash enemy trading were still an obstacle in 1812. Congress banned the practice by statute at the war's outset, but enforcement was a challenge. Criminal prosecutions were virtually useless. As Treasury Secretary Dallas reported to Congress in 1814, federal officers had a limited statutory authority to search for smuggled goods, and lived in perpetual "terror" of being sued over improper seizures, making it difficult to secure hard evidence of wrongdoing. In addition, the 1812 act defined trading with the enemy incompletely, a problem the Supreme Court comically confirmed when it ruled that oxen herded into Canada had not been "transported" across the border within the statute's meaning. Even when the government managed to bring charges, it often had to abandon the prosecution because it could not secure witnesses. And juries composed of the defendants' friends and neighbors regularly acquitted.[71]

Story understood the difficulty of quashing enemy trading better than anyone, as he witnessed its subterfuges from his perch on the circuit court. A favorite ploy was the collusive capture. Merchants who wanted to import British goods would arrange for their "capture" by an American privateer, and then share in the proceeds once the supposed "prize" was condemned in court. Sometimes the complicity was too obvious, as when a tiny privateer boat arrived in Portland, Maine riding on the deck of the 140-ton vessel it had allegedly "seized." But conspiracy was hard to prove. When a small American privateer with only one gun purportedly captured two valuable British ships (which made no apparent effort to escape), Story found the captor's tale "utterly incredible," and refused to award them the prizes. But the full Supreme Court reversed. Though Justice Johnson acknowledged that such episodes were "loaded with infamy," the paucity of direct evidence required accepting the captor's version of the events.[72]

Over time, however, Story's colleagues came to share his intolerance for Americans who sought profit at the nation's expense. It was a "melancholy truth," Justice Johnson reflected after the war, that many "unprincipled individuals" traded with the enemy. The Supreme Court unanimously agreed with Story that a capture made by a privateer with a history of collusive conduct was inherently suspicious. Story paid lip service to the idea that prior bad acts did not automatically render a privateer guilty. But judges could not simply ignore what they already knew. The sordid – and very visible – tradition of enemy trading created "a presumption of ill faith" among the captors, one they could overcome only with clear evidence that their conduct was not actually a betrayal of their nation.[73]

Story's eagerness to crack down on Americans who compromised the war effort took hold at the Court even when it went against the political tide. The thorniest cases involved Americans who had British permission to trade with the enemy. The two nations may have been at war, but political leaders on both sides of the Atlantic wanted some commerce between the nations to continue. The British government needed supplies of American grain to feed its armies on the European continent, so it issued licenses that shielded American property from capture by British armed vessels (over 600 before the war's end). Not everyone in Britain agreed with this approach. Story's idol, Sir William Scott, reportedly worried that the licensed enemy trade encouraged "simulation and dissimulation from beginning to end." But Scott affirmed the practice in his rulings on the bench; if the government gave its approval, the courts had no reason to oppose.[74]

Many Americans also embraced the licensed trade. Thomas Jefferson, still smarting from the defeat of his embargo, warned Madison in 1812 that closed markets and economic deprivation would undermine public support for the war. And if Great Britain was going to find supplies for its army regardless, the United States might as well be the beneficiary. Madison was not entirely convinced, but his administration tacitly permitted the licensed trade to go forward.[75] Attorney General William Pinkney took the view that the trade was legally permissible. Chief Justice Marshall agreed, at least under certain circumstances. In an early circuit court opinion, Marshall ruled that only American ships intending to support the British war effort against the United States were subject to capture. Marshall displayed his typical penchant for giving merchants the benefit of the doubt, speculating that an American might accept a British license merely to avoid capture by the British, not to aid them.[76]

Whatever the economic and political wisdom of allowing licensed trade, Story refused to sanction it in law. He admitted that he could find no precedent directly on point; it was one of the "novel questions" that arose out of "the extraordinary state of the world." He also appreciated the nation's deep ties to Great Britain, and conceded that licensing had been approved in "political discussions." But in Story's view neither novelty nor expediency made the practice lawful. Everyone from Vattel to William Scott agreed that trading with the enemy was illegal. The fact that the British government permitted it only proved that the trade benefited Britain. Story was unwilling to adopt Marshall's indulgent approach, and ruled on circuit that possession of a license created a "strong presumption" that the bearer intended to aid the enemy.[77]

At a deeper level, Story was offended by the very notion that the citizens of a belligerent nation could "claim to be at peace" when it suited their private interests. "Can an American citizen be permitted in this manner to carve out for himself a neutrality on the ocean," he asked rhetorically, "when his country is at war?" The answer was obvious. War, he argued, put the citizens and subjects of the belligerent nations "in a state of hostility with each other." That meant that friends and business partners were now "in all respects considered as enemies."[78]

Story's uncompromising position prevailed in the end. After a year of dithering, Congress in 1813 responded to British favoring of disgruntled merchants in the Northeast with a total ban on trading under a British license, and authorized U.S. armed vessels to seize any ship sailing with one. The following year, the Supreme Court affirmed Story's view that the same prohibition applied under the laws of war (for cases arising before Congress's ban). When Daniel Webster subsequently tried to convince the justices that his client's British-licensed shipment of flour to Spain was "as innocent as a voyage from Baltimore to Boston," Justice Washington responded for the Court in words that could have come from Story's pen. Any American who sought to "clothe himself with a neutral character," Washington wrote, had "separate[d] himself from the common character of his own country," and was to be treated as an enemy.[79]

* * *

A few years after the War of 1812 ended, Chief Justice Marshall issued a short prize opinion that contained a surprisingly gloomy passage. The case turned on a question the Supreme Court had already confronted: Were neutral-owned goods shipped in an armed British vessel lawful prize to an American privateer? The Court said no, on the strength of its earlier decision in the *Nereide*: "[T]he goods of a friend are safe in the bottom of an enemy," Marshall explained. One might think that this confirmation of a neutral's right to trade in wartime would have pleased the Chief Justice. Justice Johnson penned a long concurrence in which he dismissed the authority of a contrary decision by Sir William Scott. And Justice Story stayed silent, no doubt recognizing the futility of restarting an argument he had already lost once.[80]

Marshall, however, was in no mood to celebrate. He predicted that the rule upholding neutral rights "probably will be changed," or at least it would be "so impaired" that it would cease to have any effect. Marshall did not give reasons for his dour prediction, but the explanation seems obvious: He may have won the particular battle fought at the Court over neutral and belligerent rights in the *Nereide*, but Story had largely won the war.[81]

In hindsight, Marshall's pessimism was unwarranted, as the legal pendulum swung back in favor of free trade and neutral rights after the War of 1812 ended. Over the next several decades, international legal opinion came to take an increasingly dim view of the practice of seizing merchant ships in wartime. In the 1820s and 1830s, American officials promoted strong protections for neutral rights to their counterparts abroad – in particular, the principle that "free ships make free goods." As John Quincy Adams explained to a British minister in 1823, allowing belligerents to ransack neutral ships in search of enemy property violated the neutral's "natural right to pursue, unmolested, his peaceful commercial intercourse." In 1856, the signatories to the Declaration of Paris agreed to exempt from capture both enemy goods found on neutral ships and neutral goods found in enemy vessels.[82]

Marshall's postwar anxiety about the future of neutral rights was misguided for a more basic reason: The federal courts would not have to face such questions again until the Civil War. The end of the War of 1812 did not mean that cases arising from conflict at sea stopped appearing in American courtrooms. But because the United States itself would not formally be at war for several more decades, the federal courts would not have to balance the rights of neutrals and belligerents as they had during the conflict with Great Britain.[83]

There also were broader trends at work. The international movement to protect neutral rights was accompanied by growing doubts over the wisdom and morality of commerce raiding generally, fueled by regrets over the maritime destruction of the Napoleonic period. Prize-taking would not fully disappear until the twentieth century, but the 1856 Declaration of Paris announced that *private* commerce raiding – privateering – was no longer a legitimate form of warfare. As a result, prize law's importance as a branch of international law gradually faded over the course of the nineteenth century.[84]

Marshall can be forgiven for his lack of foresight. From the immediate postwar perspective, prize law's slow death was anything but assured. Napoleon's final defeat meant that peace reigned among the European powers. But as Henry Wheaton explained to readers of his 1815 prize treatise, it was only a matter of time before the "flames of war" rekindled, and the United States could not hope for "an exemption from its calamities." President James Monroe expressed the same view in urging Congress to expand the nation's military preparations two years later. The likelihood of future wars was high, Monroe told his audience, and "we ought not to expect to be exempted."[85]

Joseph Story's postwar mood was significantly brighter than Marshall's. In fact, in early 1815 he was positively exultant. American forces under Andrew Jackson had just routed the British in the Battle of New Orleans, and the following month the Senate ratified a treaty formally ending the war. According to Story, these developments demonstrated that the United States had "stood the contest, single-handed, against the conqueror of Europe."[86]

In truth, the war's outcome was hard to describe as a triumph. The British burning of Washington in August 1814 confirmed the United States' military vulnerability, and the British conceded no ground in the Treaty of Ghent on the issues that had prompted the United States to declare war in the first place: restrictions on free trade, impressment of American sailors, and British support for Native Americans resisting the expansion of white settlement.[87]

For enthusiasts like Story, however, the details did not matter. Britain had already repealed the hated Orders in Council, and the end of the Napoleonic Wars meant it no longer needed to impress seamen for its navy. More consequentially, the war had already proven to be a disaster for Native peoples. Andrew Jackson's campaign of terror against them in the south resulted in the cession of huge swaths of Creek and Cherokee territory, and Britain's abandonment of its Native allies in the west gave the United States a freer hand to expropriate territory in the North American interior.[88]

Like many Americans, Story thought the war's most meaningful outcome was symbolic. Across the nation, politicians, newspaper editors, and ordinary citizens celebrated the Battle of New Orleans and ratification of the treaty as double confirmation of the United States' sovereignty and independence. As one Republican member of Congress exclaimed, the war demonstrated that "[t]he men of Europe ... are not a match for the men of America." Story echoed this excitement in a February 1815 letter to his friend Nathaniel Williams. The advent of peace, Story believed, heralded a new age in American foreign relations. Having withstood the force of British arms, Story gushed, the United States was now poised to "attain to a very high character abroad."[89]

For Story, the key to cementing the nation's triumph overseas was strengthening the federal government's authority at home. He articulated an ambitious agenda in his letter to Williams, including a permanent military establishment, a national bank, and increased federal control over navigation and commerce. "If we are ever to be a great nation," he wrote to his friend William Pinkney in 1816, "it must be by giving vital operation to every power confided in the Government." In particular, this meant that the federal courts – the republic's "strong and stringent link" – should be granted "the whole constitutional powers" provided them in the Constitution. The framing generation, Story wrote, understood the importance of expansive federal jurisdiction, and would not have "suffer[ed] it to slumber."[90]

Much to Story's dismay, his dreams of plenary federal authority were never realized in his lifetime. Congress increased military funding in the postwar years, but it would be decades before the nation had anything resembling the robust establishment Story desired. The Supreme Court famously affirmed the Bank of the United States' constitutionality in *McCulloch v. Maryland*, but it did not survive Andrew Jackson's presidency. The results were mixed even regarding commerce. In *Gibbons v. Ogden*, the Court laid the foundation for broad federal authority to regulate interstate commercial activity, but Congress rarely exercised it before the Civil War.[91] Congress also failed to heed Story's call to invest the judiciary with greater power. He drafted a bill extending the courts' jurisdiction over all cases arising under federal law, including crimes "committed against the United States." But with the war over, the specter of disloyalty faded, and the dream of complete judicial authority was deferred.[92]

One area where Story was pleased with his handiwork was at sea. The courts' admiralty and maritime jurisdiction, he noted to Pinkney, "has been completely delegated." And Story was deeply gratified when Sir William Scott wrote to praise the "acuteness and learning" in Story's published circuit court opinions. In particular, Scott was happy to see that the "same principles" that he expounded on the admiralty court in Britain were being "adhered to in America."[93]

Apparently not every English judge was glad to see the resemblance between Scott's doctrines and Story's. After the war ended, Sir William Grant, Master of the Rolls and a member of the Privy Council, reportedly crossed paths with Scott at an evening club. Brandishing a volume of Story's circuit court decisions, Grant commented that "Mr. Story appears to be a promising pupil." He warned Scott, however, not to expect his doctrines "to be confined to one belligerent power," for they would inevitably "make the tour of all."[94]

For Story, the Supreme Court's adoption of international legal principles advanced by British jurists was something to be celebrated rather than feared. At the war's outset, the nation – and Story's colleagues on the Supreme Court – still held the belief that the best way to affirm the United States' independence was by protecting its maritime population, and that of other nations, from war's destruction. The nation's wartime rallying cry, after all, was "free trade and sailor's rights." But the United States was no longer the weak and vulnerable republic that Marshall had come of age defending. Story believed that the key to resisting British aggression, and to establishing the nation's sovereign legitimacy, was by adopting policies and doctrines that furthered belligerent rights. Despite Marshall's resistance, Story persuaded the Court to agree.

The pro-belligerent doctrines Story advanced did not, as Grant predicted, make a "tour of all." In the post-Napoleonic settlement the international community embraced stronger protections for neutrals. But even if Story's rulings had little lasting impact doctrinally,

Grant was right to sense in them a growing American confidence. Much like the Supreme Court's 1790s willingness to take jurisdiction over captures made by foreign privateers, Story's declaration in the War of 1812 of a broad American right to seize maritime property of both enemies and neutrals was a claim of authority over the seas. In making such claims, Story emulated the expansive wartime prerogatives asserted by France and Great Britain, heralding ever more forcefully the young republic's claim to sovereign equality with the great powers. The courts would soon be called upon to make good on that claim.

PART III

COURTS FOR A NEW EMPIRE, 1816–1825

6

Confronting Revolution

It was the first day of winter in 1817, and John Quincy Adams was in a querulous mood. This was normal for the famously irascible scion of America's most prominent political family. But the spleen Adams vented in a letter to his father seemed out of place. The nation's future, after all, seemed so bright. The United States had recently fought the world's most powerful empire to a standstill, elevating the young republic's prestige "in the eyes of all Europe," according to Adams. The postwar economy was recovering, tensions over slavery's expansion had yet to explode, and President James Monroe's goodwill tour of the northern states had inaugurated a brief but welcome "Era of Good Feelings" in the wake of the war's divisiveness. Only a few weeks earlier, in fact, Monroe had extolled to Congress the nation's uniquely "prosperous and happy condition." Adams's own prospects were equally encouraging. He was a political star, a former Senator and experienced diplomat, now Secretary of State. Many – including Adams himself – anticipated that he would succeed Monroe as president.[1]

Despite all the good omens, Adams knew that trouble was brewing at sea. He complained to his father that "ardent spirits" among their countrymen were "rushing into the conflict, without looking to the consequences," just like in the bad old days of the French Revolution. The new struggle Adams had in mind was the war for liberation then raging across Spain and Portugal's empires in the Americas. In early 1816, agents from South American revolutionary governments had arrived in Baltimore with privateering commissions authorizing raids on Spanish maritime commerce. The city's merchants and sailors were happy to resume the violent trade they plied in the War of 1812, but Iberian officials were furious. They viewed any American support for the rebels as an affront, and permitting armed vessels to raid Spanish and Portuguese shipping was tantamount to an act of war. When Adams penned his letter, frigid temperatures had just caused the Potomac River to freeze over. But the Secretary of State predicted to his father that the revolutionary Atlantic's politics would "*soon be at boiling heat.*"[2]

Adams had reason to be alarmed, for the renaissance of privateering in the United States threatened to derail the American imperial project just as it was getting started. Conditions were ripe for the emergence of what Attorney General William Wirt would soon describe to the Supreme Court as a "widely-extended empire" in North America. The Louisiana Purchase had already doubled the United States' continental footprint. The collapse of Spanish royal authority in the Americas, combined with Great Britain's recession from western territory following the War of 1812, meant that Native nations were left alone to resist westward encroachment. Adams himself was in the midst of long-running negotiations with Spain over a treaty that would resolve boundary disputes stemming from the Purchase and secure new territory in Florida and the Pacific Northwest.[3]

The postwar period was not the beginning of an inexorable march toward continental and even hemispherical hegemony that subsequent generations of Americans have imagined. From the perspective of 1817, the international situation was deeply uncertain. According to Adams, the European monarchs restored to power following Napoleon's defeat viewed the United States as a threat – "a very dangerous member of the society of nations." Great Britain, in particular, was liable to seize on any excuse to reassert its authority in North America, and its alliance with the beleaguered Spanish crown could provide one. Any American action (or inaction) that smacked of support for the South American revolutionaries not only jeopardized relations with Spain and Portugal, but also threatened to embroil the United States in a new cycle of destructive conflict. The end of the Napoleonic struggle might herald a new age of American power, or it might lead to renewed subjugation to European military and economic authority.[4]

As they had in the past, the nation's political leaders turned to the federal courts for help in controlling the maritime violence that threatened American sovereignty. Public support for the emerging South American republics was strong in the United States, at least in the abstract, and officials in the Madison and Monroe administrations deflected Iberian complaints for action by insisting that claimants go to court to recover captured ships and goods. But the new crisis was not simply a replay of the struggles of the 1790s. Adams, more than anyone, recognized that civil suits were insufficient to placate Iberian representatives. So the executive branch reached for a tool for suppressing violence on the high seas that previous administrations had largely eschewed – criminal prosecutions on grounds of piracy. Punishing rebel adventurers as pirates, the internationally recognized "enemies of all mankind," would not only give foreigners redress for violations of American neutrality. It would also show the world that the new global power emerging in North America was both willing and able to police the revolutionary Atlantic's roiled waters.

The drive to vindicate an imperial vision of American sovereignty through the courts foundered, at least initially, on obstacles old and new. As before, recalcitrant government officers and sympathetic juries made criminal convictions nearly impossible to secure. But South American privateering also presented policymakers in the United States with a new problem – uncertainty about the nature of sovereignty itself. In an age when a kaleidoscopic array of insurgent polities claimed the same right of self-determination that colonial North Americans had asserted against Britain four decades earlier, drawing a legal line between legitimate resistance to monarchical oppression and unlawful robbery on the high seas proved deeply challenging.

Federal judges also had misgivings about assuming a leading role in superintending the high seas. Familiar doubts about the proper scope of the courts' jurisdiction, combined with ambiguity about the South American republic's sovereign status, led the justices of the Supreme Court to deny that it was their responsibility to punish "offences against the human race," as John Marshall put it. The judges would eventually overcome their hesitancy, and would once again prove instrumental in securing American authority on the water. But at the time Adams expressed his fears to his father about the nation's future, his dark predictions seemed on the verge of realization.[5]

* * *

The trouble for the Madison administration began almost as soon as the War of 1812 was over. On February 27, 1815, merchant Henry Didier, Jr. wrote an anxious letter to his business partner. News of the war's end had just arrived in Baltimore, and it took Didier by surprise. Most Americans celebrated the advent of peace, but Didier was less enthusiastic. His firm, Didier and D'Arcy, was a leading privateer investor during the war, and commerce raiding had been terrific business. The profits enabled Didier's family to live comfortably in their "highly cultivated seat" at the city's western edge. Had the war lasted just two more years, Didier complained, he would have been able to retire.[6]

With hostilities ended, Didier had fifteen idle schooners sitting at the docks. There were other opportunities available. Small, fast-sailing vessels were perfect for running muskets and gunpowder through Spanish blockades into South American ports. As long as the combatants had "plenty of dollars," Didier was happy to meet their needs. But privateering offered the most profitable use of Didier's ships, and he did not want to "sacrifice" any of them. "I am in hopes that there will be a war between England, France, and some of the continental powers," Didier told his partner John D'Arcy, "that we may make use of our fast sailing schooners."[7]

The opportunity to profit from armed conflict at sea came instead from the south. In the wake of the fall of the Spanish Bourbons to Napoleon in 1808, Spain's American colonies began to rebel against the peninsular authorities who sought to replace the abdicated king. In 1810, colonial subjects in Buenos Ayres overthrew the Spanish viceroy and established a junta to govern the newly denominated United Provinces of the Río de la Plata (part of modern-day Argentina). The movement toward outright independence developed slowly, as various royalist and separatist authorities in the interior territories contested the claims to central control advanced by successive Supreme Directors based in in Buenos Ayres. In 1816, however, the United Provinces formally declared their independence from Spain under the leadership of Juan Martín de Pueyrredón. Meanwhile, Jose Gervasio Artigas consolidated a rival base of power in the Banda Oriental, the territories that roughly correspond to modern-day Uruguay. As a result, by 1816 both the United Provinces and Artigas were at war with Spain, as well as with each other. In addition, Artigas was soon at war with the Portuguese monarchy, which had relocated to Brazil in 1808 and invaded the Banda Oriental in 1816.[8]

Amid this tumult, a merchant brig Didier owned arrived in Baltimore from Buenos Ayres in January 1816, carrying precious cargo. One of the passengers was Thomas Taylor, an experienced ship captain who had recently served in the United Provinces' fledgling navy. Taylor was a mysterious figure. He claimed to have been born a British subject in the Caribbean, and to have served in the British Navy. But apparently he was originally from Delaware and emigrated to Buenos Ayres to join the independence movement. Spanish royalist forces captured and imprisoned him, though he escaped and later commanded the United Provinces' first privateer. Having gained the trust of the Buenos Ayrean leadership, he sailed to Baltimore in late 1815 on a mission to secure American assistance in the revolutionary struggle.[9]

Taylor was just one of dozens of South American representatives who came to the United States in the postwar period seeking money, weapons, and men. This was not a new phenomenon. Since the early 1800s, charismatic and ambitious men such as Francisco de Miranda and Aaron Burr had sought American support for their plans to erect new polities out of the fragmenting pieces of the Spanish Empire. But, unlike most of these adventurers, Taylor brought something of tremendous value to opportunistic merchants like Didier – blank privateering commissions from the United Provinces (Figure 6.1). Like France in 1793 and the United States in 1812, the only way the rebels could fight their royalist enemies on the water was through privateering. Taylor's shipmates also carried commissions supplied by David DeForest, a wealthy American merchant residing in Buenos Ayres. Though DeForest regretted only being able to secure a small handful, he was confident they would be "sufficient to make business for any one house."[10]

The commissions Didier's ship brought were a godsend for Baltimore's seafaring community. The War of 1812's end meant that many seamen were out of work. A typical merchant ship required far fewer hands than an armed vessel, so there were fewer jobs to go around. In addition, the winding down of the broader Napoleonic conflict meant that the British once again began to dominate transatlantic trade, leaving American maritime commerce in what President Madison described in December 1816 as a "depressed state." Resourceful businessmen such as Didier and D'Arcy found

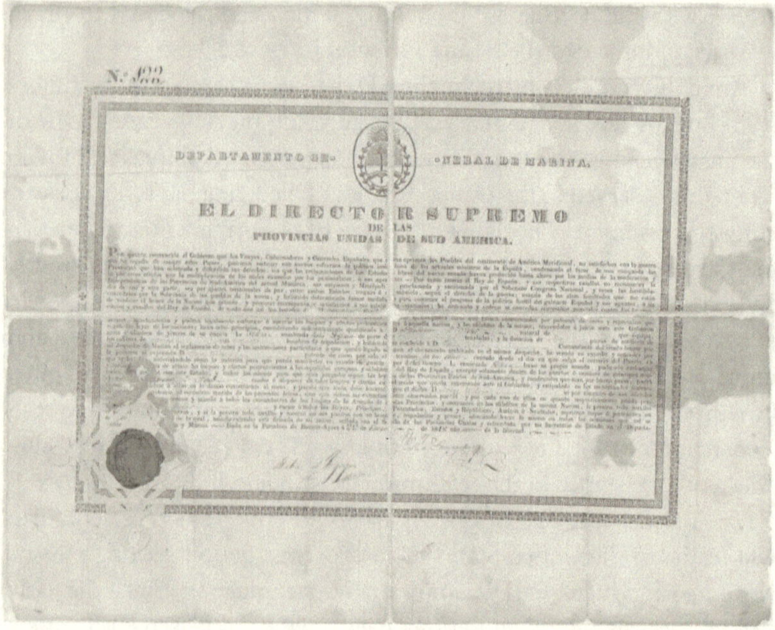

DEPARTAMENTO GENERAL DE MARINA.

EL DIRECTOR SUPREMO

DE LAS

PROVINCIAS UNIDAS DE SUD AMERICA.

FIGURE 6.1 The arrival in Baltimore of agents bearing South American privateering commissions put the United States' relationship with both Spain and Portugal in jeopardy. Courtesy of the National Archives and Records Administration.

other commercial opportunities, including the arms trade, but the end of maritime conflict was a financial disaster for many.[11]

Taylor's arrival offered Baltimore a lifeline. Spain's disputed territorial possessions still produced a host of valuable commodities destined for markets in Europe, but the Spanish monarchy's control over its American empire was crumbling. The Napoleonic Wars decimated the Spanish navy, making easy targets of the slow, heavily laden merchant ships that transported valuable colonial produce across the Atlantic. South American privateering commissions offered North American merchants and sailors an opportunity to resume their former operations, perhaps even more profitably than before. By early 1816, according to naval officer David Porter, many mariners had "turned their thoughts to South America."[12]

Taylor became one of the leaders of a resurgent wave of privateering from American ports. He purchased one of Didier and D'Arcy's best vessels, the *Romp*, and refitted it to cruise against Spanish commerce.

He engaged a famous War of 1812 privateer captain, Joseph Almeida, to take command of another Didier and D'Arcy vessel, the *Orb*. As in the late war, most Baltimore privateer vessels were owned by groups of investors. They pooled their money to fund the expense of arming and fitting out a privateer, and divided the profits from successful cruises according to their level of investment – minus DeForest's ten percent commission for managing the condemnation and sale of prizes in Buenos Ayres. For men such as Taylor, Didier, and DeForest, revolution promised to be good business.[13]

Money was not the privateers' only motivation. Some of the men who schemed on the Baltimore waterfront were true believers in the patriot cause. Taylor wore a United Provinces uniform when on board his vessels, and required that his crew take an oath pledging to support "the Independence of South America." At one point he even plotted to kidnap the Spanish consul in Baltimore and "deliver him to the patriots." Another captain, John Danels, was so moved by the revolutionary spirit that he – like other Americans – named his son "Bolivar," in honor of the Venezuelan revolutionary leader. Others had very personal reasons for taking up arms against Spain. Almeida had spent time as a Spanish prisoner, and it had not been pleasant. He was beaten, marched 140 miles, and then had his ship and goods taken from him. Taylor's commission offered an opportunity to exact revenge.[14]

Privateers' mixed motivations reflected American attitudes toward the South American revolutions more generally. Popular support in the United States was strong overall. Enthusiasm never reached the fever pitch it had during the French Revolution, but those who looked south in the 1810s once again saw themselves in the mirror, and they were comforted. The War of 1812 may have heralded the nation's arrival as a world power, but the reestablishment of monarchy in Europe left the United States isolated and vulnerable. As one newspaper anxiously pointed out, at war's end the United States was "the only free government on earth." The emergence of new democratic governments to the south reassured North Americans that their own experiment in revolutionary republicanism might survive, and they cheered their fellow-patriots' successes in speeches, pamphlets, and songs. As Henry Clay, the Speaker of the House of Representatives, put it in 1818, the rebels were "fighting for liberty and independence – for precisely what we fought for."[15]

Americans also had less lofty reasons for cheering the collapse of Iberian authority. One was economic. Spain's travails during the Napoleonic Wars had already resulted in the partial opening of Spanish ports to American ships, and northern merchants and politicians delighted at the prospect of establishing unfettered trade relations with the independent nations that would control the coffee and sugar that Americans coveted (not to mention the region's fabled gold and silver). A second reason was rivalry. Weakening Britain's Spanish ally might help combat British hemispheric influence, but it also posed risks, as Britain's economic and maritime power could easily fill the void left by Spain's imperial demise. By allying themselves with the rebels in word and deed, Americans could ensure that the British money, weapons, and men already quietly flowing into Spanish America did not result in British domination of the continent.[16]

Not all North Americans shared in the enthusiasm. Some in the United States worried that years of oppression by a corrupt and unenlightened monarchy left South Americans ill-prepared for self-government, and that widespread adherence to Catholicism rendered them vulnerable to despotic power. John Adams *père*, growing increasingly cranky in his dotage, grumbled in 1815 that such "ignorant" and "biggoted" people could no more sustain a free government than could "Beasts Birds or Fishes." Others, especially in the southern United States, worried that antislavery tendencies among some revolutionaries – and especially the arming of black soldiers – risked social chaos.[17]

But these anxieties – especially the racially motivated ones – did not crystallize into widespread opposition until the 1820s. In the immediate postwar period, Americans enthused by the spread of liberty in the hemisphere were willing to look past the "popish" leanings of their republican brothers. And the gradual emancipation movements in the Spanish empire seemed, from a safe distance, no more threatening to slavery as an institution than similar developments in the northern United States. Even a skeptic like the elder Adams confessed, after receiving a visit in 1817 from a rebel agent from Brazil, that he "could not but Sympathize" with their cause.[18]

The Spanish government made clear, however, that American sympathy for the rebels put the two nation's relations in jeopardy. The initial concern expressed by the Spanish minister to the United States, Luis de Onís, was that "insurgents and incendiaries" were allegedly raising troops in Louisiana to help liberate Mexico from Spanish rule. This was not a new problem, as John Quincy Adams knew all too well. A decade earlier, his brother-in-law William Stephens Smith had stood trial for his role in helping Francisco de Miranda launch his infamous (and ultimately disastrous) mission to bring liberty to Venezuela. But the "revolutionary squadron" of privateers fitting out in Baltimore in 1816 posed a greater threat than the rag-tag expeditions mounted by Miranda and his later imitators. Private armed ships roaming the Atlantic could do incalculable damage to Spain's economy and its tenuous hold on its American possessions.[19]

Fortunately for Onís, the law was firmly on his side. The Neutrality Act of 1794, which Congress had enacted at the height of the French privateering controversy of the 1790s (see Chapter 2), forbade Americans from participating in armed conflict against friendly nations. A 1795 treaty between Spain and the United States specifically prohibited the citizens and subjects of either nation from privateering against the other. Onís therefore demanded that the Madison administration end the "scandalous hostilities" hatching in the United States and punish any offenders "according to law."[20]

Onís saw the developments in Baltimore as not simply unlawful, but also as an insult. The South American insurgents were traitors, not patriots, and any reception in the United States short of throwing them in jail effectively legitimized their treasonous rebellions. Commissioning private armed vessels was a particularly galling act, because that was something the law of nations only allowed a sovereign state to do. By licensing privateers, the revolutionary governments proclaimed themselves, in word *and* deed, to be independent states. If the United States tolerated such brazen and unwarranted displays of sovereignty, Onís raged, it would effectively be treating the "scum of all countries" as equal to His Most Catholic Majesty.[21]

The Madison administration would have preferred to ignore Onís's protests altogether. During the War of 1812, he had hatched a plan to help Great Britain carve off a portion of United States territory, and Madison did not trust him. (The feeling was mutual; Onís suspected that Madison was an ardent Francophile, and even a closet Bonapartist.) The Spanish minister was also haughty and a bit of a bore. He had the habit of repeating the same demands over and over, to the point that his American counterparts largely stopped listening. He was also highly sensitive to any possible affront to him or his royal master. When he discovered that his daughter was seated next to DeForest's wife at a presidential reception, he stormed off in a huff.[22]

The administration also wanted to keep Onís at arm's length because of international and domestic politics. Any effort to suppress the Baltimore privateers was politically risky, given the support the rebels enjoyed in Congress and among the broader public. Henry Clay, the leader of the pro-independence faction, was a true believer in the patriot cause, but he was also deeply ambitious. In an era of one-party rule, staking out a strong position in favor of the revolutions was a way for Clay to distinguish himself from rivals and, Adams grumbled, possibly ride his "South American great horse" all the way to the presidency.[23] There was support for the rebels in the White House as well. Both Madison – who was finishing his second term just as the privateering controversy emerged – and James Monroe had doubts about South Americans' capacity for self-government. But even if Monroe believed it would "take[] a while" to get them "in the right road," he had little doubt that their journey would end in independence.[24]

But executive branch officials could not afford to alienate Onís entirely, as angering Spain came with its own risks. The once-mighty empire posed little military threat, but the complex web of post-Napoleonic treaties among European nations meant that war with Spain risked igniting a wider and more perilous conflict. Great Britain, in particular, might seize on any excuse to reassert its authority in North America, and its alliance with the beleaguered Spanish crown could provide one. Adams was already persuaded that the European monarchs recently restored to power viewed the United States as a threat. "We have enemies in almost every part of the world," Adams declared pessimistically before becoming Secretary of State, "and few or no friends anywhere."[25]

Conflict with Spain also jeopardized the realization of a long-held, and deeply contested, vision of American continental empire. One of Madison's chief postwar priorities was to negotiate a treaty with

Spain that would secure and expand the nation's boundaries. The greatest prize was Florida. The United States had already annexed its western portion, and Spain could barely administer the rest. Acquiring the entire peninsula would open new land for white settlers seeking to capitalize on the burgeoning European market for American cotton, and would prevent the territory from becoming a haven for enslaved persons trying to escape the murderous labor regime that made that market possible. A treaty would also fix the borders between Spanish and American territory left uncertain after Jefferson's purchase of Louisiana in 1803, and potentially secure U.S. claims to territory in the Pacific Northwest. For the first time, the dream of extending the nation's borders across North America seemed possible.[26]

With Spain holding the key to an expanded American domain, the Madison administration had to proceed cautiously. It was actually in no hurry to sign a treaty, however beneficial. American policymakers believed that the inevitable growth of U.S. power, and a parallel decline in Spain's, could only improve their bargaining position. As Madison put it to Jefferson just before leaving office, "delay is our ally."[27] So the administration tried to strike a delicate balance. It resisted Clay's calls to grant the revolutionary governments formal recognition. At the same time, it made clear that it would treat the warring sides on equal terms. The federal government, Monroe explained, viewed the armed struggle raging across Spain's empire not as an "ordinary insurrection," but "as a civil war between parties nearly equal." It also emphasized that this was a dispute in which the United States would not get involved. Even before Taylor's arrival in Baltimore, Madison warned U.S. citizens to steer clear of the conflict, and threatened punishment if they did not.[28]

The government also tried to mollify Spain. Monroe – who was Madison's Secretary of State before becoming president himself – explained to Onís in early 1816 that investigations by federal officials in Louisiana had not discovered armed forces assembling in U.S. territory. Nor did the Baltimore customs collector have reason to suspect that ships were being fitted out there to make war against Spain. But the government acted quickly once it discovered that one of the Baltimore armed vessels had attacked Spanish ships after leaving port. Federal officers arrested several of its crew members on their return to Virginia, and Monroe ordered the federal district attorney to prosecute the owners for violating the law. The vessel was the *Romp*, and the owner was Thomas Taylor.[29]

* * *

Like his predecessors, Monroe soon discovered that bringing privateers like Taylor to justice was harder than he imagined. The *Romp* had slipped its moorings in Baltimore harbor in April 1816 and sailed quietly down the Chesapeake. She left port under American registry with a clearance for Buenos Ayres, carrying six guns and a small crew. A few miles south of Baltimore, however, she stopped to take on an additional forty to fifty sailors. After two weeks at sea, her captain raised the Buenos Ayres flag and renamed the ship *Santafecino*. She then crossed the Atlantic and seized five Spanish vessels in the waters off the Iberian peninsula, the Canaries, and West Africa.[30]

Despite this initial success, the *Romp*'s sailors were unhappy. Some later claimed that they had been tricked into enlisting on the privateer. Whatever the reasons for their discontent, the crew mutinied, put their officers onto a passing ship, and sailed the *Romp* back to the United States. A government vessel intercepted her upon arrival in the Chesapeake, and the federal district court judge ordered eight crew members into confinement on charges of mutiny and revolt.[31]

As the *Romp*'s exploits became national news, federal officials huddled together to decide what to do. Attorney General Richard Rush and Virginia district attorney William Wirt recommended going after Taylor first. Spain would not be satisfied if the government allowed the "prime mover" behind the privateering enterprise "to go at large with impunity." But to prosecute Taylor the government first had to get its hands on him. Rumor had it that he was living in Baltimore, without fear of arrest, confident that the federal government would "wink" at his exploits. Taylor even admitted in an open letter to a newspaper that he fitted out the *Romp*, but asserted that, as a Buenos Ayrean citizen and naval officer, he had every right to do so. The government eventually tracked him down, but a Maryland justice of the peace let him go free, finding insufficient evidence to show that he was responsible for the *Romp*'s "acts of piracy."[32]

One might have thought it would be easy for federal officers to find evidence of privateering activity in a major port like Baltimore. But, as customs collector James McCulloch explained to Secretary of the

Treasury Alexander Dallas shortly after Taylor's release, it was easy to disguise intended privateers with "the appearance of Mercantile projects," and then smuggle guns and men aboard in one of the Chesapeake's countless small bays and inlets.[33] In fact, the evidence did not need to be hidden at all. It was common for merchant vessels to arm themselves for defense against pirates, and privateers masquerading as merchants could take on crew as pretended "passengers." Plus, nothing in federal law prohibited arms sales to foreign nations at war, and the Madison administration was happy to allow the trade to continue. Absent definitive proof that a ship was specifically being prepared to raid Spanish commerce, McCulloch protested, there was little that federal officers could do.[34]

José Francisco Corrêa da Serra fully understood the difficulties the government faced. In 1816, the recently appointed Portuguese envoy to the United States was also watching Baltimore with growing alarm. Portugal and the United Provinces were not at war, so privateers with Buenos Ayres commissions could not legally seize Portuguese ships. But Corrêa da Serra knew the calm would likely not last. Thomas Taylor had instructed the *Romp*'s captain to attack Portuguese shipping if he received news of war between those governments. When Corrêa da Serra caught wind of Taylor's activities, he personally went to Baltimore to investigate. What he saw on the docks convinced him that the growing menace had to be quashed.[35]

Corrêa da Serra was well equipped to persuade Washington policymakers to take a firm hand against the Baltimore privateers. He was an amiable and witty conversationalist, equally comfortable discussing politics, philosophy, or botany, and counted luminaries such as Jefferson and Madison among his personal friends. Even John Quincy Adams, who was largely immune to diplomatic charm, delighted in Corrêa da Serra's company.[36]

The Portuguese minister also had a keen sense for how best to cajole American politicians into action. In contrast to Onís, Corrêa da Serra preferred communicating in person, finding a bit of gossip over tea more effective than bombastic letters. And he rarely made demands. Instead, he appealed to Americans' pride, and to their insecurities. As the western hemisphere's "paramount powers," Corrêa da Serra suggested to Monroe, Portugal and the United States had the joint authority and obligation to maintain good order at sea.

Adopting the role of a concerned friend, Corrêa da Serra warned Monroe that the government's failure to suppress the Baltimore privateers would leave her "unworthy ... in the eyes of foreign nations." More ominously, he hinted it would also put the United States' "peace and tranquility" at risk.[37]

Corrêa da Serra knew that even if the government was able to punish "a few obscure offenders," the deeper problem lay with the law itself. The statutory regime governing neutrality had not changed since Washington's presidency, and Corrêa da Serra found the old laws maladapted to the present situation. Perhaps federal legislators had tolerated its infirmities in the past, he mused, because they never dreamed that their countrymen would engage in such egregious conduct. But now that Americans were openly preparing to make war against sovereigns with whom the United States was at peace, only new legislation "sufficient for the emergency" could rehabilitate the nation "in the eyes of the civilized world."[38]

Corrêa da Serra's inveigling prompted the executive branch to seek controversial changes to the nation's legal order that would strengthen its hand in dealing with South American privateering. In December 1816, Madison asked Congress to consider legislation to preserve the nation's "pacific relations." Because privateers could easily mask their hostile purposes behind the façade of ordinary mercantile activity, Monroe proposed a revision to the Neutrality Act of 1794 giving customs officers the power to detain vessels they believed were being prepared under questionable circumstances.[39]

The revolutionaries' supporters in Congress lambasted the proposed legislation as a betrayal of republican principles. They complained that the bill was instigated by those "devot[ed] to kingly governments," and Clay joked bitterly that the bill should be renamed "an act for the benefit of His Majesty the King of Spain." Their evidence was the provision allowing detention of vessels on "mere suspicion." According to the critics, it gave the customs officers "a greater power over their citizens than they ought to have," similar to the reviled authority exercised by British officials in the colonial period and federal customs officers under Jefferson's embargo.[40]

The legislation's opponents argued that judges, not executive branch functionaries, should decide whether evidence of wrongdoing justified detention of a suspected privateer. Americans of the revolutionary generation may have extolled the jury as the primary guarantor of individual liberties in the judicial system. But admiralty courts had no juries, so the best defense against autocracy and oppression were independent judges. The administration's proposal, the critics charged, undermined that scheme by putting into the executive branch's hands "powers that belong to the Judiciary."[41]

For a majority in Congress, however, privateering's threat to international security was greater than the proposed legislation's threat to the domestic constitutional order. Proponents noted there were similar detention provisions in laws regulating the slave trade and commerce with Haiti. Empowering the executive branch to prevent offenses before they occurred, rather than simply punish them via judicial process after the fact, was a salutary aspect of any functional law enforcement regime. As one representative put it, "[w]hy have laws that we cannot execute?" Otherwise, the actions of "a few worthless men" would "sacrifice the peace of the nation." South American privateering was too dangerous to continue unhindered, and in March 1817 a revised neutrality act was enacted into law.[42]

The new legislation also addressed another deficiency of the preexisting legal regime, one laid bare by the fractured sovereignty of the early nineteenth century. The original Neutrality Act prohibited Americans from taking up arms on behalf of a "foreign prince or state." That formulation worked fine during the Neutrality Crisis, when the law's purpose was to restrain privateers with commissions issued by revolutionary France – no longer governed by a "prince" in 1794 (having removed his head), but certainly still a "state." Now, however, a new question arose: Were the rebelling South American polities "states"? If not, the Neutrality Act simply did not apply.[43]

The confounding factor, as it often was in the Age of Revolution, was Haiti. For twenty-five years, Americans had watched events in the former French colony with a mix of fascination and horror. When a 1790s insurrection by enslaved persons on the island sparked a bloody civil war, many white Americans worried that the contagion of slave rebellion would infect the United States. Their fears were exaggerated, but not unjustified. Long before Haiti formally declared its independence from France in 1803, news of the dramatic events on the island inspired free and enslaved persons of color around the

Atlantic world to consider the possibilities for their own liberation. Fear of the rebellions a black republic might inspire led successive American presidents to refuse to acknowledge Haiti's independence, and in 1806 the Jefferson administration prohibited trade with Haiti's black population.[44]

Disdain for Haitians' claims to political equality pervaded the courts, as well. In 1808, the Supreme Court conceded that Haiti had "maintained its sovereignty" by force of arms. But until the executive branch recognized its independence, John Marshall insisted, the courts were bound to consider "the ancient state of things" – that is, black Haitians' subservience to France – as "remaining unaltered."[45]

Ironically, Americans' obstinate refusal to recognize Haiti's independence undermined the federal government's ability to control the maritime violence that subsequent revolutionary movements unleashed. In 1816, Chancellor James Kent in New York ruled that Haiti was not a "state" under the Neutrality Act, citing Supreme Court precedent and Jefferson's trade ban as evidence of Haiti's degraded sovereignty. As a result, the Act did not give the New York federal customs collector authority to prevent armed ships from serving in Haiti's ongoing civil war. The ruling technically only applied to Haiti, but Kent made clear that he had similar doubts about more recent independent movements. The "experience of this age," he declared, highlighted the transience of "newly-erected powers in revolutionary times." Before such governments could "command confidence," they first had to demonstrate their stability and legitimacy. Until that happened, they could not be considered "states" at all.[46]

In response to Kent's ruling, the 1817 Neutrality Act applied to anyone seeking to foment rebellion from the United States. The act's prohibition on arming ships extended not just to vessels intended to serve a "foreign prince or state," but also any "colony, district, or people at war." This technical-seeming additional verbiage, Chief Justice Marshall later explained, "adapt[ed] the previous laws to the actual situation of the world." Henry Clay tried to insert a disclaimer in the bill that would have prevented the government from prosecuting privateers under the Neutrality Act simply because their commissions came from governments the United States had not formally recognized. But his opponents argued that his proposal would legitimize ephemeral polities "which might have no existence," and it was not included in the final version. With a revamped Neutrality Act that applied to all who might threaten the United States' peace and security, the Baltimore privateers were squarely in the government's sights.[47]

Creating the legal tools needed to suppress privateering was one thing, but prodding the recalcitrant machinery of federal administration to use them was another. The national government had come a long way since its threadbare beginnings in the late 1780s. Thanks to three decades of war and territorial expansion, it had an army, a navy, and a host of civil officers responsible for everything from distributing land to delivering mail. In addition, the Treasury Department had thousands of officers stationed on the eastern seaboard, armed with significant authority to inspect seagoing vessels and seize them for violating the law.[48]

Customs officials' chief responsibility, however, was to collect revenue, not to prevent war. Without the taxes merchants paid on imported goods, there literally would be no government at all. This was especially true in 1817, when the United States was just beginning to crawl out of the financial deficit caused by the War of 1812. Individual officers also had a personal reason to prioritize collecting customs duties over enforcing the strictures of the Neutrality Act. They were entitled to fees for the services they provided to merchants, and to a share of the proceeds from the sale of goods they seized for smuggling and nonpayment of levies. Little wonder that some officers openly declared that regulating privateer conduct was simply not their responsibility.[49]

Rigorous law enforcement on the waterfront was also in tension with longstanding practices of early American governance. Tax evasion was common in the North American colonies long before the crises of the 1760s. The British crown perennially struggled to collect customs revenue, as did the state governments and Confederation Congress after independence. Things did not change dramatically in 1789. For decades, policymakers in the executive branch had difficulty cajoling customs officers into stricter execution of the law governing maritime commerce. Most officers came from the mercantile communities they were supposed to regulate, and were disinclined to scrutinize the activities of their friends and neighbors. When independent-minded officers did try to enforce the law, they faced

FIGURE 6.2 Federal laws prohibiting American involvement in the wars of South American liberation proved difficult to enforce in busy ports like Baltimore. "Baltimore from Federal Hill," by W. J. Bennett (c. 1831), courtesy of the Library of Congress.

defiance, lawsuits and even personal violence from people long accustomed to evading or ignoring government regulation.[50]

As a result, early customs enforcement was characterized by what one historian describes as a culture of "accommodation" between merchants and officers. As long as sufficient revenues flowed into government coffers, regulation remained light. To be sure, the early federal government was generally successful at collecting revenue, and at least some customs collectors forcefully pursued smugglers and other tax evaders. At minimum, however, law enforcement on the American waterfront was uneven (Figure 6.2).[51]

The permissive approach to maritime regulation was on full display as the controversy over South American privateering grew. James McCulloch, the Baltimore customs collector, started his career as an enthusiastic Jefferson appointee determined to vindicate Republican commercial policies. But opposition from the powerful Baltimore mercantile community during Jefferson's embargo led McCulloch to temper his approach. Almost a decade later, Spanish officials were convinced that McCulloch was showing the same leniency toward merchants invested in the privateering trade. They repeatedly complained about his failure to take action, despite clear evidence of privateer conduct that violated American neutrality. This critique was not entirely justified, but executive branch officials agreed that McCulloch was not doing his job. They believed that he was simply too enthusiastic about the patriot cause, and therefore "easily duped by knaves."[52]

Officers up and down the seaboard proved to be inconstant guardians of American neutrality. A few were in outright cahoots with privateers.[53] Some, like Boston customs collector Henry Dearborn, simply failed to enforce provisions in the Neutrality Act of 1817. Others, like Elias Glenn, the federal district attorney in Maryland, responded to Spanish demands for intervention by giving evasive answers, or sometimes not responding at all.[54] Charles Mallory, the Norfolk customs collector, was the most dogged in his hair-splitting and foot-dragging. He insisted to Antonio Argote Villalobos, the local Spanish consul, that federal officers needed "positive facts" of a privateer's unlawful intent before they could act. Mere "public notoriety" – and even prior unlawful conduct by the same vessel – was insufficient. When Villalobos supplied the facts required, Mallory proceeded to spin them in the most innocent light possible, refusing to see the wrongdoing that Villalobos insisted was "known to everybody."[55]

A mix of concerns seemed to inspire federal officers' recalcitrance. Mallory, for example, did not understand neutrality enforcement to be his primary responsibility, despite the new powers bestowed by the Neutrality Act. He told Villalobos – incorrectly and perhaps disingenuously – that as long as suspected privateers complied with the "revenue laws" when they brought prizes into port, there was little he could do.[56] Mallory may also have worried about the consequences of taking decisive action, for the threat of being sued personally for an unlawful seizure was a well-known professional hazard.[57] Mallory took the law seriously, and sought clarification from cabinet officers about what the Neutrality Act proscribed. But his interactions with Villalobos indicated he was unwilling to impede the South American "struggle for independence" (as he termed it) unless federal law unambiguously required him to.[58]

This dissembling and intransigence infuriated Spanish officials. The misdeeds of Baltimore privateers were an open secret, and the

Spaniards were unable to comprehend the respect American officials gave to pirates. When Mallory allowed a suspected privateer to leave Norfolk, Onís railed about the official salute the ship received from the government fort as it sailed out of harbor.[59] As the resentment grew, the complaints became more ominous. The Spanish made clear their expectation that the "interposition of Government" would put a stop to "iniquitous proceedings so contrary to the laws of nations." If not, Spain would hold the United States responsible.[60]

* * *

Iberian officials did not wait around for the federal government to act. Like their British predecessors more than two decades earlier, they took their complaints about privateers to court. Onís circulated a copy of the Neutrality Act of 1817 to Spain's consuls immediately after its enactment, and they responded with a coordinated and aggressive litigation campaign that dwarfed Benjamin Moodie's solitary effort against French privateers in the 1790s. Iberian representatives filed dozens of lawsuits in federal court to recover property scattered across the eastern seaboard.[61] They hired skilled and experienced lawyers to represent them, including a number of federal district attorneys (acting in their private capacities).[62] They took depositions from witnesses, sought information from government officers and the public, and kept in constant communication with each other about the progress of their litigation.[63]

Iberian officials used litigation in federal court to turn the law of American neutrality from a shield into a sword. Successful lawsuits deprived privateers of their anticipated profits, and pushed them to the brink of financial ruin. Some cases were worth tens or even hundreds of thousands of dollars, but consuls routinely pressed smaller claims that resulted in minimal gains.[64] They were willing to settle when they had trouble securing evidence, or when expenses began to outrun the likely returns.[65] But political considerations often trumped financial ones. When the captors of one Spanish ship appealed an unfavorable ruling to the Supreme Court, the Spanish consul at Boston, John Stoughton, engaged Daniel Webster to argue the case, despite his shockingly high fee. For Stoughton, the case involved a "novel" question that demanded an answer from the nation's highest tribunal.[66]

The Iberians' persistence paid off. In Massachusetts, New York, and Virginia, consuls had an almost perfect record in privateering suits. Even in Baltimore, they won at least seventy-five percent of the time. Thomas Taylor might have avoided criminal prosecution, but the Portuguese consul successfully prosecuted seven different lawsuits against property seized by one of Taylor's privateers, recouping hundreds of thousands of dollars.[67]

The privateers' legal losses made it difficult for them to stay in business, especially when the financial crisis that swept across the country in 1819 pushed a number of investors into bankruptcy. David DeForest, the American merchant who served as the privateers' agent in Buenos Ayres, returned to the United States in 1818 with hopes of increasing his wealth and standing. By 1820, suits by Spanish claimants over privateering were causing him great "anxiety." DeForest survived; he eventually settled in New Haven and became a leading benefactor of Yale University. But others were not so lucky. John Chase, a successful Baltimore privateering captain, reputedly captured over $10 million worth of ships and cargo during his career. Yet after a series of lawsuits by Portuguese officials resulted in judgments he could not pay, a federal marshal auctioned off his "very comfortable" house and furniture, and Chase ended up insolvent.[68]

Despite their success, Iberian officials did not think that private lawsuits were the solution to the privateering problem. Going to court was expensive and time-consuming, and managing litigation was a significant burden. Consuls often had to advance funds to cover expenses, and could not always rely on property owners for reimbursement. They even faced threats of personal violence. Stoughton, the Spanish consul in Boston, was a faithful champion of Spanish interests, but even he confided to his counterpart in Baltimore that he would have liked to rid himself of the whole "troublesome business."[69]

Moreover, civil litigation was, in Corrêa da Serra's estimation, "too partial and too precarious a remedy." Suits to recover captured property did not deprive privateers of their own ships, and even forfeiture actions against privateer vessels by the federal government had limited effect. Corrêa da Serra was gratified that some federal judges upheld the administration's position and restored property seized by privateers, but even a fully responsive judiciary could not "attain them all."[70]

Corrêa da Serra's frustration ultimately prompted him to try bypassing the courts altogether. He proposed to Adams that Portugal and the United States establish a bilateral commission to assess Portuguese losses at the hands of U.S.-based privateers. The details of Corrêa da Serra's proposal have not survived, but apparently he thought that the federal government's failure to suppress privateering obliged it to indemnify injured Portuguese subjects. This was not an outlandish position. Sovereigns were usually obliged to provide compensation for unlawful captures made by their own armed ships. But in the 1790s the Washington administration had accepted responsibility for any British losses stemming from the federal government's failure to suppress French privateers (see Chapter 2). Presumably, Corrêa da Serra's proposed commission would determine the financial obligation that followed from the United States' inability to protect Portuguese merchants – which Corrêa da Serra believed was more than $600,000.[71]

Adams flatly rejected Corrêa da Serra's attempt to take questions about maritime captures away from the judiciary. The Secretary of State was privately critical of the federal courts' performance in criminal cases (as we will see), but in public he defended them unequivocally. He told Corrêa da Serra that the government had diligently pursued every credible allegation, and noted that the courts had restored captured Portuguese property on a number of occasions. Congress had even updated the Neutrality Act at Corrêa da Serra's request.[72]

Adams also protested that Corrêa da Serra's commission would be unconstitutional. It would be "in its nature a judicial tribunal," and the Constitution already provided Portuguese claimants with a forum for their grievances – the federal courts. When Corrêa da Serra brought up his plan with his friend Jefferson, the former Secretary of State likewise rejected it. He conceded that Corrêa da Serra's anger about the "the piracies of Baltimore" was reasonable. And Jefferson was no defender of the federal judiciary late in life (see Chapter 4). But for all the vitriol he had directed toward the courts in the previous two decades, he declared Corrêa da Serra's scheme to be "out of the question."[73]

As both Adams and Jefferson knew, their insistence on the judiciary's exclusive authority to remedy injuries arising at sea was largely nonsense. Many countries – the United States included – regularly used bilateral commissions to determine the damages governments owed for war-related claims. As we have seen, in the 1790s the Jay Treaty established a U.S.–British commission to determine the compensation due to British victims of French-licensed privateers operating from the United States (see Chapter 3). And at the very moment Adams rejected Corrêa da Serra's suggestion, the Monroe administration was entering into arbitration with Great Britain over reparations owed to American slaveholders for enslaved persons who fled behind British lines during the War of 1812. No one suggested that the commission was unconstitutional.[74]

What Adams *meant* in rebuffing Corrêa da Serra is what Jefferson had told British officials nearly thirty years earlier: The federal courts' openness to Iberian lawsuits satisfied the United States' obligations as a neutral nation. This was the Washington administration's position during the Neutrality Crisis, and it was ratified by the Jay Treaty commission, which ruled that the United States had almost no obligation to pay compensation for French privateer seizures. Monroe assumed Corrêa da Serra was somehow ignorant of this precedent; otherwise, he would not have dared such an unprecedented attack on the judiciary's integrity.[75]

The president's indignation at Corrêa da Serra's proposal was more than a little ironic. He seemed to have forgotten the far more vituperative insults his friend Edmond-Charles Genet, the French minister, had hurled at federal judges twenty-five years earlier. But perhaps Monroe's amnesia was to be expected. In the 1790s, the federal courts were new and half-formed, and the scope of their authority under domestic and international law was legitimately subject to debate. But now, after decades of judicial intervention in the affairs of state, the courts' fitness as a forum for resolving international disputes was no longer in doubt.

* * *

The Monroe administration's bravado notwithstanding, it knew that private lawsuits alone could not guarantee American peace and security. The new Neutrality Act was only a partial measure; it did not apply retrospectively, so any privateer activity before March 1817 came under the 1794 statute, which only prohibited privateering on behalf of a "prince" or "state." In addition, the new act's strictures largely applied to those who organized and underwrote privateering ventures, so it had little deterrent effect on ordinary seamen. This was evident in the prosecution of the *Romp* crew members who had mutinied against their commander. Wirt, the Virginia district attorney, considered prosecuting them under the Neutrality Act. But it was not the *Romp*'s sailors who had accepted the United Provinces privateering commission. And they swore that they had not knowingly enlisted on a privateer – a dubious assertion, but one that would be difficult to disprove.[76]

Seeking an alternative, the Madison administration reached for a tool long favored by sovereigns seeking to assert their authority over maritime violence – a criminal prosecution for piracy. Wirt secured indictments against the *Romp*'s crew for "piratically and feloniously ... mak[ing] a revolt" on board the ship. The defendants went to trial six months later, in late 1816, before Chief Justice John Marshall in the federal circuit court for Virginia. There was only one problem: Prior to the munity, the *Romp* had apparently seized only Spanish vessels and property, and had paid "perfect respect" to the vessels of neutral nations. So Wirt would have to convince Marshall, and a jury, that the crew were pirates for some other reason.[77]

The appeal of a piracy charge was precisely its malleability. Pirates, as everyone knew, were seafarers whose depredations on peaceful commerce made them social outcasts – the "enemies of all mankind." This notion had classical roots, but it was articulated most fully in its early modern form by Alberico Gentili, an Italian-English jurist who taught at Oxford and tutored Queen Elizabeth I of England. Piracy came to dominate the European public imagination during its "Golden Age" of the late seventeenth and early eighteenth centuries, when unlicensed commerce raiders preyed on merchant ships in the Atlantic and Indian Oceans.[78]

In truth, few "pirates" ever operated entirely outside the law, either as the treasure-burying freebooters of popular culture or as the proto-anarchists depicted in some modern historical scholarship. So-called pirates were usually just privateers with questionable claims to legal authority for their actions. They had commissions that had expired, were forged, had been granted to someone else, or did not authorize them to seize the vessels and goods they captured. A pirate was often someone, like the infamous William Kidd, whose despoliations had sufficiently injured the politically powerful to result in criminal punishment.[79]

As a legal concept, piracy had two key features that made it attractive to early modern states seeking to exert authority over the seas. One was that it was punishable by death, which provided both a strong deterrent to piratical conduct and an opportunity for sovereigns to dangle (literally) their authority before audiences at home and abroad. For centuries, sovereigns flexed their maritime power by executing pirates. Few government acts could create a greater impression among seafaring people than a dockside hanging from the yardarm of a naval vessel, in full view of the crowds that thronged to bear witness.[80]

Piracy's second salutary aspect was "universal jurisdiction" – the theory that *any* sovereign could punish *any* pirate, irrespective of where or against whom he committed his crimes. As a general rule, a nation's maritime jurisdiction was territorially limited to the waters a few miles from its shoreline, unless the matter involved its subjects or citizens. But as Blackstone explained, by his very actions a pirate "declar[ed] war against all mankind," so every nation had the right, grounded in self-defense, "to inflict … punishment upon him." In practice, most piracies that ended up in court bore some connection to the sovereign doling out the punishment, if only because few governments had the incentive to pursue sea raiders whose conduct did not implicate their interests. But the *idea* of universal jurisdiction over the enemies of all humankind was rhetorically useful. States could deploy it to justify expansive assertions of authority over shared (and contested) waters, and the notion that pirates were the nemeses of civilized society justified the severe punishments they received.[81]

For all its conceptual elegance, piracy was knotty in application, as the Madison administration soon learned. The greatest challenge was figuring out what kinds of acts qualified as piratical. Because the *Romp* had behaved properly with respect to the ships it stopped, the government either had to argue that the crew's mutiny itself was criminally punishable, or that the *Romp* lacked proper authority to seize Spanish vessels. Wirt chose the second route: The *Romp*'s crew were pirates because there was no proof that Buenos Ayres was "an independent government" with authority to issue privateering licenses. Without a valid commission, the *Romp*'s seizures were nothing more than robbery on the high seas – textbook piracy.[82]

Wirt's aspersions on South American sovereignty were perhaps too clever. As the defendants' attorney pointed out, the United States itself had commissioned privateers during its struggle for independence nearly half a century earlier. Given this "exact and perfect analogy," Buenos Ayres's authority to issue privateering commissions in 1816 was legally as complete as the United States' was in 1775. Chief Justice Marshall, however, sided with Wirt, ruling that the only commissions that were valid in federal court were those issued by a government formally recognized by the executive branch (and none of the South American governments had been).[83]

Neither Wirt nor Marshall were able to persuade the jury that the *Romp*'s crew were pirates. It returned a not guilty verdict after only ten minutes' deliberation. The Chief Justice was deeply irritated. He believed the *Romp*'s conduct had been "highly illegal," and he excoriated one of the defendants before releasing him. The harsh words were small solace, however. Wirt succeeded in having the *Romp* itself forfeited to the federal government for violating the Neutrality Act, but Taylor and his associates purchased the ship at auction and sent her to Baltimore. She was back on the hunt for Spanish vessels before the legal proceedings even finished.[84]

Recalcitrant juries were not the only obstacle to securing convictions against privateers. A few months after the *Romp* acquittals, Spanish minister Onís managed to prod Maryland state authorities into arresting Joseph Almeida, who had taken dozens of Spanish prizes in his ship *Congreso*, on charges of violating federal law. But state judges set him free; they reasoned that the states, as separate sovereigns, had no authority to enforce the criminal laws of the United States. Federal judges proved no more hospitable to Onís's complaints. Supreme Court Justice Gabriel Duvall issued a federal arrest warrant for Almeida, but at the subsequent trial in the circuit court he directed the jury to acquit, for reasons unknown.[85]

These failures of the American legal system flabbergasted Onís. He refrained from commenting on the proper relationship between state and federal authority. But he made it clear to cabinet officers that Almeida's escape undermined not only "the justice due to the subjects of His Catholic Majesty," but also "the honor of the United States." Unless the federal government took effective measures to restrain Almeida and his ilk, the "friendship" that existed between Spain and the United States would not last much longer.[86]

The arrival of four men in Boston in September 1817 gave the full Supreme Court an opportunity to bring the unsettled law of piracy to bear against South American privateers. The men were discovered carrying five thousand dollars in specie, far more than your average mariner's pocket-money. When questioned by authorities, they revealed that they had served on Almeida's privateer *Congreso*, and had found the money hidden in a Spanish merchant ship captured off Madeira. Almeida had taken most of the ship's cargo into the *Congreso*, and ordered a small crew to sail the prize to Buenos Ayres for condemnation. But the prize crew steered the prize for the New England coast instead, hoping to smuggle the remaining cargo on shore.[87]

Joseph Story was no doubt delighted to see the privateersmen haled into his circuit court. Story was generally sympathetic to the South American revolutions. But he was more deeply committed to federal judicial power, especially in criminal cases. In his circuit court rulings during the War of 1812, Story gave broad effect to statutory and common law crimes, especially those committed on the water. But he had little occasion to weigh in on questions respecting South American privateers, who operated largely from the Chesapeake, forcing him into an involuntary silence that must have galled him.[88]

Story seized the opportunity the new case presented to define the scope of the federal courts' maritime authority. He appointed two leading members of the state bar as defense counsel, and proceeded to trial as soon as the grand jury rendered an indictment. As in Marshall's Virginia courtroom almost a year earlier, the Massachusetts jury voted to acquit after only "a few minutes consultation." Story, however, was unperturbed. He drew up a list of eleven legal questions relating to the case upon which he and district court judge John Davis purportedly disagreed, and "certified" them to the Supreme Court for decision and resolution.[89]

Not all of Story's colleagues were as eager to jump into the legal fray over privateering. "We are constituted to decide causes," Justice Johnson grumbled, "not to discuss themes, or digest systems."

Johnson found certification especially egregious in the Massachusetts case. Only two of Story's eleven questions actually seemed to arise from the events, but it was difficult to know for sure because no facts accompanied them. The questions were effectively hypotheticals, Johnson complained, that could arise "in any other case." Johnson had a point, but ultimately even he conceded the importance of securing the full Court's views in cases of "great importance," including those involving piracy.[90]

The first question the Court faced in *United States v. Palmer* was the same one Marshall had confronted in Virginia: When, if ever, did a self-constituted political entity like the United Provinces of the Río de la Plata enjoy full belligerent rights, including the authority to grant privateering commissions? Perhaps more important, which institution of American government was to resolve that issue? In his opinion for the Court, Marshall acknowledged that there was actually no need to address these "delicate and difficult" questions, since the justices resolved the case on other grounds (as we will see). And Marshall conceded that it was impossible to specify in the abstract what rights were due to a rebellious "part of a foreign empire," as the answer necessarily depended on each polity's particular political situation. By early 1818, however, the question had apparently become too important to put off.[91]

George Blake, the district attorney for Massachusetts, urged the Court to adopt the position Marshall had taken a year earlier in the *Romp* case: Absolute deference to the executive branch in defining the sovereign prerogatives of a rebelling colony such as Buenos Ayres. Foreign relations were delicate, Blake argued, especially when the "predatory hostilities" of private armed ships were at issue. A judicial mistake in assessing a foreign government's claim to sovereignty risked embroiling the United States in conflict. The safest course was for the courts to accord belligerent rights only to revolutionary polities that the executive or legislative branches had officially recognized. Until that happened, such rebels had no "perfect title to sovereignty," Blake argued, and no right to license privateers.[92]

Marshall, perhaps surprisingly, did not embrace the complete deference to the executive he had signaled in the *Romp* case. Instead, he wrote his favorite kind of opinion – one that extolled judicial submissiveness while quietly asserting the Court's authority to decide questions of great significance. Echoing the distinction he famously articulated in *Marbury v. Madison*, Marshall declared that decisions about the rights a self-proclaimed republic enjoyed in wartime were "rather political than legal," and therefore "entrusted" to the political branches in the first instance. Yet there was a catch. The law of nations required courts to treat belligerent acts by a government at war as legitimate, not criminal. So what mattered legally, Marshall explained, was not formal recognition by Congress or the President, but the facts on the ground. If the executive branch acknowledged "the existence of a civil war," the law of nations *obliged* the courts to give the rebelling party the same rights as its putative sovereign. Otherwise, the judiciary would effectively violate the international norms of neutral obligation by aligning the United States with one side against the other.[93]

Technically, under Marshall's formulation in *Palmer* the courts were still to follow the executive's lead as to whether a particular polity was actually in a state of civil war. But Marshall admitted that determining whether the president had "acknowledged" the existence of civil war was a fact-specific inquiry that left much to judicial discretion. This was precisely why Blake argued that courts could act on only the "most explicit" government recognition of a rebelling polity's sovereign bona fides. According belligerent rights on mere "inference and conjecture" about the executive branch's views was too uncertain, and too risky. But the justices did not seem to share his concerns.[94]

Blake's protests notwithstanding, the Monroe administration seemed quite happy to have judges ultimately decide consequential questions of sovereign rights in wartime. Just as the argument was ending, newly appointed Attorney General William Wirt spoke up. He conceded that the federal government had not formally recognized Buenos Ayres as an independent nation. But, Wirt noted, President Monroe had publicly acknowledged that it was a "distinct belligerent" in its conflict with Spain. Though Wirt did not say more, his suggestion was clear enough: Buenos Ayres was far enough along in its struggle for independence that it could exercise the rights of a sovereign nation. And, more important, federal judges could decide for themselves whether that was true.[95]

Wirt's motivations for intervening are unclear, but the Monroe administration had good reason for trying to divert questions of belligerent right to the courts. More than anything, it was studiously avoiding the question of official recognition. The president was generally inclined toward acknowledging established governments like Buenos Ayres, but Adams was more cautious. He was desperate to secure the long-sought treaty with Spain over Florida and western boundaries, and any executive branch act that smacked of recognition risked upsetting Onís and scuttling their negotiations. Public opinion, however, strongly favored the rebels, and subjecting privateers to the death penalty simply because the federal government had not formally recognized Buenos Ayrean independence would be politically unwise. Indeed, Story's haste in arranging the indictment against the *Palmer* defendants prompted criticism from a Boston newspaper, which doubted whether the defendants' mere "irregular" conduct merited "the dreadful punishment of DEATH!" Much like in the 1790s, letting the courts draw the line between legitimate privateering and unlawful banditry allowed the Monroe administration to keep divisive and hugely consequential questions at arm's length.[96]

The Monroe administration was much less pleased with the Court's other significant ruling in *Palmer*. It involved another question Story certified: whether the Crimes Act of 1790 gave the federal courts jurisdiction to punish acts of piracy committed by foreign citizens on foreign ships. This issue was of doubtful relevance to the *Palmer* case itself, as the defendants were apparently residents of the United States, and likely citizens. But Story's undeveloped factual record did not include evidence about their nationality, which allowed the Court to consider its jurisdiction over foreign pirates in the abstract.[97]

The Crimes Act itself suggested no limits on the federal judiciary's authority over pirates. It empowered the courts to punish "any person" who committed piratical acts "upon the high seas." This made sense, since piracy was a crime subject to universal jurisdiction under the law of nations (at least in theory). Blake raised this point in urging the Court to read the statute broadly. The Constitution authorized Congress to "define and punish piracies." What could be a more appropriate exercise of that power than subjecting the enemies of all nations to the federal courts' authority? Indeed, Blake argued, the United States had an obligation, "as a member of the community of nations," to punish such offenses, and Congress in 1790 would not have neglected "so important a duty."[98]

The justices, however, did not agree that it was their responsibility to police the conduct of all who committed unlawful violence at sea. Marshall conceded that the statutory text was formally "unlimited." But he concluded that Congress in 1790 could not have meant to extend the federal courts' jurisdiction to foreigners and foreign ships. Reading the statute in this way would give the courts the power to punish a foreign seaman on a foreign ship for mutiny, or for stealing as little as fifty dollars – matters Marshall believed were within the exclusive purview of the nation under whose flag the ship sailed. The Act's formal title, after all, was "An Act for the Punishment of certain Crimes *against the United States*." It was not, Marshall asserted, designed to punish "offences against the human race." A month later, the *Palmer* defendants walked free.[99]

The Court's rulings in *Palmer* highlighted the justices' ongoing ambivalence about taking a leading role in defending American sovereignty at sea. They accepted Wirt's invitation to decide whether a revolutionary government had the legitimacy required to commission privateers. But they were reluctant to assume jurisdiction over piracy cases that did not involve American citizens or vessels, even though the statutory text, the Constitution, and the law of nations all allowed it. As before, federal judges were generally supportive of the political branches' policy goals, but they were hesitant to take responsibility for cases in which Americans were not directly implicated – whether those were prize disputes between European governments in the 1790s or criminal prosecutions against South American privateers in the 1810s. And like their colleagues in the 1790s and the War of 1812, the justices seemed wary of assuming the administrative and jurisprudential burden of resolving increasingly complex and contentious cases arising from maritime war. That stance would change soon enough, but for the time being the justices' willingness to police the violence of revolution had reached its limit.

* * *

As 1818 wore on, the legal constraints on the government's ability to bring privateers to heel put the nation's international standing in deeper jeopardy. After the *Romp*'s mutinous misadventure, Thomas

Taylor took personal command of his next privateer, *El Patriota*, and seized hundreds of thousands of dollars' worth of vessels and goods. The owner of one ship sued him personally for damages, claiming Taylor tortured him on board, but the wily privateer wriggled out of trouble again.[100]

Despite Taylor's elusiveness, by late 1818 the administration was optimistic about bringing him to justice. Elias Glenn, the district attorney in Baltimore, accumulated significant evidence about Taylor's privateering operations, with help from Portuguese minister Corrêa da Serra, who was pushing "very indiscreetly" for a prosecution. Glenn believed that public opinion was turning against the privateers, and the government could expect a "fair hearing at least."[101] Wirt was even more bullish on its prospects. *El Patriota* had reportedly sailed with a commission from Artigas, the leader of the Banda Oriental rebels, whose claim to sovereign legitimacy Wirt thought was much weaker than that of Buenos Ayres. Between the Neutrality Act and the Crimes Act, Wirt was sure that federal law offered Taylor no escape.[102]

Wirt was confident enough in the government's case against Taylor that he agreed to try it himself. This was unusual, since the Attorney General typically only argued for the government in the Supreme Court. Wirt, however, had his reasons. The $1,500 in additional compensation he persuaded Monroe to pay him was nearly half his annual salary, and Wirt was always on the lookout for extra income. He was an orphan from Maryland who now moved in Virginia's highest social circles, and he was obsessed with becoming one of the gentleman lawyers he admired and envied. According to Adams, Wirt thought "more about his salary ... than of any other subject."[103]

Taylor's trial also gave Wirt a chance to burnish his professional reputation by matching wits with William Pinkney, widely regarded as the greatest American lawyer of his generation. Pinkney had just returned to Baltimore from a stint as U.S. envoy to Russia, and quickly became "standing counsel for the pirates," as Adams put it. He was a formidable opponent. Known as the "dictator of the Maryland bar," Pinkney was unafraid to cow his adversaries, and even judges, with his learning and his bombast, treating them, according to Wirt, "as if they were men made of wood."[104]

Wirt was no doubt eager to face off with Pinkney in Baltimore. He had fumbled an earlier opportunity to best his rival in the Supreme

Court by forgetting his notes. "Had I been prepared," he lamented to a friend, "how should I have gloried in that theatre, that concourse, and that adversary!" The Taylor trial was the perfect rematch. Newspapers around the country reported on the proceedings, due to the "conspicuous part" Taylor had played in the South American revolutions and the "anxiety manifested throughout the union on that subject." Overcome with excitement, one newspaper correspondent described the trial as "one of the most extraordinary ... that ever took place in this Republican land," and predicted that it would be "a fruitful source of reflection for historian and patriot."[105]

In the end, Taylor's trial was fruitful for neither Wirt nor the Monroe administration. The proceedings lasted ten days, giving Wirt and Pinkney ample time to perform for the assembled crowds. But Wirt received an unpleasant surprise when the trial began. It turned out that Taylor had cruised in *El Patriota* with a commission from Buenos Ayres, not from Artigas. Under the Supreme Court's ruling in *Palmer*, the government at Buenos Ayres could lawfully license privateers. Wirt tried to persuade the court that Taylor's privateering commission was invalid under the Neutrality Act, but Pinkney reminded the judges that Taylor was on trial for piracy, not a neutrality violation. Plus, Taylor had fitted out *El Patriota* in early 1817, so the only relevant neutrality law was the old 1794 version, which the Supreme Court had recently confirmed did not prohibit armed aid to a rebelling colony like Buenos Ayres. The judges allowed both sides to present their evidence, but they instructed the jury that Taylor's commission was lawful, and it acquitted Taylor without even retiring to deliberate.[106]

Taylor's escape left Wirt despondent. Reports suggested that the Attorney General abandoned the case before the verdict issued, convinced that the facts the government had painstakingly marshaled about Taylor's piratical conduct could not overcome the legal hurdles Pinkney threw in his way. The humiliation seemed too much for Wirt to bear. When the attorneys debated whether piratical conduct not charged in the indictment was admissible against Taylor, Pinkney's disparagement of the Virginia law of evidence as "trash" nearly resulted in a duel.[107] Wirt managed to secure a misdemeanor conviction against one of Taylor's associates for a neutrality violation, but the judges overturned it, and the government abandoned the prosecutions of the remaining defendants. Other prosecutions ended similarly.[108]

Wirt's vexation over Taylor's escape contrasted with the public's delight. The acquittal inspired rejoicing in the galleries and in the press. Friendly newspapers hailed Pinkney in particular; his eloquence and erudition in Taylor's defense, one observer claimed, exceeded even Edmund Burke's famous speeches in Parliament supporting the American colonists during the Revolution. Taylor's supporters also denounced federal officials for their craven submission to Iberian pressure. Wirt was the target of particular opprobrium. One newspaper alleged that the Attorney General acted "at the service of his most Christian Majesty," and discharged his duty "with much *loyalty*."[109]

Most cuttingly, the Monroe administration's critics derided its attempt to establish the United States' own sovereign respectability by prosecuting fellow republicans. "How manfully and loyally, we frown upon the rebellious sons of South American Liberty," a newspaper jeered after the verdict. Another mocked the international pretensions underlying the government's efforts to punish Taylor: "It seems we are assuming a *legitimate* character," it taunted. "If we progress, we shall ... not long be 'the only exception to the family of nations.'" Sarcasm aside, the detractors protested that such "vexatious prosecutions" were unbecoming of a republic with its own proud tradition of resisting royalist despotism. "[W]e hope," one declared, "that the means will soon be found to put an end to them."[110]

The failed prosecutions were a bitter pill for the Monroe administration, and for John Quincy Adams in particular (Figure 6.3). In his diary, he vented his rage at everyone involved. He believed that some federal officers in Baltimore were fully in bed with privateers, like the postmaster John Skinner (who avoided conviction along with Taylor), as well as customs inspectors and the captain of the revenue cutter. Others were simply inept. Federal district attorney Elias Glenn was a "weak, incompetent man" who bungled the indictments against Taylor's cabal, and customs collector James McCulloch was blinded by enthusiasm for the South American cause. Even Wirt did not escape Adams's acerbic pen. Thanks to his inferior performance against Pinkney, Adams grumbled, the Attorney General made American taxpayers "pay him fifteen hundred dollars for losing the causes."[111]

FIGURE 6.3 The government's inability to secure criminal convictions against Baltimore privateers infuriated Secretary of State John Quincy Adams. Portrait by Chester Harding (1828), courtesy of the Diplomatic Reception Rooms, U.S. Department of State.

Adams reserved his greatest antipathy for the lawyers and judges who let Taylor go free. He was unmoved by the fact that the judges who presided at trial – including Supreme Court Justice Gabriel Duvall – received death threats during the proceedings. He castigated them as "feeble, inefficient" jurists who allowed Pinkney to dominate them. The problem was not simply a deficiency of judicial character. Rather than pursue "truth or justice," he complained, those trained in the law exalted an "artificial system" obsessed with technicalities. Pinkney was the prime example. His "browbeating" intimidated judges, but it was his "pettifogging law quibbles" that did the real damage, by eliding the plain meaning of statutes meant to put a stop to his clients' crimes.[112]

Adams was similarly disparaging of the Supreme Court's ruling in *Palmer* limiting federal jurisdiction over piracy. It was a "disingenuous, false, and hollow" decision, a cynical example of "judicial logic" that ignored the plain meaning of the statutory text. "[I]f human language means anything," Adams railed, Congress in 1790 intended to subject all pirates to the courts' jurisdiction. By casting away this authority, the Court had left "an enormous hole in the moral garment of this nation," one the Monroe administration would struggle to repair.[113]

Adams had good reason to be angry, because the government's inability to stop the Baltimore privateers threatened potentially grave consequences. Onís and Corrêa da Serra kept up their steady drumbeat of complaints. More ominously, Portugal persuaded the European allied monarchies – who were then meeting at Aix-la-Chapelle to discuss how to restore order after decades of war and revolution – to formally express their "displeasure and indignation" over the continuing South American depredations.[114]

Adams's chief concern was the treaty with Spain. In February 1819, he and Onís finally reached an agreement in which Spain formally ceded all of Florida, as well as land north of the 42nd parallel all the way to the Pacific Coast. In return, the treaty settled the Louisiana Purchase's disputed borders, and preserved Texas as Spanish territory. What brought Spain around was its fear that, without a treaty, it might lose everything. Andrew Jackson's violent 1818 military campaign against Indians and escaped slaves in the southeast demonstrated that Spain was powerless to stop the United States from taking Florida by force if it chose. At the same time, the European allies' refusal to aid Spain in reasserting control over its rebelling colonies persuaded it to solidify its increasingly tenuous hold in the Americas wherever it could. Adams exulted in the result; the day Onís signed the treaty, Adams recorded in his diary, was "perhaps the most important ... of my life."[115]

Adams's diplomatic triumph was short lived. The Senate ratified the treaty immediately, but Spain delayed, ostensibly due to a drafting error that left the status of certain Florida lands unresolved. But in fact Spain wanted to ensure that the United States continued withholding support from the South American republics. King Fernando and his advisors knew that the Monroe administration would have little reason to continue its cautious diplomacy vis-a-vis the rebel governments once the treaty was concluded. Spanish officials also remained angry over the "scandalous system of piracy" that persisted in the United States and the "decisions of the several Courts" permitting such conduct to continue. Uncertainty over the treaty's fate was the Spaniards' best leverage for prodding the administration into action against the rebels, and they were loath to give it up.[116]

Failure to secure the treaty was a serious blow to the Monroe administration's hopes for peace and security, both at home and abroad. Monroe thought that the treaty's favorable terms would quiet domestic critics of the administration's foreign policy, and lessen public agitation for recognition of the rebelling governments. But many were not placated, especially on the question of slavery. That long-simmering issue exploded into controversy just as Adams and Onís reached their agreement, over Missouri's admission to the union. Northerners who feared slavery's expansion were leery of acquiring Florida, while Southerners and Westerners were angry that the treaty did not secure more territory for its growth.[117]

The treaty's failure also threatened international repercussions. In the absence of an agreement, Adams thought that a "rupture" with Spain was inevitable. Europe's alliance structure meant that war with Spain would likely lead to conflict with Great Britain, and perhaps with other nations. As the twin controversies over slavery and territory dragged on, Monroe saw his dreams for post-war stability dashed. He lamented to Madison that, only a few years earlier, the successful outcome of the War of 1812 had given him hope that the young United States would "escape[] all the perilous trials to which it was inevitably exposed." That happy result was now looking increasingly unlikely.[118]

7

Policing the High Seas

On May 15, 1820, Joseph Story stared down at three defendants waiting to hear what punishment he would pronounce in their case. Two years earlier, the men had been sailors on a Baltimore privateer commissioned by the revolutionary government at Buenos Ayres to raid Spanish shipping. When the privateer seized a Spanish vessel "laden with a valuable cargo," the men were ordered to sail the prize to South America for condemnation and sale.[1]

Like many sailors who suddenly found themselves in possession of profitable maritime property, the men had other ideas. On the Fourth of July, they capped off a day of patriotic "pleasure and festivity" by throwing their sailing master and his mate overboard. The mate went easily, with only a few shrieks of terror that disappeared into the night. But the master managed to grab hold of a rope and hang overboard; it took the mutineers ten minutes to dislodge him, with the help of repeated stabbings from a homemade dagger. The men then set course for Massachusetts. They were apprehended soon after arrival, and, two years later, a jury in Story's federal circuit court in Boston convicted them of piracy.[2]

The men surely knew what Story's sentence would be. Their acts were a capital offense under federal law. The Supreme Court had affirmed their convictions two months earlier, along with those of dozens of other privateers with South American commissions. The men had immediately petitioned President James Monroe for a pardon, claiming that their sole purpose in brutally murdering their shipmates had been to restore the seized vessel to its rightful Spanish owners. If the president did not intervene, the petitioners exclaimed, their fate would be "to suffer *Death*!" But Monroe had yet to respond, leaving the mariners in a state of "awful suspense" as they shuffled into Story's court.[3]

Story was not inclined to be merciful to men who perpetrated such unwarranted violence on the high seas. "[S]carcely could there be a murder more foul, gross, and abominable in its circumstances," he declared. The defendants had received a full and fair hearing, with representation by two court-appointed lawyers, and the jury's verdict was fully justified by the evidence. Now that the nation's highest tribunal had rejected their appeal, all that remained was for Story to perform what he termed his "painful duty." He closed his lecture with a warning addressed to the defendants, but aimed at a broader audience: "You thought perhaps that crimes, like these, perpetrated in a distant sea ... could go unpunished." Yet the men had forgotten that the "Almighty Being ... from whom nothing is hidden," would "*assuredly* punish the guilty."[4]

Story's invocation of divine authority elided the role that more terrestrial powers played in bringing the Fourth of July privateers to justice. Their pending execution was the culmination of a campaign by all three branches of the federal government to use its full coercive power against seafarers who threatened the United States' peace and security. In the wake of the Monroe administration's failed efforts to prosecute privateer ringleaders (see Chapter 6), executive branch officials shifted their attention to ordinary seamen. At the same time, the Supreme Court abandoned its previously constrained interpretation of federal law, finding that the federal courts' jurisdiction was not limited to "offences against the United States." Instead, the courts were responsible for punishing "offences committed against all nations."[5]

The catalyst for this freshly expansive view of judicial power was a shift in how Americans thought about privateering, and about the revolutionary governments that sponsored it. By 1819, both elite and popular opinion about the South American privateers had begun to sour. Story himself questioned whether the defendants in his courtroom had any "legitimate national character," suspecting instead that they were simply robbers and murderers who hid their avarice behind the mask of republicanism. Politicians like Secretary of State

John Quincy Adams were convinced that the insurgent regimes to the south had neither the means nor the will to control the marauding they authorized. As doubts about privateers' moral and sovereign legitimacy grew, the executive branch, Congress, and the courts proclaimed ever more boldly the United States' prerogative to police the revolutionary Atlantic's roiled waters.[6]

The courts' assertion of legal and political authority over "pirates" presaged the increasingly expansive claims to hemispherical preeminence that Americans began articulating after the War of 1812. Visions of an imperial future had entranced Americans for decades (if not centuries). But the post-war period gave new momentum to the project of extending the nation, fueled by the economic power of bonded labor, the expropriation of territory inhabited by Native people, and a belief that the extension of "civilization" by white settlers across the North American continent was mandated by divine providence.[7]

Piracy prosecutions played a key role in articulating an imperial vision of American sovereignty. At a material level, the punishment of South American privateers helped secure Spain's acceptance of the Transcontinental Treaty, which paved the way for decades of territorial expansion in North America. Ideologically, the extension of federal criminal jurisdiction over anyone who disturbed the tranquility of the seas mirrored broad claims about the United States' hegemony over the continental interior. Even when federal judges denied their own power to discipline a different category of "pirates" – those who engaged in the slave trade – they did so in ways meant to uphold sovereign rights that Americans had been asserting since independence. If a nineteenth century American empire was ultimately realized on land, some of its first stirrings were at sea.

* * *

The Monroe administration's response to a deepening diplomatic crisis with Spain and Portugal over privateering was to double down on a strategy that had initially failed – criminal prosecutions in federal court. Without the threat of jail or the hangman's noose, noted Spanish minister Luis de Onís, privateers knew the only risk they faced in preying on Iberian commerce was being forced to give back the ships and cargo they captured. The Portuguese minister, José

Francisco Corrêa da Serra, made the same point, though less directly. Great Britain, he noted to Adams, had given Portugal "ample satisfaction" by putting several alleged pirates to death – unlike the United States.[8]

The stakes were incredibly high. Onís made clear that the federal government's failure to quash South American privateering would make it impossible for Spain to conclude the long-sought treaty meant to resolve the two nations' territorial disputes and open the west to American expansion. Corrêa da Serra's warnings were less specific, but no less alarming. He told Adams that resentment in Portugal over privateering was deepening by the day. Commercial retaliation against the United States was likely, and Corrêa da Serra reported that many Portuguese would welcome open war with the United States.[9]

The Monroe administration got the message. Prior to 1819, the only criminal cases it had initiated against privateers from Baltimore were the failed efforts against Thomas Taylor, Joseph Almeida, and a few of their associates. But, as Adams explained to Maryland district attorney Elias Glenn in March 1819, the nation's "Honor," as well as its "important interests," now depended on repressing the "enormous scandal" taking place in Baltimore. That year, the government charged 100 individuals with piracy, and it sought indictments against another 130 in 1820.[10]

The administration's renewed prosecutorial campaign represented a change in how American policymakers and the broader public conceived of the South American privateering problem. The administration's focus had initially been on privateer ringleaders like Taylor. According to Adams, securing convictions against the prime movers would do more good than executing "a whole navy of common sailors." In 1819, however, the government began prosecuting ordinary seamen in much greater numbers. As the failed Taylor prosecution demonstrated, the combination of high-priced legal representation, recalcitrant witnesses, and sympathetic juries enabled privateering leaders to escape punishment. In contrast, the government was often able to procure damning evidence against ordinary crew members by turning them against each other. And those defendants often did not have the financial means to protect themselves.[11]

The new wave of prosecutions also reflected deep doubts about the practice of privateering itself. Private commerce raiding in wartime had always had its critics, but the advent of peace in Europe in 1815 created new momentum for its abolition. Nations with powerful navies, like Great Britain, had little use for private armed vessels. At the same time, a transnational movement of policymakers, journalists, and intellectuals argued that the seizure of private property in wartime was incompatible with modern political, economic, and moral thought. European nations had given up the practice of pillaging in land wars (at least in theory). Why should a merchant trading goods between Cadiz and Veracruz be a legitimate target in war, when a farmer tilling his fields in the Loire Valley was not? It was unjust in both cases "to gather by violence the fruits of another's industry," according to leading American critic John Gallison, a young lawyer who studied with both Story and Adams (and who was the reporter of Story's circuit court decisions).[12]

A related critique was that commerce raiding interfered with free trade. Joseph Story may have pushed the Supreme Court to tolerate such interference in the name of national security during the War of 1812, but internationally the postwar trend was toward liberalization. The mercantilist dogma that had dominated European thinking for centuries was ceding ground to a transatlantic ideology that opposed barriers to commercial intercourse. Free traders were convinced that a larger economic pie was "in the interest of the world," as a petition signed by Gallison and Daniel Webster put it to Congress. Obstacles to trade – whether high tariffs or seizures by armed vessels – were anathema.[13]

Perhaps the greatest nineteenth-century concern with privateering was what Justice William Johnson described in 1821 as its "demoralizing influence." For religiously inspired reformers, privateering was one of many longstanding human habits, such as slave trading and corporal punishment, that were incompatible with a newly enlightened age. Like other vices, privateering endangered not only its victims' bodily well-being but also its perpetrators' character, especially that of the young and impressionable.[14]

Gallison and his fellow-critics believed that privateering encouraged seamen's worst instincts. They were already a suspect class, especially among middle-class reformers who watched with dismay as mariners drank, cursed, gambled, and brawled. Detractors viewed privateer ships as "schools of depravity and licentiousness," where budding scholars of immorality learned "the rudiments of piracy and murder." As the South American privateering controversy dragged on, these concerns pervaded Baltimore itself. In early 1820, a grand jury noted that privateersmen on shore leave committed many of the ordinary property and violent crimes the jury confronted. Baltimore mariners, the jurors lamented, had once stood at the "proud pinnacle of honor and glory." But thanks to the "demoralizing business of privateering," they were now nothing more than "culprits and criminals."[15]

Privateers who entered the service of foreign nations were especially suspect. Critics such as renowned jurist James Kent suspected that all privateers were motivated by "plunder and profit" rather than "chivalric warfare," but they reserved special opprobrium for those who sailed under commissions from other nations. Foreign mercenaries had long formed an integral part of early modern armies, but they came under increasing suspicion in the late eighteenth century, fueled by the nationalist ideology of the French Revolution. In a republic, citizens *were* the nation. So it stood to reason, as one French revolutionary leader put it, that not only "every citizen must be a soldier," but also "every soldier a citizen."[16]

Distrust of foreign fighters was also a staple of republican discourse in the United States. According to the Declaration of Independence, one of King George's chief crimes was the employment of Hessian mercenaries in defense of his tyranny. To be sure, Americans venerated European aristocrats who fought on their side in the Revolutionary War, like the Marquis de Lafayette, and foreigners also served heroically in French and South American republican armies. But those volunteers' service was legitimate precisely because they were fighting for liberty, not lucre. Those who fought for pay rather than principle were viewed with increasing distrust across the Atlantic world.[17]

John Quincy Adams believed that questionable allegiance was exactly the problem with the South American privateers. Adams was a recent convert to the anti-privateering cause. For most of his political career he had echoed the standard American view that privateers were an indispensable resource for a nation without a large navy – a "militia moving upon the water." But his views began to change after the War of 1812, and by the 1820s he deemed privateering "a relict of the barbarous warfare of barbarous ages."[18]

The catalyst for Adams's change of heart was his doubts about privateers' character and motives. He complained to friends that the armed vessels sailing from Baltimore were manned by "the sweepings of our streets," and the crimes they committed were nothing more than "robberies wearing the mask of patriotism."[19] Others agreed. An anonymous 1819 pamphleteer – possibly Corrêa da Serra, the Portuguese minister – argued that South American privateers masked their crimes under the "false and shallow pretence of aiding the cause of liberty." Even Thomas Jefferson concurred. Like many Americans, he generally supported the South American revolutionaries. But the "renegado rovers of several nations" who enlisted on their ships, he wrote to Corrêa da Serra in 1820, were simply "lawless banditti."[20]

The deeper problem with South American privateers was the revolutionary governments themselves. Not in the abstract – it was an article of faith in the United States that self-governance was the South Americans' right and destiny. But the uncertain status of many self-proclaimed polities was deeply vexing for policymakers who had to navigate between public enthusiasm for the rebels and Iberian anger at them. The nascent republics of the Western Hemisphere, Adams lamented to Justice William Johnson, "are Chinese Shadows; they rise upon the Stage, and pass off." This ephemeral character seemed to confirm longstanding doubts about the South Americans' capacity for self-government. According to Jefferson, centuries of monarchical and papal subjugation had left South Americans in "degrading ignorance." By the late 1810s, political instability on the southern continent looked more and more like a threat to the United States, as it left South Americans vulnerable to exploitation by both home-grown despots and rapacious foreign powers.[21]

What most troubled skeptics like Adams was the way that the fractured sovereignty of the Americas promoted a "piratical spirit" on the high seas. One immediate concern was the congeries of smugglers, freebooters, and slave traders that dotted the Gulf of Mexico and Caribbean. By 1819, the Monroe administration had already dealt with the most troublesome establishment, at Amelia Island off Florida's Atlantic coast. In 1817, a small contingent of would-be revolutionaries "liberated" the island from Spanish control. They were led first by Gregor MacGregor, a charismatic Scotsman who fought with revolutionary leader Simon Bolivar in Venezuela, and then by Louis-Michel Aury, another former Bolivar ally who had recently commanded a similar outpost on Galveston Island.[22]

Sitting on the ragged border between the crumbling Spanish empire and the nascent American one, Amelia Island was the perfect location for launching maritime attacks against Spanish commerce. It was also ideal for smuggling prize goods into Georgia, including the human cargo privateers took from Spanish slave ships. The introduction of captive Africans into the United States was a blatant violation of the 1808 federal law that prohibited the international slave trade. Many slaveholders welcomed the opportunity to acquire new laborers on an unregulated market, but others worried about the pernicious influence that "foreign" enslaved persons would have on their own bondspeople. Racial fears shaped the discourse around Amelia in other ways. Supporters of South American independence defended MacGregor and Aury in the press, but the latter's recruitment of black and mulatto fighters discomfited them. The same newspapers that praised Bolivar's multiracial army when it fought at a safe distance recoiled at the proximity to the United States of Aury's "sable followers."[23]

The Amelia adventurers were only the closest manifestation of the broader sovereignty problem that haunted the Monroe administration. Its desire to avoid taking sides in the rebellions demanded a hands-off approach to the South Americans' wartime conduct (at least when it did not violate federal law). But in an era when every "petty chief" purported to be an "independent sovereign," as Adams put it, too much solicitude for rebel claims to legitimacy encouraged plunder and robbery under the fig leaf of pretended authority. For example, Aury's connection to the government of the Mexican Republic was tenuous at best (and a questionable source of authority to govern territory in East Florida anyway). But when he assumed control over the Amelia encampment he drew up a constitution (modeled after the U.S. version), set up a lawmaking body, and even established a functioning prize court. This display of governmental legitimacy was not enough to prevent Monroe from sending naval ships to clear Aury's men out of Amelia in late 1817, but the larger problem of dubious sovereignty persisted.[24]

In Adams's view, the fragility of even the most established revolutionary governments allowed maritime violence to flourish. In theory, the Monroe administration accepted the validity of privateering commissions issued by the United Provinces of the Río de la Plata (commonly referred to as Buenos Ayres) or the Republic of Venezuela. It accorded similar respect to commissions from Jose Gervasio Artigas in the Banda Oriental (roughly modern-day Uruguay), despite his more tenuous grip on territory and political power.[25]

Adams, however, thought these governments too badly organized to control the bandits they unleashed. Their prize tribunals, he complained, were supposed to ensure that privateers followed the law. But such "sham courts" could neither "punish the guilty, nor make satisfaction to the injured."[26] He noted that Juan Bautista Arismendi, another Bolivar associate, set up a court on an island off Venezuela that willingly condemned prizes taken by any South American privateer, regardless of which flag it flew. Adams contrasted this laxity in administering the laws of war with the recent U.S. experience in the War of 1812, when the federal courts' watchfulness had helped prevent the sort of "horrible outrages" that now characterized South American privateering. If the revolutionary governments could not assert similar control, Adams ominously predicted, "privateers and pirates will be synonymous."[27]

The most damning evidence of privateering's descent into piracy was a series of mutinies in late 1818 and early 1819. Insurrection was always a threat on armed vessels, both naval and private. Living conditions for sailors were often miserable, and resentment over inadequate pay, food, drink, and shore leave fostered dissension. Moreover, sailing and maritime combat required tremendous discipline and coordination, which many commanders sought to instill in their crews through fear and domination. Corporal punishments were common, and sailors chafed under the rule of tyrannical officers.[28]

Mutinies were not always the product of oppressive working conditions. Lurid tales that appeared in American newspapers confirmed suspicions that South American privateers were only in it for the money (Figure 7.1). When the sailors on a Baltimore privateer got wind of possible forced enlistment in the Venezuelan navy, they mutinied against their officers, seized a different privateer by force, and then went to sea to plunder merchant vessels. The men of another privateer reportedly turned on their captain because he was "too mild and honest" in his treatment of potential prizes.[29]

FIGURE 7.1 Mutinies like the one depicted in this 1824 engraving turned public opinion in the United States against South American privateers. "Roche and His Associates Throwing the Master and Mate overboard," from Andrew Knapp and William Baldwin, *The Newgate Calendar; Comprising Interesting Memoirs of the Most Notorious Characters Who Have Been Convicted of Outrages on the Laws of England Since the Commencement of the Eighteenth Century* (London: J. Robins and Co., 1824)

Even when crew members had defensible reasons for overthrowing their officers, their subsequent conduct seemed to reveal their innate rapacity. The men of the Baltimore privateer *Louisa* turned their captain ashore when they grew tired of his abuse. But rather than sail for home, they proceeded to pillage neutral ships, and even raided a coastal settlement, killing several people in the process. Their leader justified their actions in terms that embraced the mutineers' piratical status while inverting its legal import: Any vessel they came across was a lawful prize, he told the crew, because they "were of no nation," and therefore were "at war with all."[30]

As stories of privateer lawlessness multiplied, so did public outrage in the United States. The complaints came not only from activists such as John Gallison or partisans like Corrêa da Serra. By one newspaper's February 1819 reckoning, Americans had witnessed more cases of piracy in the previous eighteen months than in the fifteen years prior. The turmoil in South America had unleashed "unprincipled cupidity" among the nation's seafaring population, as rebel leaders doled out commissions to "every desperate adventurer, who prefers robbery to honest labor." Baltimore, in particular, had allowed itself to become "the grand depot of a horde of pirates and robbers." Even supporters of the revolutionary governments joined the chorus. "We yield to no one in our devotion to the cause of liberty in South

America," proclaimed *Niles' Weekly Register* in April 1819. But the patriot cause was disgraced by the acts of "bad men" whose "sole purpose is plunder." This "shameful traffic," warned another paper, would turn the world against the revolutionary republics, and against the United States as well.[31]

Critics demanded that the federal government do more to quell the spreading violence, for the nation's honor and well-being were at stake. As foreign newspapers decried the "villainous heterogeneous mass of ocean highwaymen" preying on peaceful traders, insurance companies in New York and Norfolk warned the Monroe administration that unchecked depredations would have dire consequences for American commerce. A Baltimore grand jury urged the administration to take action and spare the nation from "obloquy and reproach."[32]

Some doubted whether the Monroe administration was up to the task of suppressing privateering. A June 1819 newspaper letter to the editor noted the president's absence from Washington to visit southern and western states, where he was hoping to rekindle the "good feelings" generated by his 1817 northern tour. It would be just as good for the country, the writer drily suggested, if the president devoted his attention instead to the "faithful execution" of the law. A Baltimore newspaper was less sanguine about the benefit of government intervention. The cabinet was riddled with "apathy," and Congress was afflicted by "paralysis." In such a state, "the Deity alone" could save the country from disgrace.[33]

* * *

Judicial intervention, not divine, is what ultimately enabled the federal government to impose its will on those who perpetrated violence in the name of liberty. The executive branch's prosecutorial campaign resulted in a windfall of piracy convictions in the federal circuit courts. Acquittals were still common, especially for seamen who plausibly claimed to have been tricked or coerced into committing violent acts. But public opinion had turned, and juries had little difficulty condemning privateers who mutinied against their officers and plundered merchant vessels indiscriminately. By early 1820, dozens of mariners, including the defendants in Joseph Story's circuit court, faced the gallows.[34]

A serious obstacle remained to the government's assertion of authority at sea: It was unclear whether the federal courts actually had jurisdiction to punish privateers' violent acts. In 1818, the Supreme Court ruled in *United States v. Palmer* that the courts' jurisdiction did not extend to piratical acts committed by persons sailing *on* foreign vessels *against* foreign vessels (see Chapter 6). As Chief Justice Marshall put it, Congress's intent in the Crimes Act of 1790 was to punish only "offences against the United States," not "offences against the human race." That limitation was a serious problem for convicting the new crop of defendants in federal court, who had raided foreign ships (Spanish, Portuguese, and neutral) from on board privateer vessels that were formally South American (even if fitted out in Baltimore).[35]

Federal judges presiding over piracy trials recognized the difficulty the *Palmer* ruling presented. They allowed juries to hear evidence and render verdicts against the defendants, but then used the certificate of division to send the legal question of jurisdiction to the Supreme Court. By its February 1820 term, the Court had six piracy cases involving South American privateers on its docket. If the Court adhered to its narrow ruling in *Palmer*, scores of defendants would go free.[36]

Unlike before, the Court in 1820 did not let privateers go unpunished. It abandoned the restricted reading of federal law it had articulated earlier, and embraced a strikingly broad conception of judicial authority over maritime violence. The Court did not overrule *Palmer* directly. Instead, it created an exception that effectively swallowed the rule.

Unsurprisingly, it was Joseph Story who found the key that unlocked more expansive federal jurisdiction. At the circuit court trial of the Fourth of July privateers in Boston, Justice Story confronted the fact that the murder occurred on a Spanish-owned ship that had been captured by a Buenos Ayres privateer, which would mean no jurisdiction under *Palmer*. But Story was able to finesse the problem by invoking the trope that pirates were social outcasts lacking any national affiliation. In Story's view, at the time of the murders the captured prize ship was not Spanish at all, because it was in the possession of "pirates." As a result, the ship actually had "no national character," and *Palmer*'s prohibition against federal court jurisdiction over "foreign" ships did not apply.[37]

When the issue reached the full Court, Story's colleagues expanded his statelessness theory of jurisdiction to include virtually every South American privateer. Even when a foreign-owned ship was not yet in the privateers' possession, argued Attorney General William Wirt in 1820, the courts could consider the privateer vessels *themselves* to be the locus of the crime. And *they* did not belong to any particular sovereign, because pirates were "outcasts from the society of nations." The Court agreed. It conceded that, following *Palmer*, the Crimes Act of 1790 prohibited the courts from trying crimes that fell exclusively within a foreign nation's authority. But the act did not deny jurisdiction over offenses committed by persons acknowledging obedience "to no government whatever." Such persons, Chief Justice Marshall reasoned, were proper objects "for the penal code of all nations," including the United States.[38]

Using pirates' outlaw status to extend jurisdiction over foreign vessels and persons plugged the hole *Palmer* had created, but it left a critical question unanswered: What kinds of acts transformed privateers into stateless "pirates" subject to the authority of all? This question had long bedeviled international jurists, and the justices did not attempt to catalog all the conduct that would exile a privateer from the community of nations. Instead, they focused on the absence of authority justifying privateer seizures.

The idea that a privateer who lacked valid sovereign authorization was equivalent to a pirate had roots dating back at least to Gentili in the sixteenth century. Justice Story took up this idea in condemning the Fourth of July mutineers. He echoed John Quincy Adams's skepticism about privateers' national affiliations by doubting whether the privateer ship the Boston defendants sailed in was *really* from Buenos Ayres. No one could produce a valid commission, and no one involved seemed to have any connection to Buenos Ayres at all. Absent any evidence that the defendants had a "legitimate national character," the only sensible conclusion was that they were simply pirates.[39]

Before the full Court, Story's misgivings about the Boston defendants metastasized into doubts about the sovereign legitimacy of the South American republics more generally. In one 1820 case, Marshall did not ask whether the defendant actually had a commission from Louis Aury, who styled himself as "Brigadier of the Mexican Republic and Generalissimo of the Floridas." Instead, the Chief Justice doubted whether there was such a government at all. Florida, Marshall noted, was formally a Spanish province (even if Spain could barely administer it). And Mexico was "a republic of whose existence we know nothing." This was not literally true; the long-running insurgency in Mexico received less attention in the United States than the South American contests, but the public was well aware of it. What Marshall *meant* was that the Mexican Republic was not truly a sovereign nation, and therefore had no power to issue commissions. Anyone who sailed under such illegitimate authority was therefore a pirate.[40]

Marshall's equation of unrecognized sovereignty with piracy was more radical than it might have seemed. Historically, privateers risked condemnation as pirates when they exceeded the scope of their commissions, or when they had no valid license at all. Doubts about the issuing government's legitimacy were typically not grounds for conviction. For example, during the American Revolution, the British government rhetorically condemned American privateers as "pirates." But it did not actually prosecute any on the ground that the Continental Congress lacked sovereign authority to issue commissions.[41]

Marshal was a veteran of the Revolutionary War and an experienced diplomat, so he surely knew this history. If he did not, a defense attorney in his circuit court made the analogy explicit. If the self-proclaimed independent states of North America had authority to issue privateering commissions in 1776, then so did the self-proclaimed independent states of South America four decades later. But Marshall was not persuaded that the emergent republics were worthy of judicial recognition. And, unlike British officials during the Revolutionary War, he was prepared to punish the exercise of pretended authority with criminal sanctions.[42]

For the justices, extending their criminal jurisdiction to privateers with questionable legitimacy was not enough. That would allow those sailing with commissions from undoubtedly legitimate governments – Buenos Ayres, for example – to escape punishment in federal court no matter how heinous their conduct. In a subsequent 1820 case, the Court clarified that even a privateer holding "the most unquestionable commission" could be subject to prosecution for piracy under the Crimes Act of 1790 "when embarked on a piratical cruize."[43]

Again, the justices did not bother to specify what kinds of conduct rendered an otherwise-lawful privateering expedition "piratical." The defendants in the case at bar were mutineers accused of murdering innocent victims, so perhaps that was an easy case. But Marshall hinted at a broader understanding of the courts' jurisdiction. Seizure of maritime property with the goal of personal enrichment, known as *animo furandi*, was not an act of war, regardless of any national authority the captor claimed. It was simply piracy, and punishable in the courts of the United States.[44]

The Court's invocation of familiar terms of international law, like *animo furandi*, again masked the radicalism of its approach. Historically, a valid privateering commission shielded the bearer from piracy charges, even when he committed unjustified violence. The commissioning government, not the community of nations, was responsible for punishing wrongful conduct by a licensed privateer. This was not a controversial view; Story's protégé Henry Wheaton would later affirm it in his celebrated international law treatise. Jurists and publicists debated whether piracy *required* an intent to steal, but no one argued that pecuniary motivation *alone* made a sea raider a pirate. Indeed, given the continued prevalence of commerce raiding as a key facet of maritime war in the early nineteenth century, the idea was borderline nonsensical. At best, Marshall's suggestion that a court could disentangle a privateer's financial motives from his political and military ones – and punish only the former – seemed highly aspirational (if not disingenuous).[45]

At bottom, the Court's 1820 rulings reflected the same suspicions of South American privateers that animated the Monroe administration's prosecutions. Even if privateers had valid commissions from established revolutionary governments, they seemingly did not take up arms for liberty or patriotism. All they cared about was plunder. Justice Johnson made the point explicit in an 1821 opinion. The case had nothing to do with the South American revolutions, and privateers' moral failings were irrelevant to the legal issues. But Johnson made his disgust known anyway. Privateering attracted a particular "race of men" who sought only "a legal pretext" for satisfying their "appetite for blood and violence." The United States was now experiencing the "baneful effects" that inevitably resulted from "letting loose the passions of men to gratify themselves with plunder," and the time for privateering's eradication had come.[46]

The 1820 decisions also made clear the justices' embrace of a far more assertive role in policing the maritime violence that revolution had unleashed. Only two years earlier, in *Palmer*, Chief Justice Marshall concluded that Congress's intent in the Crimes Act of 1790 was to limit the courts' jurisdiction to "offences against the United States." But now the Court had "reconsidered" the question, as Marshall put it, and discovered that Congress had in fact granted the courts plenary authority over "offences committed against all nations." The Court's newly expansive interpretation of the courts' jurisdiction over piracy contrasted with its more constrained reading of the same statute in dealing with other maritime offenses, even fatal ones. In contemporaneous cases, the Court ruled that the federal judiciary did not have jurisdiction over an American citizen who murdered a cook on board a U.S. naval vessel anchored in Boston harbor, or one who killed a sailor on an American ship floating on a Chinese river. But South American privateers were subject to federal judicial authority wherever they were found.[47]

The Court's assertion of universal jurisdiction over South American privateers was in many ways unprecedented. European sovereigns had long used accusations of piracy as justification for bringing state power to bear against those who engaged in disfavored violence at sea. In practice, however, states rarely punished attacks on the subjects and property of other sovereigns. As Adams conceded only a few years later, piracies *could* be punished "by the courts of any country," but they were usually tried "by those of the country whose vessels have been the sufferers." In addition, by treating commissioned privateers as pirates, the Court denied the sovereign legitimacy of governments claiming the same right to self-determination that Americans had advanced more than four decades earlier. The Court was not explicit about what caused this change of heart, but its hints left little doubt. If the ephemeral republics to the south were incapable of controlling the bandits they licensed, then the United States – and its courts – would have to do so itself.[48]

The radicalism of the Court's 1820 decisions notwithstanding, in one sense Marshall was correct – Congress *had* given the federal courts broad power to police maritime violence. But not in the Crimes Act of 1790. In March 1819, Congress responded to the Supreme Court's earlier, constrained reading of the Crimes Act with a short statute that rewrote the federal law of piracy. The new law came too late to apply to crimes that occurred before its passage, but it heralded an even more expansive understanding of judicial authority over revolutionary privateers going forward.[49]

The 1819 act was remarkably concise. It eschewed the complicated formulations of prior law that had confounded the courts. The Crimes Act of 1790 defined piracy, in part, as any "murder or robbery," or any other crime that was punishable by death under federal law, when committed on "the high seas, or in any river, haven, basin or bay, out of the jurisdiction of any particular state" – a formulation that had caused confusion among judges about precisely what conduct was within its scope. The Piracy Act of 1819 did not mention murder or robbery, the high seas or rivers, or define as piracy specific mutinous conduct like running away with a ship or using violence against a captain. The new law simply said this: Anyone who committed "the crime of piracy, as defined by the law nations," was punishable by death in federal court.[50]

Congress's textual parsimony was a sharp departure from past practice, but it made sense. Only a week before the piracy bill was introduced, an effort to ban slavery in the would-be state of Missouri touched off a furious debate between proponents and opponents of expanding human bondage into the western territories. According to President Monroe, the slavery dispute "completely absorbed" Congress until the Missouri Compromise of 1820 resolved the issue (at least temporarily). Amid this crisis, the piracy legislation received little attention. The bill passed both houses only eight days after introduction, with minimal amendment and no recorded debate.[51]

Importing the law of nations definition of piracy into a federal statute spared preoccupied legislators the trouble of defining the crime themselves. And who better to determine what constituted piracy under international law than federal judges? Not everyone agreed; *Niles' Weekly Register* editorialized that it was improper for the nation's elected representatives to slough off their lawmaking duties "to judges and juries." But, just like in the 1790s and the War of 1812, Congress showed little hesitation in empowering judges to define the limits of their own authority over the seas.[52]

Congress's eagerness to defer to the judiciary on international issues stood in sharp contrast to the political storm gathering over the Supreme Court's rulings on domestic matters. Trouble started brewing in 1816, when the Court's declaration in *Martin v. Hunter's Lessee* that it could review state court decisions on questions of federal law angered states' rights advocates. The Court's problems deepened in 1819, only three days after Congress passed the Piracy Act. In *McCulloch v. Maryland*, the Court upheld the constitutionality of the congressionally chartered Bank of the United States.[53]

The Court's endorsement of broad federal power under the Constitution's Necessary and Proper Clause sparked a firestorm of controversy. The ruling came under immediate attack from states-righters, especially in Virginia, who denounced the *McCulloch* opinion as an assault on state sovereignty. They also castigated the courts – and the Supreme Court in particular – for anointing themselves as the supreme arbiter of constitutional meaning. The rhetorical assault was deeply unnerving for the justices. Chief Justice Marshall was so alarmed that he uncharacteristically entered the political fray with a series of public essays defending *McCulloch*, the Court, and his vision of the Constitution. But the critics persisted, egged on by Thomas Jefferson, who nursed his grievances against the federal judiciary (and Marshall personally) deep into retirement.[54]

The antipathy inspired by the Court's rulings on the scope of federal power at home, however, did nothing to shake the political branches' confidence in the judiciary when it came to delineating that power abroad. Just as the Virginia critics were publishing their first attacks, Iberian representatives expressed their doubt that a one-sentence statute sufficiently demonstrated the United States' commitment to bringing maritime criminals to justice. The act's definition of "piracy" was woefully short on specifics, Spanish minister Onís pointed out, especially on the question that mattered the most to his sovereign: Did the statute apply to seizures made by privateers with commissions from rebelling South American governments? Portuguese minister Corrêa da Serra was of a similar mind. Only a presidential declaration that Artigas's privateers were pirates under the 1819 act would put a stop to their depredations.[55]

Adams refused to take the bait. "The question, what aggression will in any individual case be deemed piratical is, by the nature of our Institutions, to be determined by the Judicial Department of the Government." This was particularly true, Adams said, with respect to disputes over the validity of privateering commissions issued by revolutionary governments. The new Piracy Act itself said nothing on that score, confirming that Congress wanted to leave thorny questions implicating the rights of foreign nations, as Adams put it, "strictly within the Province of the Tribunals."[56]

Before the courts could exercise the power granted them under the Piracy Act, however, they had to figure out whether the legislature was allowed to give it to them. The Constitution's text suggested not. Article One, Section Eight gave Congress, not the courts, authority to "define and punish" piracies and other felonies committed on the high seas. As Daniel Webster argued in defending a privateer in 1820, the framers would not have given Congress the power to "define" piracy if they thought the law of nations already did so. Webster also echoed the earlier critique in *Niles' Weekly Register*, contending that Congress could not abdicate its constitutional responsibility and leave the law's content "to be ascertained by judicial interpretation." Justice Brockholst Livingston agreed, on humanitarian grounds. The legislature had a moral obligation to define piracy with sufficient precision to warn seafarers whether their conduct might cost them their lives.[57]

Even John Marshall was unsure whether the Piracy Act was constitutional. A few months after its passage, he presided over a trial at Richmond that involved, in Marshall's words, "as notorious [a] piracy as ever occurred." But the ambiguities of international law troubled him. All nations punished high-seas robberies, he confided to Justice Bushrod Washington, but only as a matter of their own domestic law. Marshall was not persuaded that "there is any such thing as Piracy as 'defined by the law of nations.'" He was so uncertain that he urged the Richmond jury to render a special verdict that decided the facts but left the legal issue open. He and his district court colleague then certified the question to the Supreme Court for resolution.[58]

Joseph Story had no doubts about whether the Constitution allowed the courts to figure out what it meant to be a pirate. When the question came before the full Court in February 1820, he brushed aside any concerns about the judiciary's fitness for the task.

"[T]here is scarcely a writer on the law of nations," Story proclaimed, "who does not allude to piracy as a crime of settled and determinate nature." To prove his point – and perhaps to flaunt his superior learning – Story compiled an eighteen-page footnote citing dozens of definitions of piracy from law of nations publicists. Given this international authority, Story asserted, the interpretive task the Piracy Act of 1819 assigned to judges was no different than the one required by the Crimes Act of 1790. Just as the latter obliged the Court to determine what constituted "murder" or "robbery," the former simply necessitated an investigation of what acts constituted "piracy" under the law of nations. And that, of course, was the judicial function *par excellence*.[59]

Story also believed that the answer to the constitutional question resolved any doubts about the extent of the courts' jurisdiction. It was the practice of all nations, Story declared, to punish those who committed piratical offenses, everywhere and against anyone. In other words, the courts' jurisdiction over pirates under the 1819 act was universal. And there could be no doubt that the privateer defendants in the particular case before the Court *were* pirates. They had initially sailed under a valid Buenos Ayres commission, but had mutinied against their officers and then plundered a merchant ship. In Story's view, they were simply "freebooters upon the sea," not under the supervision of any "acknowledged authority." If their acts did not constitute piracy, it was hard to imagine what kind of maritime conduct would.[60]

As in the War of 1812 (see Chapter 5), Story's expansive understanding of the federal courts' authority over the seas carried the day. Livingston dissented – a rarity for him – but Marshall kept his doubts about the Piracy Act private. Perhaps Story's overwhelming erudition convinced the Chief Justice that the law of nations really did define "piracy" with sufficient precision to pass constitutional muster. Or maybe the challenge of controlling maritime violence again prompted Marshall to "reconsider" his earlier, narrower understanding of the courts' jurisdiction. Whatever the reason for Marshall's silence, the result was the same: Those who committed crimes while acting under supposed South American authority were subject to the full power the federal government could bring to bear against them.[61]

* * *

The Supreme Court's embrace of broad jurisdiction over privateers was a mixed blessing for the Monroe administration. Having broadly re-interpreted the Crimes Act of 1790 and upheld the Piracy Act of 1819, the Court affirmed all the piracy convictions it considered at its February 1820 term. By June of that year, the lower courts had sentenced fifty-four privateers to death for their crimes. Compared with the government's complete inability to secure convictions in previous years, the fact that dozens of seamen were now facing the gallows was a victory, of sorts. The condemned did not include any of the sponsors or organizers of Baltimore privateering, and Adams regretted that the hand of federal justice fell more heavily on its "mere instruments." But punishing ordinary seamen for their rapacious behavior was better than not punishing anyone at all.[62]

Putting convicted pirates to death offered the government a new opportunity to enhance the United States' standing both at home and abroad. Newspaper editors extolled the "salutary effect" executions would have on the villainous and misled, and warned that failure to demonstrate "a firm and unwavering resolution" toward convicted pirates would only embolden those who threatened the security of the high seas. The Monroe administration agreed; as the president explained to Congress in May 1820, public hangings served as "severe examples" to seafarers about the consequences of lawbreaking. The audience was international as well as domestic. Executions, according to Adams, offered "justice" to privateers' victims. Most of all, they reassured foreign governments that the United States had both the will and the means to punish those who endangered maritime peace.[63]

The raft of piracy convictions also presented the Monroe administration with a challenge. Executions in the United States – like everywhere else – were mass events, attended by thousands who came to hear addresses from ministers and magistrates, not to mention the last words of the condemned. The theme of these rituals was the preservation of social order. Criminals who broke the law threatened societal stability – an especially grave concern in a republic whose very survival depended on civic virtue in its citizenry. Yet for all their popularity, public executions were increasingly criticized in the early nineteenth century. Americans who associated sanguinary punishments with monarchical oppression questioned whether the death penalty was compatible with republican government. Some saw public executions as festivals of moral disorder that only served to brutalize the populace and desensitize them to violence. By the 1820s, Americans had begun to shun hangings altogether.[64]

The administration also had to contend with public sympathy for condemned privateers. Despite growing outrage over their conduct, many of the condemned sailors enjoyed support from prominent citizens in their home communities, who attested to the convicts' good character and their families' reputations. Friendly newspapers published extensive justifications for the defendants' behavior, and excoriated the executive branch for threatening to take their lives. Cabinet officials harbored their own sympathies. Monroe believed the government needed only to execute a few seamen to secure the "full benefit of example." Both "policy" and "humanity" counseled in favor of sparing the rest.[65]

The Monroe administration navigated the fine line between firmness and tyranny by reaching for a venerable tool of executive authority – the pardon. The cabinet decided that ten of the convicted privateers would be executed, two each in Baltimore, Charleston, New Orleans, Richmond, and Savannah. These were the places most in need of public displays of government retribution, in order to "arrest this hideous crime of piracy." The most culpable would die, and the rest would be spared, by presidential decree.[66]

The pardon power had long been a powerful instrument for promoting government legitimacy. Early modern criminal codes were rife with capital offenses for conduct that few believed warranted death, and royal officials made extensive use of pardons and commutations to soften the law's sharp edges. American presidents followed suit. Congress included relatively few capital offenses in the Crimes Act of 1790, but the death penalty remained for piracy. Maritime violence was often difficult to detect and prosecute, so meaningful deterrence required the threat of severe punishment for anyone unlucky enough to be caught. As Alexander Hamilton explained in *The Federalist*, the pardon power enabled the government to enforce the law without appearing "too sanguinary and cruel."[67]

Pardoning was not simply a matter of individual compassion. Hamilton recognized the political value of well-timed pardons, which could defuse anger over punishments meted out to "insurgents or rebels" who enjoyed public support. And pardons were as much a display of government authority as the executions they prevented. The power to spare a life, after all, was as awesome as the power to end one.[68]

The decision to pardon most of the convicted South American privateers created a new problem for the Monroe administration – figuring out whom to excuse, and whom to execute. The executive branch did not make these decisions in a vacuum. The condemned inundated the president with petitions seeking clemency. Some pleaded actual innocence, claiming that former accomplices had borne false witness to secure their own release (a plausible argument, given the government's frequent use of testimony from fellow crew members).[69] Others conceded their factual guilt, but claimed to be morally blameless, having been tricked into enlisting on a privateer or pressured into joining a mutiny. Still others pleaded their youth, poverty, or their good conduct in jail as mitigating factors. Some of the condemned were supported by petitions with thousands of signatures, including one that was purportedly signed by nearly "every female individual in the city of Richmond."[70]

It fell to John Quincy Adams, as Secretary of State, to sift through the claims to mercy and determine which were the most justified. He approached the task with his characteristic lack of sentimentality. While the more affecting petitions caused Monroe to fret over taking the "life of an individual," Adams was clear-eyed (or perhaps coldhearted). He scoffed at the privateers' "deathbed repentances." They might be good for the petitioners' immortal souls, Adams noted, but they were not reliable evidence for making the difficult decisions of statecraft.[71]

To distinguish the merely wayward from the irredeemably piratical, the Monroe administration again turned to federal judges. This was not an innovation, as presidents had always sought judicial advice on pardons. In an era before verbatim transcripts, the judges who presided over the trial of the condemned acted as the federal government's eyes and ears in the courtroom. From their perch, they were best able to assess, in Thomas Jefferson's words, "the degree of the crime, & character and deportment of the criminal." Judges also indicated which defendants the jury had recommended for clemency, serving as a conduit through which the public's views of the defendants' blameworthiness were transmitted to Washington.[72]

In 1820, the judges' input effectively decided the condemned privateers' fates. Adams had a dim view of Justice Gabriel Duvall's abilities, especially in privateering matters (see Chapter 6). Nevertheless, Duvall's opinion that two seamen convicted in Baltimore had misrepresented the facts of their case sent them to the gallows, despite a petition bearing thousands of signatures pleading for mercy.[73] In contrast, Justice William Johnson's recommendations for clemency in Charleston and Savannah resulted in pardons for the defendants he identified. The judges expected their views to carry weight; Johnson felt free to recommend pardon for two defendants in South Carolina without being asked. Even when the judges could not decide, their views prevailed. Chief Justice Marshall struggled to differentiate the prisoners at Richmond, so Monroe simply reprieved them all (Figure 7.2).[74]

The only judicial recommendation the administration did not follow was from Maryland District Judge Theodorick Bland. Perhaps it was because of persistent rumors of Bland's personal involvement with privateering. Or maybe it was simply because, as Adams explained, Baltimore was "where the necessity of making an example was the most urgent."[75]

The Monroe administration's deference to the judiciary proved fatal for the Fourth of July murderers facing Justice Story's wrath in Boston. Their court-appointed attorney, James Austin, was a well-respected lawyer, son-in-law to former Vice-President Elbridge Gerry and the future Attorney General of Massachusetts. Austin showed no hesitation in peppering cabinet officers with petitions and letters on his clients' behalf.[76]

The Boston privateers did not emphasize mitigating circumstances in order to inspire the president's "compassion." Instead, they wanted "justice," for they believed the federal courts did not have jurisdiction over them in the first place. They had originally sailed with a valid Buenos Ayres commission. In their view, that meant that only the government of the United Provinces could punish their alleged wrongdoing. Austin claimed he had not been able to produce the commission at trial because of the defendants' lack of "money, activity and

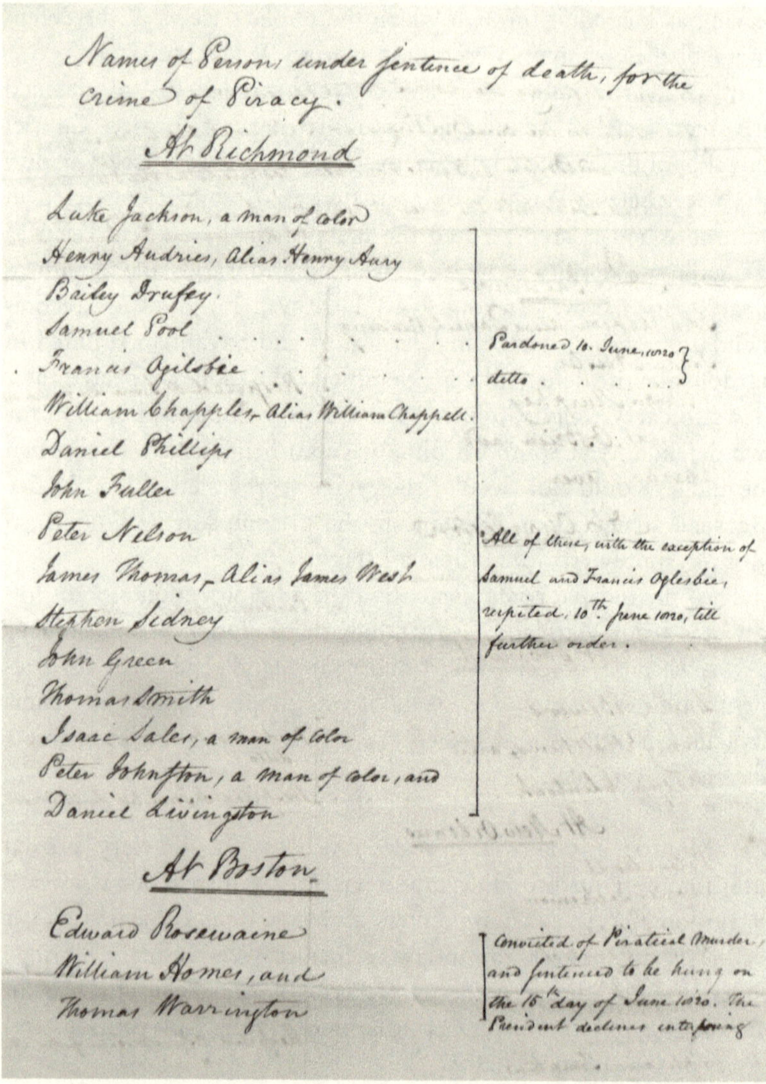
Names of Persons under sentence of death, for the crime of Piracy.

At Richmond

Luke Jackson, a man of color
Henry Audries, alias Henry Auxy
Bailey Drufey
Samuel Pool . . . . Pardoned 10. June, 1820
Francis Ogilsbie . . . . ditto
William Chappler, alias William Chappell.
Daniel Phillips
John Faller
Peter Nelson
James Thomas, alias James West
Stephen Sidney
John Green
Thomas Smith
Isaac Sales, a man of color
Peter Johnston, a man of color, and
Daniel Livingston

All of these, with the exception of Samuel and Francis Oglesbie, respited, 10th. June 1820, till further order.

At Boston

Edward Rosewaine
William Homes, and
Thomas Warrington

Convicted of Piratical Murder, and sentenced to be hung on the 15th day of June 1820. The President declines interposing

FIGURE 7.2 In deciding which South American privateers to pardon, the Monroe administration relied heavily on the views of the federal judges who presided over the trials, including Joseph Story (for Boston) and John Marshall (for Richmond). Courtesy of the National Archives and Records Administration

influence." He had submitted other evidence of the privateers' national character, but Story peremptorily rejected it for "informality," and instructed the jury to ignore it.[77]

Austin's critique of Story's conduct was bold for a Massachusetts lawyer, but it did not shake the administration's faith in the courts. Monroe was hesitant to take the men's lives if there was any doubt about their guilt, so he sought Wirt's opinion. But the Attorney General was not inclined to question Story's judgment. Wirt agreed that, in theory, a crime committed by bona fide Buenos Ayrean privateers, even a heinous murder, was not within the federal courts' jurisdiction. But the defendants had failed to establish the legitimacy of their privateering commission at trial, and now Austin was attempting to relitigate the case before the president, under a new and untested set of facts. The pardon power was formidable; it could erase criminal convictions authorized by law. Wirt was adamant, however, that it did not empower the president to revisit legal questions that had been "solemnly decided" by a court.[78]

With Story's sentence reaffirmed by the executive branch, all that remained was to put the Boston prisoners to death. Responsibility fell to the federal marshal, James Prince, who arranged the execution ceremony to ensure a "solemn and sympathizing feeling" among the many spectators. On June 15, 1820, Boston church bells tolled as the condemned made their way from jail to the scaffold, accompanied by clergy and reportedly "resigned to their doom." Prince read the death warrant signed by the president, and then addressed the assembled crowd. He acknowledged that his task was a heavy one – to secure the pirates' atonement "on the altar of publick justice." It was an especially weighty burden for Prince, as he had tried and failed to secure a pardon for one of the defendants. But as the "organ of the nation," as Prince put it, he could not shrink from his duty to ensure the safety of the seas.[79]

At twenty minutes to twelve, the machinery of federal justice sent the prisoners to their fate. Edward Rosewaine and William Holmes expired quickly. But Thomas Warrington was a large man, and needed two ropes around his neck. He struggled against them for some time, and died "a hard death." Privateering's critics were pleased nonetheless. According to a Rhode Island newspaper, the executions demonstrated that those who put the nation's peace at risk could not escape "the vigilant justice of the government."[80]

The bells that accompanied the Boston pirates to the gallows also heralded a new era of American sovereignty. A few months after the executions, Spain finally agreed to the treaty that Adams had spent years negotiating. The "Baltimore pirates" had not been the only reason for the Spanish holdout, but the criminal punishments doled out by federal judges were instrumental in securing Spain's agreement. According to Monroe, they "place[d] the conduct of the U States ... on ground which cannot be assailed." That same year, the administration secured a permanent extension of the Piracy Act of 1819 and a ban on foreign armed vessels entering most U.S. ports. Criminal indictments for piracy and civil suits by claimants seeking to recover seized ships and cargo soon dried up. Iberian officials occasionally grumbled about vessels being prepared for service to South American governments, but by 1822 the threat that privateering posed to U.S. foreign relations was effectively over.[81]

The resulting Transcontinental Treaty transformed the North American continent. Spain ceded Florida to the United States, opening new lands for American agricultural expansion and the bonded labor that made it possible, as well as eliminating any protection that Spain had offered to Native people there. The treaty also settled the long-disputed borders of the Louisiana Territory and extinguished Spanish claims to Oregon, clearing the way for westward expansion to the Pacific Ocean (Figure 7.3).[82]

The treaty did not create a continental empire on its own. The Monroe administration abandoned claims to Texas, which meant that acquiring that territory would necessitate a bloody war against independent Mexico two decades later. Asserting sovereignty over the continental interior also required more than a century of conflicts of eradication against Native people. But the treaty's conclusion was a critical moment in transforming the United States from a republic "bounded by the Mississippi," as Adams put it in his 1825 presidential inaugural address, to an empire that "extended from sea to sea."[83]

The suppression of South American privateering also enhanced the United States' international standing in less tangible ways. With the Transcontinental Treaty ratified, the Monroe administration could press ahead with recognition of the South American rebel governments. Doing so bound them more closely to their northern sibling, and counteracted the European influence in the region. In 1822, the United States recognized Chile, the United Provinces of the Río de la

FIGURE 7.3 This 1833 map symbolizes how ratification of the Transcontinental Treaty strengthened the United States' control over significant portions of North American territory (including Florida in the eagle's talons), paving the way for eventual expansion to the Pacific coast. "The eagle map of the United States" (1833), courtesy of the Library of Congress

Plata, Peru, Gran Colombia, and Mexico, with other nations soon to follow. By 1825, Spain conceded that most of its former colonies were now independent.[84]

Recognition of the revolutionary governments was a key moment for the United States. In his now-famous December 1823 message to Congress, Monroe warned European powers that the republics of the Americas, having obtained their independence by force of arms, "are henceforth not to be considered as subjects for future colonization by any European powers." Foreign attempts to "oppress" the emerging South American nations or to "control their destiny" were evidence of an "unfriendly disposition."[85]

The Monroe Doctrine (as it was later called) was not the unequivocal "diplomatic declaration of independence" that historians have deemed it, let alone the assertion of "manifest destiny" that later generations of empire-builders ascribed to it. But Monroe's implication was unmistakable. If the new polities of the Americas were outside European control, the influence of the hemisphere's most prosperous and powerful republic – the United States – would necessarily grow.[86]

* * *

There was one group of "pirates" that American sovereignty-builders were less eager to bring to justice – those who trafficked in human beings. In June 1820, two weeks after the hanging of the Boston privateers, a U.S. revenue cutter found the Spanish ship *Antelope* hovering off the Florida coast with nearly three hundred African captives on board. A South American privateer had taken the Africans from several Spanish and Portuguese slaving vessels, hoping to sell them in a friendly port. The revenue cutter brought the *Antelope* to Savannah, and the cutter's captain filed suit seeking compensation under federal law for recovery of the putative human property on board. Nearly a year later, a U.S. naval vessel seized a French-flagged vessel, *La Jeune Eugenie*, off the West African coast. There were no captives on board this ship, but the chains and manacles found lying below decks made its purpose obvious. Suspecting American ownership, the U.S. commander filed suit in Boston seeking condemnation.[87]

One might think that the Monroe administration would have welcomed these new opportunities to assert the United States' authority over those who sowed violence and disorder at sea. Both ships had allegedly violated federal law prohibiting American involvement in the international slave trade. And there was growing political support in the United States for treating slave traders as harshly as South American privateers. Up to 1820, federal law prescribed only prison terms for traders. But in May of that year Congress passed a new statute declaring that anyone involved in slave trading would be "adjudged a pirate," and put to death. A congressional committee declared that kidnapping innocent foreigners and transporting them across the Atlantic did not "differ[] in malignity from piracy." Slave traders were therefore "*hostes humani generis*" – the enemies of all humankind. President Monroe seemed to agree. His initial reaction to the *Antelope*'s seizure was to treat American citizens involved "as pirates."[88]

Equating the slave trade with gravest of maritime crimes reflected rising public opposition to what the congressional committee termed "this odious traffic." Historians have long doubted whether, prior to the Civil War, Americans really wanted to eliminate the slave trade. The Constitution famously prevented Congress from banning the "Importation" of persons into the United States before 1808, and the subsequent prohibitions Congress enacted were rarely enforced with vigor.[89] But American support for interdiction grew in the early decades of the nineteenth century. Cynically, many American slave owners knew that banning new imports would increase the value of their human property on the booming internal market. And as British-led abolitionism imbued antislavery ideas with greater "moral capital," advocating for the trade's eradication demonstrated American virtue internationally. It was also useful for American leaders seeking to build domestic political coalitions. Amid rising tensions over slavery's internal expansion, denunciation of the Middle Passage's inhumanity was valuable common ground.[90]

Zealous suppression of the slave trade, however, came with political risks, both at home and abroad. Many Americans, including wealthy and powerful merchants, continued participating in the traffic under the cover of foreign flags. And slavery's domestic defenders were wary of efforts to suppress the trade, as many of the humanitarian arguments against the practice raised doubts about the moral legitimacy of the "peculiar institution" itself.[91] Foreign governments were equally suspicious. After Napoleon's defeat, Britain persuaded smaller nations to act against the trade. But the major slaving powers – France, Portugal, and Spain – were half-hearted opponents at best, and they resented Anglo-American interference with their sovereign prerogatives. Indeed, Spanish and Portuguese officials demanded restoration of the captives on the *Antelope* to their original captors. And the French government decried American interdiction of alleged slavers like *La Jeune Eugenie* as a violation of the law of nations that "must be resisted."[92]

The Monroe administration's greatest concern was that interdiction of the slave trade threatened American sovereignty itself. As with executing "pirates" who sailed with South American privateering commissions, seizing foreign-flagged vessels on suspicion of violating the United States' slave trade laws was a bold assertion of American power over the seas. The problem was that it created a precedent for Great Britain to do the same. For over a decade, the British government had been urging the maritime nations of the Atlantic world to grant each other the right to stop and search ships suspected of slave trading. Given the ease with which slaving ships could mask their true national identities, British officials argued that only a universal search right could ferret out perpetrators.[93]

American politicians were loath to give British armed cruisers an excuse to harass U.S. ships on the high seas. After all, the two nations had recently gone to war over Britain's heavy-handed treatment of American vessels and seamen – in particular, the British practice of searching American ships to find supposed British subjects for impressment into the Royal Navy (see Chapter 4). Little wonder that Adams viewed Britain's search proposal as a "barefaced and impudent" attempt to obtain in peacetime a prerogative which Britain had "so outrageously abused during war." His dudgeon grew so high that when the British minister asked him to name a "more atrocious evil than this slave-trade," Adams did not hesitate: "[T]he right of search by foreign officers of our vessels upon the seas." Permitting such an affront to American sovereignty would be worse than allowing the continued kidnapping of Africans, Adams asserted, because it "would be making slaves of ourselves."[94]

The Monroe administration's concern for protecting American mariners from "slavery" at sea made it difficult to justify its seizure of foreign-flagged ships (even if they were actually putting humans into bondage). After *La Jeune Eugenie*'s capture, the President ordered the navy to cease such operations, but the question remained of what to do about the already-taken vessels. Monroe, for one, had no doubts: "[W]e should disclaim all right to seize foreign vessels ... engaged in the slave trade." Handing *La Jeune Eugenie* over to the French government would "settle a precedent" of limiting maritime search rights, and "avoid countenancing ... the British doctrine." Monroe recognized that federal law gave the naval officers and crew a share in the proceeds of *La Jeune Eugenie*'s forfeiture and sale (if it proved to be American-owned). But in his view the crucial question was not "what our law will sanction," it was "what policy dictates." Framed in that light, it was obvious that the officers' financial stake had to give way to "the high interests and principles that are involved."[95]

The more difficult question was *how* to restore the vessels, for they were already in judicial hands. The cabinet was split. Monroe and

Secretary of the Treasury William Crawford believed that the president had the power to simply to hand *La Jeune Eugenie* over to the French consul. Attorney General Wirt eventually concurred, at least as a legal matter. Precedent stretching back to the Neutrality Crisis confirmed the president's authority, and his obligation, to remedy injuries to the sovereign rights of other nations. But Wirt worried about the propriety of "Executive interference" in judicial proceedings, and feared that unilaterally restoring the ship would produce a "collision" between the branches. Secretary of the Navy Smith Thompson agreed, echoing the assertions that generations of cabinet officers had made regarding the sanctity of judicial decisions about ships and goods seized at sea: Foreign governments, Thompson argued, "ought to be satisfied" with whatever decisions the courts made.[96]

Adams came up with a compromise solution. The administration instructed the federal district attorney in Massachusetts to file a "suggestion" with the circuit court recommending that it turn *La Jeune Eugenie* over to French officials, but ultimately left it to the judges to do "as they should see fit." This was not a novel tactic. The Washington administration did the same thing to encourage a federal district court to release a French warship subject to suit in 1796 (see Chapter 3), as did the Madison administration in 1812. The benefits of this approach were obvious. The Monroe administration made clear its preferred outcome in the case, and demonstrated its willingness to act in defense of foreign interests. But the form of a "suggestion" formally respected the judiciary's decisional independence. And it gave judges final responsibility for resolving thorny questions of sovereign right.[97]

Adams's strategy of deferring to the judiciary came with the same risk as always – that federal judges would not rule in the way the executive branch wanted them to. Justice Story, who presided over the Massachusetts circuit court, supported the Monroe administration's position in the recently decided privateering cases. But his rulings in those cases were fully consistent with his assertive understanding of American maritime power more generally. Persuading him to *decline* jurisdiction over those who violated the law at sea was a different matter.

Story was also a vociferous critic of the slave trade. As early as 1815, he declared it to be the "most odious and horrible traffic." In grand jury charges in 1819 and 1820, he recited in vivid detail all the "human depravity" that flowed from the trade's "polluted march" across the Atlantic – the brutal kidnappings in Africa, the horrific conditions of the Middle Passage, and the terror of the slave auction. He was convinced that many Americans were "steeped up to their very mouths ... in this stream of iniquity," and he warned jurors that failure to suppress the trade put the nation's international reputation at risk. Most ominously for the Monroe administration, Story lauded the British government for its persistence in seeking cooperation from other nations to eradicate the trade: "May America not be behind her in this glorious work."[98]

The administration nevertheless pressed ahead. The French minister to the United States, Baron Jean Guillaume Hyde de Neuville, was initially unhappy with the prospect of putting his nation's sovereign interests in judicial hands. "[W]e know how long lawsuits drag on in America," he later wrote in his memoirs. But Adams insisted, in words that were by now a diplomatic mantra: "[T]he case is regularly before the judicial tribunal, from which the President has no power to take it." According to Adams, Hyde de Neuville eventually pronounced himself "entirely satisfied" with the Monroe administration's plan to let Story determine *La Jeune Eugenie*'s fate. Thirty years earlier, French diplomats had ridiculed Thomas Jefferson's assertion that the federal courts were the proper institution of American government for vindicating the rights of foreign sovereigns. But that idea apparently no longer seemed so laughable.[99]

Federal judges rewarded the Monroe administration's faith, though not before first giving it a scare. Story made clear in his 1822 circuit court decision in *La Jeune Eugenie* that he understood the case's implications. Few disputes were "more likely to excite the jealousies of a foreign government." Yet a judge was not to take such considerations into account, Story declared. Courts were obliged to administer the law "fearlessly and faithfully," regardless of any "national difficulties" that might result.[100]

Those words must have made Adams's heart skip a beat, because Story's expansive vision of judicial authority over the slave trade seemed calculated to produce precisely the sort of "national difficulties" the Monroe administration hoped to avoid. Story conceded that the law of nations sanctioned no general right of search in peacetime.

But every nation, he argued, had inherent authority to discover whether foreigners were abetting violations of domestic law on the high seas. And Story was emphatic – the slave trade *was* unlawful. It was a vocation of "corruption, plunder and kidnapping," which had "desolated Africa for the last three centuries."[101] As with other kinds of "pirates," Story also believed that slave traders' inhumanity justified virtually unfettered judicial power over them. Even if *La Jeune Eugenie* was truly a French vessel, and therefore the federal statutory ban did not apply to it, France itself had outlawed the trade (at least in theory). And "any court may take notice of the laws of a foreign country ... to enforce rights and redress wrongs." American courts, in other words, could enforce French law against French subjects, even when French courts did not.[102]

Even more controversially, Story asserted that federal courts could condemn foreign slave ships for violating the law of nations. Only a few years earlier, Story's jurisprudential hero, Sir William Scott of the British High Court of Admiralty, had concluded that international law did not prohibit the slave trade. But Story disagreed. It did not matter that some nations still permitted the trade. Just because a legal principle was not "settled by the consent or practice of nations" did not mean it was nonexistent. The law of nations, Story declared, derived "first, from the general principles of right and justice." And American judges could discern and apply that universal law for themselves.[103]

Having pushed American (and judicial) power to the very limit, Story stopped short. In a single closing paragraph, he concluded that the remedy for *La Jeune Eugenie*'s violation of universal law was not to condemn the vessel for the naval officers' benefit, as provided for by federal statute. Instead, Story handed the vessel over to the French consul, just as the Monroe administration wanted. Story took pains to note that the government's "suggestion" of this outcome was not a "direction to the court," for such a command was "beyond the reach of executive authority." But given the "difficulties" that aggressive slave trade interdiction posed, Story later explained to Scott, it was not his place to question the Monroe administration's policy choices. No doubt trying to save face, Story ended his opinion with a principled, if dubious, gloss on his decision to let suspected slave traders off the hook: "[T]he American courts," he averred, "are not hungry after jurisdiction in foreign causes."[104]

John Marshall was also conflicted about the scope of the federal courts' jurisdiction over slave traders. The case of the *Antelope* sat undisturbed on the Supreme Court's docket for three years, until the justices finally heard it in 1825. There were strong humanitarian reasons for greater haste. The hundreds of captives found on board the ship spent those years in a state of fatal limbo, bonded out to work on the plantations of local grandees around Savannah. The Monroe administration took little interest in their fate, even when presented with evidence of maltreatment by the federal marshal who was responsible for their well-being. More than 100 of the enslaved persons died while waiting for the Supreme Court to decide what would happen to them.[105]

The judicial delay was deadly for the captives, but it was convenient for the Monroe administration. In the early 1820s, debates over suppressing the slave trade were more fraught than ever. In 1824, the Monroe administration finally gave in to British pressure and agreed to allow mutual search rights to interdict the traffic. But the slave power in the United States could not stomach even this limited cession of American sovereignty. Slave owners were becoming increasingly fearful of the threat that creeping abolitionism posed to their way of life. Any proposal that reeked of antislavery was to be abjured, and their allies in the Senate succeeded in defeating the agreement.[106]

Delay also suited the justices, as they knew that any decision that questioned slavery's legitimacy would spark a firestorm of criticism. In 1823, Justice William Johnson declared unconstitutional a South Carolina law that mandated the detention of free black sailors who arrived in port, to prevent them from spreading notions of liberty among the state's enslaved population. Johnson's ruling outraged white Southerners shaken by the Denmark Vesey uprising of 1822. They saw any judicial decision that questioned a state's authority to limit black people's freedom as a mortal threat. The ensuing controversy alarmed Marshall. As he explained to Story in September 1823, he had "escaped" similar controversy by construing an analogous Virginia law in a way that avoided constitutional problems. Given the rhetorical fire that Johnson's critics were building "to roast the judicial department," he thought that a cautious approach on questions implicating slavery was the best way forward.[107]

When the Supreme Court finally got around to deciding the African captives' fate, Marshall's opinion disclaimed any American authority to interfere with foreign slave trading. The central question in the *Antelope* was whether the trade was illegal under the law of nations. If so, the captives would be freed; if not, those that had been taken from Spanish and Portuguese ships would be restored to their captors. Marshall conceded that the slave trade was "contrary to the law of nature," and that transatlantic public opinion was generally in favor of ending it. But those were considerations for a "moralist" (a comment possibly aimed at Story's opinion in *La Jeune Eugenie*). A "jurist" had to look to the actual laws and practices of sovereign nations to determine the content of international law. European nations had engaged in the slave trade for centuries "without opposition, and without censure," and it was not for the courts of the United States to "impose a rule on another." Story apparently disagreed, but he remained silent.[108]

Marshall did not wholly renounce judicial power to remedy wrongs committed at sea. He revisited the evidence presented to the lower courts, and concluded, somewhat doubtfully, that they had awarded too many captives to the Spanish claimants. In addition, he ruled that the Portuguese claimants had forfeited the right to recover any of the captives by not appearing personally in the case, even though the Portuguese consul had represented their interests all along. The result was that a number of Africans were eventually freed from captivity, though not for a while longer (and the number would have been much greater had so many not died in the interim). Marshall may have been unwilling to endorse universal authority over slave trading, but he seemed to recognize that justice and morality demanded some mitigation of its deadly effects.[109]

Story and Marshall traveled different paths, but they arrived at the same end. Ironically, Story's approach in *La Jeune Eugenie* was reminiscent of Marshall's in *Marbury v. Madison*: A sweeping assertion of judicial power, followed by an actual disposition of the case that did not exercise any real power at all. Marshall took the opposite tack in the *Antelope*; he denied the courts' authority to regulate the conduct of foreigners on the water, while reaching a result that actually deprived Spanish and Portuguese subjects of some of the human beings they claimed as property.[110] In both cases, however, the bottom line was the same. No matter how morally repugnant, slave trading by foreigners was an activity the federal courts would police lightly, if at all. As Adams wrote in a letter to Hyde de Neuville, the decisions were proof that no federal officer would presume to act "as the High Justiciar of the seas."[111]

At first blush, the contrast between the justices' rulings in the privateering and slave trading cases seems stark. In 1820, the Supreme Court announced that the federal courts had broad and unprecedented power to punish maritime violence committed by would-be revolutionaries who sought profit in the cause of human liberty. Only a few years later, the Court largely renounced any authority to regulate violence perpetrated by those who sought to profit by denying liberty to fellow humans. The discrepancy was equally apparent going forward. In 1820, the federal government executed a dozen privateers that the courts had sentenced to hang for piracy. But even though Congress made slave trading a capital crime that same year, the government did not put a single slaver to death in the subsequent four decades. Slave trading may have been equivalent to piracy in the law, but in practice it was not.[112]

The different outcomes might be explained by the faintheartedness of antislavery commitment among American political leaders in the early nineteenth century. James Monroe had deep political and moral concerns about slavery, but he never freed any of the hundreds of people he held in bondage during his lifetime. Same for John Marshall, who was a far more active acquirer of enslaved persons than historians have generally recognized. Northerners such as Joseph Story and John Quincy Adams did not own slaves, and were more outspoken in their criticisms of slavery and the slave trade. But they were not abolitionists. Preserving the union – the rights of slave owners included – was their first priority.[113]

When viewed through the lens of American sovereignty, however, the divergent treatment of privateers and slave traders was entirely consistent. Punishing foreign privateers in federal court extended American state power over the waters of the Western Hemisphere, while also facilitating the territorial expansion of the United States' nascent empire on land. *Not* punishing foreign slave traders in federal court, in contrast, spared American ships the indignity of being subject to the British Navy's roving maritime authority. Sometimes, the best way to protect American sovereignty was for the courts to stand down.

Like the piracy prosecutions, the slave trade cases also affirmed the courts' central role in steering the United States through the Age of Revolution's fraught international politics. Story's explanation for handing *La Jeune Eugenie* over to the French consul had no sound legal basis, and Marshall's decision in the *Antelope* was just as doubtful. But the awkwardness of the courts' rulings only underscored their importance. Faced with delicate and momentous questions about the rights of foreigners at sea, the Monroe administration, like its predecessors, left it to federal judges to come up with the answers.[114]

Epilogue

When John Quincy Adams learned of John Marshall's death in 1835, he gave the late Chief Justice the highest acclaim a nationalist like Adams could bestow. Adams had not always viewed Marshall favorably. In 1819, he decried the Chief Justice's initially restrictive view of federal jurisdiction over South American privateers as being "founded upon captious subtleties." But the two men grew closer in subsequent years, aided no doubt by the Court's rapid about-face, their sympathetic views on constitutional issues, and the regular walks they took in the predawn quiet of the nation's still-unfinished capital. By the time of Marshall's passing, Adams believed him to be "one of the most eminent men that this country has ever produced." In particular, Marshall's constitutional rulings of the 1820s overcame the "crafty and quixotic democracy of Jefferson," and "cemented the Union."[1]

Adams praise for Marshall was not wrong, but it was misdirected. Like many of Marshall's later admirers, Adams had in mind the Court's celebrated decisions setting forth a vision of constitutional governance in which the powers of the federal government prevailed over claims of states' rights. But in the 1830s that vision had not yet come to fruition. The Jacksonian ascendancy of the late 1820s meant that the full potential of national sovereignty latent in the Marshall Court's doctrines would be unrealized until at least the Civil War. And persistent divisions over the very nature of the American union meant that, in 1835, its integrity was anything but secure.

Where Marshall and his fellow judges actually *had* "cemented the union" was at sea. The federal judiciary kept the republic out of a catastrophic maritime conflict in the 1790s. It enabled the nation to fight a transformational war on the ocean in 1812. And its subsequent assertion of authority over the revolutionary Atlantic proved instrumental in realizing the United States' imperial future in the Americas. By the time Marshall and his colleagues began their efforts to put federal authority on firm constitutional footing at home, the courts had already established the United States' sovereignty and independence abroad.

This history of judicial sovereignty-building at sea has long been hidden, obscured by two often-told stories about the courts and the nation. One tells us that judges historically have ceded authority to the president in foreign affairs, and therefore have had little influence on the United States' international relations. The other, following Adams's eulogy, asserts that the Marshall Court's constitutional rulings laid the foundation for federal sovereignty under the Constitution. Both of these accounts have elements of truth, but only because of developments a century later. The claim that Marshall's constitutional decisions built the nation projects backward into the past an importance those rulings did not have when they were made. And the oft-repeated claim that the courts have historically had little to do with foreign affairs ignores that early judges were central participants in a cooperative effort among the three branches of government to secure the United States' place in the world. It is that legacy of judicial nation-building, rather than the stories we have inherited, that can help us think about the court's role in our constitutional government today.

* * *

There is good reason why Adams eulogy of Marshall glossed over the courts' maritime role in securing American sovereignty. By 1835, federal judicial power over the sea was in the first stages of a steady decline. Adams confirmed as much in his first presidential message to Congress in 1825. As Secretary of State, Adams had repeatedly used the courts as the conduit for asserting American authority over the water. But as president he found the judiciary "inadequate to the administration of national justice." He instead extolled the force of arms as the key to propagating American sovereignty abroad. He commended Congress for building new naval vessels to suppress Spanish-commissioned privateers around Cuba and Puerto Rico. A "military marine," Adams asserted, was "the only arm by which the power of this [nation] can be estimated or felt by foreign nations."[2]

That same year, a new federal criminal statute confirmed that the courts were no longer the "arm" of American authority on the water. The 1825 act – the first comprehensive federal criminal legislation since the Crimes Act of 1790 – was Joseph Story's brainchild. Story wanted Congress to confer on the courts a general power to define and punish common law crimes, which he believed was essential for safeguarding the nation. Instead, the act specified the conduct that qualified as a federal offense in painstaking detail. It also did not mention "piracy" anywhere. Piracy was still a crime under prior legislation, but its exclusion from a landmark criminal law confirmed that broad judicial authority over the seas was no longer a national necessity.[3]

An 1829 criminal prosecution exemplified this narrower understanding of the judiciary's international role. District Judge Joseph Hopkinson ruled that the courts had no jurisdiction over an American citizen who stole a French merchant vessel. Hopkinson acknowledged that the Piracy Act of 1819 gave the courts authority over all piracies under the laws of nations, and that the Supreme Court had interpreted such legislation broadly (see Chapter 7). But Hopkinson viewed the more recent 1825 law as evidence that Congress had "abandoned" its previous efforts to invest the courts with all the maritime power the Constitution allowed. And he worried that foreign governments would resent the expansive assertions of jurisdiction that had characterized earlier rulings. It was best to limit the courts' authority to offenses committed on American ships, and "leav[e] other nations to take care of their own."[4]

Hopkinson did not explain what motivated his constrained ruling, but the answer seems obvious. The Age of Revolution was over, and the United States' place in the world was more secure. For decades, judicial intervention in the affairs of state had enabled the government to keep faith with its commitments to foreign nations under treaty and international law, while sparing the political branches the responsibility for choosing between conflicting demands made by powerful empires. But that was no longer the state of things. A crime committed on a French ship in 1829 did not raise the same questions of sovereign right and responsibility that a similar offense against a British or Spanish vessel had in earlier years. The threat that maritime war posed to American independence was fading. With the Atlantic world in a period of relative peace, it was safe for the courts to pull back.

The courts' withdrawal from the sea in the 1820s marked the start of a gradual retreat from judicial engagement with foreign affairs. Cases arising from maritime violence did not disappear immediately. Piracy and slave trade matters occasionally appeared on the courts' dockets. So too did prize cases, especially during the Civil War. The Lincoln administration's blockade of southern ports resulted in the seizure and condemnation of more than 600 vessels, many of them British-owned. These cases raised the difficult question of whether the Confederacy was a sovereign entity (and could therefore be lawfully blockaded). In 1863, the Supreme Court upheld the president's power to declare a blockade, despite the fact that Lincoln did so before Congress formally declared war.[5]

The Court's ruling in *The Prize Cases* was in some ways a departure from earlier judicial decisions. As before, the Court affirmed claims to maritime authority advanced by the president and Congress. But neither the majority nor the dissent mentioned the cases' diplomatic context – namely, British outrage at the seizure of its ships by U.S. cruisers. The justices discussed the law of nations at length, but they seemingly did not view the dispute as implicating the rights of foreign sovereigns. Instead, the dispute was about domestic rebellion, and the legal relationship among the union's component parts.[6]

The Prize Cases also hinted at a new era of judicial deference to the executive branch in wartime. The Lincoln administration maintained that the Confederate states were still part of the union. But under the laws of war a government could not blockade its own ports. Nevertheless, the Supreme Court made clear that it would defer to the president's judgment. In a conflict of "such alarming proportions," wrote Justice Robert Grier, difficult questions of sovereign rights were "to be decided *by him*, and this Court must be governed by the[m]."[7]

In truth, judicial passivity in the international arena was not new in 1862. It had begun as soon as the wars of the Age of Revolution ended. In 1823, Chief Justice Marshall declared that the federal government's power to extinguish Native peoples' land claims was "not for the Courts of this country to question." His successor, Roger Taney, was usually unafraid to declare legislative and executive action to be unconstitutional. But in 1846 Taney similarly upheld the extension of federal criminal jurisdiction over members of Native tribes. The "right and propriety" of such jurisdiction, Taney asserted, "is a question for the law making and political department of the government, and not for the judicial."[8]

Judicial deference in foreign relations matters became more widespread in the years after the Civil War. In a series of immigration cases, the Supreme Court ruled that Congress' decision to prohibit the entry of foreign laborers (especially Chinese) was "conclusive," even though such measures contravened existing treaties between China and the United States. "It is not within the province of the judiciary," the Court declared in 1892, to "oppos[e] ... the constitutional and lawful measures of the legislative and executive branches of the national government." Around the same time, the Court declared that, in matters that "might involve war or peace," it was bound to "follow[] the action of the political branch."[9]

A general principle of judicial abstention in foreign affairs fully took root in the twentieth century. It was fueled in part by an emergent theory of "plenary power" in foreign affairs – the idea that federal government's authority included not just the powers specifically enumerated in the Constitution, but also the "inherent powers" that sovereign nations enjoyed under international law. This idea was already immanent in nineteenth-century jurisprudence regarding immigration (especially of nonwhite peoples), territorial annexation, and the status of Native nations. But twentieth-century proponents fashioned it into a general principle that loosened the constitutional limits on federal authority in "external affairs." These extraconstitutional powers belonged primarily by the president, and his exercise of them was generally not amenable to judicial review.[10]

Growing deference to the executive was also premised on the idea that judges were not competent to decide questions with significant foreign affairs implications. In 1936, the Supreme Court famously proclaimed in *United States v. Curtiss-Wright* – borrowing words from a speech John Marshall made while serving in Congress – that the president is the nation's "sole organ" in international relations. The Court extolled the president's superior understanding of international conditions, and the speed and secrecy of executive decision-making. These institutional advantages made it imperative that the president operate with a level of "discretion and freedom" from judicial limits that would not be warranted "were domestic affairs alone involved."[11]

For many judges, the existential dangers the United States faced in the twentieth century made deference to the executive a constitutional imperative. According to the *Curtiss-Wright* Court, the "complicated, delicate and manifold problems" posed by the rise of totalitarianism and global conflict meant that only the president had the power "to speak or listen as a representative of the nation." The Supreme Court's 1944 decision in *Korematsu v. United States*, which upheld the army's internment of Japanese Americans during World War II, invoked the same threats. "[W]hen under conditions of modern warfare our shores are threatened by hostile forces," the Court said, "the power to protect" – the executive's power – "must be commensurate with the threatened danger."[12]

By the Cold War's end, judicial deference in foreign affairs cases was presumed. "The conduct of foreign relations," the Supreme Court declared, "is not subject to judicial inquiry or decision." This norm found its most prominent expression in the political question doctrine, which holds that certain issues – especially those involving foreign relations – are not amenable to judicial resolution, regardless of whether jurisdiction is otherwise proper. Judges are "particularly ill suited" to make foreign policy decisions, the Court has explained, because they are "fundamentally underequipped" to do so.[13]

Two hundred years after the courts began their retreat from the world stage, their absence is understood to be an original feature of our constitutional order. "Since early in the nation's history," asserts one commentator, "courts have been reluctant to contradict the executive branch in its conduct of foreign relations." Some modern observers see signs that the era of deference may be waning, but there are doubts about the breadth and depth of this new-found judicial assertiveness. Even vociferous champions of judicial intervention concede that the courts typically accede to the other branches, "above all in foreign affairs." The legacy of the courts' first decades, it seems, has largely been forgotten.[14]

* * *

The story of judicial sovereignty-building told here has also been obscured by a more familiar, but misleading, tale about the courts' role in establishing American nationhood. Beginning in 1816, the Supreme Court became embroiled in a series of high-profile disputes over the scope of federal power under the Constitution. The cases name themselves: *Martin v. Hunter's Lessee*, *Dartmouth College v. Woodward*, *McCulloch v. Maryland*, *Cohens v. Virginia*, *Gibbons v. Ogden*, among others. This era is often described as the Marshall Court's "golden age," when the Court's rulings established a nationalist conception of the Constitution in which the powers of the federal government (and, not incidentally, the Court's own authority) typically prevailed over those of the states (Figure E.1).[15]

Lawyers and historians have long credited the Supreme Court in this period with having realized the Constitution's promise of national sovereignty. A century ago, Marshall's leading biographer declared that the Chief Justice's constitutional rulings did more "to knit the American people into an indivisible nation than any other one force in

FIGURE E.1 The famous constitutional cases of John Marshall's later years are often credited with laying the legal foundation for American nationhood. But the federal courts' resolution of cases arising from maritime war in the decades following ratification of the Constitution were more critical to the establishment American sovereignty. Portrait by Henry Inman (c. 1832), courtesy of the Diplomatic Reception Rooms, U.S. Department of State

our history, excepting only war." A decade earlier, Woodrow Wilson credited Marshall with giving the federal government "its scope and power." Marshall's most recent admirer is equally effusive: "[N]o one did more than Marshall to preserve the delicate unity of the fledgling republic." Even Marshall's critics agree that his "great service to the country" was "planting the national government on the broadest and strongest foundations."[16]

In truth, the Supreme Court's "great" cases of the 1810s and 1820s were far less transformative than such praise suggests. States-rights advocates responded to Marshall's opinions with denunciations and defiance. Southerners in particular feared that a broad construction of federal power might enable Congress to "emancipate every slave in the United States." A Virginia newspaper put the conflict in stark terms: "[T]he Judiciary power, with a foot as noiseless as time and a spirit as greedy as the grave, is sweeping to their destruction the rights of the States." Marshall saw these critiques for what they were – a refutation of his nationalist reading of the Constitution. "The attack upon the judiciary," he told Story in 1821, was "an attack upon the union" itself, and he worried that the constitutional regime he sought to advance would not be "long lived."[17]

The antipathy that greeted the Court's rulings was followed by disregard for their nationalist principles. Cases such as *McCulloch* and *Gibbons* invoked an expansive understanding of Congress's authority under Article I of the Constitution, especially on matters related to the national economy. But the actual holdings in those cases were relatively uncontroversial, and elected officials in the antebellum period did not take up the Court's invitation to expand federal power further. Presidents from James Monroe to James Polk vetoed funding for internal improvements, on constitutional grounds. In 1832, Andrew Jackson famously refused to recharter the very federal bank that the Court declared in *McCulloch* to be squarely within Congress's authority to create.[18]

The most obvious examples of the Supreme Court's impotence produced the most disastrous results. Its 1832 ruling in *Worcester v. Georgia* rejected state authority over Indian tribes, but did nothing to prevent the genocidal expulsion of Native people from the South that soon followed. In the 1850s, politicians from across the political spectrum insisted that only the Court could resolve questions over slavery's expansion that were threatening to undo the union. Chief Justice Taney accepted that invitation in *Dred Scott*, with shattering consequences. If Adams was correct in 1835 that Marshall's constitutional rulings had "cemented the Union," those bonds proved to be all too easily dissolved.[19]

It would take nearly a century before Marshall's nationalist opinions became the basis for a more expansive conception of federal power. After the Civil War, the Court rejected attempts by Radical Republicans and Progressives to mobilize Marshall's decisions in favor of a broad understanding of Congress's legislative authority. That effort only bore fruit in the New Deal and in the decades after, when the Court relied on cases like *McCulloch* to validate Congress's capacity to regulate the national economy and protect civil rights.[20]

It is this twentieth-century embrace of the Marshall Court's jurisprudence, not the nineteenth-century reality, that frames modern understandings of the early courts. What it conceals is the more tangible and impactful "foundation" the courts actually laid for the nation – the one they established at sea.

* * *

Despite two centuries of obscurity, the history of the courts' early international orientation offers insights that still have relevance today. For the past several decades, the judiciary's role in foreign affairs has been the subject of intense scholarly and judicial discussion. The end of the Cold War saw a rise in human rights litigation in the federal courts, primarily under a seldom-used provision of the Judiciary Act of 1789 known as the Alien Tort Statute. The advent of the so-called War on Terror after the 9/11 attacks subsequently gave rise to lawsuits challenging executive branch action ranging from the detention of enemy combatants to targeted killings by drone strike. Disagreements over the judiciary's role in resolving such disputes sweep broadly, encompassing issues of treaty interpretation, the extraterritorial application of U.S. law, the status of customary international law, and sovereign immunity (to name a few). But the core question is the same: When, if ever, should courts decide cases with implications for American foreign relations?[21]

Participants in this debate can roughly be divided into two camps. Those who favor presidential power argue that judicial decision-making interferes with the president's constitutional authority and undermines U.S. foreign policy. Judges lack the expertise to understand the foreign relations consequences of their decisions, and their interference disables the president from responding quickly and decisively to international developments. Proponents of a more activist judiciary, in contrast, assert that adjudication of cases raising foreign affairs issues is constitutionally permissible and normatively desirable. In particular, judicial intervention can restrain abuses of executive authority and promote adherence to the rule of law.[22]

For all its vibrancy, this debate largely elides the history of the federal courts' deep and sustained engagement with U.S. foreign affairs in the nation's first decades. The disputants tend to focus on a small handful of early cases, mainly from the early years of Marshall's tenure. And they do so primarily to argue over the allocation of foreign affairs powers between the president and Congress. This is a striking omission, given the originalist turn in judging and legal scholarship. But the courts' essential role in establishing early American sovereignty is largely invisible.[23]

Perhaps there is good reason for this ignorance of the courts' early history. Centuries-old cases applying the archaic law of prize to the capture of sailing ships may have limited application in current legal debates over the treatment of enemy combatants or suits against multinational corporations. What is more, many of the historical conditions that pushed the early courts to assume responsibility for ensuring the nation's peace and survival no longer exist. Unlike George Washington or James Monroe, modern presidents have a massive national security apparatus at their disposal. Suspected terrorists – the "pirates" of the twenty-first century – need not be criminally prosecuted when they can be indefinitely detained. The judiciary, too, is different. Early presidents could be confident that the men on the bench were versed in the nuances of domestic and international politics. But now no former ambassadors or secretaries of state sit on the Supreme Court.[24]

Despite these changed circumstances, the nation's early years may still have something to tell us about the courts' role in foreign affairs. But recognizing this requires a different conception of the relationship between the courts and the political branches, especially the executive. For modern debaters, judicial decision-making stands in opposition to executive power. Or, as a recent book puts it, the central question is which branch should "rule" in U.S. foreign affairs. The Supreme Court endorsed this view in a 2008 case regarding the detention of suspected enemy combatants at Guantanamo Bay: "Few exercises of judicial power are as legitimate or as necessary," the Court declared, "as the responsibility to hear challenges to the authority of the Executive."[25]

The lesson of the nation's first decades, in contrast, was that cooperation between the branches helped secure the nation's place in the world. By repeatedly asking the courts to resolve disputes over the rights of foreigners, Congress and the president engaged federal judges in a shared project of early American state-building. Judges were reluctant participants at times. But ultimately they accepted responsibility for helping to secure American sovereignty.

This older, cooperative understanding of the interbranch relationship in foreign affairs is worth remembering. The modern executive branch is far more powerful than it was in the nation's early years, but judicial decision-making can still serve the national interest. For example, in 1976 the State Department persuaded Congress to transfer responsibility for deciding whether to grant sovereign immunity to foreign defendants from the executive branch to federal judges. Its stated reasons were the same as the Washington administration's when it steered disputes over French privateer captures to the courts nearly two hundred years earlier. Judicial resolution of diplomatically fraught questions would relieve the executive branch of the burden of making such decisions, and reassure foreign sovereigns that they would be made impartially. Judicial involvement in foreign affairs, in other words, is not necessarily opposed to executive or legislative authority; it can be complementary.[26]

Hearkening back to the original conception of the courts' role in foreign affairs may also offer more diffuse benefits. For early American statesmen, judicial decision-making demonstrated the new nation's willingness and ability to fulfill its responsibilities under treaty and international law. Human rights advocates argue that the same is true now. Judicial resolution of legal claims against foreign governments and multinational corporations can serve as a "badge of honor," demonstrating the nation's commitment to upholding the rule of law in domestic and international affairs. Of course, we are no longer in the late eighteenth century, when proving the weak and vulnerable republic's fidelity to international legal norms was an existential imperative. But given the recent – and alarming – disregard for the rule of law by governments at home and abroad, a renewed commitment to judicial determination of rights claims made across borders might help slow the advance of autocracy.[27]

We should be mindful, however, that judicial participation in the project of nation-building has always come with considerable costs. And those costs have been borne more heavily by some than others. The Supreme Court's expansion of government power in the nation's early years had severe consequences for people caught up in maritime war. Neutral merchants had their property seized and condemned for alleged cooperation with the enemy. Ordinary seafarers who transgressed norms of maritime conduct found themselves hanging by the yardarm, while their commanders usually escaped punishment. And the end result of the courts' interventions was an aggressive vision of U.S. sovereignty that had catastrophic consequences for Native people in North America.

Cautionary tales abound in the present, as well. Many commentators lauded the Supreme Court's initial willingness to review the legality of executive branch detention of enemy combatants at Guantanamo as a victory for the rule of law. Yet in the past fifteen years the courts have actually ordered the release of very few detainees. Perhaps the mere threat of judicial review has prompted the executive branch to be more law-abiding. Or maybe it has instead given executive detention a veneer of legality that shields the government's actual practices from true scrutiny. And the Supreme Court's increasingly constrained reading of the Alien Tort Statute over the last twenty years has undermined efforts to vindicate global human rights claims in federal court.[28]

Fittingly enough, yet another twentieth-century celebration of John Marshall's legacy illustrates the promise and the peril of judicial engagement with global politics. In 1955, the American Bar Association invited President Dwight Eisenhower and Chief Justice Earl Warren to give remarks at a convention marking the bicentennial of Marshall's birth. Unsurprisingly, each of them extolled Marshall's legacy of nation-building. Warren lauded him for creating a government that would be esteemed "both at home and abroad," a feat Eisenhower claimed had enabled the United States to "survive its most perilous years." They urged their audience to follow Marshall's example. To guarantee "the freedom and security of the Republic," the nation had to prove that the rights guaranteed by the Constitution were "enforceable in our courts."[29]

Everyone in the audience understood what Eisenhower and Warren meant. The United States was in the midst of the Cold War – a "worldwide struggle between the forces of freedom and totalitarianism," according to Warren. Whether the United States would prevail in that contest, the president declared, depended on how far "the march of human progress" advanced on home soil. And that, in turn, depended heavily on the courts. The Supreme Court had ruled the year before in *Brown v. Board of Education* that segregated public schools were unconstitutional, and followed that decision by ordering that schools be integrated "with all deliberate speed." Eisenhower was a tepid supporter of civil rights, but he knew that segregationist resistance was damaging to the United States' international position, especially with newly independent post-colonial nations. He made the point explicit two years later, when ordering the National Guard to protect black students integrating schools in Little Rock. Failure to enforce the Court's rulings, Eisenhower explained in a national radio address, would damage "the prestige and influence, and indeed the safety, of our nation and the world."[30]

It is debatable whether judicial enforcement of civil rights in the twentieth century actually "command[ed] respect, both at home and abroad," as Warren put it, let alone that it proved decisive in winning the Cold War. But the United States did emerge from that conflict as the sole global superpower – an apotheosis of sovereignty that even John Marshall could not have imagined. At the same time, the failure of judicial desegregation to remedy the inequalities in American education, let alone in American society, is now – seventy years after *Brown* – plain for all to see. Perhaps that makes Eisenhower and Warren's tribute to Marshall all the more fitting. For the first thirty-five years of their existence, the federal courts were instrumental in defining the United States' place in the world, and they still are today. Whether that is for good or for ill is less clear.[31]

Notes

Introduction

1. *DHRC*, 10:1442 (Henry); William Grayson to Nathan Dane, June 19, 1788, *DHRC*, 10:1636–37; Pauline Maier, *Ratification: The People Debate the Constitution, 1787–1788* (New York: Simon and Schuster, 2010), 255–91.
2. *DHRC*, 10:1430–39 (Marshall).
3. Ibid.; Charles F. Hobson, "The Recovery of British Debts in the Federal Circuit Court of Virginia, 1790 to 1797," *Virginia Magazine of History and Biography* 92 (1984): 176–200; Thomas H. Lee, "The Safe-Conduct Theory of the Alien Tort Statute," *Columbia Law Review* 106 (2006): 830–908; Richard B. Lillich, "The Jay Treaty Commissions," *St. John's Law Review* 37 (1963): 260–83.
4. Declaration of Independence (1776). On the Declaration as an assertion of sovereignty, see Eliga H. Gould, *Among the Powers of the Earth: The American Revolution and the Making of a New World Empire* (Cambridge: Harvard University Press, 2012), 2–3, 112–15.
5. Marbury v. Madison, 5 U.S. 137, 177 (1803).
6. Randolph to Monroe, June 1, 1795, *ASPFR*, 1:705, 706; John Fiske, *The Critical Period of American History, 1783–1789* (Boston: Houghton Mifflin Company, 1916); Frederick W. Marks, *Independence on Trial: Foreign Affairs and the Making of the Constitution* (Baton Rouge: Louisiana State University Press, 1973); Peter Onuf, "Anarchy and the Crisis of the Union," in Herman Belz, et al., eds., *"To Form a More Perfect Union": The Critical Ideas of the Constitution* (Charlottesville: University Press of Virginia, 1992), 272–302; George Van Cleve, *We Have Not a Government: The Articles of Confederation and the Road to the Constitution* (Chicago: University of Chicago Press, 2017); Gordon S.

Wood, *The Creation of the American Republic, 1776–1787* (Chapel Hill: University of North Carolina Press, 1998), 393–429.

Synthetic treatments of the Age of Revolution in the Atlantic world include Jeremy Adelman, *Sovereignty and Revolution in the Iberian Atlantic* (Princeton: Princeton University Press, 2006); Laurent Dubois, *Avengers of the New World: The Story of the Haitian Revolution* (Cambridge: Belknap Press, 2004); Lester D. Langley, *The Americas in the Age of Revolution, 1750–1850* (New Haven: Yale University Press, 1996); R. R. Palmer, *The Age of the Democratic Revolution: A Political History of Europe and America, 1760–1800* (Princeton: Princeton University Press, 1959); Jaime E. Rodríguez O, *The Independence of Spanish America* (Cambridge: Cambridge University Press, 1998); Paul W. Schroeder, *The Transformation of European Politics, 1763–1848* (New York: Oxford University Press, 1994); Brian Taylor, *The Empire of the French: A Chronology of the Revolutionary and Napoleonic Wars, 1792–1815* (Stroud: Tempus, 2006).

Political and constitutional histories of the early United States that pay little attention to war include Paul E. Johnson, *The Early American Republic, 1789–1829* (New York: Oxford University Press, 2007); Jeffrey L. Pasley, Andrew W. Robertson, and David Waldstreicher, eds., *Beyond the Founders: New Approaches to the Political History of the Early American Republic* (Chapel Hill: University of North Carolina Press, 2004); Gordon S. Wood, *Empire of Liberty: A History of the Early Republic, 1789–1815* (Oxford: Oxford University Press, 2009). For a thoughtful exploration of the ubiquity of war in American history and its effect on the law, see Mary L. Dudziak, *War-Time: An Idea, Its History, Its Consequences* (Oxford: Oxford University Press, 2012).

7. Opinion on Ship Passports, May 3, 1793, *PTJ*, 25:643, 645; Hannah Farber, *Underwriters of the United States: How Insurance Shaped the American Founding* (Williamsburg: Omohundro Institute of Early American History and Culture, 2021), 151–80. Economic historians debate the actual impact that the French Revolutionary and Napoleonic Wars had on the American economy, though most conclude it was positive. Donald R. Adams, "American Neutrality and Prosperity, 1793–1808: A Reconsideration," *Journal of Economic History* 40 (1980): 713–37; Brooke Hunter, "Wheat, War, and the American Economy during the Age of Revolution," *William and Mary Quarterly* 62 (2005): 505–26; Douglass C. North, *The Economic Growth of the United States, 1760–1860* (New York: W. W. Norton & Company, 1966); James F. Shepherd and Gary M. Walton, "Economic Change after the American Revolution: Pre- and Post-War Comparisons of Maritime Shipping and Trade," *Explorations in Economic History* 13 (1976): 397–422; Claudia D. Goldin and Frank D. Lewis, "The Role of Exports in American Economic Growth during the Napoleonic Wars, 1793 to 1807," *Explorations in Economic History* 17 (1980): 6–25.

On opportunities for expansion and dispossession across the Americas, see Gregory Ablavsky, *Federal Ground: Governing Property and Violence in the First U.S. Territories* (New York: Oxford University Press, 2021); Jeremy Adelman, *Republic of Capital: Buenos Aires and the Legal Transformation of the Atlantic World* (Stanford: Stanford University Press, 1999); Stuart Banner, *How the Indians Lost Their Land: Law and Power on the Frontier* (Cambridge: Belknap Press, 2005); Ned Blackhawk, *Violence over the Land: Indians and Empires in the Early American West* (Cambridge: Harvard University Press, 2006); Paul Frymer, *Building an American Empire: The Era of Territorial and Political Expansion* (Princeton: Princeton University Press, 2017); Patrick Griffin, *American Leviathan: Empire, Nation, and Revolutionary Frontier* (New York: Hill and Wang, 2007); Peter J. Kastor, ed., *Empires of the Imagination: Transatlantic Histories of the Louisiana Purchase* (Charlottesville: University of Virginia Press, 2009).

8. Randolph to James Monroe, June 1, 1795, *ASPFR*, 1:705, 706; David Armitage, *The Declaration of Independence: A Global History* (Cambridge: Harvard University Press, 2007); David M. Golove and Daniel J. Hulsebosch, "A Civilized Nation: The Early American Constitution, the Law of Nations, and the Pursuit of International Recognition," *New York University Law Review* 85 (2010): 932–1066; Gould, *Among the Powers*; Marks, *Independence on Trial*; Peter S. Onuf and Nicholas Onuf, *Federal Union, Modern World: The Law of Nations in an Age of Revolutions, 1776–1814* (Madison: Madison House, 1993).
9. On the colonial origins of American distrust of central authority, see Thomas C. Barrow, *Trade and Empire: The British Customs Service in Colonial America, 1660–1775* (Cambridge: Harvard University Press, 1967); Justin du Rivage, *Revolution against Empire: Taxes, Politics, and the Origins of American Independence* (New Haven: Yale University Press, 2018); Edmund S. Morgan, *The Stamp Act Crisis: Prologue to Revolution* (Williamsburg: Institute of Early American History and Culture, 1953). The partisan politics of early federal governance are explored by Saul Cornell, *The Other Founders: Anti-Federalism and the Dissenting Tradition in America, 1788–1828* (Chapel Hill: University of North Carolina Press, 1999); Stanley M. Elkins and Eric L. McKitrick, *The Age of Federalism* (New York: Oxford University Press, 1993); James Roger Sharp, *American Politics in the Early Republic: The New Nation in Crisis* (New Haven: Yale University Press, 1993); Wood, *Empire of Liberty.*
10. John M. Murrin, "The Great Inversion, or Court versus Country: A Comparison of the Revolution Settlements in England (1688–1721) and America (1776–1816)," in J. G. A. Pocock, ed., *Three British Revolutions: 1641, 1688, 1776* (Princeton: Princeton University Press, 1980): 368–454; List of Civil Officers of the United States, in

American State Papers, Miscellaneous (Washington, DC: Gales and Seaton, 1834), 1:57–68; Brian Balogh, *A Government out of Sight: The Mystery of National Authority in Nineteenth-Century America* (Cambridge: Cambridge University Press, 2009); Max M. Edling, *A Hercules in the Cradle: War, Money, and the American State, 1783–1867* (Chicago: University of Chicago Press, 2015); Dwight F. Henderson, *Courts for a New Nation* (Washington, DC: Public Affairs, 1971); Gautham Rao, *National Duties: Custom Houses and the Making of the American State* (Chicago: University of Chicago Press, 2016); Craig L. Symonds, *Navalists and Antinavalists: The Naval Policy Debate in the United States, 1785–1827* (Newark: University of Delaware Press, 1980); Leonard White, *The Federalists: A Study in Administrative History* (Macmillan Co., 1948).

11. William H. Bergmann, *The American National State and the Early West* (New York: Cambridge University Press, 2012); Robin L. Einhorn, *American Taxation, American Slavery* (Chicago: University of Chicago Press, 2006); David F. Ericson, *Slavery in the American Republic: Developing the Federal Government, 1791–1861* (Lawrence: University of Kansas Press, 2011); Richard R. John, *Spreading the News: The American Postal System from Franklin to Morse* (Cambridge: Harvard University Press, 1995); Kohn, *Eagle and Sword:* John Lauritz Larson, *Internal Improvements: National Public Works and the Promise of Popular Government in the Early United States* (Chapel Hill: University of North Carolina Press, 2001); Malcolm J. Rohrbough, *The Land Office Business: The Settlement and Administration of American Public Lands, 1789–1837* (New York: Oxford University Press, 1968); Bethel Saler, *The Settlers' Empire: Colonialism and State Formation in America's Old Northwest* (Philadelphia: University of Pennsylvania Press, 2015).

    For challenges to the notion that the early American state was "weak," see Richard R. John, "Governmental Institutions as Agents of Change: Rethinking American Political Development in the Early Republic, 1787–1835," *Studies in American Political Development* 11 (1997): 347–80; William J. Novak, "The Myth of the 'Weak' American State," *American Historical Review* 113 (2008): 752–72. For a comprehensive overview of recent literature, see Gautham Rao, "The New Historiography of the Early Federal Government: Institutions, Contexts, and the Imperial State," *William and Mary Quarterly* 77 (2020): 97–128.

12. As Rachel St. John notes, "an active federal government was not necessarily a powerful one." Rachel St. John, "State Power in the West in the Early American Republic," *Journal of the Early Republic* 38 (2018): 87–94. On the difficulties of early law enforcement, see Peter Andreas, *Smuggler Nation: How Illicit Trade Made America* (New York: Oxford

University Press, 2013); Ernest Obadele-Starks, *Freebooters and Smugglers: The Foreign Slave Trade in the United States after 1808* (Fayetteville: University of Arkansas Press, 2007); Rao, *National Duties*, 132–62; Joshua M. Smith, *Borderland Smuggling: Patriots, Loyalists, and Illicit Trade in the Northeast, 1783–1820* (Gainesville: University Press of Florida, 2006). For an argument that early customs enforcement was more vigorous than is typically thought, see Aaron T. Knapp, "From Empire to Law: Customs Collection in the American Founding," *Law & Social Inquiry* 43 (2018): 554–84.

13. James E. Lewis, *The Burr Conspiracy: Uncovering the Story of an Early American Crisis* (Princeton: Princeton University Press, 2017); Andrew McMichael, *Atlantic Loyalties: Americans in Spanish West Florida, 1785–1810* (Athens: University of Georgia Press, 2008); Frank L. Owsley and Gene A. Smith, *Filibusters and Expansionists: Jeffersonian Manifest Destiny, 1800–1821* (Tuscaloosa: University of Alabama Press, 1997); William Spence Robertson, *The Life of Miranda* (Chapel Hill: University of North Carolina Press 1929).
14. Kevin Arlyck, "Plaintiffs v. Privateers: Litigation and Foreign Affairs in the Federal Courts, 1816–1822," *Law and History Review* 30 (2012): 245–78; William C. Davis, *The Pirates Laffite: The Treacherous World of the Corsairs of the Gulf* (New York: Houghton Mifflin Harcourt, 2006); David Head, *Privateers of the Americas: Spanish American Privateering from the United States in the Early Republic* (Athens: University of Georgia Press, 2015); Edgardo Pérez Morales, *No Limits to Their Sway: Cartagena's Privateers and the Masterless Caribbean in the Age of Revolutions* (Nashville: Vanderbilt University Press, 2018).
15. U.S. Const, art. III, § 2; Judiciary Act of 1789, §§ 2, 9, 1 Stat. 73. On the contested scope of federal judicial authority up to the Civil War, see Justin Crowe, *Building the Judiciary: Law, Courts, and the Politics of Institutional Development* (Princeton: Princeton University Press, 2012), 23–131; Richard E. Ellis, *The Jeffersonian Crisis; Courts and Politics in the Young Republic* (New York: Oxford University Press, 1971); Barry Friedman, *The Will of the People: How Public Opinion Has Influenced the Supreme Court and Shaped the Meaning of the Constitution* (New York: Farrar, Straus and Giroux, 2009), 44–136; Wythe Holt, "'To Establish Justice': Politics, the Judiciary Act of 1789, and the Invention of the Federal Courts," *Duke Law Journal* (1989): 1421–531; Alison L. LaCroix, *The Ideological Origins of American Federalism* (Cambridge: Harvard University Press, 2011), 175–213. On the prize system of the American Revolution, see Henry J. Bourguignon, *The First Federal Court: The Federal Appellate Prize Court of the American Revolution, 1775–1787* (Philadelphia: American Philosophical Society, 1977).
16. Jonathan M. Gutoff, "Original Understandings and the Private Law Origins of the Federal Admiralty Jurisdiction: A Reply to Professor

Casto," *Journal of Maritime Law and Commerce* 30 (1999): 361–404; Henderson, *Courts for a New Nation*, 55–63; Dwight F. Henderson, *Congress, Courts, and Criminals: The Development of Federal Criminal Law, 1801–1829* (Westport: Greenwood Press, 1985), 111–60.

17. On the importance of securing recognition from European empires, see Golove and Hulsebosch, "Civilized Nation"; Gould, *Powers of the Earth*; Onuf and Onuf, *Federal Union*; Charles Anthony Smith, "Credible Commitments and the Early American Supreme Court," *Law & Society Review* 42 (2008): 75–110.

18. Charles S. Maier, *Among Empires: American Ascendancy and Its Predecessors* (Cambridge: Harvard University Press, 2006), 101. The theoretical and historical literature on sovereignty is vast. For a recent discussion that emphasizes sovereignty's uneven and fractured quality in the early modern period, see Lauren Benton, *A Search for Sovereignty: Law and Geography in European Empires, 1400–1900* (Cambridge: Cambridge University Press, 2010), 279–99.

    There were significant questions of sovereignty and foreign affairs that the courts largely did not confront in this period – most notably, those implicating the federal government's complex relations with indigenous people in the North American interior. The federal courts constituted under Article III of the Constitution had little to say about relations with Native nations until the 1820s. Johnson v. M'Intosh, 21 U.S. 543 (1823). In Mary Bonsteel Tachau's comprehensive study of the federal district court for the borderland state of Kentucky from 1789 to 1816, she reports only a single case expressly addressing relations between Native people and white settlers. Mary K. Bonsteel Tachau, *Federal Courts in the Early Republic: Kentucky, 1789–1816* (Princeton: Princeton University Press, 1978), 127–48. The courts Congress established in the federal territories under Article I were more active in this domain, though even there their influence was limited. Ablavsky, *Federal Ground*, 109–38.

19. Stephen Skowronek, *Building a New American State: The Expansion of National Administrative Capacities, 1877–1920* (Cambridge: Cambridge University Press, 1982), 24. The burgeoning literature on the early federal state includes Ablavsky, *Federal Ground*; Balogh, *Government Out of Sight*; Edling, *Hercules in the Cradle*; John, *Spreading the News*; Peter J. Kastor, *The Nation's Crucible: The Louisiana Purchase and the Creation of America* (New Haven: Yale University Press, 2004); Kohn, *Eagle and Sword*; Rao, *National Duties*; Stephen J. Rockwell, *Indian Affairs and the Administrative State in the Nineteenth Century* (Cambridge: Cambridge University Press, 2010). A partial exception to the ignorance of the judiciary is scholarship on how the courts' exercise of judicial review has shaped American political development. Crowe, *Building the Judiciary*; Mark A. Graber, "The Nonmajoritarian Difficulty: Legislative

Deference to the Judiciary," *Studies in American Political Development* 7 (1993): 35–73; Keith E. Whittington, *Political Foundations of Judicial Supremacy* (Princeton: Princeton University Press, 2007).

There is a similar lacuna in the literature that explores the international dimensions of early American law and politics, exemplified by Armitage, *Declaration of Independence*; Anthony J. Bellia and Bradford R. Clark, *The Law of Nations and the United States Constitution* (New York: Oxford University Press, 2017); Golove and Huslebosch, "Civilized Nation"; Gould, *Powers of the Earth*. Even scholarship that directly engages with the Supreme Court's maritime war cases tends to focus on domestic disputes over the separation of powers, rather than on international politics. Michael J. Glennon, "Two Views of Presidential Foreign Affairs Power: *Little v. Barreme* or *Curtiss-Wright*," *Yale Journal of International Law* 13 (1988): 5–20; Frederick C. Leiner, "The *Charming Betsy* and the Marshall Court," *American Journal of Legal History* 45 (2001): 1–21; Jane Manners, "Executive Power and the Rule of Law in the Marshall Court: A Rereading of *Little v. Barreme* and *Murray v. Schooner Charming Betsy*," *Fordham Law Review* 89 (2021): 1941–74. The handful of exceptions include Kevin Arlyck, "The Courts and Foreign Affairs at the Founding," *Brigham Young University Law Review* (2017): 1–66; William R. Casto, *Foreign Affairs and the Constitution in the Age of Fighting Sail* (Columbia: University of South Carolina Press, 2006); David Sloss, "Judicial Foreign Policy: Lessons from the 1790s," *Saint Louis University Law Journal* 53 (2008): 145–96.

20. Albert J. Beveridge, *The Life of John Marshall: The Building of the Nation* (Boston: Houghton Mifflin Co., 1919), 4:429–30. For similar assessments, see Irving Brant, "John Marshall and the Lawyers and Politicians," in W. Melville Jones, ed., *Chief Justice John Marshall: A Reappraisal* (Ithaca: Cornell University Press, 1956), 58; Samuel R. Olken, "Chief Justice John Marshall and the Course of American Constitutional History," *John Marshall Law Review* 33 (2000): 743–79; Jean Edward Smith, *John Marshall: Definer of Nation* (New York: H. Holt & Co., 1998), 1–3; Joel Richard Paul, *Without Precedent: Chief Justice John Marshall and His Times* (New York: Riverhead Books, 2017), 1; Charles Warren, *The Supreme Court in United States History* (Boston: Little, Brown and Company, 1922), 1:vii.

21. *Marbury*, 5 U.S. at 177. Skeptics of the Marshall Court's importance include Mark A. Graber, "Establishing Judicial Review? *Schooner Peggy* and the Early Marshall Court," *Political Research Quarterly* 51 (1998): 221–39; Mark A. Graber, "Federalist or Friends of Adams: The Marshall Court and Party Politics," *Studies in American Political Development* 12 (1998): 229–66; Michael J. Klarman, "How Great Were the 'Great' Marshall Court Decisions?" *Virginia Law Review* 87 (2001): 1111–84; Farah Peterson, "Interpretation as Statecraft: Chancellor Kent and the

Collaborative Era of American Statutory Interpretation," *Maryland Law Review* 77 (2018): 712–73; David S. Schwartz, *The Spirit of the Constitution: John Marshall and the 200-Year Odyssey of McCulloch v. Maryland* (New York: Oxford University Press, 2019), 2–4.

On the federal courts' reputational difficulties, see R. B. Bernstein, "President John Adams and Four Chief Justices: An Essay for James F. Simon," *New York Law School Law Review* 57 (2012): 441–63; Dale Yurs, "The Early Supreme Court and the Challenges of Riding Circuit," *Journal of Supreme Court History* 36 (2011): 181–92. For Jeffersonian attacks on the judiciary, see Ellis, *Jeffersonian Crisis*; George Lee Haskins and Herbert Alan Johnson, *History of the Supreme Court of the United States: Foundations of Power: John Marshall, 1801–1815* (New York: Cambridge University Press, 1981), 136–81; R. Kent Newmyer, *John Marshall and the Heroic Age of the Supreme Court* (Baton Rouge: Louisiana State University Press, 2001), 146–209; Keith E. Whittington, "Reconstructing the Federal Judiciary: The Chase Impeachment and the Constitution," *Studies in American Political Development* 9 (1995): 55–116.

Marshall's political acuity is a theme in Alexander M. Bickel, *The Least Dangerous Branch: The Supreme Court at the Bar of Politics* (Indianapolis: Bobbs-Merrill, 1962), 1; Friedman, *Will of the People*, 44–71; Charles F. Hobson, *The Great Chief Justice: John Marshall and the Rule of Law* (Lawrence: University Press of Kansas, 1996), 47–54; Robert G. McCloskey, *The American Supreme Court* (Chicago: University of Chicago Press, 1960), 23–30; Paul, *Without Precedent*, 243–61.

22. According to Michael Klarman, the courts did not decide "any significant issue involving the scope of national power" before 1815. Klarman, "How Great," 1137. For similar statements about the courts' irrelevance in the 1790s, see David P. Currie, *The Constitution in the Supreme Court: The First Hundred Years, 1789–1888* (Chicago: University of Chicago Press, 1985), 61; Haskins & Johnson, *Foundations of Power*, 140.
23. William R. Casto, "The Origins of Federal Admiralty Jurisdiction in an Age of Privateers, Smugglers, and Pirates," *American Journal of Legal History* 37 (1993): 117–57; Grant Gilmore and Charles L. Black, *The Law of Admiralty* (Mineola: Foundation Press, 1975), 44.
24. Only a small handful of older studies make significant use of early federal court records. Tachau, *Federal Courts in the Early Republic*; Henderson, *Courts for a New Nation*; Henderson, *Congress, Courts, and Criminals*. On the methodological and conceptual challenges of writing the history of the lower federal courts, see Edward A. Purcell Jr., "Review: Reconsidering the Frankfurterian Paradigm: Reflections on Histories of Lower Federal Courts," *Law & Social Inquiry* 24 (1999): 679–750.
25. Hamilton to George Washington, May 15, 1793, *PGWPS*, 12:577, 582; Kate Elizabeth Brown, *Alexander Hamilton and the Development of American Law* (Lawrence: University Press of Kansas, 2017), 57–84.

26. There is a long line of scholarship treating Marshall's decision in *Marbury v. Madison* as a self-conscious assertion of judicial authority. Beveridge, *Life of Marshall*, 3:101–56; David P. Currie, "The Constitution in the Supreme Court: The Powers of the Federal Courts, 1801–1835," *University of Chicago Law Review* 49 (1982): 646–724; McCloskey, *American Supreme Court*, 40–47; Sylvia Snowiss, *Judicial Review and the Law of the Constitution* (New Haven: Yale University Press, 1990), 172–75. There is an equally extensive revisionist literature arguing that *Marbury* was a modest claim to power, one that was in keeping with preexisting understandings of the judicial role in republican government. Hobson, *Great Chief Justice*: 47–71; William Edward Nelson, *Marbury v. Madison: The Origins and Legacy of Judicial Review* (Lawrence: University Press of Kansas, 2000), 28–71; William Michael Treanor, "Judicial Review before Marbury," *Stanford Law Review* 58 (2005): 455–562. For a discussion of *Marbury*'s treatment by generations of scholars in the nineteenth and twentieth centuries, see Mary Sarah Bilder, "Idea or Practice: A Brief Historiography of Judicial Review," *Journal of Policy History* 20 (2008): 6–25; Robert Lowry Clinton, *Marbury v. Madison and Judicial Review* (Lawrence: University Press of Kansas, 1989).
27. Jefferson to Edmond Charles Genet, June 17, 1793, *PTJ*, 26:301–2; Ellis, *Jeffersonian Crisis*. On the early history of presidential and congressional war powers, see David J. Barron and Martin S. Lederman, "The Commander in Chief at the Lowest Ebb: A Constitutional History," *Harvard Law Review* 121 (2008): 941–1113; Saikrishna B. Prakash and Michael D. Ramsey, "The Executive Power over Foreign Affairs," *Yale Law Journal* 111 (2001): 231–356.
28. In 1936, the Supreme Court famously proclaimed – borrowing words John Marshall spoke before joining the Supreme Court – that the president is "the sole organ of the federal government in the field of international relations." United States v. Curtiss-Wright Exp. Corp., 299 U.S. 304, 319–20 (1936). The origins of this view are explored in Sarah Cleveland, "Powers Inherent in Sovereignty: Indians, Aliens, Territories, and the Nineteenth Century Origins of Plenary Power over Foreign Affairs," *Texas Law Review* 81 (2002): 1–284; G. Edward White, "The Transformation of the Constitutional Regime of Foreign Relations," *Virginia Law Review* 85 (1999): 1–150.

    On the extensive debate over the courts' role in foreign affairs, compare Jack L. Goldsmith, "The New Formalism in United States Foreign Relations Law," *University of Colorado Law Review* 70 (1999): 1395–438; Julian Ku and John Yoo, "*Hamdan v. Rumsfeld*: The Functional Case for Foreign Affairs Deference to the Executive Branch," *Constitutional Commentary* 23 (2006): 179–226; Jide Nzelibe, "The Uniqueness of Foreign Affairs," *Iowa Law Review* 89 (2004): 941–1010, with Martin S.

Flaherty, *Restoring the Global Judiciary: Why the Supreme Court Should Rule in U.S. Foreign Affairs* (Princeton: Princeton University Press, 2019); Thomas M. Franck, *Political Questions/Judicial Answers: Does the Rule of Law Apply to Foreign Affairs?* (Princeton: Princeton University Press, 1992); Derek Jinks and Neal Kumar Katyal, "Disregarding Foreign Relations Law," *Yale Law Journal* 116 (2007): 1230–83.

29. Jefferson to Thomas Pinckney, June 14, 1793, *PTJ*, 26:286–88. Scholars in law and political science recognize that elected officials promote and defend judicial authority when it serves their purposes, yet have rarely applied such insights to the early federal judiciary. Crowe, *Building the Judiciary*; Barry Friedman and Erin F. Delaney, "Becoming Supreme: The Federal Foundation of Judicial Supremacy," *Columbia Law Review* 111 (2011): 1137–93; Howard Gillman, "How Political Parties Can Use the Courts to Advance Their Agendas: Federal Courts in the United States, 1875–1891," *American Political Science Review* 96 (2002): 511–24; William M. Landes and Richard A. Posner, "The Independent Judiciary in an Interest-Group Perspective," *Journal of Law & Economics* 18 (1975): 875–901; Matthew C. Stephenson, "'When the Devil Turns …': The Political Foundations of Independent Judicial Review," *Journal of Legal Studies* 32 (2003): 59–89. The handful of exceptions include Graber, "Establishing Judicial Review?"; Graber, "Federalist or Friends of Adams"; Whittington, *Political Foundations*.

    On the relationship between international conflict and domestic politics in the early period, see Susan Branson, *These Fiery Frenchified Dames: Women and Political Culture in Early National Philadelphia* (Philadelphia: University of Pennsylvania Press, 2001); Caitlin Fitz, *Our Sister Republics: The United States in an Age of American Revolutions* (New York: Liveright, 2017); Eugene P. Link, *Democratic-Republican Societies, 1790–1800* (New York: Octagon Books, 1965); Sharp, *American Politics*, 69–184.

30. The Santissima Trinidad, 20 U.S. 283, 349 (1822).

1 From Confederation to Constitution

1. *Freeman's Journal* (Philadelphia), Dec. 12, 1787, p. 3; Ron Chernow, *Alexander Hamilton* (New York: Penguin Books, 2005), 243–69.
2. Federalist 22, *DHRC*, 14:436–44; U.S. Const., art. III. On Madison's disinterest in the judiciary, see Mary Sarah Bilder, *Madison's Hand: Revising the Constitutional Convention* (Cambridge: Harvard University Press, 2015), 117–18.
3. *Maryland Journal*, Aug. 5, 1788, *DHRC*, 12:887; Federalist 78, *DHRC*, 18:87–94.
4. Federalist 80, *DHRC*, 18:99; *DHRC*, 2:518 (Wilson); George Mason to Samuel Griffin, Sep. 8, 1789, in Robert A. Rutland, ed., *The Papers*

of George Mason (Chapel Hill: University of North Carolina Press, 1970), 3:1172.

5. Federalist 80, *DHRC*, 18:96–102.
6. Federalist 78, *DHRC*, 18:87–94; Julius Goebel, *History of the Supreme Court of the United States: Antecedents and Beginnings to 1801* (New York: Macmillan Publishing Co., 1971), 97. The literature detailing early debates over federal judicial authority includes Friedman, *Will of the People*, 33–42; Goebel, *Antecedents*, 196–412; Matthew P. Harrington, "The Economic Origins of the Seventh Amendment," *Iowa Law Review* 87 (2002): 145–234; Wythe Holt, "'To Establish Justice': Politics, the Judiciary Act of 1789, and the Invention of the Federal Courts," *Duke Law Journal* (1989): 1421–531; Larry D. Kramer, *The People Themselves: Popular Constitutionalism and Judicial Review* (New York: Oxford University Press, 2004), 73–92; Alison L. LaCroix, *The Ideological Origins of American Federalism* (Cambridge: Harvard University Press, 2011), 175–87.
7. Daniel A. Baugh, *British Naval Administration in the Age of Walpole* (Princeton: Princeton University Press, 1965), 113–14; Henry J. Bourguignon, *The First Federal Court: The Federal Appellate Prize Court of the American Revolution, 1775–1787* (Philadelphia: American Philosophical Society, 1977), 4–11; Matthew P. Harrington, "The Legacy of the Colonial Vice-Admiralty Courts (Part II)," *Journal of Maritime Law and Commerce* 27 (1996): 323–51; Francis R. Stark, *The Abolition of Privateering and the Declaration of Paris* (New York: Columbia University, 1897), 49–55. On state-sponsored English privateering during the reign of Elizabeth I, see Kenneth R. Andrews, *Elizabethan Privateering: English Privateering During the Spanish War, 1585–1603* (Cambridge: Cambridge University Press, 1964).
8. Benjamin Franklin to Benjamin Vaughan, Mar. 14, 1785, in Albert Henry Smyth, ed., *The Writings of Benjamin Franklin* (New York: The Macmillan Co., 1905), 9:291, 299; James G. Lydon, *Pirates, Privateers, and Profits* (Upper Saddle River: Gregg Press, 1970); John Franklin Jameson, *Privateering and Piracy in the Colonial Period: Illustrative Documents* (New York: Macmillan, 1923); Carl E. Swanson, *Predators and Prizes: American Privateering and Imperial Warfare, 1739–1748* (Columbia: University of South Carolina Press, 1991).
9. Gardner Weld Allen, *Massachusetts Privateers of the Revolution* (Boston: Massachusetts Historical Society, 1927), 18–31; Gardner Weld Allen, *A Naval History of the American Revolution* (New York: Russell & Russell, 1962), 42–48; Michael J. Crawford, "The Privateering Debate in Revolutionary America," *The Northern Mariner/Le Marin Du Nord* 21 (2011): 219–34. For general histories of privateering in the Revolutionary War, see Eric Jay Dolin, *Rebels at Sea: Privateering in the American Revolution* (New York: Liveright, 2022); Kylie A. Hulbert,

The Untold War at Sea: America's Revolutionary Privateers (Athens: University of Georgia Press, 2022); Robert H. Patton, *Patriot Pirates: The Privateer War for Freedom and Fortune in the American Revolution* (New York: Vintage Books, 2009).

10. Mark Mayo Boatner III, *Encyclopedia of the American Revolution* (New York: David McKay, 1966), s.v., Privateering; Crawford, "Privateering Debate," 220–23; "Vessels of the Continental Navy," Naval History and Heritage Command, www.history.navy.mil/research/library/online-reading-room/title-list-alphabetically/v/vessels-of-the-continental-navy.html.

11. Silas Deane to Committee of Secret Correspondence, Oct. 8, 1776, *NDAR*, 2:168; Jonathan Williams to the Committee for Foreign Affairs, Aug. 10, 1777, *NDAR*, 9:561; Adams to the President of Congress, Sep. 16, 1780, *NDAR*, 4:58; Adams to the President of Congress, Mar. 10, 1780, *NDAR*, 3:541; Abigail Adams to John Adams, Sep. 7, 1776, in L. H. Butterfield, ed., *The Adams Papers, Adams Family Correspondence* (Cambridge: Harvard University Press, 1963), 2:121–24.

12. Franklin to Richard Oswald, Jan. 14, 1783, in *Writings*, 9:3; Drew R. McCoy, "Benjamin Franklin's Vision of a Republican Political Economy for America," *William and Mary Quarterly* 35 (1978): 605–28; John Adams, *Diary and Autobiography* (Cambridge: Harvard University Press, 1962), 3:342–43; Allen, *Massachusetts Privateers*, 15–17; Crawford, "Privateering Debate," 225–26; Don Higginbotham, *The War of American Independence: Military Attitudes, Policies, and Practice, 1763–1789* (Boston: Northeastern University Press, 1983), 337–38. Franklin saw the conflicts of interest up close. The privateers he commissioned when serving as minister to France had great success in seizing valuable enemy ships and cargo, but they were less interested in capturing the British seamen that Franklin wanted to exchange for Americans languishing in enemy detention. John Paul Jones to Robert Morris, Dec. 11, 1777, *NDAR*, 10:1091–92; William Bell Clark, *Ben Franklin's Privateers: A Naval Epic of the American Revolution* (Baton Rouge: Louisiana State University Press, 1956).

13. Morris to Silas Deane, Sep. 12, 1776, *NDAR*, 6:794; Morris to William Bingham, Dec. 4, 1776, *NDAR*, 7:368; Morris to Bingham, Apr. 25, 1777, *NDAR*, 8:429; Hulbert, *Untold War*, 25–26; Charles Rappleye, *Robert Morris: Financier of the American Revolution* (New York: Simon and Schuster, 2010).

14. Bourguignon, *First Federal Court*, 274–75; Lydon, *Pirates, Privateers, and Profits*; Donald A. Petrie, *The Prize Game: Lawful Looting on the High Seas in the Days of Fighting Sail* (Annapolis: Naval Institute Press, 1999); Swanson, *Predators and Prizes*, 29–48; Stark, *Abolition of Privateering*, 11–45.

15. Lauren Benton, "Legal Spaces of Empire: Piracy and the Origins of Ocean Regionalism," *Comparative Studies in Society and History*

47 (2005): 700–24; Peter Earle, *The Pirate Wars* (London: Methuen, 2003); Steven Johnson, *Enemy of All Mankind: A True Story of Piracy, Power, and History's First Global Manhunt* (New York: Riverhead Books, 2020); Richard Pares, *Colonial Blockade and Neutral Rights, 1739–1763* (Oxford: Clarendon Press, 1938), 226–310; Nicholas Parrillo, "The De-Privatization of American Warfare: How the US Government Used, Regulated, and Ultimately Abandoned Privateering in the Nineteenth Century," *Yale Journal of Law and the Humanities* 19 (2007): 1–95; Robert Ritchie, *Captain Kidd and the War Against the Pirates* (Cambridge: Harvard University Press, 1989).

16. Arthur Lee to Committee of Foreign Affairs, Nov. 27, 1777, *RDCUS*, 2:429–31; Franklin to Ferdinand Grand, Oct. 14, 1778, *RDCUS*, 2:839–41; Lee to Committee of Foreign Affairs, Nov. 15, 1778, *RDCUS*, 2:839–41.
17. Morris to William Hooper, Jan. 24, 1777, *NDAR*, 7:1031–32; Franklin, Deane, and Lee to Committee of Foreign Affairs, Nov. 30, 1777, *RDCUS*, 2:435; Franklin to President of Congress, Dec. 3, 1780, *RDCUS*, 4:179–80; Henry J. Bourguignon, "Incorporation of the Law of Nations During the American Revolution: The Case of the San Antonio," *American Journal of International Law* 71 (1977): 270–95.
18. Felix Gilbert, *To the Farewell Address: Ideas of Early American Foreign Policy* (Princeton: Princeton University Press, 1961), 48–57; Gilje, *Free Trade*, 11–68; Daniel J. Hulsebosch, "The Revolutionary Portfolio: Constitution-Making and the Wider World in the American Revolution," *Suffolk University Law Review* 47 (2014): 759–822; Gregg L. Lint, "John Adams on the Drafting of the Treaty Plan of 1776," *Diplomatic History* 2 (1978): 313–20.
19. *JCC*, 11:486; *JCC*, 19:360–64; *JCC*, 17:672–74; *JCC*, 3:371–76; Allen, *Massachusetts Privateers*, 33–39; Franklin, Deane, and Lee to Committee of Foreign Affairs, Nov. 30, 1777, *RDCUS*, 2:435. For ongoing complaints, see Franklin to John Jay, Oct. 4, 1779, *RDCUS*, 3:361–66; John Adams to President of Congress, Apr. 7, 1780, *RDCUS*, 3:599–602; Charles Dumas to President of Congress, May 21, 1780, *RDCUS*, 3:696–97; Chevalier de la Luzerne to President of Congress, Sep. 24, 1781, *RDCUS*, 4:728; Luzerne to Robert Livingston, Feb. 18, 1782, *RDCUS*, 5:176–77; Franklin to Livingston, Mar. 4, 1782, *RDCUS*, 5:214–17.
20. Washington to Hancock, Nov. 8, 1775, in W. W Abbot, et al., eds., *The Papers of George Washington, Revolutionary War Series* (Charlottesville: University Press of Virginia, 1985), 2:330–33; Washington to Hancock, Nov. 11, 1775, ibid., 2:349–52; Washington to Hancock, Dec. 4, 1775, ibid., 2:483–87; Allen, *Naval History*, 59–74.
21. Quoted in Graydon S. Staring, "The Admiralty Jurisdiction of Torts and Crimes and the Failed Search for Its Purposes," *Journal of Maritime Law and Commerce* 38 (2007): 433–86; Bourguignon, *First Federal*

Court, 4–10; Reginald G. Marsden, ed., *Select Pleas in the Court of Admiralty* (London: B. Quaritch, 1894), 1:xi–lx; R. G. Marsden, "Early Prize Jurisdiction and Prize Law in England," *English Historical Review* 24 (1909): 675–97; Lionel H. Laing, "Historic Origins of Admiralty Jurisdiction in England," *Michigan Law Review* 45 (1946): 163–82; Frederic L. Cheyette, "The Sovereign and the Pirates, 1332," *Speculum* 45 (1970): 40–68; Thomas K. Heebøll-Holm, "Law, Order and Plunder at Sea: A Comparison of England and France in the Fourteenth Century," *Continuity and Change* 32 (2017): 37–58.

22. Pares, *Colonial Blockade*, 226–310; Cheyette, "Sovereign and the Pirates"; Heebøll-Holm, "Law, Order and Plunder"; Vincent Gabrielsen, "Warfare, Statehood and Piracy in the Greek World," in Nikolas Jaspert and Sebastian Kolditz, eds., *Seeraub im Mittelmeerraum: Piraterie, Korsarentum und maritime Gewalt von der Antike bis zur Neuzeit* (Paderborn: Verlag Ferdinand Schöningh, 2014), 133–54. For a sampling of the massive literature on the relationship between violence and modern state formation, see Max Weber, "Politics as Vocation," in David Owen and Tracy B. Strong, eds., *The Vocation Lectures* (Indianapolis: Hackett Publishing, 2004); Charles Tilly, "War Making and State Making as Organized Crime," in Peter Evans, et al., eds., *Bringing the State Back In* (Cambridge: Cambridge University Press, 1985), 169–86; Andreas Anter, "The Modern State and Its Monopoly on Violence," in Edith Hanke, et al., eds, *The Oxford Handbook of Max Weber* (New York: Oxford University Press, 2019), 226–36.

23. L'Invincible, 14 U.S. 238, 254 (1816); T. Rutherforth, *Institutes of Natural Law* (Cambridge: J. Bentham, 1754), 2:594–600; Marsden, "Early Prize Jurisdiction," 675–97.

24. Le Caux v. Eden, 99 Eng. Rep. 375 (K.B. 1781); Pares, *Colonial Blockade*, 79–80. On the difference between prize and instance jurisdiction, see Edward Stanley Roscoe, *A History of the English Prize Court* (London: Lloyd's, 1924), 44–46. Respect for the admiralty courts' exclusive jurisdiction over prize was not as complete in the colonies in the mid eighteenth century, where common law courts – often acting at the behest of captors who had lost in admiralty – were known to intervene in prize proceedings in the vice-admiralty courts, despite Privy Council decisions concluding that common law courts had no more authority to issue write of prohibition against the admiralty in the colonies than they did in England. Roscoe, *Prize Court*, 16–18; Pares, *Colonial Blockade*, 80–84.

25. Bourguignon, *First Federal Court*, 30–36; Carl Ubbelohde, *The Vice-Admiralty Courts and the American Revolution* (Chapel Hill: University of North Carolina Press, 1960); Matthew P. Harrington, "The Legacy of the Colonial Vice-Admiralty Courts (Part I)," *Journal of Maritime Law and Commerce* 26 (1995): 581–600.

26. Lindo v. Rodney, 99 Eng. Rep. 385, 388 (K.B. 1782); Henry J. Bourguignon, *Sir William Scott, Lord Stowell: Judge of the High Court of Admiralty, 1798–1828* (Cambridge: Cambridge University Press, 1987), 115–242; Pares, *Colonial Blockade*, 148–225.
27. Pares, *Colonial Blockade*, 77–84. British vice-admiralty judges in the Caribbean, in particular, were notorious for their willingness to ratify even the most legally dubious seizures, at times due to their personal involvement in the privateering business itself. Douglas R. Burgess, *The Politics of Piracy: Crime and Civil Disobedience in Colonial America* (Lebanon: University Press of New England, 2014), 26–35.
28. *JCC*, 3:371–75; Bourguignon, *First Federal Court*, 45–48.
29. Adams to Thomas Brand Hollis, Jan. 4, 1788, in Sara Georgini, et al., eds, *The Adams Papers, Papers of John Adams* (Cambridge: Harvard University Press, 2016), 19:250–51; *DHRC*, 28:150–51 (Pinckney); William Blackstone, *Commentaries on the Laws of England* (Oxford: Clarendon Press, 1768), 3:379–80. It is doubtful that juries ever protected victims of royal oppression as well as legend had it, but several high-profile cases in the seventeenth and eighteenth centuries cemented this view in England. The failed 1733 prosecution of printer John Peter Zenger in New York, though technically not a criminal case, had the same effect in the American colonies. Democratic Federalist, *Pennsylvania Herald*, Oct. 17, 1787, *DHRC*, 2:193–98; Harrington, "Economic Origins," 155–62.
30. Oliver Morton Dickerson, *The Navigation Acts and the American Revolution* (University of Pennsylvania Press, 1974); Harrington, "Vice-Admiralty, Part I," 591–600; Harrington, "Economic Origins," 163–67; Gautham Rao, *National Duties: Custom Houses and the Making of the American State* (Chicago: University of Chicago Press, 2016), 19–51; Ubbelohde, *Vice-Admiralty Courts*, 128–47.
31. Adams' Copy of the Information and Draft of His Argument: Court of Vice Admiralty, Boston, October 1768–March 1769, in L. Kinvin Wroth and Hiller B. Zobel, eds., *The Legal Papers of John Adams* (Cambridge: Harvard University Press, 1965), 2:194–210; Declaration of Independence (1776). For similar complaints about British deprivations, see C. A. Weslager, *The Stamp Act Congress* (Newark: University of Delaware Press, 1976), 12, 201–2.
32. Virginia Declaration of Rights of 1776, § 11; Akhil Reed Amar, *The Bill of Rights: Creation and Reconstruction* (New Haven: Yale University Press, 1998), 92 & n.33; Renee Lettow Lerner, "The Failure of Originalism in Preserving Constitutional Rights to Civil Jury Trial," *William & Mary Bill of Rights Journal* 22 (2014): 811–80.
33. Adams to Thomas Brand Hollis, Jan. 4, 1788, *Adams Papers*, 19:250–51; *DHRC*, 28:150–51 (Pinckney); *JCC*, 13:134–37. Both Adams and Pinckney had reason to overstate the problems that admiralty juries

caused during the war, as they made their observations when seeking to justify of the Constitution's lack of a civil jury guarantee a decade later. For details of the decisions in a number of prize cases adjudicated in state courts, see Bourguignon, *First Federal Court*, 79–82, 230–31, 276–82.

34. Quoted in J. Franklin Jameson, "The Predecessor to the Supreme Court," in J. Franklin Jameson, ed., *Essays in the Constitutional History of the United States in the Formative Period, 1775–1789* (New York: Houghton, Mifflin, 1889), 25–26; John Lowell to John Adams, Aug. 4, 1777, in Robert J. Taylor, ed., *The Papers of John Adams* (Cambridge: Harvard University Press, 2006), 5:262–65; Bourguignon, *First Federal Court*, 85–96, 179–90; Goebel, *Antecedents*, 149–57.
35. Bourguignon, *First Federal Court*, 60–75, 101–34; Goebel, *Antecedents*, 161–64; United States v. Peters, 9 U.S. 115 (1809).
36. *JCC*, 13:281–84; J. C. Bancroft Davis, *The Committees of the Continental Congress Chosen to Hear and Determine Appeals from Courts of Admiralty* (New York: Banks & Brothers, 1888), 5–6.
37. *JCC*, 14:508, 16:29–32, 61–64; Articles of Confederation, art. 9; Bourguignon, *First Federal Court*, 113–16. Even after the Articles went into effect, delegates could not agree on whether the Court of Appeals had jurisdiction over cases that arose earlier. Goebel, *Antecedents*, 179–81.
38. Quoted in Bourguignon, "Case of the *San Antonio*," 280–81; Bourguignon, *First Federal Court*, 231–33.
39. *JCC*, 25:546–48; Thomas Jefferson to Edward Church, Mar. 13, 1792, *PTJ*, 23:272–73; Bourguignon, "Case of the *San Antonio*," 292–94; Bourguignon, *First Federal Court*, 230–37, 318.
40. Franklin to John Torris, June 26, 1780, in Barbara B. Oberg, ed., *The Papers of Benjamin Franklin* (New Haven: Yale University Press, 1996), 32:602–3; Clark, *Franklin's Privateers*, 72–80.
41. Franklin to Ferdinand Grand, Oct. 14, 1778, *RDCUS*, 2:784; Franklin to President of Congress, Dec. 3, 1780, *RDCUS*, 4:179; Livingston to Franklin, Mar. 26, 1783, *RDCUS*, 6:343–45; *JCC*, 24:227–28; Bourguignon, "Case of the *San Antonio*," 280–81.
42. Historians have long debated just how critical the so-called "critical period" of the 1780s was. Charles A. Beard, *An Economic Interpretation of the Constitution of the United States* (New York: Macmillan, 1919); John Fiske, *The Critical Period of American History, 1783–1789* (Boston: Houghton Mifflin Company, 1916); Woody Holton, *Unruly Americans and the Origins of the Constitution* (New York: Macmillan, 2008); Merrill Jensen, *The New Nation: A History of the United States During The Confederation, 1781–1789* (New York: Knopf, 1950); George Van Cleve, *We Have Not a Government: The Articles of Confederation and the Road to the Constitution* (Chicago: University of Chicago Press, 2017); Gordon S. Wood, *The Creation of the American Republic, 1776–1787* (Chapel Hill: University of North Carolina Press, 1998). For

a recent overview of the literature, see "Introduction," in Christopher R. Pearl and Douglas Bradburn, eds., *From Independence to the U.S. Constitution: Reconsidering the Critical Period of American History* (Charlottesville: University of Virginia Press, 2022), 1–22.

43. John Jay's Charge to the Grand Jury, May 22, 1793, *DHSC*, 2:380–91. On the problem of taxation prior to the Constitution, see Robert A. Becker, *Revolution, Reform, and the Politics of American Taxation, 1763–1783* (Baton Rouge: Louisiana University Press, 1980); Roger H. Brown, *Redeeming the Republic: Federalists, Taxation, and the Origins of the Constitution* (Baltimore: Johns Hopkins University Press, 1993); Max M. Edling, *A Revolution in Favor of Government: Origins of the US Constitution and the Making of the American State* (New York: Oxford University Press, 2003); Leonard L. Richards, *Shays's Rebellion: The American Revolution's Final Battle* (Philadelphia: University of Pennsylvania Press, 2002).

44. Definitive Treaty of Peace (1783); Daniel J. Hulsebosch, "Confiscation Nation: Settler Postcolonialism and the Property Paradox," *Yale Journal of Law and the Humanities* 33 (2022): 1–27; Robert S. Lambert, "The Confiscation of Loyalist Property in Georgia, 1782–1786," *William and Mary Quarterly* 20 (1963): 80–94; Marcus Gallo, "Property Rights, Citizenship, Corruption, and Inequality: Confiscating Loyalist Estates during the American Revolution," *Pennsylvania History: A Journal of Mid-Atlantic Studies* 86 (2019): 474–510. The most famous exception – though only a partial one – came in *Rutgers v. Waddington*, in which a New York court narrowly interpreted a state statute giving citizens a right to sue Loyalists who had occupied their property during the British occupation for rent and damages. Daniel J. Hulsebosch, "A Discrete and Cosmopolitan Minority: The Loyalists, the Atlantic World, and the Origins of Judicial Review," *Chicago-Kent Law Review* 81 (2006): 825–66.

45. Emory G. Evans, "Private Indebtedness and the Revolution in Virginia, 1776 to 1796," *William and Mary Quarterly* 28 (1971): 350–74; Harrington, "Economic Origins," 171–72; Charles F. Hobson, "The Recovery of British Debts in the Federal Circuit Court of Virginia, 1790 to 1797," *Virginia Magazine of History and Biography* 92 (1984): 176–200; Holt, "Invention of the Federal Courts," 1421–531.

46. *JCC*, 31:784–95; Jay to Adams, Nov. 1, 1786, in *The Diplomatic Correspondence of the United States, 1783–1789* (Washington, DC: Blair & Rives, 1837), 2:674; George Mason to Patrick Henry, May 6, 1783, *Papers of George Mason*, 2:769; Christian G. Fritz, *American Sovereigns: The People and America's Constitutional Tradition before the Civil War* (2008), 80–116; Golove and Hulsebosch, "Civilized Nation," 952–61; Holt, "Invention of the Federal Courts," 1440–42, 1449; Holton, *Unruly Americans*, 145–62; Richard B. Morris, *The*

Peacemakers: The Great Powers and American Independence (New York: Harper and Row, 1965), 361, 379–80. This was not a new phenomenon; violence against lawyers over debt collection practices was also a feature of pre-Revolutionary political culture. John Fabian Witt, *Patriots and Cosmopolitans: Hidden Histories of American Law* (Cambridge: Harvard University Press, 2007), 38–44.

47. Federalist 15, *DHRC*, 14:324–31; Federalist 22, *DHRC*, 14:436–44; *JCC*, 31:781–95; Laws of The Legislature of The State of New York, In Force Against The Loyalists (London, H. Reynell, 1786); Frederic Austin Ogg, *The Opening of the Mississippi: A Struggle for Supremacy in the American Interior* (New York: Haskell House, 1969); Charles R. Ritcheson, *Aftermath of Revolution: British Policy Toward the United States, 1783–1795* (Dallas: Southern Methodist University Press, 1969), 37–39, 138–39; Van Cleve, *Not a Government*, 69–73, 148–51, 161–85.
48. Gregory Ablavsky, "Beyond the Indian Commerce Clause," *Yale Law Journal* 124 (2015): 1012–90; David M. Golove, "Treaty-Making and the Nation: The Historical Foundations of the Nationalist Conception of the Treaty Power," *Michigan Law Review* 98 (2000): 1075–319; Frederick W. Marks, *Independence on Trial: Foreign Affairs and the Making of the Constitution* (Baton Rouge: Louisiana State University Press, 1973), 142–66. For an argument that states have more robust authority in foreign affairs than is typically recognized, see Jack L. Goldsmith, "Federal Courts, Foreign Affairs, and Federalism," *Virginia Law Review* 83 (1997): 1617–716.
49. Jefferson to James Monroe, Aug. 11, 1786, *PTJ*, 10:225; Jefferson to George Wythe, Sep. 16, 1787, *PTJ*, 12:128–29; Pekka Pohjankoski, "Federal Coercion and National Constitutional Identity in the United States 1776–1861," *American Journal of Legal History* 56 (2016): 326–58.
50. *RFC*, 1:21 (Randolph); Charles F. Hobson, "The Negative on State Laws: James Madison, the Constitution, and the Crisis of Republican Government," *William and Mary Quarterly* 36 (1979): 215–35; Alison L. LaCroix, "The Authority of Federalism: Madison's Negative and the Origins of Federal Ideology," *Law and History Review* 28 (2010): 451–506.
51. Federalist 80, *DHRC*, 18:96–102; Federalist 22, *DHRC*, 14:436–44; *RFC*, 2:27 (Madison); *DHRC*, 2:46 (Randolph); *DHRC*, 10:1042–43 (Mason).
52. Federalist 81, *DHRC*, 18:102–11; Federalist 80, *DHRC*, 18:96–102; Golove & Hulsebosch, "Civilized Nation," 1001–3; Thomas H. Lee, "The Safe-Conduct Theory of the Alien Tort Statute," *Columbia Law Review* 106 (2006): 830–908.
53. Federalist 78, *DHRC*, 18:87–94; Kramer, *People Themselves*, 73–92; LaCroix, American Federalism, 158–66; Sylvia Snowiss, *Judicial Review*

and the Law of the Constitution (New Haven: Yale University Press, 1990), 38–59. Supporters of the Constitution – like Wilson – also assured skeptics that the courts would declare "null and void" any *federal* law that transgressed constitutional bounds. *DHRC*, 2:517.

54. Mary Sarah Bilder, *The Transatlantic Constitution: Colonial Legal Culture and the Empire* (Cambridge: Harvard University Press, 2004); William E. Nelson, *Marbury v. Madison: The Origins and Legacy of Judicial Review* (Lawrence: University Press of Kansas, 2018), 56–67; William Michael Treanor, "Judicial Review before Marbury," *Stanford Law Review* 58 (2005): 455–562.
55. *RFC*, 1:124 (Madison); *RFC*, 1:124 (Rutledge); Holt, "Invention of the Federal Courts," 1462–63; Michael G. Collins, "Article III Cases, State Court Duties, and the Madisonian Compromise," *Wisconsin Law Review* (1995): 39–198; Martin H. Redish and Curtis E. Woods, "Congressional Power to Control the Jurisdiction of Lower Federal Courts: A Critical Review and a New Synthesis," *University of Pennsylvania Law Review* 124 (1975): 45–109.
56. Federal Farmer, Letter II, Oct. 9, 1787, *DHRC*, 19:214–18; *RFC*, 1:124 (Rutledge); *RFC*, 1:125 (Butler).
57. George Clinton's Remarks Against Ratifying the Constitution, July 11, 1788, *DHRC*, 22:2146; A Columbian Patriot: Observations on the Constitution, *DHRC*, 16:279; *DHRC*, 10:1447 (Grayson); Charles Warren, "New Light on the History of the Federal Judiciary Act of 1789," *Harvard Law Review* 37 (1923): 49–132.
58. George Clinton's Remarks Against Ratifying the Constitution, July 11, 1788, *DHRC*, 22:2146; Federal Farmer: An Additional Number of Letters to the Republican, New York, May 2, 1788, *DHRC*, 20:1044; *DHRC*, 10:1442 (Henry); Dissent of the Minority of the Pennsylvania Convention, Dec. 18, 1787, *DHRC*, 15:24. For similar concerns, see Melancton Smith to Abraham Yates, Jr., Jan. 23, 1788, *DHRC*, 20:638; Brutus XII, Brutus XV, *DHRC*, 20:871–76. On the identity of Federal Farmer, see *DHRC*, 19:203–7.
59. Brutus XI, *DHRC*, 20:680–86.
60. *DHRC*, 10:1402 (Mason); Brutus V, *DHRC*, 19:410–15; Federal Farmer, Letter IV, Oct. 12, 1787, *DHRC*, 19:231–37; Michael J. Klarman, *The Framers' Coup: The Making of the United States Constitution* (New York: Oxford University Press, 2016), 257–304; John Mikhail, "McCulloch v. Maryland, Slavery, the Preamble, and the Sweeping Clause," *Constitutional Commentary* 36 (2021): 131–47.
61. U.S. Const., art. II, § 2; art. III, § 1.
62. Federalist 78, *DHRC*, 18:87–94; Thomas Jefferson, *Notes on the State of Virginia* (Philadelphia: Mathew Carey, 1794), 171; Wood, *Creation*, 160–61; Charles Gardner Geyh and Emily Field Van Tassel, "The Independence of the Judicial Branch in the New Republic," *Chicago-Kent*

Law Review 74 (2000): 31–89; Joseph Smith, "An Independent Judiciary: The Colonial Background," *University of Pennsylvania Law Review* 124 (1975): 1104–56.

63. Brutus XV, *DHRC*, 20:871–76; Melancton Smith to Abraham Yates, Jr., Jan. 23, 1788, *DHRC*, 20:638; Wood, *Empire*, 400–8, Gerhard Casper, "The Judiciary Act of 1789 and Judicial Independence," in Maeva Marcus, ed., *Origins of the Federal Judiciary: Essays on the Judiciary Act of 1789* (New York: Oxford University Press, 1992), 281–98.
64. *RFC*, 2:587–88 (Mason); *RFC*, 628, 632–33, 640; U.S. Const. art. III, § 2, cl. 3; Federalist 83, *DHRC*, 18:115–27; Harrington, "Economic Origins," 168, 180–81.
65. Georgia v. Brailsford, 3 U.S. 1, 4 (1794); Federal Farmer: An Additional Number of Letters to the Republican, May 2, 1788, *DHRC*, 20:1049. On jury law-finding and nullification, see Matthew P. Harrington, "The Law-Finding Function of the American Jury," *Wisconsin Law Review* (1999): 377–440; Lerner, "Civil Jury Trial," 819–21; William E. Nelson, "The Lawfinding Power of Colonial American Juries," *Ohio State Law Journal* 71 (2010): 1003–30; William E. Nelson, "The Province of the Judiciary," *John Marshall Law Review* 37 (2004): 325–56. On civil juries generally, see Stephan Landsman, "The Civil Jury in America: Scenes from an Unappreciated History," *Hastings Law Journal* 44 (1993): 579–620; Forrest McDonald, *Novus Ordo Seclorum: The Intellectual Origins of the Constitution* (Lawrence: University Press of Kansas, 1985), 40–41, 289–91.
66. An Old Whig VIII, *Philadelphia Independent Gazetteer*, Feb. 6, 1788, *DHRC*, 16:55; Federal Farmer: An Additional Number of Letters to the Republican, May 2, 1788, *DHRC*, 20:1049; A Democratic Federalist, *Pennsylvania Herald*, Oct. 17, 1787, *DHRC*, 2:196; A Farmer IV, *Baltimore Maryland Gazette*, Mar. 21, 1788, *DHRC*, 9:408. For a similar perspective, see Centinel II, *Philadelphia Freeman's Journal*, Oct. 24, 1787, *DHRC*, 13:463. On the less-than-complete exclusion of black people from jury service before the Civil War, see Thomas Ward Frampton, "The First Black Jurors and the Integration of the American Jury," *New York University Law Review* 99 (2024): 515–77.
67. Federalist 83, *DHRC*, 18:115–27; Dunlop v. Ball, 6 U.S. 180, 182–84 (1804); *RFC*, 1:124 (Madison); Harrington, "Economic Origins," 173; F. Thornton Miller, *Juries and Judges Versus the Law: Virginia's Provincial Legal Perspective, 1783–1828* (Charlottesville: University Press of Virginia, 1994), 7.
68. *DHRC*, 2:519 (Wilson); A Citizen of America, Oct. 17, 1787, *DHRC*, 20:787–91; Harrington, "Economic Origins," 168
69. Federalist 83, *DHRC*, 18:115–27; Hamilton to Morris, May 19, 1777, *PAH*, 1:254–56.
70. U.S. Const., amend. VII; Judiciary Act of 1789, §§ 9, 12, 22; Harrington, "Economic Origins," 199–217.

71. *RFC*, 1:124 (Wilson); *DHRC*, 10:1414 (Madison); *DHRC*, 37:255 (Virginia); *DHRC*, 22:2125 (New York); *DHRC*, 37:268 (North Carolina); Pauline Maier, *Ratification: The People Debate the Constitution, 1787–1788* (New York: Simon and Schuster, 2010), 286–91, 449–54. On the general unanimity, see Holt, "Invention of the Federal Courts," 1477; John Frank, "Historical Bases of the Federal Judicial System," *Law and Contemporary Problems* 13 (1948): 3–28; Felix Frankfurter and John Landis, *The Business of the Supreme Court: A Study in the Federal Judicial System* (New York: Macmillan, 1928), 8 n.14.
72. Civis Rusticus, *Virginia Independent Chronicle*, Jan. 30, 1788, *DHRC*, 8:331–40.
73. Goebel, *Antecedents*, 458–63; Holt, "Invention of the Federal Courts," 1477–89. There is a massive literature exploring whether the Constitution requires Congress to create inferior federal tribunals and vest them with the jurisdiction conferred by Article III. Richard H. Fallon, et. al., *Hart and Wechsler's The Federal Courts and the Federal System* (St. Paul: Foundation Press, 2015), 307–14; Christopher Jon Sprigman, "Congress's Article III Power and the Process of Constitutional Change," *New York University Law Review* 95 (2020): 1778–859.
74. Judiciary Act of 1789, §§ 1, 4, 11, 21; *Annals*, 1:783 (Tucker); *Annals*, 1:797 (Livermore); *Annals*, 1:803 (Jackson); *Annals*, 1:805–6 (Sedgwick); *Annals*, 1:813 (Madison); William R. Casto, "The First Congress's Understanding of its Authority Over the Federal Courts' Jurisdiction," *Boston College Law Review* 26 (1985):1107–8, 1133–35; Wythe Holt, "'The Federal Courts Have Enemies in All Who Fear Their Influence on State Objects': The Failure to Abolish Supreme Court Circuit-Riding in the Judiciary Acts of 1792 and 1793," *Buffalo Law Review* 36 (1987): 301–40.
75. Judiciary Act of 1789, §§ 9, 11–13, 22; Holt, "Invention of the Federal Courts," 1484–86.
76. *Annals*, 1:810 (Stone); Judiciary Act of 1789, §§ 2, 3, 9, 21; Goebel, *Antecedents*, 474; Thomas H. Lee, "Article IX, Article III, and the First Congress: The Original Constitutional Plan for the Federal Courts, 1787–1792," *Fordham Law Review* 89 (2021): 1895–940. The decision to make the federal districts coextensive with the states was a concession to those who wanted the state courts to serve as the trial forum for cases arising under federal law. Goebel, *Antecedents*, 471.
77. The district courts also had exclusive jurisdiction over certain federal crimes and suits against foreign consuls. Judiciary Act of 1789, § 9. The district court's admiralty jurisdiction was not wholly "exclusive." Section 9 included perplexing language "saving to suitors ... the right of a common law remedy, where the common law is competent to give it." This clause has caused much confusion, but its purpose seems to have been to allow plaintiffs to bring common law actions in state courts – say in contract or tort – for injuries bearing a connection to the water. The

clause rarely arose in cases implicating the nation's foreign affairs, and did not become a matter of serious interest for the federal courts until well into the nineteenth century. Waring v. Clarke, 46 U.S. 441 (1847); New Jersey Steam Nav. Co. v. Merchant's Bank of Boston, 47 U.S. 344 (1848); Goebel, *Antecedents*, 474–75; Jonathan M. Gutoff, "Admiralty, Article III, and Supreme Court Review of State-Court Decisionmaking," *Tulane Law Review* 70 (1996): 2169–94.

78. Judiciary Act of 1789, § 9, 12; United States v. The Betsey and Charlotte, 8 U.S. 443, 446 n. (1808).
79. James Madison to Samuel Johnson, July 31, 1789, *DHSC*, 4:491, 491; Edgar S. Maclay, ed., *Journal of William Maclay* (New York: D. Appleton & Co., 1890), 91, 91, 101, 117.
80. *RFC*, 1:66 (Randolph); H.R. Res., 1st Cong., 2d Sess. (Aug. 5, 1790), *Journal of the House of Representatives of the United States*, (Washington, DC: Gales and Seaton, 1826), 1:289; Wythe Holt, "Federal Courts as the Asylum to Federal Interests: Randolph's Report, the Benson Amendment, and the Original Understanding of the Federal Judiciary," *Buffalo Law Review* 36 (1987): 341–72. On Randolph as a national politician, see John J. Reardon, *Edmund Randolph: A Biography* (New York: Macmillan, 1974), 96–150; John Garry Clifford, "A Muddy Middle of the Road: The Politics of Edmund Randolph, 1790–1795," *Virginia Magazine of History and Biography* 80 (1972): 286–311.
81. Randolph to Speaker of the House of Representatives, Dec. 27, 1790, in *American State Papers: Miscellaneous* (Washington, DC: Gales and Seaton, 1834), 21–36; Holt, "Asylum to Federal Interests," 347–54.
82. Randolph to Speaker, 22, 26, 35.
83. Ibid., 22.
84. Ibid.
85. Holt, "Asylum to Federal Interests," 345–47, 354–57.
86. Madison to Samuel Johnson, July 31, 1789, *DHSC*, 4:491, 491; Madison to Edmund Pendleton, Sep. 14, 1789, in Charles F. Hobson and Robert A. Rutland, eds., *The Papers of James Madison* (Charlottesville: University Press of Virginia, 1979), 12:402, 402.
87. Jay to Edward Rutledge, Nov. 16, 1789, quoted in Holt, "Invention of the Federal Courts," 1517; Edmund Randolph to James Madison, June 30, 1789, *DHSC*, 4:432, 433; Randolph's Report, 21.

2 War Comes to America

1. William R. Casto, *Foreign Affairs and the Constitution in the Age of Fighting Sail* (Columbia: University of South Carolina Press, 2006), 45–49, 85–86, 91, 100.
2. Genet to Jefferson, June 1, 1793, *PTJ*, 26:159; Memorial from Edmond Charles Genet, May 27, 1793, *PTJ*, 26:130–31; Jefferson to James

Monroe, May 5, 1793, *PTJ*, 25:660–63; Harry Ammon, *The Genet Mission* (New York: W. W. Norton & Company, 1973), vii–ix.

3. Jefferson to Genet, June 1, 1793, *PTJ*, 26:160–61; Jefferson to Edward Telfair, Sep. 9, 1793, *PTJ*, 27:73–74.
4. Randolph to John Laurance, Aug. 12, 1794, *DHSC*, 6:527.
5. On war and foreign affairs power during Washington's presidency, see David J. Barron and Martin S. Lederman, "The Commander in Chief at the Lowest Ebb: A Constitutional History," *Harvard Law Review* 121 (2008): 941–1112; Curtis A. Bradley & Martin S. Flaherty, "Executive Power Essentialism and Foreign Affairs," *Michigan Law Review* 102 (2004): 545–688; Steven G. Calabresi and Christopher S. Yoo, *The Unitary Executive: Presidential Power from Washington to Bush* (New Haven: Yale University Press, 2008), 39–57; H. Jefferson Powell, *The President's Authority Over Foreign Affairs: An Essay in Constitutional Interpretation* (Durham: Carolina Academic Press, 2002), 34–76; Saikrishna B. Prakash and Michael D. Ramsey, "The Executive Power over Foreign Affairs," *Yale Law Journal* 111 (2001): 231–356; Robert J. Reinstein, "Executive Power and the Law of Nations in the Washington Administration," *University of Richmond Law Review* 46 (2012): 373–456.

   The little scholarship on the courts' role in the Neutrality Crisis includes Kevin Arlyck, "Courts and Foreign Affairs at the Founding," *BYU Law Review* (2017): 1–64; Casto, *Fighting Sail*, 59–82; William R. Casto, "Foreign Affairs Crises and the Constitution's Case or Controversy Limitation: Notes from the Founding Era," *American Journal of Legal History* 46 (2004): 237–70; David Sloss, "Judicial Foreign Policy: Lessons from the 1790s," *Saint Louis University Law Journal* 53 (2008): 145–96.
6. Gouverneur Morris to George Washington, Dec. 28, 1792, *PGWPS*, 11: 559–63; Ammon, *Genet Mission*, 1–20; Alexander DeConde, *Entangling Alliance: Politics and Diplomacy under George Washington* (Durham, NC, 1958), 183–85; Stanley M. Elkins and Eric L. McKitrick, *The Age of Federalism* (New York: Oxford University Press, 1993), 331.
7. *National Gazette*, May 4, 1793, p. 2; Ammon, *Genet Mission*, 19–29; Carol Berkin, *A Sovereign People: The Crises of the 1790s and the Birth of American Nationalism* (New York: Basic Books, 2017), 91–93; Casto, *Fighting Sail*, 16–17.
8. Relatif aux instructions de Genet, Dec. 1792, *CFM*, 201; Mémoire pour servir d'instruction au Citoyen Genet, Dec. 1792, *CFM*, 202–7; Supplement aux instructions donnés au Citoyen Genet, Dec. 1792, *CFM*, 207–11; Gouverneur Morris to Thomas Jefferson, Mar. 7, 1793, *ASPFR*, 1:354; Wesley J. Campbell, "The Origin of Citizen Genet's Projected Attack on Spanish Louisiana: A Case Study in Girondin Politics," *French Historical Studies* 33 (2010): 515–44; Casto, *Fighting Sail*, 14–18.
9. Supplement aux instructions donnés au Citoyen Genet, Dec. 1792, *CFM*, 207–11; Genet to consuls, May 1793, AMAE-CP, 37:384–85;

Gouverneur Morris to Thomas Jefferson, Mar. 7, 1793, *ASPFR*, 1:354; Adet to Pickering, May 18, 1796 (29 Floréal An 4), *ASPFR*, 1:650–51; Melvin H. Jackson, *Privateers in Charleston, 1793–1796: An Account of a French Palatinate in South Carolina* (Washington, DC: Smithsonian Institution Press, 1969), 1–2; William S. Cormack, *Revolution and Political Conflict in the French Navy, 1789–1794* (Cambridge: Cambridge University Press, 1995).

A note about French sources: For ease of following their chronology, I have converted all dates in French documents from the French Republican calendar into standard dates, but have provided the Republican date in parentheses for reference. All translations from the French are mine.

10. Genet to LeBrun, May 31, 1793, *CFM*, 216; Monroe to Jefferson, May 9, 1793, *PTJ*, 25:696; Genet to Ministère des Affaires Étrangères, Apr. 16, 1793, *CFM*, 211–13; Francois Furstenberg, *When the United States Spoke French: Five Refugees Who Shaped a Nation* (New York: Penguin Press, 2014), 45–53; Ammon, *Genet Mission*, 51–55; David Waldstreicher, *In the Midst of Perpetual Fetes: The Making of American Nationalism, 1776–1820* (Chapel Hill: University of North Carolina Press, 1997), 133–36.
11. Supplement aux instructions donnés au Citoyen Genet, Dec. 1792, *CFM*, 207–11; Genet to Jefferson, May 27, 1793, *PTJ*, 26:124–29. Memorandum of Conversations with Edmond Charles Genet, July 26, 1793, *PTJ*, 26:571–73. On sailors and citizenship in the Age of Revolution, see Nathan Perl-Rosenthal, *Citizen Sailors: Becoming American in the Age of Revolution* (Cambridge: Harvard University Press, 2015).
12. Genet to Minister of Foreign Affairs, Apr. 16, 1793, *CFM*, 211–13; Robert Alderson, *This Bright Era of Happy Revolutions: French Consul Michel-Ange-Bernard Mangourit and International Republicanism in Charleston, 1792–1794* (Columbia: University of South Carolina Press, 2008), 110–11; Ammon, *Genet Mission*, 8, 44–45. For details on the fitting out of privateer vessels in Charleston, see Casto, *Fighting Sail*, 45–49; Jackson, *Privateers in Charleston*, 5.
13. Washington to Hamilton, Apr. 12, 1793, *PAH*, 14:314–15; Washington to Jefferson, Apr. 12, 1793, *PTJ*, 12:448–49; A Proclamation by the President of the United States, Apr. 22, 1793, *ASPFR*, 1:140; Lindsay Chervinsky, *The Cabinet: George Washington and the Creation of an American Institution* (Cambridge: Harvard University Press, 2020), 196–97.
14. David Brion Davis, *Revolutions: Reflections on American Equality and Foreign Liberations* (Cambridge: Harvard University Press, 1990), 33–38; DeConde, *Entangling Alliance*, 178–80; Eliga H. Gould, *Among the Powers of the Earth: The American Revolution and the Making of a New World Empire* (Cambridge: Harvard University Press, 2012), 145–77.

15. Jefferson to Madison, May 13, 1793, *PTJ*, 26:25–27; Lance Banning, *The Jeffersonian Persuasion: Evolution of a Party Ideology* (Ithaca: Cornell University Press, 1980), 126–78; Elkins and McKitrick, *Age of Federalism*, 77–132, 257–302; Drew McCoy, *The Elusive Republic: Political Economy in Jeffersonian America* (Chapel Hill: University of North Carolina Press, 2012), 120–35, 152–61; James Roger Sharp, *American Politics in the Early Republic: The New Nation in Crisis* (New Haven: Yale University Press, 1993), 69–91.
16. *City Gazette and Daily Advertiser* (Charleston), Sep. 7, 1793, p. 3; Jefferson to Harry Innes, May 23, 1793, *PTJ*, 26:99–100; Furstenberg, *Spoke French*, 50–53; Robert W. Tucker and David C. Hendrickson, *Empire of Liberty: The Statecraft of Thomas Jefferson* (New York: Oxford University Press, 1992), 39–42, 45; Waldstreicher, *Perpetual Fetes*, 126–41.
17. Adams to Richard Price, Apr. 19, 1790, in Sara Georgini, et al., eds., *The Adams Papers, Papers of John Adams* (Cambridge: Harvard University Press, 2020), 20:321–23; Enclosure: Answer to Question the 3d. Proposed by the President of the United States, May 2, 1793, *PAH*, 14:367–96; DeConde, *Entangling Alliance*, 174–78, 181.
18. Washington to Daniel Morgan, Oct. 8, 1794, *PGWPS*, 17:29–40; Nathaniel Chipman to Alexander Hamilton, June 9, 1794, *PAH*, 16:465–70; DeConde, *Entangling Alliance*, 256–69; Eugene P. Link, *Democratic-Republican Societies, 1790–1800* (New York: Octagon Books, 1965), 10–12; Rachel H. Cleves, *The Reign of Terror in America: Visions of Violence from Anti-Jacobinism to Antislavery* (New York: Cambridge University Press, 2009), 58–103.
19. Samuel Eliot Morison, ed., *The Life and Letters of Harrison Gray Otis, Federalist, 1765–1848* (Boston: Houghton Mifflin, 1913), 1:51; Davis, *Revolutions*, 49–54; DeConde, *Entangling Alliance*, 178, 255 n. 52; Ashli White, *Encountering Revolution: Haití and the Making of the Early Republic* (Baltimore: Johns Hopkins University Press, 2010), 124–65.
20. Jefferson to Madison, July 7, 1793, *PTJ*, 26:443–44; Casto, *Fighting Sail*, 59–82; Elkins & McKitrick, *Age of Federalism*, 339–40; Chervinsky, *Cabinet*, 201–4; Christopher J. Young, "Connecting the President and the People: Washington's Neutrality, Genet's Challenge, and Hamilton's Fight for Public Support," *Journal of the Early Republic* 31 (2011): 435–66.
21. Edmund Randolph to James Monroe, June 1, 1795, *ASPFR*, 1:705, 706; James Monroe to Thomas Jefferson, May 28, 1793, *PTJ*, 26:135–37; Casto, *Fighting Sail*, 16–17.
22. Opinion on Ship Passports, May 3, 1793, *PTJ*, 25:643, 645; Jefferson to Alexander Donald, Aug. 29, 1790, *PTJ*, 17:473; Tucker and Hendrickson, *Empire of Liberty*, 55–56.

23. Hamilton, "Report on a Plan for the Further Support of Public Credit," Jan. 16, 1795, *PAH*, 18:56–129; Gautham Rao, *National Duties: Custom Houses and the Making of the American State* (Chicago: University of Chicago Press, 2016), 1–4, 105–6.
24. Thomas Jefferson, *Notes on the State of Virginia* (Philadelphia: Mathew Carey, 1794), 253–54; Jefferson to Edward Rutledge, July 4, 1790, *PTJ*, 16:600–1; Mlada Bukovansky, "American Identity and Neutral Rights from Independence to the War of 1812," *International Organization* 50 (1997): 209–43; Brooke Hunter, "Wheat, War, and the American Economy during the Age of Revolution" *William and Mary Quarterly* 62 (2005): 505–26; McCoy, *Elusive Republic*, 76–104.
25. Jefferson to Gouverneur Morris, Apr. 20, 1793, *PTJ*, 25:575–76; Jefferson to Madison, Mar. 24, 1793, *PTJ*, 25:442–43; James Madison, "Helvidius" Number 4, Sep. 14, 1793, *PJM*, 15:106–10; Tucker & Hendrickson, *Empire of Liberty*, 39–46.
26. Lord Grenville to Hammond, Jan. 4, 1793, in Bernard Mayo, ed., *Instructions to the British Ministers to the United States* (Washington, DC: Government Printing Office, 1941), 33; Grenville to Hammond, July 5, 1793, ibid., 40–42; Hammond to Jefferson, May 2, 1793, *PTJ*, 25:637; Hammond to Jefferson, May 8, 1793, *PTJ*, 25:685–86; Notes on Neutrality Questions, July 13, 1793, *PTJ*, 26:498–500; Hammond to Jefferson, Aug. 30, 1793, *PTJ*, 26:789–90; Casto, *Fighting Sail*, 45–58. Spanish representatives similarly protested what they called Genet's "perverse scheme." Josef de Jaudenes and Josef Ignacio de Viar to Jefferson, Oct. 2, 1793, *PTJ*, 27:176–80.
27. Memorial from George Hammond, May 8, 1793, *PTJ*, 25:685–86; Jefferson to Genet, June 5, 1793, *PTJ*, 26:195–97; Hammond to Jefferson, June 14, 1793, *PTJ*, 26:284–85; Casto, *Fighting Sail*, 40–51.
28. Emmerich de Vattel, *The Law of Nations or the Principles of Natural Law*, §§ 103–104 (Washington, DC: Carnegie Institution, 1916), 3:268; Cornelius van Bynkershoek, *Quaestionum Juris Publici Libri Duo* (Oxford: Clarendon Press, 1930), 2:60–65; Hugo Grotius, *The Rights of War and Peace* (Washington, DC: M. Walter Dunne, 1901), 377–78; Christian Wolff, *Jus Gentium Methodo Scientifica Pertractatum* (Oxford: Clarendon Press, 1934), 2:346–54; Jefferson to Gouverneur Morris, Aug. 16, 1793, *PTJ*, 26:697–715; Charles S. Hyneman, *The First American Neutrality: A Study of the American Understanding of Neutral Obligations During the Years 1792 to 1815* (Urbana: University of Illinois, 1934), 14. For a discussion of the publicists favored by Jefferson and other founders, see Brian Richardson, "The Use of Vattel in the American Law of Nations," *American Journal of International Law* 106 (2012): 547–71.
29. Geoffrey Butler and Simon Maccoby, *The Development of International Law* (London: Longmans, Green and Co., 1928), 162–66; Samuel Flagg Bemis, *The Diplomacy of the American Revolution* (Edinburgh: Oliver

and Boyd, 1957), 53–55; Jonathan R. Dull, *A Diplomatic History of the American Revolution* (New Haven: Yale University Press, 1984), 60–61; Elkins and McKitrick, *Age of Federalism*, 330–35.

30. Vattel, *Law of Nations*, 268; van Bynkershoek, *Quaestionum Juris*, 61–63; Reinstein, "Executive Power," 385; Treaty of Amity and Commerce (1778), art. 17, 22.

31. Genet to Jefferson, June 22, 1793, *PTJ*, 26:339–42; Genet to Jefferson, May 27, 1793, *PTJ*, 26:124–27; Memorial from Edmond Charles Genet, May 27, 1793, *PTJ*, 26:130; Memorandum of Edmund Randolph, May 17, 1793, *PGWPS*, 12:602–5; Thomas, *American Neutrality*, 118–64. For similar views expressed by other French officials, see Protest of Citizen Hauterive, June 21, 1793, *ASPFR*, 1:153; Alexandre Maurice d'Hauterive to Jefferson, Sep. 10, 1793, *PTJ*, 27:83.

32. Jefferson to Jean Baptiste Ternant, May 15, 1793, *PTJ*, 26:42–44; Jefferson to Gouverneur Morris, Aug. 16, 1793, *PTJ*, 26:697–715; Circular to French Consuls and Vice-Consuls, Sep. 7, 1793, *PTJ*, 26:51. The 1788 consular convention between the two nations – signed by Jefferson – did not include jurisdiction over prizes. Convention Defining and Establishing the Functions and Privileges of Consuls and Vice Consuls, art. 8 (1788).

33. Washington to Hamilton, Apr. 12, 1793, *PGWPS*, 12:447–48; Grotius, *Rights of War and Peace*, 394; Vattel, *Law of Nations*, 13–37; Manuel R. Garcia-Mora, *International Responsibility for Hostile Acts of Private Persons against Foreign States* (The Hague: Martinus Nijhoff, 1962), 17–24; Reinstein, "Executive Power," 431.

34. Casto, *Fighting Sail*, 22; Charles G. Fenwick, *The Neutrality Laws of the United States* (Washington, DC: The Carnegie Endowment, 1913), 6, 27–28; William Edward Hall, *International Law* (Oxford: Clarendon Press, 1880), 540–50; Hyneman, *First Neutrality*, 13–16; Philip C. Jessup, *American Neutrality and International Police* (Boston: World Peace Foundation, 1928), 7–12; Jules Lobel, "The Rise and Decline of the Neutrality Act: Sovereignty and Congressional War Powers in United States Foreign Policy," *Harvard International Law Journal* 24 (1983): 1–72; Reinstein, "Executive Power," 384–400.

35. Washington to Jefferson, July 11, 1793, *PTJ*, 26:481–82; Thomas Jefferson's Notes on a Conversation with Edmond Genet, July 10, 1793, *PGWPS*, 13:202–7; Jefferson to Thomas Mann Randolph, Jr., June 24, 1793, *PTJ*, 26:355–56; Cabinet Opinion on the Little Sarah, July 8, 1793, *PGWPS*,13:180–85; Casto, *Fighting Sail*, 103–7; Chervinsky, *Cabinet*, 211–16.

36. Jefferson to the Justices of the Supreme Court, July 18, 1793, *PTJ*, 26:520.

37. Jefferson to Thomas Mann Randolph, Jr., June 24, 1793, *PTJ*, 26:355–56; Phineas Bond to Lord Grenville, June 8, 1793, in *Annual Report*

of the American Historical Association for the Year 1897 (Washington, DC: Government Printing Office, 1898), 528–31; DeConde, *Entangling Alliance*, 269. On Genet's recall, see Ammon, *Genet Mission*, 94–110.

38. Jefferson to Genet and Hammond, July 12, 1793, *PTJ*, 26:487; Jefferson to the Justices of the Supreme Court, July 18, 1793, *PTJ*, 26:520. Casto, *Fighting Sail*, 109–11; Stewart Jay, *Most Humble Servants: The Advisory Role of Early Judges* (New Haven: Yale University Press 1997), 159.
39. John Jay's Charge to the Grand Jury, May 22, 1793, *DHSC*, 2:380–91; Iredell to Randolph, May 2, 1794, *DHSC*, 2:451–52. On the early federal judges, see William R. Casto, *The Supreme Court in the Early Republic: The Chief Justiceships of John Jay and Oliver Ellsworth* (Columbia: University of South Carolina Press, 1995), 54–70; Jay, *Most Humble*, 71–112; Maeva Marcus, "George Washington's Appointments to the Supreme Court," *Journal of Supreme Court History* 24 (1999): 243–54.
40. On Jay's advice in the Neutrality Crisis, see Hamilton to Jay, Apr. 9, 1793, *PAH*, 14:297, 297–98; Hamilton to Jay, Apr. 9, 1793, *PAH*, 14:299, 300; Jay to Hamilton, Apr. 11, 1793, *PAH*, 14:307, 307–10; Casto, *Fighting Sail*, 27–28. On the practice of giving advice generally, see Jay, *Most Humble Servants*, 10–112; Casto, *Supreme Court*, 97–98, 147–57, 178–83.
41. Supreme Court Justices to Washington, July 20, 1793, *PGWPS*, 13:256–57; Supreme Court Justices to Washington, Aug. 8, 1793, *PGWPS*, 13:392.
42. Clinton v. Jones, 520 U.S. 681, 700 (1997); John Marshall, *The Life of George Washington* (Philadelphia: C.P. Wayne, 1804): 5:441; Julius Goebel, *History of the Supreme Court of the United States: Antecedents and Beginnings to 1801* (New York, Macmillan Publishing Co., 1971), 1:626 n. 68; Charles Marion Thomas, *American Neutrality in 1793: A Study in Cabinet Government* (New York: Columbia University Press, 1931), 150; Robert J. Pushaw, Jr., "Why the Supreme Court Never Gets Any 'Dear John' Letters: Advisory Opinions in Historical Perspective," *Georgetown Law Journal* 87 (1998): 473–97; Jay, *Most Humble*, 1–2.
43. U.S. Const., art. II, § 2; Russell Wheeler, "Extrajudicial Activities of the Early Supreme Court," *Supreme Court Review* (1973): 144–58; Jay, *Most Humble*, 10–112; Casto, *Fighting Sail*, 117–21.
44. David M. Golove and Daniel J. Hulsebosch, "A Civilized Nation: The Early American Constitution, the Law of Nations, and the Pursuit of International Recognition," *New York University Law Review* 85 (2010): 932–1066. Similarly, arguments that the justices declined to answer in order to strengthen the executive branch's role in foreign affairs (and specifically to empower Hamilton) give too little weight to the fact that the Washington administration directly requested their aid. Jay, *Most Humble*, 167–70; Casto, *Fighting Sail*, 117–21; Golove and Hulsebosch, "A Civilized Nation," 1027 n. 60.

45. *National Gazette*, July 27, 1793, p. 2. Relatedly, Christian Burset posits that late eighteenth-century British doubts about advisory opinions' legal authority may have prompted the justices to refrain from taking a position on the fraught questions the administration raised. Christian R. Burset, "Advisory Opinions and the Problem of Legal Authority," *Vanderbilt Law Review* 74 (2021): 621–80.
46. Hayburn's Case, 2 U.S. 408 (1792); Susan Low Bloch, "Early Role of the Attorney General in Our Constitutional Scheme: In the Beginning There Was Pragmatism," *Duke Law Journal* (1989): 561–653; Maeva Marcus and Robert Teir, "Hayburn's Case: A Misinterpretation of Precedent," *Wisconsin Law Review* (1988): 527–46.
47. Chisholm v. Georgia, 2 U.S. 419 (1793); *National Gazette*, July 3, 1793, p. 3; Goebel, *Antecedents*, 725–37; Jay, *Most Humble*, 161–66.
48. Letter from the Justices of the Supreme Court to the Congress of the United States, Aug. 9, 1792, *DHSC*, 2:289–90; Iredell to Hannah Iredell, Oct. 2, 1791, *DHSC*, 2:212–13; *Annals*, 11:38 (Morris). James Pfander situates the advisory opinion episode in the broader debate over judicial compensation in "Judicial Compensation and the Definition of Judicial Power in the Early Republic," *Michigan Law Review* 107 (2008): 1–51.
49. Edward Rutledge to Henry Middleton Rutledge, Nov. 1, 1796, *DHSC*, 3:139; Clare Cushman, *Courtwatchers: Eyewitness Accounts in Supreme Court History* (Lanham: Rowan & Littlefield, 2011), 5–8; Joshua Glick, "On the Road: The Supreme Court and the History of Circuit Riding," *Cardozo Law Review* 24 (2003): 1753–843; Maeva Marcus, et al., "'It is my wish as well as my Duty to attend the court': The Hardships of Supreme Court Service, 1790–1800," *Yearbook: Supreme Court Historical Society* (1984): 118–26; Dale Yurs, "The Early Supreme Court and the Challenges of Riding Circuit," *Journal of Supreme Court History* 36 (2011): 181–92.
50. Supreme Court Justices to Washington, Aug. 8, 1793, *PGWPS*, 13:392; Supreme Court Justices to Washington, Aug. 9, 1792, *PGWPS*, 10:643–45; Thomas Johnson to James Iredell, Mar. 9, 1793, *DHSC*, 2:244–45; Casto, *Supreme Court*, 90; Marcus, "Washington's Appointments," 246–47.
51. Jefferson to Richard Harison, June 12, 1793, *PTJ*, 26:261–63; Jefferson to Henry Lee, May 21, 1793, *PTJ*, 26: 76–77; Notes on Alexander Hamilton and the Enforcement of Neutrality, May 6, 1793, *PTJ*, 25: 667–68; Edmund Randolph to William Channing, May 12, 1793, Manuscripts and Archives Division, New York Public Library.
52. Notes on Neutrality Questions, July 13, 1793, *PTJ*, 26:498–500; Judiciary Act of 1789, §§ 4, 11, 1 Stat. 73, 74–79. On the early federal grand jury, see *DHSC*, 2:4–6; Holt, "Federal Courts Have Enemies," 301–40.
53. William Paterson's Notes for Remarks on Judiciary Bill, June 23, 1789, *DHSC*, 4:416; Ralph Lerner, "The Supreme Court as Republican Schoolmaster," *Supreme Court Review* (1967): 127–80. There is relatively little scholarship exploring the circuit courts' role in the nation's

legal and political life. Maeva Marcus and Emily Field Van Tassel, "Judges and Legislators in the New Federal System, 1789–1800," in Robert A. Katzmann, ed., *Judges and Legislators: Toward Institutional Comity*, (Washington, DC: Brookings Institution Press, 1988), 31–53. Volumes 2 and 3 of *DHSC* contain many examples of the justices' grand jury charges during the early period. For an example of a response, see Reply of the Grand Jury of the Circuit Court for the District of New Jersey, Apr. 2, 1796, *DHSC*, 3:102–4.

54. Jefferson to Gouverneur Morris, Aug. 16, 1793, *PTJ*, 26:697–715; Jefferson to Morris, Aug. 26, 1793, *PTJ*, 26:760; Jefferson to Randolph, May 8, 1793, *PTJ*, 26:691–92.
55. Notes on Neutrality Questions, July 13, 1793, *PTJ*, 26: 498–500; Memorandum from Edmund Randolph, May 17, 1793, *PGWPS*, 12:602–5; Jefferson to Hammond, Sep. 5, 1793, *PTJ*, 27:35–38; John Jay's Charge to the Grand Jury, May 22, 1793, *DHSC*, 2:380–91.
56. Vattel, *Law of Nations*, 136–37; Garcia-Mora, *International Responsibility*, 17–24.
57. Hamilton to Washington, May 15, 1793, *PGWPS*, 12:577–84; Federalist 11, *DHRC*, 14:209–15. For an argument that early modern prohibitions against foreign military service can be seen as an assertion of state control over the use of violence, see Janice E. Thomson, *Mercenaries, Pirates, and Sovereigns: State-Building and Extraterritorial Violence in Early Modern Europe* (Princeton: Princeton University Press, 1994), 77–88.
58. "An Act for establishing an Executive Department," 1 Stat. 28 (1789); Richard Dobbs Spaight to Washington, June 24, 1793, *PGWPS*, 13:142–44. For a list of federal officers in 1792, see *American State Papers, Miscellaneous* (Washington, DC: Gales and Seaton, 1834), 1:57–68. On the early federal government's small size, see Homer S. Cummings and Carl McFarland, *Federal Justice: Chapters in the History of Justice and the Federal Executive* (New York: Macmillan, 1937); Dwight F. Henderson, *Courts for a New Nation* (Washington, DC: Public Affairs, 1971); Leonard White, *The Federalists: A Study in Administrative History* (New York: Macmillan Co., 1948); Brian Balogh, *A Government Out of Sight: The Mystery of National Authority in Nineteenth-Century America* (Cambridge: Cambridge University Press, 2009). On the early military, see Max M. Edling, *A Hercules in the Cradle: War, Money, and the American State, 1783–1867* (Chicago: University of Chicago Press, 2015).
59. William Vans Murray to Hamilton, May 8, 1793, *PAH*, 14:425–28; Thomas Sim Lee to Jefferson, May 20, 1793, *PTJ*, 26: 67–68; Thomas Newton, Jr. and William Lindsay to George Washington, May 5, 1793, *PGWPS*, 12: 521–22.
60. Randolph to Jefferson, May 9, 1793, *PTJ*, 25:700–2; Randolph to James Monroe, June 1, 1795, *ASPFR*, 1:705–6; Jefferson to Zebulon Hollingsworth, June 25, 1793, *PTJ*, 26:363.

61. Notes on Alexander Hamilton and the Enforcement of Neutrality, May 6, 1793, *PTJ*, 26:667–68; Jefferson to Madison, May 13, 1793, *PTJ*, 26:25–27; Chervinsky, *Cabinet*, 193–96; Thomas, *American Neutrality*, 53–90. Decision-making in the Neutrality Crisis was further complicated by an outbreak of yellow fever in the summer of 1793, which prompted thousands of Philadelphians to flee the city, including cabinet members. Jefferson to Madison, Sep. 1, 1793, *PJM*, 15:88–91; J. M. Powell, *Bring Out Your Dead: The Great Plague of Yellow Fever in Philadelphia in 1793* (Philadelphia: University of Pennsylvania Press, 1949).
62. Jefferson to Madison, Sep. 21, 1795, *PTJ*, 28:475–77. Hamilton prevailed in debates over the creation of a national bank and the federal government's assumption of state debts, but his efforts to centralize control over the customs officers under his supervision met with mixed results. Edling, *Hercules in the Cradle*, 50–107; Aaron T. Knapp, "From Empire to Law: Customs Collection in the American Founding," *Law & Social Inquiry* 43 (2018): 554–84; Rao, *National Duties*, 75–99.
63. Notes on Alexander Hamilton and the Enforcement of Neutrality, May 6, 1793, *PTJ*, 26:667–68; Jefferson to Randolph, May 8, 1793, *PTJ*, 26:691–92; Chervinsky, *The Cabinet*, 219–25. On the American tradition of distrusting customs officers, see Thomas C. Barrow, *Trade and Empire: The British Customs Service in Colonial America, 1660–1775* (Cambridge: Harvard University Press, 1967); T. H. Breen, *The Marketplace of Revolution: How Consumer Politics Shaped American Independence* (New York: Oxford University Press, 2004); Edmund S. Morgan, *The Stamp Act Crisis: Prologue to Revolution* (New York: Collier Books, 1963).
64. Randolph to Jefferson, May 9, 1793, *PTJ*, 25:700–2; Treasury Department Circular to the Collectors of the Customs, *PAH*, 15:178–81; Edmund Randolph to William Channing, May 12, 1793, Manuscripts and Archives Division, New York Public Library; Notes on Alexander Hamilton and the Enforcement of Neutrality, May 6, 1793, *PTJ*, 26:667–68.
65. John K. Mahon and Romana Danysh, *Infantry Part I: Regular Army* (Washington, DC: Office of the Chief of Military History, 1972), 13; "An Act to provide for calling forth the Militia," 1 Stat. 264 (1792). Washington would famously call out the militia to deal with the Whiskey Rebellion in Pennsylvania in 1794. Saul Cornell, *The Other Founders: Anti-Federalism and the Dissenting Tradition in America, 1788–1828* (Chapel Hill: University of North Carolina Press, 1999), 200–18; Elkins and McKitrick, *Age of Federalism*, 461–88; William Hogeland, *The Whiskey Rebellion: George Washington, Alexander Hamilton, and the Frontier Rebels Who Challenged America's Newfound Sovereignty* (New York: Scribner, 2006).
66. Jefferson to Knox, May 21, 1793, *PTJ*, 26:75–76; Knox to Samuel Huntington, Aug. 7, 1793, Connecticut Historical Society, Jonathan

Trumbull Jr. Papers; Jefferson to Hammond, Sep. 5, 1793, *PTJ*, 27:35; Jefferson to the District Attorneys, Nov. 10, 1793, *PTJ*, 27:338–39; Instructions to the District Attorneys, [undated], *PTJ*, 27:340.

67. John Temple to Samuel Huntington, Aug. 29, 1793, NAFO 5, 2:69; Huntington to Temple, Sep. 3, 1793, NAFO 5, 2:69; Henry Knox to Jefferson, Sep. 9, 1793, *PTJ*, 27:72; Richard Dobbs Spaight to Washington, Feb. 8, 1794, *PGWPS*,15:197–98. George Clinton in New York was particularly proactive, at times taking action with no prompting from the local British consul, though that did not prevent British officials from complaining about his performance. Temple to Clinton, June 9, 1793, NAFO 5, 2:33; Hammond to Randolph, Sep. 3, 1794, NAFO 5, 5: 303. By September 1793, Hammond was able to report to London that several French privateers had been disarmed, and their prizes restored to their owners. Hammond to Grenville, Sep. 17, 1793, NAFO 5, 1:290.
68. Jefferson to Hammond, Nov. 14, 1793, *PTJ*, 27:368–71; Hammond to Grenville, June 27, 1794, NAFO 5, 5:131; Hammond to Grenville, Nov. 5, 1794, NAFO 5, 5:345; Hamilton to Dundas, Feb. 19, 1794, NAFO 5, 6:160.
69. Memorandum from Thomas Jefferson, July 26, 1793, *PGWPS*, 13: 287–90; *Federal Gazette*, Oct. 24, 1793, p. 3; Hamilton to Isaac Holmes, June 2, 1794, *PAH*, 16:446–447; Moultrie to Knox, Jan. 23, 1794, AMAE-MD, 39:124; C. L. Bragg, *Crescent Moon Over Carolina: William Moultrie and American Liberty* (Columbia: University of South Carolina Press, 2013), 255–57.
70. James Wilson's Charge to the Grand Jury, July 22, 1793, *DHSC*, 2:414–23; Mark David Hall, "Notes and Documents: James Wilson's Law Lectures," *Pennsylvania Magazine of History and Biography* 128 (2004): 63–76; Aaron T. Knapp, "Law's Revolutionary: James Wilson and the Birth of American Jurisprudence," *Journal of Law and Policy*, 29 (2013): 189–94.
71. James Wilson's Charge to the Grand Jury, July 22, 1793, *DHSC*, 2:414–23.
72. Genet to Jefferson, June 1, 1793, *PTJ*, 26:159; Henfield's Case, 11 F. Cas. 1099, 1120 (C.C. Pa. 1793); Jefferson to Rawle, May 15, 1793, *PTJ*, 26:40–41; Edmund Randolph's Opinion on the Case of Gideon Henfield, May 30, 1793, *PTJ*, 26:145–46; Jefferson to Monroe, July 14, 1793, *PTJ*, 26:501–2; Casto, "Foreign Affairs Crises," 246–47; Golove and Hulsebosch, "A Civilized Nation," 1028–30.
73. Stephen B. Presser, "A Tale of Two Judges: Richard Peters, Samuel Chase, and the Broken Promise of Federalist Jurisprudence," *Northwestern University Law Review* 73 (1978): 26–111; Kathryn Preyer, "Jurisdiction to Punish: Federal Authority, Federalism and the Common Law of Crimes in the Early Republic," *Law and History Review* 4 (1986): 223–65.

74. Henfield's Case, 11 F. Cas. 1099, 1117 (C.C. Pa. 1793).
75. Henfield's Case, 11 F. Cas. 1099, 1121 (C.C. Pa. 1793); Hamilton to Washington, Aug. 5, 1793, *PAH*, 15:194; Jefferson to Gouverneur Morris, Aug. 16, 1793, *PTJ*, 26:697–711; Randolph to Washington, Aug. 21, 1793, *PGWPS*, 13:524–25; Casto, *Fighting Sail*, 97.
76. Jefferson to Gouverneur Morris, Aug. 16, 1693, *PTJ*, 26:697–715; Jefferson to Morris, Aug. 26, 1693, *PTJ*, 26:760; Francis Wharton, *State Trials of the United States During the Administrations of Washington and Adams* (Carey and Hart, 1849), 49 n.*; Casto, *Fighting Sail*, 99–100.
77. *Dunlap's American Daily Advertiser*, Dec. 10, 1793, p. 2; *Connecticut Journal*, Sep. 4, 1793, p. 3; Stephen Higginson to Hamilton, Aug. 24, 1793, *PAH*, 15:273–76: Christopher Gore to Jefferson, Oct. 21,1793, *PTJ*, 27:261; Thomas, *American Neutrality*, 212–19; Warren, *Supreme Court*, 1:114–15.
78. Casto, *Fighting Sail*, 98–102; *The Diary* (New York), Aug. 7, 1793, p. 2; Henry Knox to Washington, Aug. 17, 1793, *PGWPS*, 13:476–78, n. 1; John Marshall, *The Life of George Washington* (Philadelphia: C.P. Wayne, 1807), 5:435; Thomas, *American Neutrality*, 173–76.
79. Hamilton to Washington, May 15, 1793, *PAH*, 14:454–60; Jefferson to Hammond, June 5, 1793, *PTJ*, 26:197–98.
80. Jefferson to Hammond, June 5, 1793, *PTJ*, 26:197–98; Jefferson to Hammond, June 13, 1793, *PTJ*, 26:270–71.
81. Jefferson to Thomas Pinckney, June 14, 1793, *PTJ*, 26:286–88; Jefferson to Genet, June 17, 1793, *PTJ*, 26:297–300.
82. Genet to Jefferson, June 14, 1793, *PTJ*, 26:281; Genet to Jefferson, June 22, 1793, *PTJ*, 26:339; Protest of Citizen Hauterive, June 21, 1793, *ASPFR*, 1:153; Hamilton to Washington, May 15, 1793, *PGWPS*, 12:577, 582. On Hamilton's willingness to support and exploit judicial authority in service of his policy goals in other contexts, see Kate Elizabeth Brown, *Alexander Hamilton and the Development of American Law* (Lawrence: University Press of Kansas, 2017), 57–84.
83. Phineas Bond to Lord Grenville, June 8, 1793, *Annual Report of the American Historical Association*, 528–31; Hammond to Jefferson, Mar. 5, 1792, *PTJ*, 23:196–213.
84. Hamilton to Rufus King, June 15, 1793, *PAH*, 14:547–49; Hammond to Lord Grenville, May 17, 1793, NAFO 5, 1:137; Hammond to Grenville, June 10, 1793, NAFO 5, 1:175; Hammond to Grenville, July 7, 1793, NAFO 5, 1:193, 201.
85. Findlay v. The William, record, USDC-PA, roll 2; Phineas Bond to Lord Grenville, June 8, 1793, *Annual Report of the American Historical Association*, 528; Affidavit of Pierre Barriere, June 7, 1793, *ASPFR*, 1:152; Genet to Jefferson, June 14, 1793, *PTJ*, 26:281.
86. *Federal Gazette*, June 19, 1793, p. 2; *Federal Gazette*, June 21, 1793, pp. 2–3; Treaty of Amity and Commerce (1778), art. 17. On the capturing

nation's exclusive jurisdiction over prizes, see L'Invincible, 14 U.S. 238, 254 (1816); T. Rutherforth, *Institutes of Natural Law* (Cambridge: J. Bentham, 1754), 594–600.

87. *Federal Gazette*, June 19, 1793, p. 2; *Federal Gazette*, June 24, 1793, p. 2; Findlay v. The William, 9 F. Cas. 57, 58–59 (D. Pa. 1793).
88. Findlay v. The William, 9 F. Cas. 57, 59–61 (D. Pa. 1793). On Peters' reputation, see Stephen Presser, *The Original Misunderstanding: The English, the Americans, and the Dialectic of Federalist Jurisprudence* (Durham: Carolina Academic Press, 1991), 56–57, 60–61.
89. Findlay v. The William, 9 F. Cas. 57, 59–61 (D. Pa. 1793).
90. Cabinet Opinions on Privateers and Prizes, Aug. 5, 1793, *PTJ*, 26:620; Jefferson to Gouverneur Morris, Aug. 16, 1793, *PTJ*, 26:697–715; Moxon v. The Fanny, 17 F. Cas. 942 (D. Pa. 1793); James Duane, *Decree on the Admiralty Side of the District Court of New York* (New York: Francis Childs and John Swaine, 1794), 9, 19–35; William Paca's District Court Opinion, Aug. 15, 1793, *DHSC*, 6:324–32; Castello v. Bouteille, 5 F. Cas. 278, 279 (D.S.C. 1794). The North Carolina district court also dismissed a suit for lack of jurisdiction. *Boston Gazette*, Aug. 5, 1793, p. 2. The one exception came in Massachusetts, where the district court concluded that it had jurisdiction over the property of an American citizen shipped on board a British vessel that was captured by a French privateer. *Columbian Centinel*, Jan. 4, 1794, p. 1.
91. Findlay v. The William, 9 F. Cas. 57, 59–61 (D. Pa. 1793); Duane, *Decree on the Admiralty Side*, 34–35.
92. Findlay v. The William, 9 F. Cas. 57, 59–61 (D. Pa. 1793).
93. Genet to consuls, May 29, 1793, AMAE-CP, 37:467; Memorial from George Hammond, Sep. 6, 1793, *PTJ*, 27:44–46; John Hamilton to Lord Grenville, June 29, 1793, NAFO 5, 2:214; Hamilton to Grenville, Aug. 8, 1794, NAFO 5, 6:243; *DHSC*, 3:89 n. 15.
94. Notes of Cabinet Meeting on Edmond Charles Genet, *PTJ*, 26:601–3; John Alexander Carroll and Mary Wells Ashworth, *George Washington: A Biography* (New York: Charles Scribner's Sons, 1957), 7:117.
95. Jefferson to James Monroe, July 14, 1793, *PTJ*, 26:501–3; Jefferson to Gouverneur Morris, Aug. 16, 1793, *PTJ*, 26:697–715.
96. Washington to Jefferson, July 11, 1793, *PTJ*, 26:481–82; Ammon, *Genet Mission*, 97–104, 132–46.
97. Hammond to Lord Grenville, Oct. 12, 1793, NAFO 5, 1:329; Hammond to James Bland Burges, Oct. 12, 1793, quoted in William R. Casto, "The Early Supreme Court Justices' Most Significant Opinion," *Ohio Northern University Law Review* 29 (2002): 179 n. 58; Hammond to Grenville, June 10, 1793, NAFO 5, 1: 175; John Hamilton to Grenville, June 26, 1794, NAFO 5, 6:219; Phineas Bond to Grenville, Apr. 17, 1794, NAFO 5, 6:44.

98. To the United States Senate and House of Representatives, Dec. 3, 1793, *PGWPS*, 14:462–67; Notes of Cabinet Meeting on Neutrality, Aug. 3, 1793, *PTJ*, 26:607–8; Thomas, *Cabinet Government*, 235–45.
99. Phineas Bond to Lord Grenville, Apr. 17, 1794, NAFO 5, 6:44; Casto, *Fighting Sail*, 159–60.
100. Hamilton to Jay, June 4, 1794, *PAH*, 16:456, 457; Randolph to Hammond, June 2 1794, *ASPFR*, 1:464; Casto, *Fighting Sail*, 158–59; Elkins and McKitrick, *Age of Federalism*, 381–90; Tucker and Hendrickson, *Empire of Liberty*, 62–63.
101. Thomas MacDonogh to Lord Grenville, July 24, 1794, NAFO 5, 6:282; Hammond to Grenville, Apr. 17, 1794, NAFO 5, 4:173; DeConde, *Entangling Alliance*, 94–98; Elkins and McKitrick, *Age of Federalism*, 388–96, 451–61; Charles R. Ritcheson, *Aftermath of Revolution: British Policy Toward the United States, 1783–1795* (New York: W. W. Norton & Company, 1971), 299–305.
102. Phineas Bond to Lord Grenville, Nov. 23, 1794, NAFO 5, 6:112; John Hamilton to Grenville, Mar. 31, 1794, NAFO 5, 6:173; Elkins and McKitrick, *Age of Federalism*, 375–96. For discussions of the problems that prompted Jay's mission, see Samuel Flagg Bemis, *Jay's Treaty: A Study in Commerce and Diplomacy* (New York: The Macmillan Company, 1922); Jerald A. Combs, *The Jay Treaty: Political Battleground of the Founding Fathers* (Berkeley: University of California, 1970).
103. Genet to Ministre des Affaires Étrangères, Dec. 10, 1793, *CFM*, 277–79; Instructions to the Commissioners, Nov. 15, 1793 (25 Brumaire An 2), *CFM*, 288–94; Ammon, *Genet Mission*, 153–61, 171–72.
104. Duane, *Decree on the Admiralty Side*, 1.
105. Ibid., 4. Judge Peters in the *William* case also noted the possibility of an appeal from his decision to a "superior tribunal." Findlay v. The William, 9 F. Cas. 57, 61 (D. Pa. 1793).

3 The Courts as Compromise

1. Moodie to Lord Grenville, Mar. 4, 1794, NAFO 5, 6:127; Moodie to Grenville, Dec. 17, 1794, NAFO 5, 6:140; Victor Dupont to Pierre-Auguste Adet, Apr. 12, 1796 (23 Germinal An 4), VDP, box 2, folder 309; Dupont to Adet, Apr. 15, 1796 (26 Germinal An 4), VDP, box 2, folder 309.
2. Ellsworth to Abigail Ellsworth, Mar. 20, 1796, *DHSC*, 3:99–101.
3. Treaty of Amity, Commerce, and Navigation, art. 24 (1795); Moodie to George Miller, May 14, 1796, NAFO 5, 15:90; Victor Dupont to Pierre-Auguste Adet, May 10, 1796 (21 Floréal An 4), VDP, box 2, folder 309; Adet to Timothy Pickering, Oct. 12, 1796 (21 Vendémaire An 4), *ASPFR*, 1:654; *DHSC*, 3:89 & n. 16; William R. Casto, "Oliver Ellsworth," *Journal of Supreme Court History* 21 (1996): 73–91.

4. Jefferson to Edmond Charles Genet, Sep. 9, 1793, *PTJ*, 27:67.
5. For an argument that American constitutional law is "dependent throughout on the contingencies of time and political circumstance," see H. Jefferson Powell, *A Community Built on Words: The Constitution in History and Politics* (Chicago: University of Chicago Press, 2002), 7; see also Stephen M. Griffin, *American Constitutionalism: From Theory to Politics* (Princeton: Princeton University Press, 1996), 5; Barry Friedman and Scott B. Smith, "The Sedimentary Constitution," *University of Pennsylvania Law Review* 147 (1998): 1–90. On historical contingency in the development of judicial authority specifically, see Barry Friedman, *The Will of the People: How Public Opinion Has Influenced the Supreme Court and Shaped the Meaning of the Constitution* (New York: Farrar, Straus and Giroux, 2009).
6. Richard Harison to Jefferson, July 24, 1793, *PTJ*, 26:560; Richard Söderström to Jefferson, [July 3, 1793], *PTJ*, 26:432; Richard Söderström to Edmond Charles Genet, July 6, 1793, *DHSC*, 6:313; *DHSC*, 6:300–1.
7. Lucas Gibbes and Alexander S. Glass to Jefferson, July 8, 1793, *PTJ*, 26:453; *DHSC*, 6:305; William Paca's District Court Opinion, Aug. 15, 1793, *DHSC*, 6:324–32; Jefferson to Alexander S. Glass, Sep. 10, 1793, *PTJ*, 27:79; Knox to Jefferson, Sep. 11, 1793, *PTJ*, 27:90.
8. Knox thought that the *Betsey* was not eligible for restoration by the executive branch because she had been captured prior to Aug. 5, 1793. Knox to Jefferson, Sep. 11, 1793, *PTJ*, 27:90. But nothing in the surviving records of the administration's deliberations suggests that this fact was relevant. Under the administration's rules, prizes made before *June* 5th would not be restored (because the president had not ordered that all French privateers commissioned in the United States depart from American ports before that date). Cabinet Opinion on Prizes and Privateers, Aug. 5, 1793, *PTJ*, 26:603. Jefferson may have thought that the *Betsey* did not qualify for executive restoration because, in his view, the administration's executive restoration policy applied only to British property, and Sweden was a neutral. Jefferson to Richard Söderström, Aug. 20, 1793, *PTJ*, 26:733.
9. Jefferson to Gouverneur Morris, Aug. 16, 1793, *PTJ*, 26:697, 704; Jefferson to Richard Söderström, Nov. 20, 1793, *PTJ*, 27:409; *DHSC*, 6:302–3.
10. Edmund Randolph to George Washington, May 18, 1793, *PGWPS*, 12:608–9; Notes on Neutrality Questions, July 13, 1793, *PTJ*, 26:498–500; Jefferson to George Hammond, Sep. 5, 1793, *PTJ*, 27:35–38.
11. Randolph to Washington, May 18, 1793, *PGWPS*, 12:608–9; Notes on Neutrality Questions, July 13, 1793, *PTJ*, 26:498–500.
12. Jefferson to Hammond, June 13, 1793, *PTJ*, 26:270–71; Circular to French Consuls and Vice-Consuls, Sep. 7, 1793, *PTJ*, 26:51; Hammond to Jefferson, Sep. 6, 1793, *PTJ*, 27:44–45; Deposition of Isaac Jean, Sep. 4, 1793, NAFO 5, 1:306; Thomas MacDonogh to Lord Grenville, Nov.

11, 1793, NAFO 5, 2:269; Revocation of Duplaine's Exequatur, Oct. 3, 1793, *PTJ*, 27:185–86; *DHSC*, 3:89 n. 15; William R. Casto, *Foreign Affairs and the Constitution in the Age of Fighting Sail* (Columbia: University of South Carolina Press, 2006), 103–8; Lindsay Chervinsky, *The Cabinet: George Washington and the Creation of an American Institution* (Cambridge: Harvard University Press, 2020), 193–235.

13. Cushing to Increase Sumner, Feb. 24, 1794, *DHSC*, 6:350; Tracy to Ephraim Kirby, Feb. 24, 1794, *DHSC*, 6:350–51; Glass v. Sloop Betsey, 3 U.S. 6, 6, 12 (1794). Justice James Iredell later expressed regret over having been absent for a ruling "of so much importance." Penhallow v. Doane's Administrators, 3 U.S. 54, 97 (1795).
14. Glass, 3 U.S. at 7–8, 12–13.
15. Jefferson to Genet, June 17, 1793, *PTJ*, 26:301–2; Jefferson to Genet, Sep. 9, 1793, *PTJ*, 27:67; Jefferson to Gouverneur Morris, Aug. 16, 1793, *PTJ*, 26:697, 704.
16. James Duane, *Decree on the Admiralty Side of the District Court of New York* (New York: Francis Childs and John Swaine, 1794), 30. Judges Peters and Paca also doubted that privateering cases were matters of private right. Findlay v. The William, 9 F. Cas. 57, 61 (D. Pa. 1793); William Paca's District Court Opinion, Aug. 15, 1793, *DHSC*, 6:324–32.
17. Glass, 3 U.S. at 13–14.
18. Glass, 3 U.S. at 16; William R. Casto, *The Supreme Court in the Early Republic: The Chief Justiceships of John Jay and Oliver Ellsworth* (Columbia: University of South Carolina Press, 1995), 82–87. The Court may have proclaimed that the federal district courts possessed full admiralty powers in response to DuPonceau's argument that the Judiciary Act of 1789 did not specifically given them authority to sit as *prize* courts. Glass, 3 U.S. at 7–8. On the distinction between "prize" and "instance" jurisdiction in English admiralty courts, see Lindo v. Rodney, 99 Eng. Rep 385, 386 (1782); Edward Stanley Roscoe, *A History of the English Prize Court* (London: Lloyd's, 1924), 44–46; Richard Pares, *Colonial Blockade and Neutral Rights, 1739–1763* (Oxford: Clarendon Press, 1938), 78–79.
19. Casto, *Supreme Court*, 82–87, 109; *DHSC*, 6:296, 309–11; David M. Golove and Daniel J. Hulsebosch, "A Civilized Nation: The Early American Constitution, the Law of Nations, and the Pursuit of International Recognition," *New York University Law Review* 85 (2010): 932–1066; Maeva Marcus, "Is the Supreme Court a Political Institution?" *George Washington Law Review* 72 (2003): 95–112. On Jay and Wilson's support, see Chapter 2; on John Blair, see Christopher Gore to Jefferson, Oct. 21, 1793, *PTJ*, 26:261.
20. Glass, 3 U.S. at 16. A copy of the *Glass* opinion in the French foreign ministry's files noted that it concerned their consuls' "admiralty powers." Décisions de la cour suprème des E.U., Feb. 19, 1794 (1 Ventôse An 2), AMAE-CP, 40:103.

21. Hammond to Lord Grenville, Feb. 22, 1794, NAFO 5, 4:43; Talbot v. Jansen, 3 U.S. 133, 138 (1795); Orders of the Committee of Public Safety, Oct. 16, 1793 (25 Vendémaire An 2), *CFM*, 287–89. It is possible the Court addressed the consular jurisdiction question because the French consul at Baltimore had already condemned the *Betsey*. If that decision was valid, it arguably had preclusive effect against the rulings of any other courts. Casto, *Supreme Court*, 86–87.
22. Examples of seriatim opinions in important early cases include Chisholm v. Georgia, 2 U.S. 419 (1793), and Calder v. Bull, 3 U.S. 386 (1798). On the Court's early opinion practice generally, see John P. Kelsh, "The Opinion Delivery Practices of the United States Supreme Court 1790–1945," *Washington University Law Quarterly* 77 (1999): 137–82.
23. Hamilton to Isaac Holmes, June 2, 1794, *PAH*, 16: 446–47; George Hammond to Thomas Jefferson, May 8, 1793, *PTJ*, 26:685–86; List of French Privateers Outfitted and Armed in the United States, Aug. 30, 1793, *PTJ*, 26:791; Melvin H. Jackson, *Privateers in Charleston, 1793–1796: An Account of a French Palatinate in South Carolina* (Smithsonian Institution Press, 1969), 63–66.
24. Michel-Ange Bernard Mangourit to Edmond Charles Genet, Mar. 1, 1794, AMAE-CCC, Charleston, 2:228; Antoine-Louis Fonspertuis to Antoine de Laforest, May 31, 1794 (12 Prairial An 2), AMAE-AC, Philadelphia, box 56; Jackson, *Privateers in Charleston*, 68–86.
25. Hammond to Read Admiral Murray, Jan. 18, 1795, NAFO 116, 2:303; Phineas Bond to Lord Grenville, Nov. 16, 1795, NAFO 5, 10:237; John Hamilton to Grenville, June 29, 1793, NAFO 5, 2:214; Hammond to Grenville, Aug. 28, 1794, NAFO 5, 6:243; Benjamin Moodie to Grenville, Dec. 17, 1794, NAFO 5, 6:140; Joseph Fauchet to Commissaire des Rélations Extérieures, Sep. 5, 1794 (19 Fructidor An 2), *CFM*, 411–18.
26. Hammond to Lord Grenville, Nov. 5, 1794, NAFO 5, 5:345; Hammond to Lord Dorchester, May 26, 1794, NAFO 116, 2:221; Hammond to Grenville, June 27, 1794, NAFO 5, 5:131; Edmund Randolph to Hammond, July 28, 1794, NAFO 5, 5:243; John Hamilton to Grenville, June 26, 1794, NAFO 5, 6:219.
27. Randolph to Hammond, June 21, 1794, NAFO 5, 5:156; Randolph to Hammond, July 28, 1794, NAFO 5, 5:241; Hammond to John Graves Simcoe, Aug. 10, 1794, NAFO 116, 2:239.
28. Hammond to Randolph, Feb. 13, 1794, NAFO 116, 2:181; Randolph to Governors of the Several States, Oct. 22, 1794, *ASPFR*, 1:589, 589–90.
29. Phineas Bond to Lord Grenville, Jan. 27, 1795, NAFO 5, 10:35; Hammond to Grenville, June 8, 1794, NAFO 5, 5:59; Hammond to Grenville, Mar. 7, 1793, NAFO 5, 1:78; Hammond to Grenville, Jan. 1, 1793, NAFO 5, 1:29; Hammond to Jefferson, June 20, 1793, *PTJ*, 26: 329–30; Charles F. Hobson, "The Recovery of British Debts in the Federal Circuit Court of Virginia, 1790 to 1797," *Virginia Magazine of History and Biography*

92 (1984): 176–200; Dwight F. Henderson, *Courts for a New Nation* (Washington, DC: Public Affairs, 1971), 72–83; Mary K. Bonsteel Tachau, *Federal Courts in the Early Republic: Kentucky, 1789–1816* (Princeton: Princeton University Press, 1978), 155–58.

30. Federalist 70, *DHRC*, 16:396–402; J. D. Bailey and H. Li, "'Decision, Activity, Secrecy and Dispatch': The Intellectual Origins of Hamilton's Rhetoric in Federalist No. 70," *History of Political Thought* 42 (2021): 318–41.
31. Henry Lee to Thomas Jefferson, May 13, 1793, *PTJ*, 26:25; Jefferson to Thomas Pinckney, June 14, 1793, *PTJ* 26:286–88; Thomas Sim Lee to Jefferson, Sep. 3, 1793, *PTJ*, 27:25; Lee to Washington, Oct. 11, 1793, *PGWPS*, 14:199–200.
32. Hammond to Lord Grenville, June 8, 1794, NAFO 5, 5:59; Victor Dupont to Pierre-Auguste Adet, Apr. 12, 1796 (23 Germinal An 4), VDP, box 2, folder 309; Findlay v. The William, libel, June 3, 1793, NARA, USDC-PA; Moxon v. The Fanny, libel, June 3, 1793, NARA, USDC-PA; McCurach v. The Mary, libel, July 25, 1793, NARA, USDC-PA.
33. Hammond to Smith and Icars, Feb. 13, 1794, NAFO 116, 2:179; Hammond to Edmund Randolph, Feb. 13, 1794, NAFO 116, 2:181. For instance, Judge Duane in New York ruled on a claim to the British vessel *Catherine* seven months after the libel was first filed. Hammond to Jefferson, June 14, 1793, *PTJ*, 26:284–85; Duane, *Decree on the Admiralty Side*, 1.
34. Moodie to Benjamin Miller, Jun 23, 1794, NAFO 5, 6:137; Moodie to Miller, Nov. 28, 1794, NAFO 5, 11:88; List of British Vessels Carried into Charleston South Carolina as Prizes, NAFO 5, 11:90; *DHSC*, 7:51.
35. Moodie to Phineas Bond, Apr. 28, 1795, NAFO 5, 11:101; Moodie to Jacob Read, Dec. 29, 1795, *DHSC*, 7:62; Jean Bouteille to Représentans, Apr. 15, 1795 (26 Germinal An 3), AMAE-MD, 39:15. Though there is no record of Hamilton representing British claimants in privateering cases, he did participate in a suit brought by the Spanish consul in New York. *DHSC*, 7:525–37; Julius Goebel, *The Law Practice of Alexander Hamilton* (New York: Columbia University Press, 1969), 2:790–808.
36. Moodie to Phineas Bond, Apr. 28, 1795, NAFO 5, 11:101; Moodie to David Leonard Barnes, Aug. 28, 1795, *DHSC*, 7:819–20; Moodie to George Miller, Nov. 28, 1794, NAFO 5, 11:88; Miller to James Bland Burges, July 16, 1794, NAFO 5, 11:92.
37. Phineas Bond to Lord Grenville, Jan. 27, 1795, NAFO 5, 10:35.
38. Hollingsworth v. The Betsey, 12 F. Cas. 348, 351 n. 3 (D. Pa. 1795); Dubois v. Brig Kitty, decree, Mar. 25, 1794, NARA, USDC-PA. The Georgia district court similarly dismissed a suit over the French capture of a Spanish vessel. Trabudua v. Ship Transmarana, decree, Jan. 2, 1795, National Archives and Records Administration, Index Books, 1789–1928, and Minutes and Bench Dockets, 1789–1870 for the District Court Southern District of Georgia, microfilm M1172.

39. Castello v. Bouteille, 5 F. Cas. 278, 279 (D.S.C. 1794). The *Glass* decree was not published in South Carolina until a week after Judge Bee's decision in *Castello*, so it is possible he was not aware of the Supreme Court's ruling. *City Gazette & Daily Advertiser* (Charleston), Mar. 26, 1794, p. 3.
40. Stannick v. Brig Friendship, 22 F. Cas. 1056, 1057 (D.S.C. 1794); Reid v. Ship Vere, 20 F. Cas. 488, 488 (D.S.C. 1795). For a detailed discussion of the events surrounding Judge Bee's decisions, see Jackson, *Privateers in Charleston*, 47–62.
41. Jansen v. Vrow Christina Magdalena, 13 F.Cas. 356, 359 (D.S.C. 1794); Kelley v. Schooner Prosperity, in *Reports of Cases Adjudged in the District Court of South Carolina* (Philadelphia: William P. Farrand, 1810), 1:38–39.
42. Jansen, 13 F.Cas. at 359; Salderondo v. Ship Nostra Signora del Camino, 21 F. Cas. 225, 226 (D.S.C. 1794).
43. Washington to the U.S. Senate and House of Representatives, May 20, 1794, *PGWPS*, 16:97–98; Edmund Randolph's Draft Bill, Jan. 1794, Stephen C. Strong Collection, Forbes Library; Neutrality Act of 1794, §§ 1–4, 6, 1 Stat. 381, 382–84.
44. Neutrality Act of 1794, §§ 1–4, 6, 1 Stat. 381, 382–84 (1794).
45. Moodie v. The Betty Carthcart, 17 F. Cas. 651, 651–53 (D.S.C. 1795); British Consul v. The Mermaid, 4 F. Cas. 169, 171 (D.S.C. 1795).
46. *The Betty Carthcart*, 17 F. Cas. at 653; British Consul v. The Nancy, 4 F. Cas. 171, 171 (D.S.C. 1795).
47. Moodie to Vice Admiral Murray, Apr. 6, 1796, NAFO 5, 15:78; *DHSC*, 7:116.
48. The Mermaid, 4 F. Cas. at 171; Moodie v. The Brothers, 17 F. Cas. 653, 654 (D.S.C. 1795).
49. British Consul v. Schooner Favourite (1795), in *Reports of Cases Adjudged in the District Court of South Carolina* (Philadelphia: William P. Farrand, 1810), 1:39.
50. Moodie to Phineas Bond, Apr. 28, 1795, NAFO 5, 11:101; Moodie to George Miller, May 8, 1795, NAFO 5, 11:94; Charleston Privateers to National Convention, Apr. 14, 1795 (25 Germinal An 3), AMAE-MD, 39:8.
51. Instructions to the Commissioners, Nov. 15, 1793 (25 Brumaire An 2), *CFM*, 288–94; Fauchet to Randolph, June 8, 1795 (20 Prairial An 3), *ASPFR*, 1:614, 615; Robert J. Alderson, *This Bright Era of Happy Revolutions: French Consul Michel-Ange-Bernard Mangourit and International Republicanism in Charleston, 1792–1794* (Columbia: University of South Carolina Press, 2008), 20–21, 164–65; Alexander DeConde, *Entangling Alliance: Politics and Diplomacy under George Washington* (Durham, NC, 1958), 395–98; Stanley M. Elkins and Eric L. McKitrick, *The Age of Federalism* (New York: Oxford University Press, 1993), 330–33, 365–72.

52. DuPonceau to Joseph Fauchet, Apr. 14, 1795, *DHSC*, 7:20–21; DuPonceau to Citizen Arcambal, July 9, 1794, PSDP, 1:36; DuPonceau to Fauchet, June 9, 1795, PSDP, 1:97; Peter S. DuPonceau, *A Dissertation on the Nature and Extent of the Jurisdiction of the Courts of the United States* (Philadelphia: A. Small, 1824); William E. Butler, "Peter Stephen Du Ponceau: Pennsylvania Lawyer Extraordinaire," *Pennsylvania Bar Association Quarterly* (2018): 156–65; John F. Witt, *Lincoln's Code: The Laws of War in American History* (New York: Simon & Schuster, 2012), 81.

    DuPonceau represented the captors in most of the cases argued before Judge Peters in Philadelphia, and in nearly all those in the Supreme Court from 1794 to 1797. Findlay v. The William, plea to jurisdiction, June 11, 1793; Clark v. Couture, plea to jurisdiction, Aug. 20, 1793; Dubois v. Brig Kitty, plea to jurisdiction, Feb 25, 1794; Glass v. Citizen Genet, stipulation, [undated], NARA, USDC-PA; *DHSC*, 7:946. He also gave extensive strategic advice to French officials, litigants, and attorneys in the cases they were defending in federal courts. Jean-Baptiste Petry to Pierre Barriere, May 9, 1794 (20 Floréal An 2), AMAE-AC, Philadelphia, box 29; DuPonceau to Citoyen Arcambal, July 9, 1794, Historical Society of Pennsylvania, PSDP, 1:36; DuPonceau to Fauchet, Apr. 14, 1795, *DHSC*, 7:20–21; DuPonceau to Philippe André Joseph de Letombe, Aug. 14, 1795, PSDP, 1:128; Opinion of Jared Ingersoll, John Coxe, and Peter S. DuPonceau, July 26, 1796, PSDP, 1:168.

53. Opinion of J. S. Martin, July 7, 1794, AMAE-AC, Boston, box 71, *La Catherine*; Opinion of J. S. Martin, July 10, 1794, AMAE-AC, Boston, box 71, *La Catherine*; DuPonceau to John Y. Noel, Aug. 1, 1795, PSDP, 1:108; DuPonceau to Citoyen Arcambal, July 9, 1794, PSDP, 1:36; Opinion of Peter S. DuPonceau, July 9, 1794, AMAE-AC, Boston, box 71, *La Catherine*; DuPonceau to Martin Jorris, Apr. 8, 1795, PSDP, 1:58; DuPonceau to Joseph Fauchet, Apr. 14, 1795, *DHSC*, 7:20–25; Dubois v. Brig Kitty, plea to jurisdiction, Feb. 25, 1794, NARA, USDC-PA; Dubois v. Brig Kitty, decree, Mar. 25, 1794, NARA, USDC-PA; Hollingsworth v. The Betsey, 12 F. Cas. 348 (D. Pa. 1795).

54. Fauchet to Commissioner of Foreign Relations, Sep. 3, 1794 (17 Fructidor An 2), *Annual Report of the American Historical Association for the Year 1903* (Washington, DC: Government Printing Office, 1904), 2:411; Etat K, AMAE-MD, 39:150; John Hamilton to Lord Grenville, June 26, 1794, NAFO 5, 6:219; Theodore Charles Mozard to Pierre-Auguste Adet, Sep. 10, 1795 (24 Fructidor An 3), AMAE-AC, Boston, box 13; Victor Dupont to Adet, Dec. 15, 1795 (24 Frimaire An 4), VDP, box 2, folder 309.

55. Michel-Ange Bernard Mangourit to Ministère des Affaires Étrangères, Feb. 21, 1794, AMAE-CCC, Charleston, 2:204; Joseph Fauchet to Edmund Randolph, Aug. 26, 1794, (9 Fructidor An 2), *ASPFR*, 1:588;

Etat C, AMAE-MD, 39:79; Théric to the Comité de Salut Public, Apr. 14, 1795 (25 Germinal An 3), AMAE-MD, 39:21; Jackson, *Privateers in Charleston*, 117–26. For more examples of French complaints, see Pierre-Auguste Adet to Randolph, Aug. 2, 1795, *ASPFR*, 1:621; Thomas Dannery to Commissaire de la Marine, [undated], AMAE-CCC, Philadelphia, 3:301; Duhail to Ministère des Relations Extérieures, Oct. 2, 1795 (10 Vendémaire An 4), AMAE-CCC, Baltimore, 1:136; Commissaires de la Republique Francaise près des États-Unis to Commisaire des Relations Extérieures, May 6, 1795 (17 Floréal An 3), *CFM*, 681–83; Theodore Charles Mozard to Ministère des Relations Extérieures, Aug. 15, 1796 (18 Thermidor An 4), AMAE-CCC, Boston, 3:397.

56. Quoted in Isser Woloch, *The New Regime: Transformations of the French Civic Order, 1789–1820s* (New York: W. W. Norton & Company, 1994), 297–300, 307; John Philip Dawson, *The Oracles of the Law* (Ann Arbor: University of Michigan Law School, 1968), 350–78; Nicolas Derasse, "Words and Liberty: Hopes for Legal Defence during the French Revolution," *Quaderni Storici* 47 (2012): 745–70; Amalia D. Kessler, *Inventing American Exceptionalism: The Origins of American Adversarial Legal Culture, 1800–1877* (New Haven: Yale University Press, 2017), 202–5.

57. Theodore Charles Mozard to Ministère des Relations Extérieures, Aug. 15, 1796 (18 Thermidor An 4), AMAE-CCC, Boston, 3:397; Thomas Dannery to Commissaire de la Marine, [undated], AMAE-CCC, Philadelphia, 3:301; Louis Arcambal to Mozard, Feb. 22, 1796 (3 Ventôse An 4), AMAE-AC, Boston, box 23; Lucien Karpik, "Lawyers and Politics in France, 1814–1950: The State, the Market, and the Public," *Law & Social Inquiry* 13 (1988): 707–36. For additional complaints, see Michel-Ange Bernard Mangourit to Ministère des Affaires Étrangères, Feb. 21, 1794, AMAE-CCC, Charleston, 2:204; Duhail to Ministère des Relations Extérieures, Oct. 2, 1795 (10 Vendémaire An 4), AMAE-CCC, Baltimore, 1:136; Pierre-Auguste Adet to Timothy Pickering, Sep. 22, 1795, *ASPFR* 1:632–33; Mangourit to Edmond Charles Genet, Feb. 15, 1794, AMAE-CCC, Charleston, 2:191; Adet to Victor Dupont, Oct. 22, 1795 (30 Vendémaire An 4), VDP, box 2, folder 309; Arcambal to Mozard, Feb. 16, 1796 (27 Pluviôse An 4), AMAE-AC, Boston, box 23.

58. Fauchet to Randolph, Oct. 17, 1794 (26 Vendemaire An 3), *ASPFR*, 1:589; Fauchet to Randolph, June 8, 1795 (20 Prairial An 3), *ASPFR*, 1:614–15.

59. Randolph to Fauchet, Sep. 3, 1794, *ASPFR*, 1:588; Randolph to Fauchet, June 13, 1795, *ASPFR*, 1:617–20; Jefferson to Genet, June 17, 1793, *PTJ*, 26:301–2; Jefferson to Genet, Sep. 9, 1793, *PTJ*, 27:67–69.

60. Yard v. Ship Cassius, suggestion of William Rawle, Aug. 21, 1795, USDC-PA; *DHSC*, 6:720; Pickering to Pierre-Auguste Adet, Aug. 25,

1795, Oct. 1, 1795, *ASPFR*, 1:631–34. Randolph used virtually identical language in corresponding with Adet. Randolph to Adet, Aug. [14], 1795, *DHSC*, 6:731.

61. Jefferson to Genet, Sep. 9, 1793, *PTJ*, 27:67–69; Jefferson to Abraham Runnels, Sep. 1, 1793, *PTJ*, 27:9–10; Pinckney to Robert Liston, Oct. 5, 1796, NAFO 5, 14:155.
62. Jefferson to Genet, June 17, 1793, *PTJ*, 26:297–300; Jefferson to Genet, June 17, 1793, *PTJ*, 26:301–2.
63. Findlay v. The William, 9 F. Cas. 57, 61 (D. Pa. 1793); Jefferson to Genet, June 17, 1793, *PTJ*, 26:301–2.
64. On the invention of judicial supremacy, see Kevin Arlyck, "The Executive Branch and the Origins of Judicial Independence," *Journal of American Constitutional History* 1 (2023): 343–77. On the invention of historical traditions generally, see Eric Hobsbawm, "Introduction: Inventing Traditions," in Eric Hobsbawm and Terence Ranger eds., *The Invention of Tradition* (Cambridge: Cambridge University Press, 1983), 1–14.
65. David Sloss, "Judicial Foreign Policy: Lessons from the 1790s," *Saint Louis University Law Journal* 53 (2008): 145–96; Ariel N. Lavinbuk, "Rethinking Early Judicial Involvement in Foreign Affairs: An Empirical Study of the Supreme Court's Docket," *Yale Law Journal* 114 (2004): 855–904. During this period the Court also heard two cases that arose from captures made by French national warships, not privateers. *DHSC*, 6:719–27; 7:11–17. Once the Neutrality Crisis ended, it would be nearly a decade before the Court's workload reached the same heights. Lavinbuk, "Early Judicial Involvement," 897.
66. Talbot v. Jansen, 3 U.S. 133, 152–55 (1795) (Paterson, J.); *DHSC*, 6:650–59. Only Justice Iredell addressed the jurisdictional question directly. Given the captors' flagrant violation of "our law" as well as "the law of nations generally," Iredell had not "the slightest doubt" that jurisdiction was proper. *Talbot*, 3 U.S. at 161.
67. *Talbot*, 3 U.S. at 153, 155 (Paterson, J.); James Iredell's Draft of a Supreme Court Opinion, [Mar. 12–14, 1796], *DHSC*, 7:180–87; *DHSC*, 6:650–55. In one case, the Court concluded that the owners of an American merchant ship looted and abandoned by a French privateer could be compensated from the proceeds from the sale of a British prize lawfully seized by the same captor. Arnold v. Delcol, 3 U.S. 333, 333–35 & n.* (1796). In another, the Court affirmed a circuit court ruling that a mercantile firm involved in the sale of British property captured by American-led privateers had to pay damages originally assessed against captors themselves. Hills v. Ross, 3 U.S. 331, 332 (1796). Peter DuPonceau was generally clear-eyed about the politics surrounding the French privateering cases, but he was shocked by the *Hills* decision, and two decades later the Court concluded that the *Delcol* ruling "certainly require[d] an apology." DuPonceau to John Y. Noel, Aug. 1, 1795,

DHSC, 7:700; DuPonceau to Abraham Sasportas, Mar. 1, 1796, PSDP, 1:142; L'Invincible, 14 U.S. 238, 259 (1816).

68. Neutrality Act of 1794, § 3, 1 Stat. 381, 383; Moodie v. The Ship Phoebe Anne, 3 U.S. 319, 319 (1796); James Iredell's Notes for a Supreme Court Opinion, [Mar. 1, 1796], *DHSC*, 7:112–13; Moodie v. Ship Alfred, 3 U.S. 307, 307 (1796); The Mermaid, 4 F. Cas. 169, 171 (D.S.C. 1795); James Iredell's Draft of a Supreme Court Opinion, [Mar. 12–14, 1796], *DHSC*, 7:184–86. The only specific remedies the Neutrality Act provided for violations were criminal penalties against violators, plus authority for the government (not private parties) to seize and condemn offending vessels.
69. *The Phoebe Anne*, 3 U.S. at 319.
70. Phineas Bond to Moodie, Mar. 3, 1796, NAFO 5, 15:76; Sloss, "Judicial Foreign Policy," 176–83.
71. Iredell to Hannah Iredell, Aug. 13, 1795, *DHSC*, 1:780; British Consul v. The Mermaid, 4 F. Cas. 169 (D.S.C. 1795); Moodie v. The Brothers, 17 F. Cas. 653 (D.S.C. 1795); Moodie v. The Betty Carthcart, 17 F. Cas. 651 (1795). The other mode of review was on a "writ of error," in which the superior tribunal only addressed errors of law apparent of the face of the record. Judiciary Act of 1789, § 25. For a contemporaneous discussion of the difference, see United States v. Goodwin, 11 U.S. 108, 110–11 (1812). Article III of the Constitution did not specify a mode of appeal, but it did give the Supreme Court appellate jurisdiction "both as to law and fact." Similarly, section 21 of the Judiciary Act specified that "appeals" from the district to circuit court were allowed in admiralty cases. But Section 22 provided that all "civil actions" were to be "re-examined ... in the Supreme Court" on writ of error only. U.S. Const, art. III, § 2; Judiciary Act of 1789, § 22, 1 Stat. 73, 84–85; Robert Feikema Karachuk, "Error or Appeal? Navigating Review Under the Supreme Court's Admiralty Jurisdiction, 1789–1800," *Journal of Supreme Court History* 27 (2002): 94–101.
72. Thomas Johnson to George Washington, Jan. 16, 1793, *DHSC*, 2:344–45; *DHSC*, 2:288–92, 434 n. 1, 438; James F. Pfander, "Judicial Compensation and the Definition of Judicial Power in the Early Republic," *Michigan Law Review* 107 (2008): 1–52.
73. Iredell to Hannah Iredell, Mar. 11, 1796, *DHSC*, 3:94–95; Iredell to James Wilson, Nov. 24, 1794, *DHSC*, 2:497–98; John Blair to William Cushing, June 12, 1795, *DHSC*, 3:61–62. For other instances of Iredell's complaints, see Iredell to Hannah Iredell, Oct. 2, 1791, *DHSC*, 2:212; Nov. 27, 1795, *DHSC*, 3:82; Apr. 10, 1798, *DHSC*, 3:245.
74. James Iredell's Draft of a Supreme Court Opinion [Mar. 12–14, 1796], *DHSC*, 7:184–87; John Blair to William Cushing, June 12, 1795, *DHSC*, 3:61–62.
75. Judiciary Act of 1789, § 19, 1 Stat. 73, 83; Wiscart v. Dauchy, 3 U.S. 321, 324 (1796); Jennings v. The Brig Perseverance, 3 U.S. 336, 337 (1797); Karachuk, "Error or Appeal?," 103–8. *Wiscart* was not a French privateering case, but it is clear from the context of the Aug. 1796 term

that the rule it announced was informed by the privateering cases the Court was considering at the time. *DHSC*, 7:734.

76. *DHRC*, 10:1420 (Henry); Federal Farmer, Letter XV, Jan. 18, 1788, *DHRC*, 20:1048; Federalist 83, *DHRC*, 18:115–27; *DHRC*, 2:521 (Wilson).
77. *Wiscart*, 3 U.S. at 327; *Jennings*, 3 U.S. at 337; *DHSC*, 7:817–18; Henry J. Bourguignon, *The First Federal Court: The Federal Appellate Prize Court of the American Revolution, 1775–1787* (Philadelphia: American Philosophical Society, 1977), 329–30. On Wilson's financial and personal collapse, see John Fabian Witt, *Patriots and Cosmopolitans: Hidden Histories of American Law* (Cambridge: Harvard University Press, 2007), 75–80.
78. Bourguignon, *First Federal Court*, 338–40.
79. *Jennings*, 3 U.S. at 329–30; William R. Casto, *Oliver Ellsworth and the Creation of the Federal Republic* (New York: Second Circuit Committee on History and Commemorative Events, 1997), 58–76; Casto, *Supreme Court*, 27–28.
80. *Wiscart*, 3 U.S. at 329–30. In 1803, Congress effectively overruled the Court's decision in *Wiscart*. It repealed Sections 19 and 22 of the Judiciary Act of 1789 and explicitly provided that "new evidence" could be introduced in the Supreme Court in admiralty and prize cases. "An Act in addition to an act entitled 'An act to amend the judicial system of the United States,'" 2 Stat. 244 (1803).
81. Moodie to George Miller, Apr. 27, 1796, NAFO 5, 15:86; Moodie to Phineas Bond, Apr. 23, 1796, NAFO 5, 15:80; Moodie to Vice Admiral Murray, Apr. 6, 1796, NAFO 5, 15:78; *DHSC*, 7:116; Treaty of Amity, Commerce, and Navigation, art. 24 (1795); Alexander Hamilton to Jay, June 4, 1794, *PAH*, 16:456, 457; George Hammond to Lord Grenville, June 9, 1794, NAFO 5, 5:65; Samuel Flagg Bemis, *Jay's Treaty, a Study in Commerce and Diplomacy* (New York: The Macmillan Company, 1922), 289–95, 390.
82. Moodie to Charles Cotesworth Pinckney, Apr. 8, 1796, NAFO 5, 15:82; Victor Dupont to Pierre-Auguste Adet, Apr. 12, 1796 (23 Germinal An 4), VDP, box 2, folder 309; Dupont to Adet, Apr. 15, 1796 (26 Germinal An 4), VDP, box 2, folder 309; Elkins and McKitrick, *Age of Federalism*, 375–449; DeConde, *Entangling Alliance*, 101–36; Jerald A. Combs, *The Jay Treaty: Political Battleground of the Founding Fathers* (Berkeley: University of California, 1970), 171–88; Todd Estes, *The Jay Treaty Debate, Public Opinion, and the Evolution of Early American Political Culture* (Amherst: University of Massachusetts Press, 2006). One of the Republicans' chief constitutional complaints was that the Washington administration and its Senate allies used the treaty power to exclude the House from domestic lawmaking. They argued that treaty provisions addressing issues within Congress's legislative authority only had the force of law if Congress passed legislation

enacting them. Golove and Hulsebosch, "Civilized Nation," 1048–61; Martin S. Flaherty, "History Right?: Historical Scholarship, Original Understanding, and Treaties as 'Supreme Law of the Land,'" *Columbia Law Review* 99 (1999): 2095–153.

83. William Lee to Moodie, Apr. 12, 1796, NAFO 5, 15:84; Moodie to Charles Cotesworth Pinckney, Apr. 8, 1796, NAFO 5, 15:82; Pinckney to Moodie, Apr. 10, 1796, NAFO 5, 15:82; Moodie to John Julius Pringle, Apr. 11, 1796, NAFO 5, 15:83; Pringle to Moodie, Apr. 11, 1796, NAFO 5, 15:83; Moodie v. Ship Amity, 17 F. Cas. 650 (1796).
84. *City Gazette and Daily Advertiser* (Charleston), May 10, 1796, p. 3; *DHSC*, 3:89–91; *DHSC*, 4:201–2; Casto, *Supreme Court*, 115–16; Stanley Morrison, "The Remedial Powers of the Admiralty," *Yale Law Journal* 43 (1933): 1–33.
85. Oliver Ellsworth's Charge to the Grand Jury of the Circuit Court for the District of Georgia, Apr. 25, 1796, *DHSC*, 3:119–20; Casto, *Ellsworth*, 37–76; Casto, *Supreme Court*, 115–17.
86. Ware v. Hylton, 3 U.S. 199 (1796); Golove and Hulsebosch, "Civilized Nation," 1057–59.
87. James Iredell's Draft of a Supreme Court Opinion [Mar. 12–14, 1796], *DHSC*, 7:180, 185, 186.
88. Robert Liston to Pickering, June 29, 1796, NARA, Notes from British Legation to the United States, microfilm M50; Liston to Lord Grenville, July 3, 1796, NAFO 5, 14:63; James Shoolbred to Hammond, June 23, 1796, NAFO 5, 15:88; *DHSC*, 3:90 n. 19; Casto, *Supreme Court*, 115–17; DeConde, *Entangling Alliance*, 139–40.
89. Duhail to Ministère des Relations Extérieures, June 25, 1796 (7 Messidor An 4), AMAE-CCC, Baltimore, 1:158. Adet hoped to stir popular outrage over the treaty by publicizing it when the administration was keeping it secret. He bought a copy from Senator Stevens Thomson Mason, and had Benjamin Bache publish it in his newspaper. Deconde, *Entangling Alliance*, 427–28.
90. Victor Dupont to Adet, May 10, 1796 (21 Floréal An 4), VDP, box 2, folder 309; Adet to Dupont, June 16, 1796 (28 Prairial An 4), VDP, box 2, folder 309; *DHSC*, 3:89 n. 16; Opinion of Jared Ingersoll, John Coxe, and Peter S. DuPonceau, July 26, 1796, PSDP, 1:168; Adet to Dupont, Aug. 9, 1796 (22 Thermidor An 4), VDP, box 2, folder 309; Adet to Timothy Pickering, Oct. 12, 1796 (21 Vendémaire An 4), *ASPFR*, 1:654–55; Pickering to Adet, Nov. 15, 1796, *ASPFR*, 1:655–56; Duhail to Ministère des Relations Extérieures, Aug. 29, 1796 (12 Fructidor An 4), AMAE-CCC, Baltimore, 1:164.
91. Charles Delacroix to James Monroe, Mar. 9, 1796, *ASPFR*, 1:732–33; Robert W. Tucker and David C. Hendrickson, *Empire of Liberty: The Statecraft of Thomas Jefferson* (New York: Oxford University Press, 1992), 70–73.

92. Delacroix to Monroe, Mar. 9, 1796, *ASPFR*, 1:732; Adet to Pickering, Nov. 15, 1796, *ASPFR*, 1:580.
93. DeConde, *Entangling Alliance*, 342–91.
94. Monroe to Delacroix, Mar. 5, 1796, *ASPFR*, 1:733.
95. Delacroix to Monroe, Mar. 9, 1796, *ASPFR*, 1:732; Alexander DeConde, *The Quasi-War; the Politics and Diplomacy of the Undeclared War with France, 1797–1801* (New York: Scribner, 1966), 8–12.
96. John Hamilton to Lord Grenville, June 26, 1794, NAFO 5, 6:219.
97. Treaty of Amity, Commerce, and Navigation, art. 7 (1795); John Bassett Moore, *International Adjudications, Ancient and Modern* (New York: Oxford University Press, 1929), 4:81, 160–61.
98. Moore, *International Adjudications*, 4:36–61; Richard B. Lillich, "The Jay Treaty Commissions," *St. John's Law Review* 37 (1963): 260–83.
99. Jefferson to Hammond, Sep. 5, 1793, *PTJ*, 27:35.
100. Moore, *International Adjudications*, 4:547, 549–50.
101. Lillich, "Jay Treaty Commissions," 268–76; Charles H. Brower, II, "The Functions and Limits of Arbitration and Judicial Settlement Under Private and Public International Law," *Duke Journal of Comparative & International Law* 18 (2008): 259–309. On the debt commission generally, see Moore, *International Adjudications*, vol. 3.
102. Williams' Case, 29 F. Cas. 1330, 1331 (C.C.D. Conn. 1799).
103. Williams' Case, 29 F. Cas. at 1331.
104. DeConde, *The Quasi-War*, 8–12; Elkins and McKitrick, *Age of Federalism*, 643–61.

4 The Problems of Prize

1. Memorial of Baltimore Merchants and Owners of Private Armed Commissioned Vessels of War, Nov. 10, 1812, *ASPNA*, 1:273–74; Jefferson to James Monroe, Jan. 1, 1815, *PTJRS*, 8:176–79. On the expense of fitting out a privateer, see Jerome R. Garitee, *The Republic's Private Navy: The American Privateering Business as Practiced by Baltimore During the War of 1812* (Middletown: Wesleyan University Press, 1977), 103–13.
2. Memorial of Baltimore Merchants, Nov. 10, 1812, *ASPNA*, 1:273–74; "An Act concerning Letters of Marque, Prizes, and Prize Goods," § 6, 2 Stat. 759, 761 (1812).
3. "Additional Note on the Principles and Practices in Prize Causes," in Henry Wheaton, *Reports of Cases Argued and Adjudged in the Supreme Court of the United States* (New York: Robert Donaldson, 1817), 2:app. 5; "On the Practice in Prize Causes," ibid., 1:494.
4. *Columbian Phenix* (Providence), July 4, 1812, p. 2; Committee of Foreign Relations, *Report, or Manifesto of the Causes and Reasons of War with Great Britain* (Washington, DC: A. & G. Way, 1812), 16; Donald R. Hickey, *The War of 1812: A Forgotten Conflict* (Urbana: University of

Illinois Press, 2012). More expansive recent treatments of the War of 1812 include Carl Benn, *The Iroquois in the War of 1812* (Toronto: University of Toronto Press, 1998); Nicole Eustace, *1812: War and the Passions of Patriotism* (Philadelphia: University of Pennsylvania Press, 2012); Gene Allen Smith, *The Slaves' Gamble: Choosing Sides in the War of 1812* (New York: Palgrave Macmillan, 2013); Alan Taylor, *The Civil War of 1812: American Citizens, British Subjects, Irish Rebels, and Indian Allies* (New York: Alfred A. Knopf, 2010). For an overview of trends in historical scholarship on the war, see "Interchange: The War of 1812," *Journal of American History* 99 (2012): 520–55.

5. In Charles Tilly's memorable phrasing, "the state made war, and war made the state." Charles Tilly, "War Making and State Making as Organized Crime," in Peter B. Evans, Dieter Rueschemeyer, and Theda Skocpol, eds., *Bringing the State Back In* (Cambridge: Cambridge University Press, 1985), 169–91. For similar perspectives, see M. J. Braddick, *State Formation in Early Modern England, C. 1550–1700* (Cambridge: Cambridge University Press, 2000), 233–54; John Brewer, *The Sinews of Power: War, Money, and the English State, 1688–1783* (Cambridge: Harvard University Press, 1990); Max Edling, *A Revolution in Favor of Government: Origins of the U.S. Constitution and the Making of the American State* (Oxford: Oxford University Press, 2003); Don Higginbotham, "War and State Formation in Revolutionary America," in Eliga H. Gould and Peter S. Onuf, eds., *Empire and Nation: The American Revolution in the Atlantic World* (Baltimore: Johns Hopkins University Press, 2005), 54–71; Charles Tilly, "Reflections on the History of European State-Making," in Gabriel Ardant and Charles Tilly, eds., *The Formation of National States in Western Europe* (Princeton: Princeton University Press, 1975), 3–83.
6. Max M. Edling, *A Hercules in the Cradle: War, Money, and the American State, 1783–1867* (Chicago: University of Chicago Press, 2015), 113–17; Leonard J. Sadosky, "How the Jeffersonians Learned to Love the State: Consumption, Finance, and Empire in the Madison Administration," in Joanne B. Freeman and Johann N. Neem, eds., *Jeffersonians in Power: The Rhetoric of Opposition Meets the Realities of Governing* (Charlottesville: University of Virginia Press, 2019), 148–77; Jasper M. Trautsch, "The Causes of the War of 1812: 200 Years of Debate," *Journal of Military History* 77 (2013): 273–93.
7. James Madison, Fourth Annual Message, Nov. 4, 1812, *PJMPS*, 5:427–35; Troy Bickham, *The Weight of Vengeance: The United States, The British Empire, and the War of 1812* (New York: Oxford University Press, 2012), 28–29; Hickey, *War of 1812*, 5–28; Bradford Perkins, *Prologue to War: England and the United States, 1805–1812* (Berkeley: University of California Press, 1963); J. C. A. Stagg, *Mr. Madison's War: Politics, Diplomacy, and Warfare in the Early American Republic, 1783–1830* (Princeton: Princeton University Press, 1983), 3–119.

8. Denver Brunsman, "Subjects vs. Citizens: Impressment and Identity in the Anglo-American Atlantic," *Journal of the Early Republic* 30 (2010): 557–86; Paul A. Gilje, *Free Trade and Sailors' Rights in the War of 1812* (New York: Cambridge University Press, 2013), 99–102. On the connection between sailors and citizenship generally, see Nathan Perl-Rosenthal, *Citizen Sailors: Becoming American in the Age of Revolution* (Cambridge: Belknap Press, 2015).
9. An Address to the Independent Electors of the State of New York (Albany: Argus, 1813), 6; Taylor, *Civil War*, 135–36; Eustace, *Passions of Patriotism*, 88–92.
10. Bickham, *Weight of Vengeance*, 26–31. On the broader challenge of fully separating from Great Britain in the decades after the Revolution, see Sam W. Haynes, *Unfinished Revolution: The Early American Republic in a British World* (Charlottesville: University of Virginia Press, 2010); Kariann Akemi Yokota, *Unbecoming British: How Revolutionary America Became a Postcolonial Nation* (Oxford: Oxford University Press, 2010).
11. James G. Cusick, *The Other War of 1812: The Patriot War and the American Invasion of Spanish East Florida* (Gainesville: University Press of Florida, 2003); Julius W. Pratt, *Expansionists of 1812* (New York: The Macmillan Company, 1925). For a recent refutation of the argument that expansionism drove the war, see Richard W. Maass, "Difficult to Relinquish Territory Which Had Been Conquered," *Diplomatic History* 39 (2015): 70–97.
12. *Annals*, 23:456 (Johnson); Monroe to Jonathan Russell, June 26, 1812, quoted in Perkins, *Prologue to War*, 416.
13. Adams to John Adams Smith, June 15, 1812, quoted in Stephen Budiansky, "The War of 1812 and the Rise of American Military Power," in Pietro S. Nivola and Peter J. Kastor, eds., *What So Proudly We Hailed: Essays on the Contemporary Meaning of the War of 1812* (Washington, DC: Brookings Institution Press, 2012), 36–38; Francis R. Stark, *The Abolition of Privateering and the Declaration of Paris* (New York: Columbia University, 1897), 127.
14. On war and state-building in Europe, see Braddick, *State Formation*; Brewer, *Sinews of Power*; Tilly, "European State-Making"; on the American capacity, see Edling, *Hercules in the Cradle*.
15. Denver Brunsman, "De-Anglicization: The Jeffersonian Attack on an American Naval Establishment," in Ignacio Gallup-Diaz, et al., eds., *Anglicizing America: Empire, Revolution, Republic* (Philadelphia: University of Pennsylvania Press, 2015), 205–25; Budiansky, "American Military Power," 36–43; Frederick C. Leiner, *Millions for Defense: The Subscription Warships of 1798* (Annapolis: Naval Institute Press, 2000).
16. Robert W. Tucker and David C. Hendrickson, *Empire of Liberty: The Statecraft of Thomas Jefferson* (New York: Oxford University Press, 1992), 39–42; Craig L. Symonds, *Navalists and Antinavalists: The Naval*

Policy Debate in the United States, 1785–1827 (Newark: University of Delaware Press, 1980); Walter Russell Mead, *Special Providence: American Foreign Policy and How It Changed the World* (New York: Alfred A. Knopf, 2001), 182–94. On Madison's views, see Drew R. McCoy, *The Last of the Fathers: James Madison and The Republican Legacy* (New York: Cambridge University Press, 1991), 12–14; Ralph Ketcham, "James Madison: The Unimperial President," *Virginia Quarterly Review* (1978): 116–36.

17. *Annals*, 23:841 (McKee); Budiansky, "American Military Power," 41–42; William P. Leeman, *The Long Road to Annapolis: The Founding of the Naval Academy and the Emerging American Republic* (Chapel Hill: University of North Carolina Press, 2010), 20–21, 110–11; Symonds, *Navalists and Antinavalists*, 12–14, 233–35; Nicholas R. Parrillo, *Against the Profit Motive: The Salary Revolution in American Government, 1780–1940* (New Haven: Yale University Press, 2013), 317–18.
18. Gautham Rao, *National Duties: Custom Houses and the Making of the American State* (Chicago: University of Chicago Press, 2016), 141–58; Louis Martin Sears, *Jefferson and the Embargo* (New York: Octagon Books, 1978), 3–31; Tucker and Hendrickson, *Empire of Liberty*, 173–228.
19. Jefferson to William Duane, Aug. 4, 1812, *PTJRS*, 5:293–94; Peter J. Kastor, "Toward 'the Maritime War Only': The Question of Naval Mobilization, 1811–1812," *Journal of Military History* 61 (1997): 455–80; Budiansky, "American Military Power," 42–43.
20. Monroe to Gallatin, June 10, 1812, quoted in Kastor, "Maritime War Only," 472–80.
21. *Annals*, 6:2130 (Gallatin); "An Act Declaring War between the United Kingdom of Great Britain and Ireland and the Dependencies Thereof and the United States of America and Their Territories," 2 Stat. 755 (1812); Prize Act of 1812, 2 Stat. 759. Jefferson is quoted in George Coggeshall, *History of the American Privateers and Letters-of-Marque* (New York: C.T. Evans, 1856), xliv; for similar sentiments, see *Annals*, 28:518 (Robertson). On the navy's exploits in the war, see A. T. Mahan, *Sea Power in Its Relations to the War of 1812* (Boston: Little, Brown and Company, 1905), 1:74–75; George C. Daughan, *1812: The Navy's War* (New York: Basic Books, 2011), 53–71.
22. Jefferson to William Duane, Aug. 4, 1812, *PTJRS*, 5:293–94; Budiansky, "American Military Power," 49–50; Hickey, *War of 1812*, 97; Mahan, *Sea Power*, 1:285.
23. Jefferson quoted in Coggeshall, *History of American Privateers*, xliv; Alan Taylor, "Dual Nationalisms: Legacies of the War of 1812," in Nivola and Kastor, *What So Proudly We Hailed*, 67–96; Peter S. Onuf, *Jefferson's Empire: The Language of American Nationhood*

(Charlottesville: University Press of Virginia, 2000), 107–8, 117–21; Nicholas Parrillo, "The De-Privatization of American Warfare: How the U.S. Government Used, Regulated, and Ultimately Abandoned Privateering in the Nineteenth Century," *Yale Journal of Law & the Humanities* 19 (2007), 1–95.

24. Garitee, *Private Navy*, 24–25.
25. *Columbian Phenix* (Providence), July 4, 1812, p. 2; Abner Bosent to Albert Gallatin, July 4, 1812; William Ferson to James Monroe, July 7, 1812; David Gelston to Monroe, Aug. 24, 1812, National Archives and Records Administration, War of 1812 Papers of the Department of State, microfilm M588; Garitee, *Private Navy*, xvi, 83.
26. Didier to John D'Arcy, Dec. 6, 1814, Maryland Center for History and Culture, Henry Didier Letterbook; Garitee, *Private Navy*, 32–46, 65–82; Faye M. Kert, *Privateering: Patriots and Profits in the War of 1812* (Baltimore: Johns Hopkins University Press, 2015), 71–80.
27. For examples of courts restoring neutral property, see decree, Oct. 19, 1812, Charretton v. Concord, USDC-NY, roll 2; libel, June 15, 1813, Patrullo v. Saratoga, USDC-NY, roll 4; claim, Dec. 13, 1814, Stevenson et al. v. Prudence, USDC-NY, roll 6; The Concord, 13 U.S. 387 (1815).
28. *New York Mercantile Advertiser*, Jan. 22, 1813, p. 3; Case 201, National Archives and Records Administration, Records of General Courts Martial and Courts of Inquiry of the Navy Department, 1799–1867, microfilm M273, roll 8; *Rhode-Island American*, Apr. 11, 1815, p. 2.
29. Garitee, *Private Navy*, 65–102.
30. Case 196, National Archives and Records Administration, Records of General Courts Martial and Courts of Inquiry of the Navy Department, 1799–1867, microfilm M273, roll 6; Case 131, ibid. For other instances of mutinous plunder, see Case 201, ibid., roll 8; affidavit, Dec. 27, 1815, Cazeaux v. Emulation, USDC-NY, roll 3; The Matilda, 26 F. Cas. 1200 (C.C.D.N.C. 1813); C. S. Forester, *The Age of Fighting Sail: The Story of the Naval War of 1812* (Garden City: Doubleday, 1956), 87.
31. Georg Friedrich von Martens, *An Essay on Privateers, Captures, and Particularly on Recaptures, According to the Laws, Treaties, and Usages of the Maritime Powers of Europe* (London: E. and R. Brooke and J. Rider, 1801), 23–24; Franklin to David Hartley, May 8, 1783, in in Albert Henry Smyth, ed., *The Writings of Benjamin Franklin* (New York: The Macmillan Co., 1905), 9:40; William Paterson's Supreme Court Opinion, Aug. 11, 1796, *DHSC*, 6:680–81.
32. William Paterson's Supreme Court Opinion, Aug. 11, 1796, *DHSC*, 6:680–81; Nelson quoted in Rubin, *Law of Piracy*, 236.
33. Marshall to Rufus King, Sep. 20, 1800, *PJM*, 4:283–97; The Thomas Gibbons, 12 U.S. 421, 429 (1814).
34. Marshall to Rufus King, Sep. 20, 1800, *PJM*, 4:283–97; Elizabeth Feaster Baker, *Henry Wheaton, 1785–1848* (Philadelphia: University

of Pennsylvania Press, 1937), 14–15; Patrick Crowhurst, *The French War on Trade: Privateering, 1793–1815* (Aldershot: Gower Publishing Co., 1989), 144–72; J. R. Hill, *The Prizes of War: The Naval Prize System in the Napoleonic Wars, 1793–1815* (Portsmouth: Royal Naval Museum Publications, 1998); Faye Margaret Kert, *Prize and Prejudice: Privateering and Naval Prize in Atlantic Canada in the War of 1812* (Liverpool: Liverpool University Press, 1997), 55–76; Jeppe Mulich, *In a Sea of Empires: Networks and Crossings in the Revolutionary Caribbean* (Cambridge: Cambridge University Press, 2020), 81–101; Bradford Perkins, "Sir William Scott and the Essex," *William and Mary Quarterly* 13 (1956): 169–83.

35. "An Act to provide for the more convenient organization of the Courts of the United States," § 7, 2 Stat. 89, 90 (1801); "An Act to amend the Judicial System of the United States," § 4, 2 Stat. 156, 157 (1802); Jay to Adams, Jan. 2, 1801, in Elizabeth M. Nuxoll, et al., eds., *The Selected Papers of John Jay* (Charlottesville: University of Virginia Press, 2021), 7:128–29. Aside from Marshall, Bushrod Washington was the only Federalist-appointed judge who remained on the Court in 1812. On difficulty of persuading nominees, and Story's nomination as Madison's fourth choice, see R. Kent Newmyer, *Supreme Court Justice Joseph Story: Statesman of the Old Republic* (Chapel Hill: University of North Carolina Press, 1985), 70–71.

36. Benjamin Henry Latrobe to James Madison, Sep. 8, 1809, *PJMPS*, 361–64; George L. Haskins and Herbert A. Johnson, *Foundations of Power: John Marshall, 1801–15* (New York: Macmillan, 1981), 74–82.

37. Barry Friedman, *The Will of the People: How Public Opinion Has Influenced the Supreme Court and Shaped the Meaning of the Constitution* (New York: Farrar, Straus and Giroux, 2009), 48–50; Joel Richard Paul, *Without Precedent: Chief Justice John Marshall and His Times* (New York: Penguin Publishing, 2018), 221–26; Geoffrey Stone, *Perilous Times: Free Speech in Wartime* (New York: W. W. Norton & Company, 2004), 15–79.

38. Thomas Jefferson to John Dickinson, Dec. 19, 1801, *PTJPS*, 165–66; Monroe to Jefferson, Mar. 3, 1801, *PTJPS*, 126–28; Morris to Robert R. Livingston, Feb. 20, 1801, in Jared Sparks, ed., *The Life of Gouverneur Morris* (Boston: Gray & Bowen, 1832), 3:153–54.

39. The most comprehensive treatment of the Jeffersonian attacks on the judiciary remains Richard E. Ellis, *The Jeffersonian Crisis; Courts and Politics in the Young Republic* (New York: Oxford University Press, 1971); see also Friedman, *Will of the People*, 44–77; Keith E. Whittington, "Reconstructing the Federal Judiciary: The Chase Impeachment and the Constitution," *Studies in American Political Development* 9 (1995): 55–116. On the rivalry between Jefferson and Marshall, see James E. Simon, *What Kind of Nation: Thomas Jefferson, John Marshall, and the Epic*

Struggle to Create a United States (New York: Simon & Schuster, 2003). On the threat of impeachment after Burr's treason trial, see R. Kent Newmyer, *The Treason Trial of Aaron Burr* (New York: Cambridge University Press, 2012), 176–77. On Justice William Johnson's 1808 ruling that the president had limited authority to direct how customs officers enforced the embargo laws passed by Congress, see Rao, *National Duties*, 147–50. On the theory of departmentalism, see Larry D. Kramer, *The People Themselves: Popular Constitutionalism and Judicial Review* (New York: Oxford University Press, 2004), 106–8; David N. Mayer, *The Constitutional Thought of Thomas Jefferson* (Charlottesville: University of Virginia Press, 1994), 257–94.

40. Stuart v. Laird, 5 U.S. 299 (1803). *Marbury* proclaimed the Court's authority "to say what the law is," but ultimately ruled that it could not compel the executive branch to deliver a commission to one of Adams's judicial appointees. Marbury v. Madison, 5 U.S. 137 (1803); William Michael Treanor, "The Story of Marbury v. Madison: Judicial Authority and Political Struggle," in Vicki C. Jackson and Judith Resnik, eds., *Federal Courts Stories* (New York: Foundation Press, 2010), 29–56. For a similar account of the political dynamics that shaped other Marshall Court decisions, see Mark A. Graber, "Establishing Judicial Review? Schooner Peggy and the Early Marshall Court," *Political Research Quarterly* 51 (1998): 221–39.

41. United States v. Peters, 9 U.S. 115 (1809). *Peters*'s facts are complex, but its origins lay in Pennsylvania's refusal to abide by a 1779 decision by the Court of Appeals in Cases of Capture that overturned a Pennsylvania admiralty court's prize ruling during the Revolutionary War. Because of the CACC's inability to compel state court compliance (discussed in Chapter 1), the case festered for years, with all three branches of the Pennsylvania government repeatedly defying federal court judgments (including one from the Supreme Court). Haskins and Johnson, *Foundations of Power*, 322–31.

42. *Martin v. Hunter's Lessee* was the culmination of decades of litigation over a huge tract of Virginia land claimed by numerous parties, including John Marshall. When the Supreme Court (with Marshall recused) reversed a Virginia state court ruling in favor of the non-Marshall side, the Virginia Court of Appeals refused to comply. It declared unconstitutional Section 25 of the Judiciary Act of 1789, which gave the Supreme Court the power to review state court judgments that involved questions of federal law. In 1816, the Supreme Court again reversed, in an opinion by Justice Story that articulated a broad understanding of the Court's power to review state court judgments. Martin v. Hunter's Lessee, 14 U.S. 304 (1816); Haskins and Johnson, *Foundations of Power*, 357–65.

43. Judiciary Act of 1789, § 12, 1 Stat. 73, 79; "An Act to determine the jurisdiction of circuit courts of the United States," § 1, 18 Stat. 470, 470

(1875); Haskins and Johnson, *Foundations of Power*, 454–92; Dwight F. Henderson, *Courts for a New Nation* (Washington, DC: Public Affairs, 1971), 55–63; Ariel N. Lavinbuk, "Rethinking Early Judicial Involvement in Foreign Affairs: An Empirical Study of the Supreme Court's Docket," *Yale Law Journal* 114 (2005): 855–904.

44. Story to Nathaniel Williams, Aug. 24, 1812, *LLJS*, 1:228–30; La Vengeance, 3 U.S. 297 (1796); United States v. Schooner Sally, 6 U.S. 406 (1805); United States v. The Betsey and Charlotte, 8 U.S. 443 (1808); DeLovio v. Boit, 7 F. Cas. 418 (C.C.D. Mass. 1815).
45. Marshall to Richard Söderström, Nov. 26, 1800, *PJM*, 6:21; Söderström to Madison, June 10, 1801, in Robert J. Brugger, et al., eds., *The Papers of James Madison, Secretary of State Series* (Charlottesville: University Press of Virginia, 1986), 1:290–96; Madison to Söderström, July 23, 1801, ibid., 1:461.
46. United States v. Schooner Peggy, 5 U.S. 103 (1801); Restitution under Treaty with France, 1 U.S. Op. Atty. Gen. 119 (1802); Graber, "Establishing Judicial Review?"
47. Prize Act of 1812, § 6, 2 Stat. 759, 761; The Anne, 16 U.S. 435 (1818); "Additional Note," appx. 11–15.
48. Prize Act of 1812, §§ 2, 3, 9, 2 Stat. 759, 759–61; "An Act in addition to the act concerning letters of marque, prizes, and prize goods," 2 Stat. 792 (1813).
49. Wheaton, *Reports of Cases*, 2:80–81; The Thomas Gibbons, 12 U.S. 421, 429 (1814); Garitee, *Private Navy*, 92–93.
50. In his careful study of Baltimore privateering in the War of 1812, Jerome Garitee reports only one instance in which the president revoked a specific privateering commission. In 1814, the Secretary of State revoked the commissions of all privateers with fewer than twenty officers and crew, but apparently due to their proclivity for smuggling and trading with the enemy, not because they made unlawful captures. *Niles' Weekly Register*, Feb. 26, 1814, pp. 423–24. Garitee contends that the Baltimore customs collector was "thoroughgoing" in his evaluation of privateering applications, but the basis for this conclusion is unclear. Garitee, *Private Navy*, 90–92. The leading study of federal criminal prosecutions in the early nineteenth century devotes two chapters to the War of 1812, but does not mention any piracy prosecutions. Henderson, *Courts, Congress, and Criminals*, 99–122. It appears that on the very few occasions when the government did institute a prosecution, the jury acquitted. United States v. Jones, 26 F. Cas. 659 (C.C. D. Pa. 1814). Nicholas Parrillo points out that merit-based promotion was a significant tool for regulating the conduct of naval officers, but the executive branch had no analogous power with respect to privateers. Parrillo, "De-Privatization," 27–33.
51. Prize Goods Act of 1662, 14 Cha. 2, c. 14; Prize Act of 1691, 3 Will. & Mar., c. 4; Naval Prize Act of 1739, 13 Geo. 2, c. 4; Prize Goods Act of 1757, 30 Geo. 2, c. 18; Manning of the Navy Act, 1805, 45 Geo. 3, c.

72; *JCC*, 31:1153–58; Wheaton, *Reports of Cases*, 5:103–29 (appx.); Richard Pares, *Colonial Blockade and Neutral Rights, 1739–1763* (Oxford: Clarendon Press, 1938), 42–76, 226–310; James G. Lydon, *Pirates, Privateers, and Profits* (Upper Saddle River: Gregg Press, 1970), 82–106. For example, the Continental Congress's 1780 instructions specified that property belonging to residents of Bermuda was exempt from capture, as was any property belonging to persons intending to settle in the United States. Contraband goods belonging to neutrals, however, were eligible as prize, as were goods being traded to the enemy. Wheaton, *Reports of Cases*, 5:112 (appx.).

52. Prize Act of 1812, § 15, 2 Stat. 759, 763; Manning of the Navy Act, 1805, art. 26, 45 Geo. 3, c. 72; William Jones to William Pinkney, May 8, 1813, NARA-NL, 11:267; Jones to Richard Rush, May 23, 1814, ibid., 12:169; Stephen Budiansky, "Giant Killer," *MHQ: The Quarterly Journal of Military History* 21 (2009): 50–60; Reuben Elmore Stivers, *Privateers & Volunteers: The Men and Women of Our Reserve Naval Forces, 1766 to 1866* (Annapolis: Naval Institute Press, 1975), 123–24.

53. William Jones to Richard Rush, May 23, 1814, NARA-NL, 12:169; Jones to Richard Rush, Nov. 8, 1814, ibid., 12:240; Case 196, National Archives and Records Administration, Records of General Courts Martial and Courts of Inquiry of the Navy Department, 1799–1867, microfilm M273, roll 7; Case 201, ibid., roll 8; Parrillo, "De-Privatization," 33–34. James Valle suggests that there were thirty-two court martial cases against privateers in 1813 and 1814, but it is unclear whether those were separate cases or the total number of defendants. James E. Valle, *Rocks & Shoals: Order and Discipline in the Old Navy, 1800–1861* (Annapolis: Naval Institute Press, 1980), 93–94. Congress formally instructed the House committee on naval affairs to research an alternative mode of discipline, but none emerged. Jones to Burwell Bassett, Feb. 3, 1813, *ASPNA*, 1:286; *Annals*, 25:167.

54. Hickey, *War of 1812*, 80–88, 112–17, 303–6. Max Edling argues that the Madison administration's efforts to finance the war were theoretically sound, but failed due to a lack of political will and the war's unexpectedly high cost. Edling, *Hercules in the Cradle*, 108–44.

55. Congress gave the courts jurisdiction over captures made in the Quasi-War, but there were no privateers commissioned during that conflict and American naval vessels were only permitted to seize armed French ships. "An Act further to protect the commerce of the United States," §§ 1, 2, 1 Stat. 578, 578–79 (1798). Pamphlet descriptions of the extant case records suggest the courts heard few prize cases during this period. National Archives and Records Service, *Admiralty Case Files of the U.S. District Court for the Eastern District of Pennsylvania, 1789–1840* (Washington, DC: General Services Administration, 1975), 10–13; National Archives and Records Service, *Admiralty Case Files of the*

U.S. District Court for the Southern District of New York, 1790–1842 (Washington, DC: General Services Administration, 1973), 6. Only a handful of cases from the Quasi-War reached the Supreme Court, and none addressed the question of whether a prize was lawful. Bas v. Tingy, 4 U.S. 37 (1800); Talbot v. Seeman, 5 U.S. 1 (1801); United States v. Schooner Peggy, 5 U.S. 103 (1801); Haskins and Johnson, *Foundations of Power*, 409; J. Gregory Sidak, "The Quasi War Cases – and Their Relevance to Whether 'Letters of Marque and Reprisal' Constrain Presidential War Powers," *Harvard Journal of Law & Public Policy* 27 (2005): 465–99.

56. In 1796, the Supreme Court indicated in passing that all admiralty cases *in rem* were to be tried without a jury, and it affirmed that view in 1808. La Vengeance, 3 U.S. 297, 301 (1796); United States v. The Betsey and Charlotte, 8 U.S. 443 (1808). However, the unpublished records of the lower federal courts reveal at least a few instances in the early period where juries heard such cases. Kevin Arlyck, "The Founders' Forfeiture," *Columbia Law Review* 119 (2019): 1449–518; Henderson, *New Nation*, 55–56.
57. Owners, Officers and Crew of Privateer Nonsuch v. Schooner Perseverance, Aug. 19, 1812, USDC-SC, roll 2; Dill v. Schooner Perseverance, Aug. 21, 1812, USDC-SC, roll 2. On the *Nonsuch*, see Garitee, *Private Navy*, 202, 251. Other early cases include Graw v. Polacre San Francisco de Paula, libel, July 25, 1812, National Archives and Records Administration, Records of the U.S. District Court for the Eastern District of Louisiana, 1806–1814, microfilm M1082, roll 12; United States v. Ship Continencia, Aug. 14, 1812, USDC-SC.
58. *City Gazette and Commercial Daily Advertiser* (Charleston), Aug. 25, 1812, p. 3; Gavit v. Ship Mary and Ann, Sep. 2, 1812, Sep. 7, 1812, USDC-SC; Beaufeau v. Ship Grenada, Sep. 2, 1812, Sep. 7, 1812, USDC-SC; Chazal v. Brig Amelia, Aug. 21, 1812, Aug. 27, 1812, USDC-SC.
59. Court order, Oct. 28, 1812, USDC-SC; Letter from Judge Drayton to Robert E. Cochran, Oct. 22, 1812, USDC-SC; order, Aug. 14, 1812, National Archives and Records Administration, Records of the U.S. District Court for the Eastern District of Louisiana, 1806–1814, microfilm M1082, roll 1.
60. Leveley v. Schooner Perseverance, Sep. 14, 1812, Sep. 22, 1812, USDC-SC. On probable cause and damages under the laws of maritime war, see The Apollon, 22 U.S. 362, 373 (1824); Jane Manners, "Executive Power and the Rule of Law in the Marshall Court: A Rereading of Little v. Barreme and Murray v. Schooner Charming Betsy," *Fordham Law Review* 89 (2021): 1941–74.
61. The Anna Maria, 15 U.S. 327, 334 (1817).
62. The Lively, 15 F. Cas. 631, 635 (C.C.D. Mass. 1812).

63. The Lively, 15 F. Cas. at 635; The Amiable Nancy, 16 U.S. 546, 559 (1818); Hannah Farber, *Underwriters of the United States: How Insurance Shaped the American Founding* (Williamsburg: Omohundro Institute of Early American History and Culture, 2021), 151–80; Su Jin Kim and James Oldham, "Insuring Maritime Trade with the Enemy in the Napoleonic Era," *Texas International Law Journal* 47 (2012): 561–86.
64. Taylor v. Cargo of Ship Continencer, Oct. 6, 1812, USDC-SC; Coggeshall, *History of American Privateers*, 60; Garitee, *Private Navy*, 92–93, 239; Edgar Stanton Maclay, *A History of American Privateers* (Freeport: Books for Libraries Press, 1970), 460–61.
65. Examination of the records of four district courts – New York, South Carolina, Virginia, and Louisiana – reveals only three instances of damage awards. Connelly v. Schooner Maria, Feb. 9, 1813, USDC-SC; Megrath v. Brown, Oct. 25, 1813, USDC-SC; Zebulon Miller v. Georgia, USDC-NY, roll 3.
66. "Additional Note," appx. 9–11, 16; Parrillo, "De-Privatization," 45–48. In cases where captors sold a prize without a court order, the purchaser's legal claim was vulnerable and could be challenged later in court by the rightful owner. As a result, unadjudicated prizes sold at a steep discount. William R. Casto, "Regulating the New Privateers of the Twenty-First Century," *Rutgers Law Journal* 37 (2006): 671–702.

    It is possible that fear of losing the bonds posted as security for good behavior prompted privateers' restraint. Adams to John M. Forbes, July 11, 1820, *DCUS*, 1:138–39; Parrillo, "De-Privatization," 48–49. But punishing privateer misbehavior by bond revocation was cumbersome and uncertain. While privateers effectively had to subject themselves voluntarily to judicial supervision in order to profit from their captures, government officers had to sue in court to recover monies owed under bonds. Knapp, "Empire to Law," 570–71. Garitee reports that not a single Baltimore surety was called to account for privateer misconduct during the war. Garitee, *Private Navy*, 91–93.
67. On the distribution of prize money, see Garitee, *Private Navy*, 183–209.
68. The Brutus, 4 F. Cas. 490, 497–99 (C.C.D. Mass. 1815); Garitee, *Private Navy*, 129–30. When there was no written agreement, the court allocated the proceeds according to a federal statute specifying prize distributions to officers and crew of naval ships. Prize Act of 1812, § 4, 2 Stat. 759, 759–60.
69. Herve v. Brown, Aug. 6, 1813, USDC-SC; Ex parte John Egleston, Sep. 24, 1813, USDC-SC; Chautraud v. Brown and D'Irou, Oct. 13, 1813, USDC-SC; Garitee, *Private Navy*, 195–97.
70. Kane v. Caroline, affidavit of Kane, Apr. 5, 1813, USDC-NY, roll 1.
71. Constitution v. Susannah, affidavit of John McCauley, June 19, 1815, USDC-NY, roll 7; Cazeaux v. Adeline, claim of John Carrere, Aug. 6, 1814, decree, Nov. 4, 1814, USDC-NY, roll 1; Johnson v. Mary and Susan, order, Sep. 9, 1814, USDC-NY, roll 5.

72. Dobson v. Stranger, libel of David S. Jones, Jan. 22, 1816, USDC-NY, roll 7; Eveningham v. British Brig Tartar, motion of Thomas Parker, June 4, 1813, USDC-SC.
73. Adams v. Venus, rule of court, Nov. 16, 1812, rule of court [undated], USDC-NY, roll 8; Engersoll v. Industry, clerk's report, Mar. 10, 1813, USDC-NY, roll 3; Jenkins v. Union, clerk's report, USDC-NY, roll 8; Adams v. Jenny, clerk's report, USDC-NY, roll 3; Campan v. Young Adella, clerk's report, USDC-NY, roll 8.
74. Burch v. Goods from Schooner Meadow and Brig Lord Wellington, decree, Mar. 5, 1813, USDC-SC. The same was true in other courts. Vial v. Brig Edward, decree, National Archives and Records Administration, Admiralty Case Files of the U.S. District Court for the Eastern District of Virginia, 1801–1861, microfilm M1300, roll 6; Quarles v. Ship Windsor Castle, decree, May 8, 1815, ibid., roll 6; Garitee, *Private Navy*, 189–92.
75. Ferlat v. Brig Perola, decree, Oct. 28, 1812; Ferlat and Allen v. Schooner Woodburne, decree, Oct. 29, 1812; Sicard and Ferlat v. Ship Antrim, decree, July 16, 1813, National Archives and Records Administration, Records of the U.S. District Court for the Eastern District of Louisiana, 1806–1814, microfilm M1082, roll 1.
76. Adams v. Venus, affidavit of Robert Finn, Jan. 4, 1816; order to show cause, Jan. 8, 1816; affidavit of Samuel Craig, Jan. 13, 1816, USDC-NY, roll 8. The challenge of accounting was not simply a New York problem. Hennequin v. Brown and LeChartier, Jan. 24, 1814, USDC-SC. New York clerk's reports from the war's later years no longer included detailed prize distributions. Ward v. Mary, clerk's report, Dec. 9, 1814, USDC-NY, roll 4; Taylor v. Star, clerk's report, Mar. 20, 1815, USDC-NY, roll 7; Schenck v. Helena, clerk's report, Sep. 8, 1815, USDC-NY, roll 3; Dennet v. Jane, clerk's report, June 15, 1815, USDC-NY, roll 3; Schenck v. Harmony, clerk's report, May 23, 1816, USDC-NY, roll 3.
77. Memorial of Baltimore Merchants, *ASPNA*, 1:273–74; Reduction of Duties on Prize Goods, Dec. 21, 1812, in *American State Papers, Finance* (Washington, DC: Gales and Seaton, 1834), 2:591–94.
78. Memorial of Baltimore Merchants, *ASPNA*, 1:273–74.
79. "An Act to regulate Processes in the Courts of the United States," § 2, 1 Stat. 93, 93–94 (1789); "An Act for regulating processes in the Courts of the United States," § 2, 1 Stat. 275, 276 (1792); Memorial of Baltimore Merchants, *ASPNA*, 1:273–74. For instance, the New York district court took more than two years to resolve a case involving over twenty separate claims to the cargo. White v. Cargo of Independence, USDC-NY, roll 3. In another case, it took almost four months for the privateers to receive the prize proceeds, even though their libel went unopposed. White v. The Rio Nova, USDC-NY, roll 3. On federal court procedural rules, see Goebel, *Antecedents*, 509–51; *DHSC*, 4:108–21, 176–98; Thomas

H. Lee, "Article IX, Article III, and the First Congress: The Original Constitutional Plan for the Federal Courts, 1787–1792," *Fordham Law Review* 89 (2021): 1895–940.

80. Memorial of Baltimore Merchants, *ASPNA*, 1:273–74; "Additional Note," appx. 17, 51, 71; Hill, *Prizes of War*, 9; The St. Lawrence, 21 F. Cas. 182, 184 (C.C.D.N.H. 1814).

81. Beaufeau v. Grenada and Shaddock, Sep. 15, 1812; Ex parte Philip Cohen, Sep. 29, 1812; Oct. 5, 1812; Gavit v. Ship Mary and Ann, Oct. 5, 1812; Ex parte Captors of Schooner Shaddock, Oct. 19, 1812, USDC-SC; Browns v. Schooner Mary Ann, minute book entry, National Archives and Records Administration, Admiralty Case Files of the U.S. District Court for the Eastern District of Virginia, 1801–1861, microfilm M1300, roll 1; *Annals*, 25:144; Almeida v. Certain Slaves, 1 F. Cas. 538, 538 (D.S.C. 1814); Jeffrey Orenstein, "Joseph Almeida: Portrait of a Privateer, Pirate & Plaintiff, Part I," *Green Bag* 10 (2007): 312–14; Pedersen to Monroe, May 23, 1816, National Archives and Records Administration, Notes from the Danish Legation in the United States to the Department of State, 1801–1906, microfilm M52, roll 1.

82. "An Act regulating pensions to persons on board private armed ships," § 2, 2 Stat. 799, 799 (1813); "An Act giving pensions to the orphans and widows of persons slain in the public or private armed vessels of the United States," § 1, 3 Stat. 103, 103 (1814); "An Act making further provision for military services during the late war, and for other purposes," § 1, 3 Stat. 285, 285 (1816); Extension of the Privateer Fund, Feb. 2, 1824, *ASPNA*, 1:931–32; William H. Glasson, *Federal Military Pensions in the United States* (New York: Oxford University Press, 1918), 100–2; Robert L. Clark, Lee A. Craig, and Jack W. Wilson, "Privatization of Public-Sector Pensions: The U.S. Navy Pension Fund, 1800–1842," *The Independent Review* 3 (1999): 549–64.

On the importance of military pensions in the nineteenth century generally, see Kristin Collins, "'Petitions Without Number': Widows' Petitions and the Early Nineteenth-Century Origins of Public Marriage-Based Entitlements," *Law and History Review* 31 (2013): 1–60; Laura Jensen, *Patriots, Settlers, and the Origins of American Social Policy* (New York: Cambridge University Press, 2003); John Resch, *Suffering Soldiers: Revolutionary War Veterans, Moral Sentiment, and Political Culture in the Early Republic* (Amherst: University of Massachusetts Press, 1999); Theda Skocpol, *Protecting Soldiers and Mothers: The Political Origins of Social Policy in the United States* (Cambridge, MA: Harvard University Press, 1992).

83. William Jones to James Prince, Sep. 27, 1813, *ASPNA*, 1:382–83; William Jones to Clerk of North Carolina District Court, July 6, 1814, NARA-NL, 12:1; Benjamin Crowninshield to Carlton Walker, June 13,

1815, NARA-NL, 12:330; Crowninshield to the Attorney General, June 8, 1815, NARA-NL, 12:328. An 1814 report on district court prize condemnations noted that the federal marshal in Georgia was the only one to have rendered a proper accounting. Account of sales, Aug. 17, 1814, *ASPNA*, 1:392.

84. Connelly v. Schooner Erin, Apr. 15, 1813, Apr. 23, 1813, USDC-SC; Bulkley v. Brig Pelican, May 5, 1813, USDC-SC; United States v. Robert E. Cochran, May 7, 1813; May 11, 1813, USDC-SC.
85. Navy Department Circular, Mar. 30, 1813, Nov. 29, 1815, *ASPNA*, 1:535, 537; Benjamin Crowninshield to Carlton Walker, June 13, 1815, NARA-NL, 12:330; Crowninshield to John Eppinger, June 20, 1815, NARA-NL, 12:332.
86. James Dill to Benjamin Crowninshield, Dec. 21, 1815, *ASPNA*, 1:388; Nathan Sanford to William Jones, Sep. 30, 1813, *ASPNA*, 1:544; William S. Shaw to Secretary of the Navy, Oct. 13, 1813, *ASPNA*, 1:540; George Blake to Crowninshield, June 26, 1816, *ASPNA*, 1:543; John Eppinger to Crowninshield, June 20, 1815, *ASPNA*, 1:542.
87. "An Act in addition to an act, entitled 'An act in relation to the navy pension fund,'" §§ 2, 3, 4, 6, 3 Stat. 287, 287–88 (1816); Benjamin Crowninshield to Speaker of the House of Representatives, Jan. 5, 1816, *ASPNA*, 1:380; Crowninshield to Joseph Story, Jan. 10, 1817, *ASPNA*, 1:539; *Annals*, 32:1692–94.
88. Memorandum by the Court on the Letter of the Secretary of the Navy, Jan. 20, 1816, *ASPNA*, 1:546; Crowninshield to Theron Rudd, Jan. 1, 1815, *ASPNA*, 1:536; Crowninshield to John Smith, Apr. 28, 1815, NARA-NL, 12:310; Crowninshield to Smith, May 4, 1815, *ASPNA*, 1:391; Crowninshield to Smith, June 7, 1815, NARA-NL, 12:326; Crowninshield to Smith, Dec. 1, 1815, NARA-NL, 12:373.
89. Report on the Official Conduct of the Judge of the Southern District of New York, Feb. 17, 1819, *American State Papers: Miscellaneous* (Washington, DC: Gales and Seaton, 1834), 2:542–43; Thomas N. Baker, "'An Attack Well Directed': Aaron Burr Intrigues for the Presidency," *Journal of the Early Republic*, 31 (2011): 553–98; John L. Brooke, *Columbia Rising: Civil Life on the Upper Hudson from the Revolution to the Age of Jackson* (Raleigh: University of North Carolina Press, 2013), 477.
90. Prize Act of 1813, § 1, 2 Stat. 792, 792; The St. Lawrence, 21 F. Cas. 182, 183 (C.C.D.N.H. 1814).
91. "An Act for reducing the duties payable on prize goods captured by the private armed vessels of the United States," 3 Stat. 75 (1813); "An Act to relinquish the claims of the United States to certain goods, wares, and merchandise, captured by private armed vessels," § 1, 3 Stat. 4, 4–5 (1813); Prize Act of 1813, § 1, 2 Stat. 792, 792; "An Act in addition to an act entitled 'An Act allowing a bounty to the owners, officers, and crews of the private armed vessels of the United States,'" § 1, 3 Stat. 105,

105 (1814); Memorial of Baltimore Merchants and Ship Owners, Feb. 4, 1814, *ASPNA*, 1:300; Garitee, *Private Navy*, 168–69.

92. Jones to Charles Harris, July 6, 1814, NARA-NL, 12:190. For similar sentiments, see Jones to Robert Cochrane, Feb. 19, 1814, NARA-NL, 12:118; Jones to Richard Rush, June 27, 1814, NARA-NL, 12:169; Benjamin Homans to Agents of Private Armed Vessel Prince de Neufchatel, Jan. 2, 1815, NARA-NL, 12:256. Some federal officers seemingly took Jones's admonitions to heart. The South Carolina district attorney routinely appeared in court to ensure that monies owed to the United States were actually paid. Beaufeau v. Grenada and Shaddock, Sep. 15, 1812; Jervy v. Boat Brothers, Nov. 16, 1812; Connelly v. Schooner Erin, Jan. 28, 1813; Connelly v. Cargo of Schooner Maria, Jan. 28, 1813; D'Irou v. Ship London Trader, Aug. 25, 1813, USDC-SC.

93. Joseph Rademaker to Monroe, Mar. 27, 1813, NARA-PL, roll 1; Luis de Onís to Monroe, Dec. 28, 1812, Oct. 27, 1813, Jan. 7, 1813, NARA-SL, roll 5; Richard Söderström to Monroe, Aug. 31, 1812, National Archives and Records Administration, Notes from Foreign Consuls in the United States to the Department of State, 1789–1906, microfilm M664, roll 1.

94. Monroe to Joseph Rademaker, May 1, 1814; Monroe to M. De Kantrou, Nov. 20, 1813; Secretary of the Treasury to Monroe, May 11, 1814; Monroe to Anthony St. John Baker, July 15, 1815, National Archives and Records Administration, Notes from the Department of State to Foreign Ministers and Consuls in the United States, 1793–1834, microfilm M38, roll 2.

95. Richard Teasdale to Charles Smedberg, Oct. 28, 1813; Teasdale to Smedberg, Nov. 1, 1813; M. De Kantrou to Monroe, Nov. 12, 1813, Notes from the Swedish Legation in the United States to the Department of State, 1813–1906, microfilm M60, roll 1; Monroe to M. De Kantrou, Nov. 20, 1813, Notes from the Department of State to Foreign Ministers and Consuls in the United States, 1793–1834, microfilm M38, roll 2.

It is possible Madison thought he could not interfere with the naval officers personal right to the prize, vested by statute. But this was doubtful. Under the law of nations, all rights of prize belonged originally to the government, and were only granted to the captors by sovereign grace. "Additional Note," appx. 71. Plus, it was arguable that the president's pardon power extended to officer shares of seizures in prize and customs cases. Power of the Executive to Remit Forfeitures, 4 U.S. Op. Atty. Gen. 573, 574–77 (1847); Passenger Laws-Pardoning Power, 6 U.S. Op. Atty. Gen. 393, 406 (1854).

96. Monroe to Anthony St. John Baker, July 15, 1815; Monroe to Baker, Apr. 14, 1815, Notes from the Department of State to Foreign Ministers and Consuls in the United States, 1793–1834, microfilm M38, roll 2.

97. Glass v. Sloop Betsey, 3 U.S. 6, 13–14 (1794), U.S. Const, art. III, § 2.

98. Story to Nathaniel Williams, Aug. 24, 1812, *LLJS*, 1:228, 229; Newmyer, *Statesman*, 64–77.

99. "On the Practice in Prize Causes," in Wheaton, *Reports of Cases*, 1:494; The Lively, 15 F. Cas. 631, 633, 638 (C.C.D. Mass. 1812); The Ann Green, 1 F. Cas. 958, 961 (C.C.D. Mass. 1812); Story to Henry Wheaton, May 25, 1816, *LLJS*, 1:281; The Liverpool Packet, 15 F. Cas. 641, 642–43 (C.C.D. Mass. 1813). Story did not specify which southern courts were guilty of "irregularities," but the Louisiana district court's habit of allowing the parties to present extensive eyewitness testimony prompted him to write a scathing opinion after the war ended. Graw v. Polacre San Francisco de Paula, minute entries, Jan. 1813, National Archives and Records Administration, Records of the U.S. District Court for the Eastern District of Louisiana, 1806–1814, microfilm M1082, roll 1; The Dos Hermanos, 15 U.S. 76, 81 (1817).
100. "On the Practice in Prize Causes," 496–99, 504–6; The Sally, 21 F. Cas. 243, 246 (C.C.D. Mass. 1813); The Ann Green, 1 F. Cas. at 961. For similar complaints, see "Additional Note," appx. 19; The Julia, 14 F. Cas. 27, 28 (C.C.D. Mass. 1813); The Adeline, 13 U.S. 244, 284 (1815).
101. The Euphrates, 8 F. Cas. 815, 815 (C.C.R.I. 1813); The Dos Hermanos, 15 U.S. at 80–81; *LLJS*, 1:226–27; "Additional Note," appx. 80. On the dearth of legal sources available to early American lawyers, see Michael H. Hoeflich, *Legal Publishing in Antebellum America* (New York: Cambridge University Press, 2010); John D. III Gordan, "Publishing Robinson's Reports of Cases Argued and Determined in the High Court of Admiralty," *Law and History Review* 32 (2014): 525–73.
102. Story to Henry Wheaton, Sep. 5, 1815, *LLJS*, 1:266–69; The Dos Hermanos, 15 U.S. at 81; The Pizarro, 15 U.S. 227, 240 (1817).
103. Story to William Scott, Jan. 14, 1819, *LLJS*, 1:318; "On the Practice in Prize Causes," 495; "Additional Note," appx. 1.
104. DeLovio v. Boit, 7 F. Cas. 418 (C.C.D. Mass. 1815); Newmyer, *Statesman*, 123–25; "Extension of Federal Jurisdiction Over State Canals," *American Law Review* 37 (1903): 911–16.
105. "Additional Note," appx. 3–5, 75–79; The St. Lawrence, 21 F. Cas. 182, 182 (C.C.D.N.H. 1814); The Dove, 7 F. Cas. 979, 981 (C.C.D. Mass. 1813); The Emulous, 8 F. Cas. 697, 701 (C.C.D. Mass. 1813); "Additional Note," appx. 1.
106. "Additional Note," appx. 51, 68, 71; The Lively, 15 F. Cas. 631, 632 (C.C.D. Mass. 1812).
107. Story to Scott, Jan. 14, 1819, *LLJS*, 1:318–21.
108. Ibid.

5 A Belligerent Court

1. Story to Williams, Aug. 24, 1812, *LLJS*, 1:228–29.
2. Story to Williams, May 8, 1815, *LLJS*, 1:255, 255–56; The Nereide, 13 U.S. 388, 413–36 (1815).

3. Story to Henry Wheaton, Apr. 8, 1818, *LLJS*, 1:303, 304; The Nereide, 13 U.S. 388, 448–49 (1815) (Story, J., dissenting).
4. On war, violence, and territorial expansion in the early republic, see Gregory Ablavsky, *Federal Ground: Governing Property and Violence in the First U.S. Territories* (New York: Oxford University Press, 2021); Fred Anderson and Andrew Cayton, *The Dominion of War: Empire and Liberty in North America, 1500–2000* (East Rutherford: Penguin, 2005), 160–246; Ned Blackhawk, *Violence over the Land: Indians and Empires in the Early American West* (Cambridge: Harvard University Press, 2006); Patrick Griffin, *American Leviathan: Empire, Nation, and Revolutionary Frontier* (New York: Hill and Wang, 2007); Francis Paul Prucha, *The Sword of the Republic: The United States Army on the Frontier, 1783–1846* (New York: Macmillan, 1968); Alan Taylor, *American Republics: A Continental History of the United States, 1783–1850* (New York: W. W. Norton & Company, 2021), 106–49; Steven Watts, *The Republic Reborn: War and the Making of Liberal America, 1790–1820* (Baltimore: Johns Hopkins University Press, 1987).

   Studies emphasizing the Supreme Court's pro-neutrality stance include Eric A. Belgrad, "John Marshall's Contributions to American Neutrality Doctrines," *William and Mary Law Review* 9 (1967): 430–51; George Lee Haskins and Herbert Alan Johnson, *History of the Supreme Court of the United States: Foundations of Power: John Marshall, 1801–1815* (New York: Cambridge University Press, 1981); R. Kent Newmyer, *John Marshall and the Heroic Age of the Supreme Court* (Baton Rouge: Louisiana State University Press, 2001), 286; Charles Anthony Smith, "Credible Commitments and the Early American Supreme Court," *Law & Society Review* 42 (2008): 75–110; John Fabian Witt, *Lincoln's Code: The Laws of War in American History* (New York: Free Press, 2012), 54–60; Benjamin Munn Ziegler, *The International Law of John Marshall: A Study of First Principles* (Chapel Hill: University of North Carolina Press, 1939), 23, 110–274.

   On early American promotion of neutral rights, see Mlada Bukovansky, "American Identity and Neutral Rights from Independence to the War of 1812," *International Organization* 50 (1997): 209–43; Charles G. Fenwick, *The Neutrality Laws of the United States* (Washington, DC: Carnegie Endowment, 1913); Philip C. Jessup and Francis Deak, *Neutrality: Its History, Economics, and Law, Vol. 1: The Origins* (New York: Columbia University Press, 1936); Arnold W. Knauth, "Prize Law Reconsidered," *Columbia Law Review* 46 (1946): 69–93; W. Alison Phillips and Arthur H. Reade, *Neutrality: Its History, Economics, and Law, Vol. 2: The Napoleonic Period* (New York: Columbia University Press, 1936); Harold Scott Quigley, "The American Attitude Toward Capture at Sea," *American Journal of International Law* 11 (1917): 820–38.

Some scholars have noted the Supreme Court's reliance on the pro-belligerent prize decisions of the High Court of Admiralty authored by Sir William Scott, though generally without exploring the degree to which the Supreme Court's adoption of British precedent dovetailed with growing hostility to neutral rights. David Golove, "The Supreme Court, the War on Terror, and the American Just War Constitutional Tradition," in David L. Sloss, Michael D. Ramsey, and William S. Dodge, eds., *International Law in the U.S. Supreme Court: Continuity and Change* (Cambridge: Cambridge University Press, 2011), 561–74.

5. Ted White explores the relationship between the Court's jurisprudence and "the sense that the Revolutionary generation had passed" in his history of the Marshall Court's latter decades, though he does not extend that insight to the Court's wartime cases. G. Edward White, *The Marshall Court and Cultural Change, 1815–1835* (New York: Oxford University Press, 1991), 6, 11–75. On the generational dynamics of the post-revolutionary years more generally, see Joyce Oldham Appleby, *Inheriting the Revolution: The First Generation of Americans* (Cambridge: Belknap Press, 2000); Watts, *Republic Reborn.*
6. On the Marshall Court's general unanimity, see Ruth Bader Ginsburg, "Speaking in a Judicial Voice," *New York University Law Review* 67 (1992): 1185–209; M. Todd Henderson, "From Seriatim to Consensus and Back Again: A Theory of Dissent," *Supreme Court Review* (2007): 283–344; Percival E. Jackson, *Dissent in the Supreme Court: A Chronology* (Buffalo: William S. Hein, 1991), 20–40; John P. Kelsh, "The Opinion Delivery Practices of the United States Supreme Court, 1790–1945," *Washington University Law Quarterly* 77 (1999): 137–82; Newmyer, *Heroic Age*, 413; Thomas P. Schmidt, "Courts in Conversation," *Michigan State Law Review* (2022): 411–26; Melvin I. Urofsky, *Dissent and the Supreme Court: Its Role in the Court's History and the Nation's Constitutional Dialogue* (New York: Pantheon Books, 2015), 55–81; G. Edward White, "The Working Life of the Marshall Court, 1815–1835," *Virginia Law Review* 70 (1984): 1–52. In their volume covering the Marshall Court's first fifteen years, George Haskins and Herbert Johnson raise the possibility that internal divisions in admiralty and prize cases served to undermine Marshall's "preeminence" with respect to opinion delivery more broadly, but do not explore the idea. Haskins and Johnson, *Foundations of Power*, 387.
7. Quoted in James Sterling Young, *The Washington Community, 1800–1828* (New York: Columbia University Press, 1966), 76; Haskins and Johnson, *Foundations of Power*, 74–82; White, *Cultural Change*, 158–62.
8. Story to Ezekiel Bacon, Mar. 12, 1818, *LLJS*, 1:310; Story to Nathaniel Williams, Feb. 16, 1812, *LLJS*, 1:214; Story to Samuel Fay, Feb. 24, 1812, *LLJS*, 1:215–16; Story to Sarah W. Story, Mar. 5, 1812, *LLJS*,

1:217–18; Taylor, *American Republics*, 53–54. Marshall wrote to his wife of regular dinners, balls, and other functions, and, in 1818, a New York newspaper reported that the capital's "greatest season of festivity" only began once the Court was in session. *Commercial Advertiser*, Feb. 7, 1818, p. 2; White, *Cultural Change*, 160–61. On the importance of boardinghouses for early Washington's social and political life, see Young, *Washington Community*, 98–109.

9. Haskins and Johnson, *Foundations of Power*, 380; Kelsh, "Opinion Delivery," 146–47.
10. The Mary and Susan, 14 U.S. 25 (1816); Bank of the United States v. Dandridge, 25 U.S. 64, 90 (1827) (Marshall, C.J., dissenting); Mason v. Haile, 25 U.S. 370, 379 (1827) (Washington, J., dissenting); Haskins and Johnson, *Foundations of Power*, 383–85; White, *Cultural Change*, 186–89.
11. Ex parte Bollman, 8 U.S. 75, 101 (1807) (Johnson, J., dissenting); Johnson to Thomas Jefferson, Dec. 10, 1822, *FO*; Urofsky, *Dissent*, 49–53; Jackson, *Dissent*, 26; Donald G. Morgan, *Justice William Johnson: The First Dissenter: The Career and Constitutional Philosophy of a Jeffersonian Judge* (Columbia: University of South Carolina Press, 1954).
12. James Bradley Thayer, *John Marshall* (Boston: Houghton, Mifflin, 1901), 54–55; "A Friend to the Union, No. 1," *PJM*, 8:287–98; Paul W. Kahn, *The Reign of Law: Marbury v. Madison and the Construction of America* (New Haven: Yale University Press, 2008), 106.
13. Madison to Spencer Roane, Sep. 2, 1819, *PJMRS*, 1:500–4; Jefferson to Thomas Ritchie, Dec. 25, 1820, *PTJRS*, 16:482–84.
14. Jefferson to William Johnson, Mar. 4, 1823, *FO*; Jefferson to James Pleasants, Dec. 26, 1821, *PTJRS*, 18:79–82; Jefferson to William Johnson, June 12, 1823, *FO*; Jefferson to James Madison, June 13, 1823, *FO*; Urofsky, *Dissent*, 40–41, 47–54; Henderson, "Seriatim to Consensus," 303.
15. Talbot v. Seeman, 5 U.S. 1, 43–45 (1801); "An Act for the Government of the Navy of the United States," § 7, 1 Stat. 709, 716 (1799); Witt, *Lincoln's Code*, 56–57.
16. Commissioners to the French Minister of Foreign Affairs, Jan. 27, 1798, *ASPFR*, 2:169–82; Albert J. Beveridge, *The Life of John Marshall* (Boston: Houghton Mifflin, 1944), 2:96–98; Bukovansky, "American Identity and Neutral Rights," 222–38; Isabel De Madariaga, *Britain, Russia, and the Armed Neutrality of 1780: Sir James Harris's Mission to St. Petersburg During the American Revolution* (New Haven: Yale University Press, 1962); Sandra Moats, *Navigating Neutrality: Early American Governance in the Turbulent Atlantic* (Charlottesville: University of Virginia Press, 2021), 9–40.
17. Washington to the States, June 8, 1783, *FO*; Robert Feenstra, ed., *Hugo Grotius, Mare Liberum 1609–2009: Original Latin Text and*

English Translation (Leiden: Brill, 2009); Gilbert, *To the Farewell Address*, 57–66; Paul A. Gilje, *Free Trade and Sailors' Rights in the War of 1812* (New York: Cambridge University Press, 2013), 13–31; David Hancock, *Citizens of the World: London Merchants and the Integration of the British Atlantic Community, 1735–1785* (Cambridge: Cambridge University Press, 1995); Douglas A. Irwin, *Against the Tide: An Intellectual History of Free Trade* (Princeton: Princeton University Press, 1996).

18. Jefferson to Thomas Pinckney, Dec. 20, 1793, *PTJ*, 27:55; Banning, *Jeffersonian Persuasion*, 214–38; McCoy, *Elusive Republic*, 76–104; Onuf and Onuf, *Federal Union*, 103–8; J. G. A. Pocock, "Virtue and Commerce in the Eighteenth Century," *Journal of Interdisciplinary History* 3 (1972): 119–134; Ralph Lerner, "Character and Commerce: The Anglo-American as New-Model Man," *William and Mary Quarterly* 36 (1979): 3–16.

19. Witt, *Lincoln's Code*, 55; Alexander DeConde, *The Quasi-War; the Politics and Diplomacy of the Undeclared War with France, 1797-1801* (New York: Scribner, 1966), 8–9. In his Berlin and Milan Decrees, Napoleon banned the importation of British goods into European countries allied with or dependent upon France, and authorized French armed ships to capture neutral vessels sailing to or from any British-controlled port. In response, the British government issued Orders in Council declaring a theoretical blockade of all French-controlled European ports, subjecting any neutral vessel that attempted to trade with any such port to capture and condemnation as prize of war. Francois Crouzet, "Wars, Blockade, and Economic Change in Europe, 1792–1815," *Journal of Economic History* 24 (1964): 567–88. In the 1805 case of the *Essex*, the Lords Commissioners of Appeal extended the Rule of 1756 to hold that French goods imported by Americans to the United States for immediate re-export to Europe were subject to seizure, under the theory that transshipment was the true purpose and therefore both legs should be considered a single "continuous voyage." Bradford Perkins, "Sir William Scott and the Essex," *William and Mary Quarterly* 13 (1956): 169–83.

20. Rose v. Himely, 8 U.S. 241, 272–81 (1808). The Court also sought to minimize the degree to which the European powers could use naval blockades as a tool for regulating neutral commerce. In insurance cases, it declined to follow British precedent holding that a mere intent to enter a blockaded port subjected a ship to seizure. Fitzsimmons v. Newport Ins. Co., 8 U.S. 186 (1808); Yeaton v. Fry, 9 U.S. 335 (1809); Maryland Ins. Co. v. Wood, 10 U.S. 29 (1810); Ziegler, *International Law*, 219–39.

21. "An Act further to protect the commerce of the United States," 1 Stat. 578 (1798); Murray v. The Charming Betsy, 6 U.S. 64 (1804); Maley v. Shattuck, 7 U.S. 458 (1806). In a contemporaneous case, the

Court – again with Marshall writing – ruled against American naval officers who seized an ostensibly Danish ship for alleged violations of the rules prohibiting American trade with French possessions. Little v. Barreme, 6 U.S. 170 (1804). For an argument that the Court in *Little* and *Charming Betsy* was promoting legislative preeminence in matters of war, see Jane Manners, "Executive Power and the Rule of Law in the Marshall Court: A Rereading of *Little v. Barreme* and *Murray v. Schooner Charming Betsy*," *Fordham Law Review* 89 (2021): 1941–74. For an exploration of the ways in which Congress indemnified federal officers found personally liable for unlawful seizures, see James E. Pfander and Jonathan L. Hunt, "Public Wrongs and Private Bills: Indemnification and Government Accountability in the Early Republic," *New York University Law Review* 85 (2010): 1862–939.

In the *Charming Betsy*, Marshall endorsed the proposition that an act of Congress should never to be construed to violate the law of nations "if any other possible construction remains," instantiating a canon of statutory interpretation still in force today. Curtis A. Bradley, "The 'Charming Betsy' Canon and Separation of Powers: Rethinking the Interpretive Role of International Law," *Georgetown Law Journal* 86 (1998): 479–537. For a detailed reconstruction of the case, see Frederick C. Leiner, "The *Charming Betsy* and the Marshall Court," *The American Journal of Legal History* 45 (2001): 1–21.

22. Kelsh, "Opinion Delivery," 146–48.
23. Croudson v. Leonard, 8 U.S. 434 (1808); Hudson v. Guestier, 10 U.S. 281 (1810); Durousseau v. United States, 10 U.S. 307 (1810); The Venus, 12 U.S. 253 (1814); Speake v. United States, 13 U.S. 28 (1815); Otis v. Watkins, 13 U.S. 339 (1815); The Commercen, 14 U.S. 382 (1816); Kelsh, "Opinion Delivery," 147–48.
24. Hudson, 10 U.S. at 285.
25. Speake, 13 U.S. at 39.
26. R. Kent Newmyer, *Supreme Court Justice Joseph Story: Statesman of the Old Republic* (Chapel Hill: University of North Carolina Press, 1985), 71, 74–114; R. Kent Newmyer, "Justice Joseph Story on Circuit and a Neglected Phase of American Legal History," *American Journal of Legal History* 14 (1970): 112–35; Hiller B. Zobel, "Those Honorable Courts-Early Days on the First First Circuit," *Federal Rules Decisions* 73 (1977): 511–30.
27. Story to Webster, Jan. 4, 1824, *LLJS*, 1:435–36; Story to Nathaniel Williams, Aug. 3, 1813, *LLJS*, 1:246–48; John Gallison, *Reports of Cases Argued and Determined in the Circuit Court of the United States for the First Circuit* (Boston: Wells and Lilly, 1815); Newmyer, *Statesman*, 99. In 1810, an anonymous reporter published a collection of cases decided by Judge Thomas Bee of the South Carolina district court, which included a handful of other noteworthy opinions. *Reports of Cases Adjudged in*

the District Court of South Carolina (Philadelphia: William P. Farrand, 1810).

28. Story to Nathaniel Williams, July 14, 1813, *LLJS*, 1:245–46; "An Act to amend the Judicial System of the United States," Apr. 29, 1802, § 6, 2 Stat. 156, 159–61; Jonathan Remy Nash and Michael G. Collins, "The Certificate of Division and the Early Supreme Court," *Southern California Law Review* 94 (2021): 733–84; Newmyer, "Story on Circuit," 132; White, *Cultural Change*, 173–81. Certification was especially important in criminal cases, where the Court had no federal appellate jurisdiction. United States v. More, 7 U.S. 159 (1805); David Rossman, "'Were There No Appeal': The History of Review in American Criminal Courts," *Journal of Criminal Law & Criminology* 81 (1990): 518–66.
29. Story to Samuel P. P. Fay, Apr. 24, 1814, *LLJS*, 1:261; Marshall to Story, May 27, 1819, *PJM*, 8:313–14; Marshall to Story, July 13, 1819, *PJM*, 8:353–54; "Distinguished Lawyers," *Albany Law Journal* 2 (1870): 126–27. As Edward Corwin noted in relating the same anecdote, "[w]hether true or not, the tale at least illustrates the truth." Edward S. Corwin, *John Marshall and the Constitution* (New Haven: Yale University Press, 1919), 119; Newmyer, *Statesman*, 93.
30. Story to Nathaniel Williams, Dec. 3, 1815, *LLJS*, 1:269–70. Examples of Story's erudition include The Emulous, 8 F. Cas. 697 (C.C.D. Mass. 1813); The Adeline, 13 U.S. 244 (1815); The Julia, 12 U.S. 181 (1814); The Commercen, 14 U.S. 382 (1816); Gelston v. Hoyt, 16 U.S. 246 (1818).
31. The Nereide, 13 U.S. 388, 423–29 (1815); ibid., 436 (Johnson, J., concurring).
32. *The Nereide*, 13 U.S. at 440–41, 448–49, 454–55 (Story, J., dissenting). On the effectiveness of convoys, see Kert, *Privateers*, 32.
33. The Commercen, 14 U.S. 382, 391–94 (1816); ibid., 397–98 (Marshall, J., dissenting). The dispute in this case was not about the vessel or cargo; everyone agreed that the British-owned grain was lawful prize to the American captors, and the neutral Swedish vessel was not. The question was whether the privateers had to pay the vessel owner the shipping fees, called "freight," that the owner would have received had the grain reached its destination in Spain. Courts usually awarded freight, on the theory that neutrals should not be penalized for the lawful act of transporting belligerent property that is later seized. Courts denied freight, however, when the neutral's conduct injured the capturing nation by directly aiding their enemy's war effort. The Frances, 12 U.S. 418, 419 (1814).
34. The St. Nicholas, 14 U.S. 417, 419, 431 (1816).
35. Story to Nathaniel Williams, Aug. 3, 1813, *LLJS*, 1:246–48; Joseph Story, "Life, Character, and Services of Chief Justice Marshall," *MWJS*, 639–97; Newmyer, *Heroic Age*, 407–8; Newmyer, *Statesman*, 76–81, 208–9.

36. "Infringements of the Neutral Trade of the United States," *MWJS*, 43–57; "Literature of the Maritime Law," ibid., 93–94; Newmyer, "Judicial Nationalist"; Newmyer, *Statesman*, 33–34.
37. Newmyer, *Statesman*, 58–63. On the challenges of embargo enforcement, see Gautham Rao, *National Duties: Custom Houses and the Making of the American State* (Chicago: University of Chicago Press, 2016), 132–62; Louis Martin Sears, *Jefferson and the Embargo* (New York: Octagon Books, 1978), 73–142.
38. "Infringements of the Neutral Trade of the United States," *MWJS*, 57; Newmyer, *Statesman*, 62–63.
39. Beveridge, *Life of John Marshall*, 4:1–6; Marshall to Timothy Pickering, Dec. 19, 1808, *PJM*, 7:188; Marshall to Robert Smith, July 27, 1812, *PJM*, 7:337–39; Newmyer, *Heroic Age*, 273–76.
40. Quoted in Newmyer, *Heroic Age*, 3; John Marshall, *The Life of George Washington* (Philadelphia: C.P. Wayne, 1807), 5:25; John Stokes Adams, ed., *An Autobiographical Sketch by John Marshall*, (Ann Arbor: University of Michigan Press, 1937), 9–10; Jean Edward Smith, *John Marshall: Definer of a Nation* (New York: H. Holt & Co., 1998), 37–69.
41. Quoted in Smith, *Definer*, 49; Marshall, *Life of Washington*, 2:345, 4:261.
42. Watts, *Republic Reborn*, 161–216.
43. *The Declaration of the American Citizens, on the Mobile, with Relation to British Aggressions* (Mobile, 1807), 5; Richard Rush, *An Oration, Delivered in the Hall of the House of Representatives, July 4, 1812* (Washington, D.C., 1812), 21; *Richmond Enquirer*, Jan. 11, 1810, p. 3. On the gendered language of war and patriotism in 1812, see Nicole Eustace, *1812: War and the Passions of Patriotism* (Philadelphia: University of Pennsylvania Press, 2012).
44. "Address on Resigning the Speaker's Chair," Jan. 17, 1812, *MWJS*, 1:63–65.
45. The Nereide, 13 U.S. 388, 423–29 (1815); The Venus, 12 U.S. 253, 297 (1814); Thirty Hogsheads of Sugar v. Boyle, 13 U.S. 191, 198 (1815).
46. Joseph Story, "Chief Justice Marshall," *MWJS*, 693; Edward Samuel Corwin, *John Marshall & the Constitution: A Chronicle of the Supreme Court* (New Haven: Yale University Press, 1919), 42; Beveridge, *Life of Marshall*, 1:148–199; Joel Richard Paul, *Without Precedent: Chief Justice John Marshall and His Times* (New York: Penguin Publishing, 2018), 21–23. On Marshall's legal practice before appointment to the bench, see Newmyer, *Heroic Age*, 72–102.
47. The Rapid, 20 F. Cas. 297, 301 (C.C.D. Mass. 1812); Joseph Story, "Literature of the Maritime Law," *MWJS*, 93–121; *The Nereide*, 13 U.S. at 437 (Story, J., dissenting).
48. Joseph Story, "Progress of Jurisprudence," *MWJS*, 198–241; G. Blaine Baker, "Story'd Paradigms for the Nineteenth-Century Display of

Anglo-American Legal Doctrine," in Angela Fernandez and Markus Dubber, eds., *Law Books in Action: Essays on the Anglo-American Legal Treatise* (London: Bloomsbury Publishing, 2012), 103; Newmyer, *Statesman*, 44–45; White, *Cultural Change*, 81–83.

On the nineteenth-century concept of "legal science" generally, see Perry Miller, *The Life of the Mind in America from the Revolution to the Civil War* (New York: Harcourt Brace, 1965), 156–85; James R. Hackney, *Under Cover of Science: American Legal-Economic Theory and the Quest for Objectivity* (Durham: Duke University Press, 2006); Roger Berkowitz, *The Gift of Science: Leibniz and the Modern Legal Tradition* (Cambridge: Harvard University Press, 2005); Howard Schweber, "The Science of Legal Science: The Model of the Natural Sciences in Nineteenth Century American Legal Education," *Law and History Review* 17 (1999): 421–66.

49. William Kent, *Memoirs and Letters of Chancellor Kent, 1763–1847* (Boston: Little, Brown, 1898), 117. On the dearth of legal sources available to early American lawyers, see Michael H. Hoeflich, *Legal Publishing in Antebellum America* (New York: Cambridge University Press, 2010).
50. Baker, "Story'd Paradigms," 85–86; Daniel J. Hulsebosch, "An Empire of Law: Chancellor Kent and the Revolution in Books in the Early Republic," *Alabama Law Review* 60 (2009): 377–424; Michael H. Hoeflich, "American Blackstones," in Wilfred Prest, ed., *Blackstone and His Commentaries: Biography, Law, History* (Oxford: Hart, 2009), 171–84; John H. Langbein, "Chancellor Kent and the History of Legal Literature," *Columbia Law Review* 93 (1993): 547–94.
51. James Kent, *Commentaries on American Law* (New York: O. Halsted, 1826); Joseph Story, *Commentaries on the Constitution of the United States* (Boston: Hilliard, Gray and Company, 1833); H. Jefferson Powell, "Joseph Story's Commentaries on the Constitution: A Belated Review," *Yale Law Journal* 94 (1985): 1294–99; White, *Cultural Change*, 95; Baker, "Story'd Paradigms," 82.
52. Michael Kent Curtis, "St. George Tucker and the Legacy of Slavery," *William and Mary Law Review* 47 (2006): 1157–212; White, *Cultural Change*, 81–86, 96–98.
53. Kent, *Commentaries*, 3:88–89; Story, *Commentaries on the Constitution*, 1:v–vii; Story to Simon Greenleaf, Sep. 5, 1819, *LLJS*, 1:328–29; Baker, "Story'd Paradigms," 89–93; Morton J. Horwitz, *The Transformation of American Law, 1780–1860* (Cambridge: Harvard University Press, 1977), 245–52; Daniel J. Hulsebosch, "Writs to Rights: 'Navigability' and the Transformation of the Common Law in the Nineteenth Century," *Cardozo Law Review* 23 (2002): 1049–106.
54. The Rapid, 20 F. Cas. 297, 299–300 (C.C.D. Mass. 1812). For similar critiques, see The Emulous, 8 F. Cas. 697, 699 (C.C.D. Mass. 1813); Brown v. United States, 12 U.S. 110, 135 (1814) (Story, J., dissenting).

55. Henry J. Bourguignon, *Sir William Scott, Lord Stowell: Judge of the High Court of Admiralty, 1798–1828*, (Cambridge: Cambridge University Press, 1987), 241–48.
56. Kent, *Commentaries*, 1:66–68; Henry Wheaton, *A Digest of the Law of Maritime Captures and Prizes* (New York: McDermut and Arden, 1815), vi. On Scott's influence on American jurists such as Kent, Story, and Henry Wheaton, see Bourguignon, *Sir William Scott*, 280–85; John D. Gordan III, "Publishing Robinson's Reports of Cases Argued and Determined in the High Court of Admiralty," *Law and History Review* 32 (2014): 525–73; Newmyer, *Statesman*, 96–97.
57. The Ann Green, 1 F. Cas. 958, 965 (C.C.D. Mass. 1812); "Course of Legal Study," *MWJS*, 66; Brown, 12 U.S. at 135 (Story, J., dissenting).
58. The Venus, 12 U.S. 253, 299 (1814); Thirty Hogsheads of Sugar v. Boyle, 13 U.S. 191, 198 (1815); The Atalanta, 16 U.S. 409, 423, 431 (1818).
59. *The Venus*, 12 U.S. at 299; *The Atalanta*, 16 U.S. at 426; *Niles' Weekly Register*, Oct. 2, 1813, pp. 84–85; Bourguignon, *Sir William Scott*, 49, 169, 215–23, 235–42; Wheaton, *Digest*, vi; Perkins, "Sir William Scott and the *Essex*," 169–83; Nicholas Parrillo, "The De-Privatization of American Warfare: How the U.S. Government Used, Regulated, and Ultimately Abandoned Privateering in the Nineteenth Century," *Yale Journal of Law & the Humanities* 19 (2007): 1–95.
60. The Nereide, 13 U.S. 388, 440–42 (1815) (Story, J., dissenting); The Commercen, 14 U.S. 382, 393–94 (1816). Story also relied on Scott in deciding cases of alleged trading with the enemy. The Sally, 21 F. Cas. 243, 246–47 (C.C.D. Mass. 1813). The most famous instance of Story disagreeing with Scott was in *La Jeune Eugenie*, in which Story declared that the international slave trade was contrary to the law of nations (see Chapter 7). Even then, Story declared his "reverence" for Scott's "profound learning and talents." La Jeune Eugenie, 26 F. Cas. 832, 848 (C.C.D. Mass. 1822).
61. Story to Nathaniel Williams, May 27, 1813, *LLJS*, 1:244–45; Edmund Burke, "A Letter to a Member of the National Assembly, May 1791," in D. E. Ritchie, ed., *Further Reflections on the Revolution in France* (Indianapolis: Liberty Fund, 1992), 55–56; David A. Bell, *The First Total War: Napoleon's Europe and the Birth of Warfare as We Know It* (Boston: Houghton Mifflin Co., 2007).
62. Alan Taylor, *The Civil War of 1812: American Citizens, British Subjects, Irish Rebels, and Indian Allies* (New York: Alfred A. Knopf, 2010), 3–12; John Brewer, et al., "The Civil War of 1812 by Alan Taylor," *Huntington Library Quarterly* 74 (2011): 99–124; Gene A. Smith, *The Slaves' Gamble: Choosing Sides in the War of 1812* (New York: Palgrave Macmillan, 2013).
63. J. C. A. Stagg, *Mr. Madison's War: Politics, Diplomacy, and Warfare in the Early American Republic, 1783–1830* (Princeton: Princeton

University Press, 1983), 22–28; Newmyer, *Statesman*, 83–84. For book-length treatments of the Federalist-Republican rivalry, see Roger H. Brown, *The Republic in Peril: 1812* (New York: W. W. Norton & Company, 1971); Richard Buel, *America on the Brink: How the Political Struggle over the War of 1812 Almost Destroyed the Young Republic* (New York: Palgrave Macmillan, 2005).

64. Jefferson to Madison, June 29, 1812, *PTJRS*, 5:191–92; Gerry to Henry Dearborn, Sep. 2, 1811, quoted in Stagg, *Madison's War*, 254; George Billias, *Elbridge Gerry: Founding Father and Republican Statesman* (New York: McGraw-Hill Publishers, 1976); Donald R. Hickey, *The War of 1812: A Forgotten Conflict* (Urbana: University of Illinois Press, 2012), 48–65; Taylor, *Civil War*, 177–78.
65. Story to Nathaniel Williams, Aug. 24, 1812, *LLJS*, 1:228–30; Buel, *America on the Brink*, 199–226; Hickey, *War of 1812*, 259–60; Taylor, *Civil War*, 130–31.
66. The Bolina, 3 F. Cas. 811 (C.C.D. Mass. 1812); United States v. Sears, 27 F. Cas. 1006 (C.C.D. Mass. 1812); Newmyer, *Statesman*, 85–88; Buel, *America on the Brink*, 230–31. On the handful of failed treason prosecutions the government instituted against ordinary citizens, see Dwight F. Henderson, *Congress, Courts, and Criminals: The Development of Federal Criminal Law, 1801–1829* (Westport: Greenwood Press, 1985), 111–13.
67. Story to Nathaniel Williams, Oct. 8, 1812, *LLJS*, 1:243; Story to Nathaniel Williams, May 27, 1813, *LLJS*, 1:244–45; Story to Nathaniel Williams, Aug. 3, 1813, *LLJS*, 1:246–48; Newmyer, *Statesman*, 103.
68. United States v. Hudson, 11 U.S. 32 (1812); United States v. Coolidge, 25 F. Cas. 619, 620 (C.C.D. Mass. 1813); United States v. Coolidge, 14 U.S. 415, 416 (1816); Stephen B. Presser, "A Tale of Two Judges: Richard Peters, Samuel Chase, and the Broken Promise of Federalist Jurisprudence," *Northwestern University Law Review* 73 (1978): 26–111; Kathryn Preyer, "Jurisdiction to Punish: Federal Authority, Federalism and the Common Law of Crimes in the Early Republic," *Law and History Review* 4 (1986): 223–65.
69. Quoted in Henderson, *Courts, Congress, and Criminals*, 116; *Columbian Centinel*, Sep. 1, 1813, p. 2; *National Aegis*, Jan. 5, 1814, p. 3; Dallas to J. W. Eppes, Nov. 19, 1814, *Annals*, 28:757–61; Walter Ronald Copp, "Nova Scotia Trade during the War of 1812," *Canadian Historical Review* 18 (1937): 141–55; Hickey, *War of 1812*, 169–75; Bradford Perkins, *Castlereagh and Adams: England and the United States, 1812–1823* (Los Angeles: University of California Press, 1964), 34.
70. Thomas C. Barrow, *Trade and Empire; the British Customs Service in Colonial America, 1660–1775* (Cambridge: Harvard University Press, 1967); Douglas Lamar Jones, "'The Caprice of Juries': The Enforcement of the Jeffersonian Embargo in Massachusetts," *American Journal of Legal*

History 24 (1980): 307–30; Rao, *National Duties*, 103–62; Sears, *Jefferson and the Embargo*; Thomas M. Truxes, *Defying Empire: Trading with the Enemy in Colonial New York* (New Haven: Yale University Press, 2010).

71. Dallas to J. W. Eppes, Nov. 19, 1814, *Annals*, 28:757–61; "An Act to prohibit American vessels from proceeding to, or trading with, the enemies of the United States," 2 Stat. 778 (1812); United States v. Sheldon, 15 U.S. 119 (1817); Henderson, *Courts, Congress, and Criminals*, 111–21.
72. The Bothnea, 3 F. Cas. 962, 964, 966 (C.C.D. Mass. 1814); The Bothnea, 15 U.S. 169, 177 (1817); Kert, *Privateering*, 12; Newmyer, *Statesman*, 89–92.
73. The George, 15 U.S. 278, 280–81 (1817); The Experiment, 21 U.S. 261, 268 (1823).
74. Scott quoted in Su Jin Kim and James Oldham, "Insuring Maritime Trade with the Enemy in the Napoleonic Era," *Texas International Law Journal* 47 (2012): 561–86; Bourguignon, *Sir William Scott*, 165–67; W. Freeman Galpin, "The American Grain Trade to the Spanish Peninsula, 1810–1814," *American Historical Review* 28 (1922): 24–44; Henderson, *Courts, Congress, and Criminals*, 121 n. 12. On the eighteenth-century history of trade between nations at war, see John Shovlin, *Trading with the Enemy: Britain, France, and the 18th-Century Quest for a Peaceful World Order* (New Haven: Yale University Press, 2021).
75. Jefferson to Madison, Aug. 5, 1812, *PTJRS*, 5:96; Jefferson to James Ronaldson, Jan. 12, 1813, *PTJRS*, 5:560–61; Farber, *Underwriters*, 173–80; Galpin, "American Grain Trade," 35–37; Garitee, *Republic's Private Navy*, 50; Hickey, *War of 1812*, 113–20. In July 1812 Congress prohibited Americans from accepting licenses to trade with ports in British dominions, but the ban did not extend to other parts of Europe where the British were fighting, like Spain or Portugal. Enemy Trade Act of 1812, §7, 2 Stat. 778, 780–81.
76. Story to Nathaniel Williams, Aug. 3, 1813, *LLJS*, 1:246–48; The Matilda, 26 F. Cas. 1200, 1204 (C.C.D.N.C. 1813).
77. The Julia, 14 F. Cas. 27, 31–32 (C.C.D. Mass. 1813).
78. *The Julia*, 14 F. Cas. at 31–32; The Rapid, 20 F. Cas. 297, 300–301 (C.C.D. Mass. 1812).
79. "An Act to prohibit the use of licenses or passes granted by the authority of the government of the United Kingdom of Great Britain and Ireland," 3 Stat. 84 (1813); The Julia, 12 U.S. 181 (1814); The Ariadne, 15 U.S. 143, 144, 147–48 (1817).
80. The Atalanta, 16 U.S. 409, 415 (1818); Ibid., 431–32 (Johnson, J. concurring).
81. The Atalanta, 16 U.S. at 415.
82. Adams to George Canning, June 24, 1823, in John Bassett Moore, *A Digest of International Law* (Washington, DC: Government Printing

Office, 1906), 7:445; Francis R. Stark, *The Abolition of Privateering and the Declaration of Paris* (New York: Columbia University, 1897), 136–52. On the development of the American and international position as to whether "free ships made free goods" from the Revolution to the Civil War, see Moore, *Digest of International Law*, 7:434–53.

83. On the Civil War prize cases, see Carl B. Swisher, *History of the Supreme Court of the United States: The Taney Period, 1836–64* (New York: Macmillan, 1974), 877–900; Witt, *Lincoln's Code*, 150–55.
84. Parrillo, "De-Privatization," 52–64.
85. Wheaton, *Digest*, iii; "First Annual Message," Dec. 2, 1817, *WJM*, 6:33–44.
86. Story to Nathaniel Williams, Feb. 22, 1815, *LLJS*, 1:253–54.
87. Jon Latimer, *1812: War with America* (Cambridge: Harvard University Press, 2010).
88. Troy Bickham, *The Weight of Vengeance: The United States, The British Empire, and the War of 1812* (New York: Oxford University Press, 2012), 229–80; Colin G. Calloway, *Crown and Calumet: British-Indian Relations, 1783–1815* (Norman: University of Oklahoma Press, 1987); Gregory A. Dowd, *A Spirited Resistance: The North American Indian Struggle for Unity, 1745–1815* (Baltimore: Johns Hopkins University Press, 1992); David Stephen Heidler and Jeanne Heidler, *Old Hickory's War: Andrew Jackson and the Quest for Empire* (Baton Rouge: Louisiana State University Press, 2003); Hickey, *War of 1812*, 282–302; Taylor, *Civil War*, 409–40.
89. *Annals*, 28:1156 (Troup); Story to Nathaniel Williams, Feb. 22, 1815, *LLJS*, 1:254; George Dangerfield, *The Era of Good Feelings* (New York: Harcourt, 1952), 64–94; Eustace, *1812*, 211–35; Daniel Walker Howe, *What Hath God Wrought: The Transformation of America, 1815–1848* (New York: Oxford University Press, 2007), 8–90; Carl Edward Skeen, *1816: America Rising* (Lexington: University Press of Kentucky, 2003), 17–34.
90. Story to Nathaniel Williams, Feb. 22, 1815, *LLJS*, 1:254; Story to Pinkney, [1816], *LLJS*, 1:293–96.
91. McCulloch v. Maryland, 17 U.S. 316 (1819); Gibbons v. Ogden, 22 U.S. 1 (1824); Michael J. Klarman, "How Great Were the Great Marshall Court Decisions?," *Virginia Law Review* 87 (2001): 1111–1184. Congress also did not extend federal admiralty jurisdiction to inland waterways until after Story's death. "An Act extending the jurisdiction of the district courts to certain cases," 5 Stat. 726 (1845); Hulsebosch, "Writs to Rights," 1049–106.
92. "A bill further to extend the judicial system of the United States," § 11 (1816), in *Early American Imprints*, Series 2, no. 39265; *LLJS*, 1:297; William W. Crosskey, *Politics and the Constitution in the History of the United States* (Chicago: University of Chicago Press, 1953), 783.

93. Story to Pinkney, [1816], *LLJS*, 1:293–96; Story to Scott, Jan. 14, 1819, *LLJS*, 1:318–21; Scott to Story, July 2, 1818, *LLJS*, 1:307–8.
94. *LLJS*, 1:306–9. This anecdote was related third-hand to Story's son, so its historical accuracy is somewhat doubtful.

6 Confronting Revolution

1. Adams to A. H. Everett, Mar. 16, 1816, "Letters of John Quincy Adams to Alexander Hamilton Everett, 1811–1837," *American Historical Review* 11 (1905): 88–116; James Monroe, First Annual Message, Dec. 2, 1817, *WJM*, 6:33–44. On postwar optimism and the "Era of Good Feelings," see George Dangerfield, *The Era of Good Feelings* (New York: Harcourt, 1952); Caitlin Fitz, "The Hemispheric Dimensions of Early U.S. Nationalism: The War of 1812, Its Aftermath, and Spanish American Independence," *Journal of American History* 102 (2015): 356–79; Carl Edward Skeen, *1816: America Rising* (Lexington: University Press of Kentucky, 2003).
2. Adams to John Adams, Dec. 21, 1817, *FO*. On the South American missions to the United States, see Samuel Flagg Bemis, *Early Diplomatic Missions from Buenos Aires to the United States, 1811–1824* (Worcester: American Antiquarian Society, 1940); Caitlin Fitz, *Our Sister Republics: The United States in an Age of American Revolutions* (New York: Liveright, 2017), 46–79, 160–69; Charles Griffin, *The United States and the Disruption of the Spanish Empire, 1810–1822* (New York: Columbia University Press, 1937), 50–55, 99–106; Benjamin Keen, *David Curtis De Forest and the Revolution of Buenos Aires* (New Haven: Yale University Press, 1947), 103–57.
3. M'Culloch v. Maryland, 17 U.S. 316, 353 (1819); Philip Coolidge Brooks, *Diplomacy and the Borderlands: The Adams-Onís Treaty of 1819* (Berkeley: University of California Press, 1939); Daniel Walker Howe, *What Hath God Wrought: The Transformation of America, 1815–1848* (New York: Oxford University Press, 2007), 63–124; James E. Lewis, *The American Union and the Problem of Neighborhood: The United States and the Collapse of the Spanish Empire, 1783–1829* (Chapel Hill: University of North Carolina Press, 1998), 126–54.
4. Adams to William Plumer, Jan. 17, 1817, *WJQA*, 6:139–144; Daniel J. Burge, *A Failed Vision of Empire: The Collapse of Manifest Destiny, 1845–1872* (Lincoln: University of Nebraska Press, 2022); Paul Frymer, *Building an American Empire: The Era of Territorial and Political Expansion* (Princeton: Princeton University Press, 2017); David Stephen Heidler and Jeanne Heidler, *Manifest Destiny* (Westport: Greenwood Press, 2003); William Earl Weeks, *Building the Continental Empire: American Expansion from the Revolution to the Civil War* (Chicago: Ivan R. Dee, 1996).

5. United States v. Palmer, 16 U.S. 610, 631 (1818).
6. Didier to D'Arcy, Dec. 6, 1814, Maryland Center for History and Culture, Henry Didier Letterbook; *Federal Gazette and Baltimore Daily Advertiser*, Jan. 27, 1825, p. 3.
7. Didier to D'Arcy, Feb. 27, 1815, Mar. 27, 1815, May 16, 1815, May 18, 1815, Maryland Center for History and Culture, Henry Didier Letterbook; Jerome R. Garitee, *The Republic's Private Navy: The American Privateering Business as Practiced by Baltimore during the War of 1812* (Middletown: Wesleyan University Press, 1977), 40, 114–17, 165–66, 218–22. On the arms trade between the United States and South America, see Fitz, *Sister Republics*, 160–166; Rafe Blaufarb, "Arms for Revolutions: Military Demobilization after the Napoleonic Wars and Latin American Independence," in Alan Forrest, Karen Hagemann, Michael Rowe, eds., *War, Demobilization and Memory: The Legacy of War in the Era of Atlantic Revolutions* (London: Palgrave Macmillan, 2016), 100–18.
8. John Lynch, *The Spanish American Revolutions, 1808–1826* (New York: W. W. Norton & Company, 1973), 37–104; Jaime E. O. Rodríguez, *The Independence of Spanish America* (Cambridge: Cambridge University Press, 1998), 36–58, 123–35. On United States' involvement, see Charles Griffin, *The United States and the Disruption of the Spanish Empire, 1810–1822* (New York: Columbia, 1937); Arthur Whitaker, *The United States and the Independence of Latin America, 1800–1830* (Baltimore: Johns Hopkins University Press, 1941).
9. Juando v. Taylor, 13 F. Cas. 1179 (S.D.N.Y. 1818); David Head, *Privateers of the Americas: Spanish American Privateering from the United States in the Early Republic* (Athens: University of Georgia Press, 2015), 63; Keen, *DeForest*, 103–4, 112; Bemis, *Early Diplomatic Missions*, 29–30.
10. Keen, *DeForest*, 103–12. On early pan-American adventuring, see Matthew Brown, *Adventuring through Spanish Colonies: Simón Bolívar, Foreign Mercenaries and the Birth of New Nations* (Liverpool: Liverpool University Press, 2006); Matthew McCarthy, *Privateering, Piracy and British Policy in Spanish America, 1810–1830* (Woodbridge: Boydell Press, 2013); R. Kent Newmyer, *The Treason Trial of Aaron Burr: Law, Politics, and the Character Wars of the New Nation* (Cambridge: Cambridge University Press, 2012); Frank L. Owsley and Gene A. Smith, *Filibusters and Expansionists: Jeffersonian Manifest Destiny, 1800–1821* (Tuscaloosa: University of Alabama Press, 1997); Harris Gaylord Warren, *The Sword Was Their Passport: A History of American Filibustering in the Mexican Revolution* (Baton Rouge: Louisiana State University Press, 1943).
11. Annual Message to Congress, Dec. 3, 1816, *PJMPS*, 11:532–40; Fitz, *Sister Republics*, 169–72; Garitee, *Private Navy*, 218–21; Jeffrey Orenstein, "Joseph Almeida: Portrait of a Privateer, Pirate & Plaintiff,

Part I," *Green Bag* 10 (2007): 307–25. On Baltimore's working-class economy in the early nineteenth century, see Seth Rockman, *Scraping By: Wage Labor, Slavery, and Survival in Early Baltimore* (Baltimore: Johns Hopkins University Press, 2009).

12. Quoted in Fitz, *Sister Republics*, 170; John D. Harbron, *Trafalgar and the Spanish Navy* (Annapolis: Naval Institute Press, 1988). On the relationship between early modern piracy and the cycles of warfare, see David Starkey, "Pirates and Markets," in C. R. Pennell, ed., *Bandits at Sea: A Pirates Reader* (New York: New York University Press, 2001); Lauren Benton, "Legal Spaces of Empire: Piracy and the Origins of Ocean Regionalism," *Comparative Studies in Society and History* 47 (2005): 700–24.
13. Head, *Privateers*, 63–73; Orenstein, "Almeida, Part I," 314–21; Keen, *DeForest*, 106–7.
14. *New Bedford Mercury*, Apr. 12, 1816; Head, *Privateers*, 122–48; David Head, "Baltimore Seafarers, Privateering, and the South American Revolutions, 1816–1820," *Maryland Historical Magazine* 105 (2008): 269–93; Fitz, *Sister Republics*, 172–74; Orenstein, "Almeida, Part I," 315–16. On the motivations of South American privateers more generally, see Edgardo Pérez Morales, *No Limits to Their Sway: Cartagena's Privateers and the Masterless Caribbean in the Age of Revolutions* (Nashville: Vanderbilt University Press, 2018).
15. *National Advocate*, Dec. 23, 1814; *Annals*, 32:1614 (Clay); Fitz, *Sister Republics*, 64–67.
16. Fitz, *Sister Republics*, 19–21, 139–41; Lewis, *American Union*, 71–78.
17. Adams to James Lloyd, Mar. 27, 1815, *FO*; Piero Gleijeses, "The Limits of Sympathy: The United States and the Independence of Spanish America," *Journal of Latin American Studies* 24 (1992): 481–505.
18. Adams to Thomas Jefferson, May 26, 1817, *PTJRS*, 11:382–85; Fitz, *Sister Republics*, 83–118; Lawrence S. Kaplan, *Entangling Alliances with None: American Foreign Policy in the Age of Jefferson* (Kent: Kent State University Press, 1987), 165–84.
19. Onís to James Monroe, Dec. 30, 1815, *DCUS*, 3:1891–94; Onís to Monroe, May 30, 1816, July 3, 1816, July 22, 1816, Aug. 29, 1816, NARA-SL, roll 6; Peter P. Hill, "An Expedition to Liberate Venezuela Sails from New York, 1806," *The Historian* 78 (2016), 671–89; Karen Racine, *Francisco de Miranda: A Transatlantic Life in the Age of Revolution* (Wilmington: Scholarly Resources, 2003); Lindsay Schakenbach, "Schemers, Dreamers, and a Revolutionary Foreign Policy: New York City in the Era of Second Independence, 1805–1815," *New York History* 94 (2013): 267–82.
20. Onís to Monroe, July 22, 1816, NARA-SL, roll 6; Neutrality Act of 1794, 1 Stat. 381; Treaty of Friendship, Limits, and Navigation between Spain and the United States, art. XIV (1795).

21. Onís to Monroe, Mar. 26, 1817, *DCUS*, 3:1923. On the sovereignty claims implicit (and sometimes explicit) in commissioning privateers, see Lauren Benton, "Una soberanía extraña: la Provincia Oriental en el mundo Atlántico," *20/10 El Mundo Atlántico y la Modernidad Iberoamericana, 1750–1850* 1 (2012): 89–107; Morales, *No Limit to Their Sway*, 86–92.
22. Madison to James Monroe, July 13, 1816, *PJM*, 11:193–94; Keen, *DeForest*, 145.
23. Adams diary, Jan. 22, 1818, *MJQA*, 4:47; Charles N. Edel, *Nation Builder: John Quincy Adams and the Grand Strategy of the Republic* (Cambridge: Harvard University Press, 2014), 130–31; Fitz, *Sister Republics*, 176–84; Lewis, *American Union*, 108–110.
24. Monroe to Adams, Aug. 11, 1820, *WJQA*, 7:63 n. 1; Monroe to Adams, Dec. 10, 1815, *DCUS*, 1:17; Griffin, *Disruption*, 46–50.
25. Adams to William Plumer, Jan. 17, 1817, *WJQA*, 6:139–44; Adams to George William Erving, June 10, 1816, *WJQA*, 6:45; Lewis, *American Union*, 70–80. On the particular fears Americans had about Great Britain, see Edel, *Nation Builder*, 134–38.
26. On the treaty negotiations and Florida question, see Howe, *What Hath God Wrought*, 96–116; J. C. A. Stagg, *Borderlines in Borderlands: James Madison and the Spanish-American Frontier, 1776–1821* (New Haven: Yale University Press, 2009); William Earl Weeks, *John Quincy Adams and American Global Empire* (Lexington: University Press of Kentucky, 1992).
27. Madison to Jefferson, Feb. 15, 1817, *PJM*, 11:667–69; Lewis, *American Union*, 85–90, 115–18.
28. James Monroe, First Annual Message, Dec. 2, 1817, *WJM*, 6:33–44; James Madison, Presidential Proclamation, Sep. 1, 1815, *PJMPS*, 9:580–81; Lewis, *American Union*, 108–14.
29. Monroe to Onís, Jan. 19, 1816, June 10, 1816, July 30, 1816, *DCUS*, 1:19–21, 31–36.
30. *The Repertory* (Boston), Dec. 28, 1816, p. 2; *American Beacon* (Norfolk), Apr. 22, 1817, p. 2. At least one of the prizes was sent on to Buenos Ayres, but wrecked off the coast of Africa en route. Several of the crew of the wrecked prize were captured and sold into slavery by "Arabs"; two were ransomed and one – a former U.S. Army officer headed to Buenos Ayres to "join the Patriots" – died of starvation while in captivity. *Richmond Herald*, June 6, 1817, p. 1.
31. United States v. Hitchings, declaration, May 24, 1816, order, June 18, 1816, Library of Virginia, United States Circuit Court (5th Circuit) Records, 1790–1861, Ended Cases; *Baltimore Patriot*, June 27, 1816, p. 2; *Essex Register*, July 10, 1816, p. 3.
32. Opinion of the Attorney General, July 23, 1816, NARA-AG, Legal Opinions, 1790–1870; Wirt to Monroe, July 11, 1816, Library of

Congress, William Wirt Papers (microfilm); *New York Evening Post*, Aug. 3, 1816, p. 2; Elias Glenn to Madison, Sep. 7, 1816, *Annals*, 30:1084–85.

33. McCulloch to Dallas, Sep. 2, 1816, National Archives and Records Administration, Correspondence of the Secretary of the Treasury with Collectors of Customs, 1789–1833, microfilm M178, roll 3; Chacón v. 89 Bales of Cochineal, Charles Mallory to Richard Rush, Apr. 3, 1817, Library of Virginia, United States Circuit Court Records (5th Circuit), 1790–1861, Ended Cases; Head, *Privateers*, 277–78. Collector McCulloch was not the same James McCulloch who was a party to the landmark Supreme Court case *McCulloch v. Maryland*. David S. Schwartz, *The Spirit of the Constitution: John Marshall and the 200-Year Odyssey of McCulloch v. Maryland* (New York: Oxford University Press, 2019), 46.
34. Madison to Congress, Dec. 26, 1816, *Annals*, 30:1079–80; Gautham Rao, *National Duties: Custom Houses and the Making of the American State* (Chicago: University of Chicago Press, 2016), 119–31; Fitz, *Sister Republics*, 160–66.
35. Corrêa da Serra to Monroe, Dec. 20, 1816, NARA-PL, roll 1; Fitz, *Sister Republics*, 58.
36. Richard Beale Davis, "The Abbé Corrêa da Serra in America, 1812–1820," *Transactions of the American Philosophical Society* 45 (1955): 95–103; Adams diary, Mar. 29, 1819, Apr. 8, 1819, *MJQA*, 4:314, 325–27. Corrêa da Serra visited Jefferson at Monticello so frequently that the room in which he stayed was known as "Corrêa da Serra's room" for years afterward.
37. Corrêa da Serra to Adams, Dec. 20, 1816, Oct. 15, 1818, Nov. 14, 1818, Mar. 17, 1819, June 8, 1820, NARA-PL, roll 1; Adams diary, Apr. 8, 1819, *MJQA*, 4:325–27; Fitz, *Sister Republics*, 58.
38. Corrêa da Serra to Adams, Dec. 20, 1816, NARA-PL, roll 1.
39. Madison to Congress, Dec. 26, 1816, *Annals*, 30:1079–80; Monroe to John Forsyth, Jan. 6, 1817, Jan. 10, 1817, *Annals*, 30:1080–82. Monroe later gave Corrêa da Serra credit for the act's passage, noting that Onís could never have had similar success. Monroe to Adams, Aug. 3, 1820, *WJM*, 6:145–50.
40. *Annals*, 30:745 (Wright), 32:1403 (Clay), 30:736 (Robertson). On the embargo, see Rao, *National Duties*, 133–56.
41. *Annals*, 32:1421 (Tucker).
42. *Annals*, 32:1410 (Forsyth), 30:750 (Hopkinson), 30:724 (Smith), 30:736 (Sheffey); "An Act more effectually to preserve the neutral relations of the United States," 3 Stat. 370 (1817). The act was modified in 1818, which caused Congress to revisit many of the controversies surrounding the 1817 enactment. "An Act in addition to the 'Act for the punishment of certain crimes against the United States,'" 3 Stat. 447 (1818).
43. Neutrality Act of 1794, § 3, 1 Stat. 381, 383.

44. Gordon S. Brown, *Toussaint's Clause: The Founding Fathers and the Haitian Revolution* (Jackson: University Press of Mississippi, 2005); Tim Matthewson, *A Proslavery Foreign Policy: Haitian-American Relations during the Early Republic* (Westport: Praeger, 2003); Robert J. Reinstein, "Slavery, Executive Power and International Law: The Haitian Revolution and American Constitutionalism," *American Journal of Legal History* 53 (2013): 141–237; Julius S. Scott, *A Common Wind: Afro-American Currents in the Age of the Haitian Revolution* (London: Verso, 2018); Ashli White, *Encountering Revolution: Haiti and the Making of the Early Republic* (Baltimore: Johns Hopkins University Press, 2010).
45. Rose v. Himely, 8 U.S. 241, 272 (1808). The *Rose* case's international context is discussed further in Chapter 5.
46. Gelston v. Hoyt, 13 Johns. 561, 588 (N.Y. 1816).
47. Neutrality Act of 1817, § 1, 3 Stat. 370, 370; The Gran Para, 20 U.S. 471, 489 (1822); *Annals*, 32:1429 (Clay amendment); *Annals*, 32:1431 (Forsyth); Neutrality Act of 1818, 3 Stat. 447.
48. Jerry L. Mashaw, *Creating the Administrative Constitution: The Lost One Hundred Years of American Administrative Law* (New Haven: Yale University Press, 2012), 79–144; Nicholas R. Parrillo, *Against the Profit Motive: The Salary Revolution in American Government, 1780–1940* (New Haven: Yale University Press, 2013), 221–54; Leonard D. White, *The Jeffersonians: A Study in Administrative History, 1801–1829* (New York: Macmillan, 1951).
49. Peter Pedersen to John Quincy Adams, Aug. 11, 1818, National Archives and Records Administration, Notes from the Danish Legation in the United States to the Department of State, 1801–1906, microfilm M52, roll l; Charles Mallory to Antonio Argote Villalobos, Dec. 16, 1816, NARA-SL, roll 6; Mallory to Villalobos, Apr. 11, 1817, *DCUS*, 3:1937; Head, *Privateers*, 53; Max M. Edling, *A Hercules in the Cradle: War, Money, and the American State, 1783–1867* (Chicago: University of Chicago Press, 2015), 126–42; Rao, *National* Duties, 2–3, 68.
50. Rao, *National Duties*, 19–47, 75–99.
51. Ibid., 81–99, 139–56; Kevin Arlyck, "The Founders' Forfeiture," *Columbia Law Review* 119 (2019): 1449–518; Aaron T. Knapp, "From Empire to Law: Customs Collection in the American Founding," *Law & Social Inquiry* 43 (2018): 554–84. According to Rao, things began to change after the War of 1812, though it would not be until Andrew Jackson's presidency that authority over customs collection would flow centrally from Washington, rather than being negotiated in American seaports. Rao, *National Duties*, 167–96.
52. Onís to Monroe, Jan. 15, 1817, in *The Case of Great Britain as Laid before the Tribunal of Arbitration Convened at Geneva* (Washington, DC: Government Printing Office, 1872), 3:169–70; Luis de Onís to Richard Rush, Mar. 29, 1817, ibid., 180–81; Chacón v. 89 Bales of

Cochineal, McCulloch to [Surrey?], Dec. 13, 1816, Library of Virginia, United States Circuit Court Records (5th Circuit), 1790–1861, Ended Cases; John Quincy Adams to James Monroe, Aug. 2, 1820, *WJQA*, 7:59–60; Monroe to Adams, Aug. 11, 1820, *WJQA*, 7:60 n. 1; Adams diary, *MJQA*, 4:318; Rao, *National Duties*, 101–2, 142–62.

53. John Skinner, the federal postmaster in Baltimore, was a privateering investor, though he was never convicted of any crime. David Head, "Sailing for Spanish America: The Atlantic Geopolitics of Foreign Privateering from the United States in the Early Republic" (Ph.D. dissertation, SUNY Buffalo, 2010), 72; Walker Lewis, "John Quincy Adams and the Baltimore Pirates," *American Bar Association Journal* 67 (1981): 1011–14. The Savannah customs collector allegedly conspired with privateers to secrete captured goods into port unlawfully, though Adams doubted he would ever be punished for it. Adams diary, June 14, 1820, *MJQA*, 5:150–52; Adams to James Monroe, Aug. 21, 1820, *WJQA*, 7:61–64.

54. Thomas Coles to Dearborn, Oct. 13, 1817, National Archives and Records Administration (Waltham), Boston, Customs Collectors, Letters Received, Collectors and Others, 1772–1882; Pablo Chacón to Glenn, Sep. 3, 1816, Luis de Onís to James Monroe, Sep. 11, 1816, Chacón to Glenn, Jan. 6, 1817, Glenn to Chacón, Jan. 14, 1817, NARA-SL, roll 6; Onís to Monroe, Mar. 14, 1817, *Case of Great Britain*, 3:175.

55. Mallory to Villalobos, Apr. 11, 1817, *DCUS*, 3:1937; Villalobos to Mallory, Apr. 12, 1817, *DCUS*, 3:1937–38; Mallory to Villalobos, Apr. 14, 1817, *DCUS*, 3:1938–40.

56. Mallory to Villalobos, Apr. 11, 1817, Apr. 14, 1817, *DCUS*, 3:1937–40; Mallory to Pablo Chacón, July 23, 1817, PSC, section 11, box 1, *America Libre*.

57. Chacón v. 89 Bales of Cochineal, William Wirt to Mallory, Apr. 14, 1817, Library of Virginia, United States Circuit Court Records (5th Circuit), 1790–1861, Ended Cases; Mallory to Villalobos, Apr. 16, 1817, PSC, section 3, box 5, folder 62; James E. Pfander and Jonathan L. Hunt, "Public Wrongs and Private Bills: Indemnification and Government Accountability in the Early Republic," *New York University Law Review* 85 (2010): 1862–939; Jerry L. Mashaw, "Recovering American Administrative Law: Federalist Foundations, 1787–1801," *Yale Law Journal* 115 (2006): 1256–343.

58. Mallory to Villalobos, Apr. 14, 1817, *DCUS*, 3:1938–40; Chacón v. 89 Bales of Cochineal, Mallory to William Wirt, Apr. 10, 1817, Mallory to Richard Rush, Apr. 3, 1817, Mallory to William Crawford, Mar. 22, 1817, Library of Virginia, United States Circuit Court Records (5th Circuit), 1790–1861, Ended Cases.

59. Onís to Richard Rush, Mar. 29, 1817, Apr. 4, 1817, Apr. 5, 1817, *DCUS*, 3:1925–30; Antonio Argote Villalobos to Charles Mallory, Apr. 12, 1817, *DCUS*, 3:1937–38; Onís to James Monroe, Mar. 26, 1817, *DCUS*, 3:1923.

60. Luis de Onís to Richard Rush, Apr. 18, 1817, *DCUS*, 3:1934–35; John Stoughton to Pablo Chacón, Jan. 24, 1817, JSP.
61. Onís to consuls, Mar. 13, 1817, PSC, section 3, box 5, folder 64. For example, the Spanish consul in Boston instituted at least five lawsuits in Massachusetts and Maine to recover the specie and cargo from a single prize, and also defended against salvage lawsuits by locals who claimed to have "rescued" goods from the ship before it sank. Stoughton v. Sundry specie from Industria Raffaelli; Stoughton v. 280 Spanish dollars; Stoughton v. 42 pipes of rum, USDC-MA; Stoughton v. Three boxes segars; Stoughton v. Thomas McLellan, USCC-MA; John McLellan v. 42 pipes of rum; George Knights v. Three Anchors, USDC-MA.
62. Pablo Chacón to William Stanard, Dec. 12, 1820, PSC, section 11, box 19, folder 82; Statement of legal expenses, June 29, 1818, PSC, section 11, box 19, folder 84; Zamorano v. Sundry Goods, National Archives and Records Administration (Philadelphia), Records of the Circuit Court for Maryland, Appeals Docket, Nov. 1819; Stoughton v. McLellan, deposition of Thomas McLellan, USCC-MA, 13:182–84.
63. Stoughton v. Sundry specie from Industria Raffaelli, USDC-MA, 10:100–2, 10:145–59, 10:159–68; Pablo Chacón to Charles Mallory, July 21, 1817, PSC, Pablo Chacón letterbook, Apr. 17, 1817-Aug. 16, 1827; *Columbian Centinel*, Jan. 9, 1819, p. 2; John Stoughton to Pablo Chacón, Apr. 18, 1818, JSP; John Stoughton to James Stoughton, May 27, 1819, JSP; John Stoughton to John Bernabeu, May 28, 1819, JSP. On the Iberian litigation campaign generally, see Kevin Arlyck, "Plaintiffs v. Privateers: Litigation and Foreign Affairs in the Federal Courts, 1816–1822," *Law and History Review* 30 (2012): 245–78; Sean T. Perrone, "John Stoughton and the *Divina Pastora* Prize Case, 1816–1819," *Journal of the Early Republic* 28 (2008): 215–42.
64. Stoughton v. 42 pipes of rum, USDC-MA, 11:17–27; George Knights v. Three Anchors, USDC-MA, 10:529–31; Vasques v. The Brig Paqueta de Oporto and Cargo, National Archives and Records Administration (Waltham), United States District Court for Maine, Final Record Books, 5:11–13; Chacón v. Ship Providencia, National Archives and Records Administration (Philadelphia), Admiralty Cases of the United States District Court for Virginia, Order book 1811–1819, 292–93. On the value of prizes taken by Baltimore privateers, see Luis de Onís to John Quincy Adams, Nov. 2, 1817, June 9, 1818, *DCUS*, 3:1951–1952, 1967–1969; Mangoree and Esperanza, deposition of Peckner, National Archives and Records Administration, Admiralty Case Files of the U.S. District Court for the Southern District of New York, 1790–1842, microfilm M919, roll 24; Head, "Sailing," 92, 189–97; Perrone, "John Stoughton," 224.
65. John Stoughton to James Stoughton, May 27, 1819, JSP; John Stoughton to James Drake, June 15, 1818, JSP; Hugh Davey v. 60 boxes of sugar, USDC-MA, 10:340–41; John Stoughton to the Widow Roberts, May 23, 1817, June 28, 1817, JSP.

66. Stoughton to Onís, Jan. 24, 1818, JSP; Stoughton to the Widow Roberts, Jan. 23, 1818, Mar. 12, 1818, JSP. Stoughton's colleague in Norfolk, Pablo Chacón, similarly refused a privateer's offer to settle a case, as it involved "a nice legal point" Chacón hoped the Supreme Court would resolve. James Chaytor to Chacón, Dec. 10, 1817, PSC, section 11 box 19 folder 83; Chacón to Chaytor, Dec. 15, 1817, PSC, section 11, box 19, folder 82; Chacón to Littleton Tazewell, July 26, 1817, PSC, section 11, box 17, folder 57.
67. Head, "Sailing," 115–16; Head, *Privateers*, 89–91.
68. Adams diary, Jan. 22, 1819, *MJQA*, 4:225; Keen, *DeForest*, 154–55, 164–67; Vasques v. Chase, National Archives and Records Administration (Philadelphia), Records of the District Court for Maryland, Case Files, 1817–1818; *Baltimore Patriot*, Oct. 16, 1822, p. 3; *Baltimore Patriot*, Dec. 31, 1822, p. 4, Head, *Privateers*, 89–90.
69. Stoughton to Pablo Chacón, Jan. 24, 1817, JSP; Arlyck, "*Plaintiffs* v. *Privateers*," 268–69; Keen, *DeForest*, 129–30.
70. Corrêa da Serra to Adams, Mar. 17, 1819, Nov. 23, 1819, Aug. 26, 1820, NARA-PL, roll 1. Privateers bought libeled ships at auction and sent them out on new cruises before the legal proceedings against them had finished. Corrêa da Serra to Adams, June 8, 1820, NARA-PL, roll 1; Luis de Onís to James Monroe, Mar. 26, 1817, *Case of Great Britain*, 3:177; The Santissima Trinidad, 20 U.S. 283, 344–45 (1822).
71. Corrêa da Serra to Adams, July 16, 1820, *Annals*, 42:3042; Adams to Monroe, Aug. 30, 1820, *WJQA*, 7:68.
72. Adams to Corrêa da Serra, Sep. 30, 1820, *WJQA*, 7:73; Adams to John Graham, Apr. 24, 1819, *DCUS*, 1:98–101.
73. Adams to Monroe, Aug. 30, 1820, *WJQA*, 7:68; Adams to Corrêa da Serra, Sep. 30, 1820, *WJQA*, 7:73; Jefferson to William Short, Aug. 4, 1820, *PTJRS*, 16:163–68; Adams diary, Sep. 19, 1820, *MJQA*, 5:175–78.
74. Bennett Ostdiek and John Fabian Witt, "The Czar and the Slaves: Two Puzzles in the History of International Arbitration," *American Journal of International Law* 113 (2019): 535–67.
75. Monroe to Adams, Sep. 4, 1820, *WJQA*, 7:69 n. 1; Monroe to Adams, Sep. 25, 1820, *WJQA*, 7:73 n. 1.
76. Wirt to James Monroe, July 11, 1816, Library of Congress, William Wirt Papers (microfilm).
77. United States v. Hitchings, grand jury indictments, Nov. 1816, Dec. 6, 1816, Library of Virginia, United States Circuit Court (5th Circuit) Records, 1790–1861, Ended Cases. The case was reported as United States v. Hutchings in Albert Brunner, *Reports of Cases Argued and Determined in the Circuit Courts of the United States* (San Francisco: S. Whitney, 1884), 489–93.
78. Daniel Heller-Roazen, *The Enemy of All: Piracy and the Law of Nations* (New York: Zone Books, 2009), 13–22, 105–15.

79. Lauren Benton, "Toward a New Legal History of Piracy: Maritime Legalities and the Myth of Universal Jurisdiction," *International Journal of Maritime History* 23 (2011): 225–40; Richard Blakemore, *Enemies of All: The Rise and Fall of the Golden Age of Piracy* (New York: Pegasus Books, 2024); Mark G. Hanna, *Pirate Nests and the Rise of the British Empire, 1570–1740* (Chapel Hill: University of North Carolina Press, 2015); Marcus Rediker, *Villains of All Nations: Atlantic Pirates in the Golden Age* (Boston: Beacon Press, 2005); Robert Ritchie, *Captain Kidd and the War against the Pirates* (Cambridge: Harvard University Press, 1989).
80. Lauren Benton, *A Search for Sovereignty: Law and Geography in European Empires, 1400–1900* (Cambridge: Cambridge University Press, 2010), 104–61; Erica Burleigh, "Coercion, Conviction, Conversion: Sovereign Selves and Interior States in Colonial Piracy Trials and Narratives," 24 *Law & Literature* (2012): 151–73; Peter Earle, *The Pirate Wars* (London: Methuen, 2003), 181–208; Guy Chet, *The Ocean Is a Wilderness: Atlantic Piracy and the Limits of State Authority, 1688–1856* (Amherst: University of Massachusetts Press, 2014), 27–50.
81. William Blackstone, *Commentaries on the Laws of England* (Oxford: Clarendon Press, 1768), 2:71; Alfred P. Rubin, *The Law of Piracy* (Newport: Naval War College Press, 1988), 91–105; Sonja Schillings, *Enemies of All Humankind: Fictions of Legitimate Violence* (Hanover: Dartmouth College Press, 2016), 25–103; Mark Chadwick, *Piracy and the Origins of Universal Jurisdiction: On Stranger Tides?* (Boston: Brill, 2019), 131.
82. Brunner, *Reports of Cases*, 490–91; Henry Wheaton, *Elements of International Law* (Oxford: Clarendon Press, 1936), 161–64.
83. United States v. Hutchings, 26 F. Cas. 440, 440–41 (C.C.D. Va. 1817).
84. *The Repertory* (Boston), Dec. 28, 1816, p. 2; United States v. Hutchings, 26 F. Cas. 440, 442 (C.C.D. Va. 1817); Taylor v. United States, Library of Virginia, United States Circuit Court (5th Circuit) Records, 1790–1861, Ended Cases; Luis de Onís to James Monroe, Mar. 26, 1817, *Case of Great Britain*, 3:177; "Case of the Romp," *American Beacon* (Norfolk), Apr. 22, 1817, p. 2; The Santissima Trinidad, 20 U.S. 283, 345 (1822).
85. *Niles' Weekly Register*, Apr. 19, 1817, pp. 114–21; Charles Warren, "Federal Criminal Laws and the State Courts," *Harvard Law Review* 38 (1925): 545–98; *Commercial Advertiser* (New York), May 12, 1817, p. 2; "Trial of Captain Almeida," *Alexandria Herald*, May 14, 1817, p. 3.
86. Onís to Richard Rush, Apr. 18, 1817, *Case of Great Britain*, 3:185.
87. *National Advocate* (Boston), Sep. 15, 1817, p. 2; *Columbian Centinel*, Sep. 13, 1817, p. 2; United States v. Palmer, 16 U.S. 610, 617 (1818); Stoughton v. Sundry specie from Industria Raffaelli, libel of Stoughton, claim of Diggs, USDC-MA, 10:95–99, 108–11; *Newburyport Herald*, Sep. 16, 1817, p. 2.
88. Joseph Story, "Characteristics of the Age," *MWJS*, 1:343; United States v. Tully, 28 F. Cas. 226 (C.C.D. Mass. 1812); United States v. Ross, 27 F. Cas. 899 (C.C.D.R.I. 1813); Rubin, *Law of Piracy*, 135–38. The

federal court records reveal only two civil suits by the Spanish consul that reached the Massachusetts circuit court in 1817, and neither resulted in a ruling. Stoughton v. Divina Pastora, USCC-MA, 10:31; United States v. 49 bags of cocoa, USCC-MA, 10:111.

89. *Salem Gazette*, Oct. 31, 1817, p. 2; *New-Bedford Mercury*, Nov. 14, 1817, p. 2; Palmer, 16 U.S. at 612–17.
90. Palmer, 16 U.S. at 640–41; United States v. Furlong, 18 U.S. 184, 189 (1820); Bank of the U.S. v. Planters' Bank of Ga., 22 U.S. 904, 910 (1824) (Johnson, J., dissenting). On Story and Johnson's certification practices, see Jonathan Remy Nash and Michael G. Collins, "The Certificate of Division and the Early Supreme Court," *Southern California Law Review* 94 (2021): 733–84. Ironically, a decade later Story appeared to regret the Court's permissiveness in allowing certified questions to function as an alternate appeal mechanism in criminal cases, which he worried was contrary to Congress's intent and an "obstruction of public justice." United States v. Gooding, 25 U.S. 460, 467–68 (1827).
91. *Palmer*, 16 U.S. at 614–17, 634. According to Henry Clay, Story had no doubt that the commission at issue in *Palmer* was valid, but he certified the question because he wanted the full Court to decide it. *Annals*, 32:1425.
92. *Palmer*, 16 U.S. at 622–25.
93. *Palmer*, 16 U.S. at 634–35.
94. *Palmer*, 16 U.S. at 616, 625.
95. *Boston Weekly Messenger*, Apr. 9, 1818, p. 2.
96. *Boston Patriot and Daily Chronicle*, Nov. 4, 1817, p. 2; Dwight F. Henderson, *Courts, Congress, and Criminals: The Development of Federal Criminal Law, 1801–1829* (Westport: Greenwood Press, 1985), 129. Wirt suggested that he spoke up because the defendants were unrepresented, but it seems doubtful that the government's senior attorney would undermine its argued position purely for the sake of procedural fairness. *Boston Weekly Messenger*, Apr. 9, 1818, p. 2.
97. *Palmer*, 16 U.S. at 611; *National Advocate* (Boston), Sep. 15, 1817, p. 2.
98. U.S. Const., art. II, § 8; *Palmer*, 16 U.S. at 620–21.
99. *Palmer*, 16 U.S. at 630–32; *New-Bedford Mercury*, Apr. 24, 1818, p. 4. On the idea that ships on the high seas were floating pockets of national jurisdiction, see Benton, *Search for Sovereignty*, 104–61.
100. Juando v. Taylor, 13 F. Cas. 1179, 1183–84 (S.D.N.Y. 1818); Head, *Privateers*, 76.
101. Glenn to William Wirt, Oct. 9, 1818, NARA-AG, Letters Received, 1813–1870; Corrêa da Serra to John Quincy Adams, Nov. 14, 1818, NARA-PL, roll 1; Adams diary, Nov. 7, 1818, *MJQA*, 4:164.
102. Wirt to Elias Glenn, Nov. 6, 1818, 1 U.S. Op. Atty. Gen. 249, 250–253.
103. Adams diary, Apr. 28, 1818, *MJQA*, 4:82; Adams diary, Nov. 7, 1818, *MJQA*, 4:164; Elias Glenn to Wirt, Nov. 13, 1818, NARA-AG, Letters Received, 1813–1870. Upon becoming the federal district attorney in Virginia in 1816, Wirt admitted to a friend that he

only accepted the position because of "the profits" it promised by bolstering his private practice, not "the honor" that government office bestowed. Wirt to Littleton Waller Tazewell, Mar. 15, 1816, Library of Virginia, Tazewell Family Papers, 1623–1930, box 3, folder 11. On how financial anxiety shaped Wirt's career, see Alison L. LaCroix, *The Interbellum Constitution: Union, Commerce, and Slavery in the Age of Federalisms* (New Haven: Yale University Press, 2024), 29–73.

104. Joseph Story to Stephen White, Feb. 26, 1816, *LLJS*, 1:278–79; Adams diary, Aug. 21, 1819, *MJQA*, 4:415, 416: Wirt to Francis W. Gilmer, Apr. 1, 1816, in John Pendleton Kennedy, *Memoirs of the Life of William Wirt, Attorney General of the United States* (Philadelphia: Lea and Blanchard, 1849), 1:357.

105. Wirt to Dabney Carr, Apr. 7, 1816, in Kennedy, *Wirt Memoirs*, 1:359; Francis Walker Gilmer to Wirt, May 4, 1816, Library of Virginia, Francis Walker Gilmer Letters, 1812–1825; *New-York Spectator*, Dec. 1, 1818, p. 3; *Baltimore Patriot*, Nov. 30, 1818, p. 2. For accounts of other encounters between Wirt and "this Antaeus Pinkney," see Gilmer to Carr, Feb. 21, 1819, Apr. 26, 1821, Library of Virginia, Francis Walker Gilmer Letters, 1818–1824; LaCroix, *Interbellum Constitution*, 63–65.

106. Letter to the Editor, *Baltimore Patriot*, Nov. 30, 1818, p. 2; Gelston v. Hoyt, 16 U.S. 246, 324–25 (1818); *Commercial Advertiser* (New York), Dec. 8, 1818, p. 2; *Alexandria Gazette*, Dec. 10, 1818, pp. 2, 3; Adams diary, Mar. 29, 1819, *MJQA*, 4:319.

107. *Times* (Hartford), Dec. 15, 1818, p. 2; *Gazette of Maine*, Dec. 15, 1818, p. 2; *Alexandria Herald*, Dec. 16, 1818, p. 3.

108. *Alexandria Gazette*, Dec. 18, 1818, p. 2; *American Beacon* (Norfolk), Dec. 25, 1818, p. 2; Robert Swift to Wirt, Dec. 17, 1818, NARA-AG, Letters Received, 1813–1870; *New York Evening Post*, July 29, 1818, p. 2; *An Appeal to the Government and Congress of the United States against the Depredations Committed by American Privateers on the Commerce of Nations at Peace with Us* (New York, 1819), 70–71; Henderson, *Courts, Congress, and Criminals*, 130–35.

109. *Commercial Advertiser* (New York), Dec. 8, 1818, p. 2; *National Advocate* (New York), Dec. 8, 1818, p. 2; Henderson, *Courts, Congress, and Criminals*, 132.

110. *Republican Agriculturalist* (Norwich), Dec. 17, 1818, p. 2; *Eastern Argus* (Portland), Dec. 29, 1818, p. 2.

111. Adams diary, Mar. 19, 1819, Mar. 29, 1819, *MJQA*, 4:308, 319.

112. Adams diary, Mar. 29, 1819, May 11, 1819, *MJQA*, 4:319, 362–63; *Alexandria Gazette*, Dec. 10, 1818, pp. 2, 3. Adams's scorn for the judges may have been warranted. One newspaper reported that they stayed in the same rooming house as Taylor during the trial, and dined

together companionably after court adjourned for the day. *New York Evening Post*, Dec. 2, 1818, p. 2.

113. Adams diary, May 11, 1819, *MJQA*, 4:362–363.
114. Adams diary, Mar. 29, 1819, *MJQA*, 4:317; Mark Jarrett, *The Congress of Vienna and Its Legacy: War and Great Power Diplomacy after Napoleon* (London: I.B. Tauris, 2013).
115. Adams diary, Feb. 22, 1819, *MJQA*, 4:274; Dangerfield, *Good Feelings*, 137–56.
116. Adams to William Lowndes, Dec. 21, 1819, *DCUS*, 1:108–10; Francisco Dionisio Vives to Adams, Apr. 14, Apr. 24, May 5, 1820, *DCUS*, 3:1988–93; Lewis, *American Union*, 136–38.
117. Adams diary, Mar. 29, 1819, *MJQA*, 4:320; Adams diary, Mar. 31, 1820, *MJQA*, 5:53; Howe, *What Hath God Wrought*, 147–60; Lewis, *American Union*, 136.
118. Adams diary, May 26, 1819, *MJQA*, 4:374; Monroe to Madison, Feb. 19, 1820, *PJMRS*, 2:14–15.

7 Policing the High Seas

1. *The Trial of William Holmes, Thomas Warrington, and Edward Rosewain, on an Indictment for Murder on the High Seas* (Boston: Joseph C. Spear, 1820), 5–8, 16–17.
2. Ibid.
3. Crimes Act of 1790, § 8, 1 Stat. 112, 113–14; United States v. Holmes, 18 U.S. 412 (1820); Petition of Edward Rosewaine, Apr. 4, 1820, James Austin to John Quincy Adams, May 16, 1820, NARA-PP, Box 16.
4. *Trial of William Holmes*, 15–20.
5. United States v. Palmer, 16 U.S. 610, 631 (1818); United States v. Klintock, 18 U.S. 144, 152 (1820).
6. *Trial of William Holmes*, 11–12.
7. For land-focused explorations of early American empire, see Gregory Ablavsky, *Federal Ground: Governing Property and Violence in the First U.S. Territories* (New York: Oxford University Press, 2021); Stuart Banner, *How the Indians Lost Their Land: Law and Power on the Frontier* (Cambridge: Belknap Press, 2005); Ned Blackhawk, *Violence over the Land: Indians and Empires in the Early American West* (Cambridge: Harvard University Press, 2006); Lisa Ford, *Settler Sovereignty: Jurisdiction and Indigenous People in America and Australia, 1788–1836* (Cambridge: Harvard University Press, 2010); Paul Frymer, *Building an American Empire: The Era of Territorial and Political Expansion* (Princeton: Princeton University Press, 2017); Patrick Griffin, *American Leviathan: Empire, Nation, and Revolutionary Frontier* (New York: Hill & Wang, 2007); Bethel Saler, *The Settlers' Empire: Colonialism and State Formation in America's Old Northwest* (Philadelphia: University of Pennsylvania Press, 2015).

Studies that attend to the maritime dimensions of American empire include Eliga H. Gould, *Among the Powers of the Earth: The American Revolution and the Making of a New World Empire* (Cambridge: Harvard University Press, 2012); David C. Hendrickson, *Union, Nation, or Empire: The American Debate over International Relations, 1789–1941* (Lawrence: University Press of Kansas, 2009); Brian Rouleau, *With Sails Whitening Every Sea: Mariners and the Making of an American Maritime Empire* (Ithaca: Cornell University Press, 2014). On the interaction of geography and empire generally, see Lauren Benton, *A Search for Sovereignty: Law and Geography in European Empires, 1400–1900* (Cambridge: Cambridge University Press, 2010).

8. Onís to Adams, Nov. 16, 1818, *DCUS*, 3:1980–83; Adams diary, Aug. 29, 1820, *MJQA*, 5:171.
9. Onís to James Monroe, Feb. 10, 1817, in *The Case of Great Britain as Laid before the Tribunal of Arbitration Convened at Geneva* (Washington, DC: Government Printing Office, 1872), 3:171–72; Onís to Adams, Nov. 16, 1818, Dec. 12, 1818, *DCUS*, 3:1980–84; Adams to Monroe, Aug. 30, 1820, *WJQA*, 7:68.
10. Adams diary, Mar. 29, 1819, *MJQA*, 4:318; Dwight F. Henderson, *Courts, Congress, and Criminals: The Development of Federal Criminal Law, 1801–1829* (Westport: Greenwood Press, 1985), 137–38, 146.
11. Adams to Charles S. Todd, June 5, 1820, *DCUS*, 1:126–30; Adams to Monroe, Aug. 21, 1820, *WJQA*, 7:62; David Head, "Baltimore Seafarers, Privateering, and the South American Revolutions, 1816–1820," *Maryland Historical Magazine* 105 (2008): 269–93. Defendants in capital cases were statutorily entitled to an attorney. Crimes Act of 1790, § 29, 1 Stat. 112, 118. But their penury could make it difficult for attorneys to procure exculpatory evidence from far-flung places. James Austin to Adams, May 16, 1820, NARA-PP, Box 16; Austin to William Wirt, June 2, 1820, NARA-AG, Letters Received, 1813–1870.
12. John Gallison, "Privateering," *North American Review* 11 (1820): 166–96; "Memoir of John Gallison, Esq.," *Christian Disciple and Theological Review* 3 (1821): 15–26; Pat O'Malley, "The Discipline of Violence: State, Capital, and the Regulation of Naval Warfare," *Sociology* 22 (1988): 253–70; Nicholas Parrillo, "The De-Privatization of American Warfare: How the U.S. Government Used, Regulated, and Ultimately Abandoned Privateering in the Nineteenth Century," *Yale Journal of Law & the Humanities* 19 (2007): 1–95; Bernard Semmel, *Liberalism and Naval Strategy: Ideology, Interest, and Sea Power During the Pax Britannica* (Boston: Allen & Unwin, 1986); Francis R. Stark, *The Abolition of Privateering and the Declaration of Paris* (New York: Columbia University, 1897), 13–45.
13. "Application to Abolish Privateering in Time of War," Jan. 26, 1821, *ASPNA*, 1:723–24; Douglas A. Irwin, *Against the Tide: An Intellectual*

History of Free Trade (Princeton: Princeton University Press, 1996), 75–98; Carl E. Swanson, *Predators and Prizes: American Privateering and Imperial Warfare, 1739–1748* (Columbia: University of South Carolina Press, 1991), 16–21.

14. The Amiable Isabella, 19 U.S. 1, 87–88 (1821); Stuart Banner, *The Death Penalty: An American History* (Cambridge: Harvard University Press, 2002), 88–143; Christopher Leslie Brown, *Moral Capital: Foundations of British Abolitionism* (Chapel Hill: University of North Carolina Press, 2006); David Brion Davis, *Inhuman Bondage: The Rise and Fall of Slavery in the New World* (New York: Oxford University Press, 2006), 231–67; Edward Dorr Griffin, *The Claims of Seamen: A Sermon Preached November 7, 1819, in the Brick Church, New-York* (New York: J. Seymour, 1819), 7; Rebecca M. McLennan, *The Crisis of Imprisonment: Protest, Politics, and the Making of the American Penal State, 1776–1941* (New York: Cambridge University Press, 2008), 14–86; Ronald G. Walters, *American Reformers, 1815–1860* (New York: Hill & Wang, 1978).

15. Gallison, "Privateering," 194; "Application to Abolish Privateering in Time of War," Jan. 4, 1820, *ASPNA*, 1:628; *Dedham Gazette*, Feb. 5, 1819, p. 3; *Baltimore Patriot*, Feb. 10, 1820, p. 2; Paul A. Gilje, *Liberty on the Waterfront: American Maritime Culture in the Age of Revolution* (Philadelphia: University of Pennsylvania Press, 2004), 6–12, 195–227; Rouleau, *With Sails Whitening*, 102–33.

16. James Kent, *Commentaries on American Law* (New York: O. Halsted, 1826), 1:92; Edmond-Louis-Alexis Dubois de Crancé, Dec. 1789, quoted in Christopher J. Tozzi, *Nationalizing France's Army: Foreign, Black, and Jewish Troops in the French Military, 1715–1831* (Charlottesville: University of Virginia Press, 2016), 3, 17–48; Peter H. Wilson, "Foreign Military Labour in Europe's Transition to Modernity," *European Review of History* 27 (2020): 12–32. On nationalism and mass mobilization, see Deborah Avant, "From Mercenary to Citizen Armies: Explaining Change in the Practice of War," *International Organization* 54 (2000): 41–72; David A. Bell, *The First Total War: Napoleon's Europe and the Birth of Warfare as We Know It* (Boston: Houghton Mifflin, 2007); Alan I. Forrest, *The Legacy of the French Revolutionary Wars: The Nation-in-Arms in French Republican Memory* (Cambridge: Cambridge University Press, 2009).

17. Declaration of Independence, July 4, 1776; Nir Arielli, *From Byron to bin Laden: A History of Foreign War Volunteers* (Cambridge: Harvard University Press, 2018), 27–42; James C. Carey, "Lord Cochrane: Critic of San Martín's Peruvian Campaign," *The Americas* 18 (1962): 340–51; Karen Racine, *Francisco de Miranda: A Transatlantic Life in the Age of Revolution* (Wilmington: Scholarly Resources, 2003); Graciela Iglesias Rogers, *British Liberators in the Age of Napoleon: Volunteering under*

the Spanish Flag in the Peninsular War (London: Bloomsbury Publishing, 2013); Tozzi, *Nationalizing France's Army*, 116–21.

18. Adams to George Canning, June 24, 1823, Adams to Richard Rush, July 28, 1823, in Carlton Savage, *Policy of the United States Toward Maritime Commerce in War* (Washington, DC: Government Printing Office, 1934), 1:303–4, 307; Samuel Flagg Bemis, *John Quincy Adams and the Foundations of American Foreign Policy* (New York: A.A. Knopf, 1949), 436–44.
19. Adams to Alexander Hill Everett, Dec. 29, 1817, *WJQA*, 6:280–83; Adams to John B. Prevost, July 10, 1820, *DCUS*, 1:134–37; Adams to Charles S. Todd, June 5, 1820, *DCUS*, 1:126–30; Adams to Monroe, July 11, 1820, *WJQA*, 7:45–46 n. 2.
20. *An Appeal to the Government and Congress of the United States against the Depredations Committed by American Privateers on the Commerce of Nations at Peace with Us* (New York, 1819), vi; Jefferson to Corrêa da Serra, Oct. 24, 1820, *PTJRS*, 16:367–69; Zoltán Vajda, "Thomas Jefferson on the Character of an Unfree People: The Case of Spanish America," *American Nineteenth Century History* 8 (2007): 273–92. On the pamphlet's authorship, see Rafe Blaufarb, "The Western Question: The Geopolitics of Latin American Independence," *American Historical Review* 112 (2007): 742–63; Richard Beale Davis, "The Abbé Corrêa da Serra in America, 1812–1820," *Transactions of the American Philosophical Society* 45 (1955): 90–121.
21. Adams to Johnson, Sep. 5, 1820, quoted in James E. Lewis, *The American Union and the Problem of Neighborhood: The United States and the Collapse of the Spanish Empire, 1783–1829* (Chapel Hill: University of North Carolina Press), 162; Adams to Charles S. Todd, June 5, 1820, *DCUS*, 1:126–30; Jefferson to Pierre Samuel Du Pont de Nemours, Apr. 15, 1811, *PTJRS*, 3:559–61; Caitlin Fitz, *Our Sister Republics: The United States in an Age of American Revolutions* (New York: Liveright, 2017), 33–34.
22. Adams to Alexander Hill Everett, Dec. 29, 1817, *WJQA*, 6:280–83; Rafe Blaufarb, *Bonapartists in the Borderlands: French Exiles and Refugees on the Gulf Coast, 1815–1835* (Tuscaloosa: University of Alabama Press, 2006), 86–116; Frank Lawrence Owsley and Gene A. Smith, *Filibusters and Expansionists: Jeffersonian Manifest Destiny, 1800–1821* (Tuscaloosa: University of Alabama Press, 1997), 118–40.
23. "An Act to prohibit the importation of Slaves into any port or place within the jurisdiction of the United States," 2 Stat. 426 (1807); Fitz, *Sister Republics*, 109–13; David Head, *Privateers of the Americas: Spanish American Privateering from the United States in the Early Republic* (Athens: University of Georgia Press, 2015), 108–14, 147; Christopher Ward, "The Commerce of East Florida during the Embargo, 1806–1812: The Role of Amelia Island," *Florida Historical Quarterly* 68 (1989): 160–79.

24. Adams to Alexander Hill Everett, Dec. 29, 1817, *WJQA*, 6:280–83; Beverly Chew to William Crawford, Aug. 30, 1817, *Annals*, 32:1793–95; Head, *Privateers*, 107–12.
25. Monroe to Congress, Nov. 6, 1818, *ASPFR*, 4:212; Adams to Richard Rush, Jan. 1, 1819, *DCUS*, 1:85–88; Adams to Smith Thompson, May 20, 1819, *DCUS*, 1:101–7; Adams to John Graham, Apr. 24, 1819, *DCUS*, 1:98–101.
26. James Monroe to Adams, Aug. 11, 1820, *WJQA*, 7:63 n. 1; Adams to John M. Forbes, July 11, 1820, *DCUS*, 1:138–39; Adams to Monroe, July 11, 1820, *WJQA*, 7:45 n. 2.
27. Adams to John B. Prevost, July 10, 1820, *DCUS*, 1:134–37; Head, *Privateers*, 145; Adams to John M. Forbes, July 11, 1820, *DCUS*, 1:138–39.
28. Adams to John M. Forbes, July 11, 1820, *DCUS*, 1:138–39; Gilje, *Liberty on the Waterfront*, 83–89; Clare Anderson, ed., *Mutiny and Maritime Radicalism in the Age of Revolution: A Global Survey* (Cambridge: Cambridge University Press, 2014); Bonamy Dobree and G. E. Manwaring, *Floating Republic: An Account of the Mutinies at Spithead and the Nore in 1797* (Barnsley: Pen and Sword Military Classics, 2004); Peter Linebaugh and Marcus Rediker, *The Many-Headed Hydra Sailors, Slaves, Commoners, and the Hidden History of the Revolutionary Atlantic* (Boston: Beacon Press, 2000), 143–73. For a contemporary critique of shipboard conditions, see William McNally, *Evils and Abuses in the Naval and Merchant Service, Exposed; With Proposals for Their Remedy and Redress* (Boston: Cassady and March, 1839), 62–72.
29. *Appeal to the Government and Congress*, 73–79; *Richmond Enquirer*, Feb. 4, 1819, p. 3; *National Advocate*, June 23, 1820, p. 2; Head, *Privateers*, 138–39.
30. *Dedham Gazette*, Feb. 5, 1819, p. 2; *Baltimore Patriot*, Jan, 27, 1819, pp. 2–3; *Richmond Enquirer*, Feb. 4, 1819, p. 3.
31. *Dedham Gazette*, Feb. 5, 1819, p. 3; *Baltimore Patriot*, Nov, 30, 1819, p. 2; *Niles' Weekly Register*, Apr. 3, 1819, p. 112; *New York Evening Post*, June 12, 1819, p. 2.
32. *Baltimore Patriot*, Feb. 10, 1820, p. 2; John P. Mumford to John Quincy Adams, Jan. 8, 1819, NARA-PP, Box 15; James Young to Adams, Feb. 9, 1819, ibid.; Peter Earle, *The Pirate Wars* (London: Methuen, 2003), 214, 234.
33. *Dedham Gazette*, Feb. 5, 1819, p. 3; Henderson, *Courts, Congress, and Criminals*, 139. On Monroe's regional tours, see Sandra Moats, *Celebrating the Republic: Presidential Ceremony and Popular Sovereignty, from Washington to Monroe* (DeKalb: Northern Illinois University Press, 2010).
34. Henderson, *Courts, Congress, and Criminals*, 137–46.

35. United States v. Palmer, 16 U.S. 610, 617 (1818).
36. United States v. Klintock, 18 U.S. 144 (1820); United States v. Smith, 18 U.S. 153 (1820); United States v. Furlong, 18 U.S. 184 (1820); United States v. Griffen and Brailsford, 18 U.S. 188 (1820); United States v. Bowers and Matthews, 18 U.S. 189 (1820); United States v. Holmes, 18 U.S. 412 (1820).
37. *Trial of William Holmes*, 10–12.
38. *Klintock*, 18 U.S. at 147, 152–53.
39. *Trial of William Holmes*, 10–12; Daniel Heller-Roazen, *The Enemy of All: Piracy and the Law of Nations* (New York: Zone Books, 2009), 13–22, 105–15; Lauren Benton, "Toward a New Legal History of Piracy: Maritime Legalities and the Myth of Universal Jurisdiction," *International Journal of Maritime History* 23 (2011): 225–40.
40. *Klintock*, 18 U.S. at 152–53; Fitz, *Sister Republics*, 42–44.
41. Silas Deane to Committee of Secret Correspondence, Nov. 27, 1776, *RDCUS*, 2:195–96; Joseph Yorke to States-General, Oct. 29, 1779, *RDCUS*, 3:396; Alfred P. Rubin, *The Law of Piracy* (Newport: Naval War College Press, 1988), 154.
42. United States v. Hutchings, 26 F. Cas. 440, 440–42 (C.C.D. Va. 1817); *Klintock*, 18 U.S. at 149.
43. United States v. Furlong, 18 U.S. 184, 193, 202 (1820).
44. *Furlong*, 18 U.S. at 192–202; *Klintock*, 18 U.S. at 149–50.
45. Henry Wheaton, *Elements of International Law* (London: B. Fellowes, 1836), 1:162–63; Rubin, *Law of Piracy*, 82–85.
46. The Amiable Isabella, 19 U.S. 1, 87–88 (1821).
47. United States v. Palmer, 16 U.S. 610, 631 (1818); *Klintock*, 18 U.S. at 152; United States v. Bevans, 16 U.S. 336 (1818); United States v. Wiltberger, 18 U.S. 76 (1820); George L. Haskins and Herbert A. Johnson, *Foundations of Power: John Marshall, 1801–15* (New York: Macmillan, 1981), 633–46; G. Edward White, *The Marshall Court and Cultural Change, 1815–1835* (New York: Oxford University Press, 1991), 870.
48. Adams to Richard Rush, June 24, 1823, in *Message from the President of the United States Transmitting the Information Required by a Resolution of the House of Representatives, of 27th February last, in Relation to the Suppression of the African Slave Trade* (Washington, DC: Gales and Seaton, 1824), 22–27.
49. Adams diary, May 11, 1819, *MJQA*, 4:363; United States v. Kessler, 26 F. Cas. 766, 772 (C.C.D. Pa. 1829).
50. "An Act to protect the commerce of the United States, and to punish the crime of piracy," § 5, 3 Stat. 510, 513 (1819). The confusion under the Crimes Act of 1790 stemmed from the fact that "robbery" was not punishable by death under federal law when committed on land, so the statute left some doubt as to whether a robbery *at sea* qualified as piracy. Rubin, *Law of Piracy*, 139–150. The Court held in 1818 that robberies

at sea were punishable, but apparently Congress wanted to avoid the possibility of further confusion about the scope of the courts' authority. United States v. Palmer, 16 U.S. 610, 626–30 (1818).

51. *Annals*, 33:1169–1216; Monroe to George Hay, Feb. 10, 1820, quoted in Lewis, *American Union*, 133; Sean Wilentz, *No Property in Man: Slavery and Antislavery at the Nation's Founding* (Cambridge: Harvard University Press, 2018), 223–24. The piracy bill only appeared in the congressional record a handful of times. *Annals*, 33:246, 253, 256, 464; 34:1403, 1410, 1415–417.
52. *Niles' Weekly Register*, Aug. 7, 1819, p. 395.
53. Martin v. Hunter's Lessee, 14 U.S. 304 (1816); McCulloch v. Maryland, 17 U.S. 316 (1819).
54. R. Kent Newmyer, "John Marshall, McCulloch v. Maryland, and the Southern States' Rights Tradition," 33 *John Marshall Law Review* 33 (2000): 875–934; David S. Schwartz, *The Spirit of the Constitution: John Marshall and the 200-Year Odyssey of McCulloch v. Maryland (New York: Oxford University Press, 2019), 59–83; Charles Warren, The Supreme Court in United States History, 1789–1835* (Boston: Little, Brown, 1926), 499–564.
55. Onís to John Quincy Adams, Mar. 9, 1819, NARA-SL, roll 8; Corrêa da Serra to Adams, Mar. 17, 1819, NARA-PL, roll 1.
56. Adams to Luis de Onís, Apr. 17, 1819, *DCUS*, 1:97. Attorney General Wirt parroted this deference back to Adams a few months later. When the Secretary of State asked Wirt to assess the new Piracy Act's "defects" and propose revisions for Congress's consideration, he declined. Questions about the act's scope were already before the federal courts, Wirt noted, and it was better to let judges answer them. Wirt to Adams, Jan. 29, 1820, NARA-AG, Letters Sent, 1793–1870.
57. United States v. Smith, 18 U.S. 153, 156–57 (1820); Ibid., 164–83 (Livingston, J., dissenting). Webster was probably wrong about the framers; as Justice Story pointed out, James Madison indicated in Federalist 42 that the definition of piracies under the Offenses Clause could properly be "left to the law of nations." Ibid., 158–59.
58. Marshall to Washington, Aug. 3, 1819, Oct. 31, 1819, *PJM*, 8:373–74; United States v. Smith, Charge to Jury, July 27, 1819, *PJM*, 8:370–72.
59. *Smith*, 18 U.S. at 159–62. For an in-depth discussion of the *Smith* case, see Joel Samuels, "The Full Story of *United States v. Smith*, America's Most Important Piracy Case," *Penn State Journal of Law & International Affairs* 1 (2012): 320–62.
60. *Smith*, 18 U.S. at 154, 162–63.
61. *Smith*, 18 U.S. at 169–76 (Livingston, J., dissenting); White, *Cultural Change*, 876–77.
62. Adams to Charles S. Todd, June 5, 1820, *DCUS*, 1:126–30; Adams to James Monroe, Aug. 21, 1820, *WJQA*, 7:62; Statement of Persons Sentenced to

Suffer Death, NARA-PP, Box 7, Case Folder 416–424, 444–447, 467–470, 478, 527. It appears that only one privateer captain or investor – Thomas Taylor's associate Joseph Karrick – was ever convicted (for a misdemeanor), and his conviction was later overturned. Head, *Privateers*, 86.

63. *Dedham Gazette*, Feb. 5, 1819, p. 3; *Boston Daily Advertiser*, June 20, 1820, p. 2; Monroe to House of Representatives, May 9, 1820, *DCUS*, 1:124–26; Adams diary, Mar. 13, 1820, *MJQA*, 5:19–22; Adams to Francisco Dionisio Vives, May 3, 1820, *DCUS*, 1:111–115.
64. Banner, *The Death Penalty*, 144–68; Louis P. Masur, *Rites of Execution: Capital Punishment and the Transformation of American Culture, 1776–1865* (Oxford University Press, 1989), 25–116. On changing attitudes toward executions in England, see Simon Devereaux, *Execution, State and Society in England, 1660–1900* (Cambridge: Cambridge University Press, 2023).
65. James Monroe, Second Inaugural Address, Mar. 5, 1821, *WJM*, 6:163–74; Ezekiel Whitman to John Quincy Adams, Jan. 3, 1820, NARA-PP, Box 8, Case Folder 513; Petition of Mezick Baptist, NARA-PP, Box 7, Case Folder 421; Petition of Baltimore citizens, Mar. 3, 1820, NARA-PP, Box 7, Case Folder 416; The Recommendations of the Bar, Mar. 3, 1820, NARA-PP, Box 7, Case Folder 416; *Richmond Enquirer*, June 6, 1820, p. 3. Testimonials from "respectable" citizens were a staple of pardon applications in the period. Margaret Colgate Love, "The Twilight of the Pardon Power," *Journal of Criminal Law & Criminology* 100 (2010): 1169–212.
66. Adams diary, Mar. 13, 1820, June 9, 1820, June 12, 1820, *MJQA*, 5:19–22, 146–47, 149–50.
67. Federalist 74, *DHRC*, 16:478–81; Crimes Act of 1790, 1 Stat. 112; Frank McLynn, *Crime and Punishment in Eighteenth Century England* (Oxford: Oxford University Press, 1989), xi, 258; J. M. Beattie, *Crime and Courts in England, 1600–1800* (Princeton: Princeton University Press, 1986), 451–55, 530–38.
68. Federalist 74, *DHRC*, 16:478–81; Scott Ingram, "Presidents, Politics, and Pardons: Washington's Original (Mis?)use of the Pardon Power," *Wake Forest Journal of Law and Policy* 8 (2018): 259–318; George Jr. Lardner and Margaret Colgate Love, "Mandatory Sentences and Presidential Mercy: The Role of Judges in Pardon Cases, 1790–1850," *Federal Sentencing Reporter* 16 (2004): 212–21.
69. Petition of Edward Rosewaine, NARA-PP, Box 16; James Prince to John Quincy Adams, May 22, 1820, NARA-PP, Box 16; James Austin to William Wirt, June 2, 1820, NARA-AG, Letters Received, 1813–1870. On the government's use of privateers as witnesses, see Robert Stanard to Adams, Feb. 3, 1820, NARA-PP, Box 8, Case Folder 513; Petition of John Ferguson, NARA-PP, Box 7, Case Folder 416.
70. Affidavit of James Griffin and Benjamin Brailsford, Affidavit of Morris Goldsmith, NARA-PP, Box 7, Case Folder 421; James Prince to John

Quincy Adams, May 22, 1820, NARA-PP, Box 16; William Fenwick to Adams, June 24, 1820, Letter of Samuel Poole, June 22, 1820, NARA-PP, Box 8, Case Folder 513; Adams diary, June 12, 1820, *MJQA*, 5:149–50; Charles Cook to James Monroe, June 13, 1820, NARA-PP, Box 8, Case Folder 513.

71. Adams diary, June 8, 1820, June 12, 1820, *MJQA*, 5:144–46, 149–50.
72. Quoted in Lardner and Love, "Presidential Mercy," 220 n. 21, 213–18; John Drayton to John Quincy Adams, Mar. 21, 1820, NARA-PP, Box 7, Case 421.
73. William Wirt to Duvall, Jan. 17, 1820, NARA-AG, Letters Sent, 1793–1870; Duvall to Wirt, Feb. 16, 1820, NARA-PP, Box 7, Case 416; Adams diary, Mar. 13, 1820, June 12, 1820, *MJQA*, 5:149–50; Statement of Persons Sentenced to Suffer Death, NARA-PP, Box 7, Case Folder 416–424, 444–447, 467–470, 478, 527.
74. William Johnson and John Drayton to John Quincy Adams, Dec. 10, 1819, NARA-PP, Box 7, Case 421; Marshall to William Wirt, May 30, 1820, NARA-PP, Box 8, Case 513; Adams diary, June 9, 1820, *MJQA*, 5:146–47; Adams to James Monroe, July 11, 1820, *WJQA*, 7:43–46; Statement of Persons Sentenced to Suffer Death, NARA-PP, Box 7, Case Folder 416–424, 444–447, 467–470, 478, 527.
75. Adams diary, Mar. 13, 1820, *MJQA*, 5:20–21. On the rumors about Bland, see Peter Graham Fish, *Federal Justice in the Mid-Atlantic South: United States Courts from Maryland to the Carolinas, 1789–1835* (Washington, DC: Administrative Office of U.S. Courts, 2002), 225–28.
76. For Austin's background, see Austin to Thomas Jefferson, July 12, 1811, *PTJRS*, 4:37–38.
77. Petition of Edward Rosewaine, NARA-PP, Box 16; Austin to John Quincy Adams, May 16, 1820, NARA-PP, Box 16; Austin to William Wirt, June 2, 1820, NARA-AG, Letters Received, 1813–1870.
78. Adams diary, June 8, 1820, *MJQA*, 5:144–46; Pardon of Piratical Murder, May 9, 1820, 1 U.S. Op. Atty. Gen. 359, 360. Wirt's concession on the jurisdictional point is curious, since the Supreme Court had recently clarified – in cases that Wirt argued for the government – that even "the most unquestionable commission" did not put those who committed piratical acts beyond the courts' reach. United States v. Furlong, 18 U.S. 184, 202 (1820). In all likelihood, Wirt had not immediately grasped the full implications of the Court's recent rulings.
79. *Christian Watchman* (Boston), June 17, 1820, p. 3; *National Aegis* (Worcester), June 21, 1820, p. 2; Prince to John Quincy Adams, May 22, 1820, NARA-PP, Box 16.
80. *Village Register and Norfolk County Advertiser*, June 23, 1820, p. 3; *Concord Observer*, June 19, 1820. p. 3; *Manufacturers' and Farmers' Journal* (Providence), June 15, 1820, p. 2.

81. Monroe to John Quincy Adams, Aug. 3, 1820, *WJM*, 6:145–50; Joseph Amado Grehon to Adams, Dec. 4, 1820, NARA-PL, roll 1; Hugh Nelson to Adams, June 18, 1824, *DCUS*, 3:2047; Francisco Hilario de Rivas y Salmon to Daniel Brent, Sep. 29, 1824, *DCUS*, 3:2049; Philip Coolidge Brooks, *Diplomacy and the Borderlands: The Adams-Onís Treaty of 1819* (New York: Octagon Books, 1970), 186–91; Henderson, *Courts, Congress, and Criminals*, 147–48; David Head, "Sailing for Spanish America: The Atlantic Geopolitics of Foreign Privateering from the United States in the Early Republic" (Ph.D. dissertation, SUNY Buffalo, 2010), 228–32.
82. Bemis, *John Quincy Adams*, 334–38.
83. Inaugural address of John Quincy Adams, Mar. 4, 1825, *ASPFR*, 5:753–55; Ned Blackhawk, *Violence over the Land: Indians and Empires in the Early American West* (Cambridge: Harvard University Press, 2006); Brooks, *Diplomacy and the Borderlands*, 191–96; Daniel Walker Howe, *What Hath God Wrought the Transformation of America, 1815–1848* (New York: Oxford University Press, 2007), 107–10, 744–91; William Earl Weeks, *John Quincy Adams and American Global Empire* (Lexington: University Press of Kentucky, 1992), 176–99.
84. Lewis, *American Union*, 164–72; Bemis, *John Quincy Adams*, 341–62; Arthur Whitaker, *The United States and the Independence of Latin America, 1800–1830* (Baltimore: Johns Hopkins, 1941), 317–95.
85. James Monroe, Seventh Annual Message, Dec. 2, 1823, *WJM*, 6:325–42.
86. Daniel J. Burge, *A Failed Vision of Empire: The Collapse of Manifest Destiny, 1845–1872* (Lincoln: University of Nebraska Press, 2022); Dexter Perkins, *The Monroe Doctrine, 1826–1867* (Baltimore: Johns Hopkins Press, 1933); Jay Sexton, *The Monroe Doctrine: Empire and Nation in Nineteenth-Century America* (New York: Hill & Wang, 2011), 3–14, 47–84.
87. The Antelope, 23 U.S. 66, 67–69 (1825); United States v. La Jeune Eugenie, 26 F. Cas. 832, 832–34 (C.C.D. Mass. 1822); John Thomas Noonan, *The Antelope: The Ordeal of the Recaptured Africans in the Administrations of James Monroe and John Quincy Adams* (Berkeley: University of California Press, 1977), 28–33; "International Norms and Politics in the Marshall Court's Slave Trade Cases," *Harvard Law Review* 128 (2015): 1184–205.
88. *Annals*, 36:2207–11; Monroe to Adams, Aug. 3, 1820, *WJM*, 6:145–50; Slave Trade Act of 1807, § 5, 2 Stat. 426, 427; "An Act in addition to 'An act to prohibit the introduction (importation) of slaves,'" § 4, 3 Stat. 450, 451 (1818); "An Act to continue in force 'An act to protect the commerce of the United States, and punish the crime of piracy,' and also to make further provision for punishing the crime of piracy," § 4, 3 Stat. 600, 601 (1820).

89. U.S. Const. art. I, § 9. On the American commitment to slave trade suppression (or lack thereof), see W. E. B. Du Bois, *The Suppression of the African Slave-Trade to the United States of America, 1638–1870* (New York: Longmans, Green, 1896); Don E. Fehrenbacher, *The Slaveholding Republic: An Account of the United States Government's Relations to Slavery* (Oxford: Oxford University Press, 2001); Craig B. Hollander, "Against a Sea of Troubles: Slave Trade Suppressionism During the Early Republic" (Ph.D. diss., Johns Hopkins University, 2013); Ernest Obadele-Starks, *Freebooters and Smugglers: The Foreign Slave Trade in the United States after 1808* (Fayetteville: University of Arkansas Press, 2007).
90. Brown, *Moral Capital*; David Brion Davis, *The Problem of Slavery in the Age of Revolution* (Ithaca: Cornell University Press, 1975); Seymour Drescher, *Econocide: British Slavery in the Era of Abolition* (University of North Carolina Press, 1977); Fehrenbacher, *Slaveholding Republic*, 201–4; Philip Gould, *Barbaric Traffic: Commerce and Antislavery in the Eighteenth-Century Atlantic World* (Cambridge: Harvard University Press, 2003); Hollander, "Sea of Troubles," 12–25; Jenny Martinez, *The Slave Trade and the Origins of the International Human Rights Law* (Oxford: Oxford University Press, 2012).
91. Jay Coughtry, *The Notorious Triangle: Rhode Island and the African Slave Trade, 1700–1807* (Philadelphia: Temple University Press, 1981); Charles Rappleye, *Sons of Providence: The Brown Brothers, the Slave Trade and the American Revolution* (New York: Simon & Schuster, 2006); Hollander, "Sea of Troubles," 525–39; Edward Bartlett Rugemer, *The Problem of Emancipation: The Caribbean Roots of the American Civil War* (Baton Rouge: Louisiana State University Press, 2008).
92. Adams diary, Oct. 15, 1821, Nov. 1, 1821, *MJQA*, 5:359–63, 377–80; Albert Gallatin to Adams, Nov. 16, 1821, in Henry Adams, ed., *The Writings of Albert Gallatin* (Philadelphia: J.B. Lippincott, 1879), 2:212–13; Hollander, "Sea of Troubles," 330–32, 413–16.
93. Martinez, *Slave Trade*, 18–37; Matthew Mason, "Keeping Up Appearances: The International Politics of Slave Trade Abolition in the Nineteenth-Century Atlantic World," *William and Mary Quarterly* 66 (2009): 809–32.
94. Adams diary, June 6, 1817, *MJQA*, 3:556–60; Adams diary, June 19, 1823, *MJQA*, 6:148–545; Paul A. Gilje, *Free Trade and Sailors' Rights in the War of 1812* (New York: Cambridge University Press, 2013), 288–96; Martinez, *Slave Trade*, 38–66; Hugh G. Soulsby, *The Right of Search and the Slave Trade in Anglo-American Relations, 1814–1862* (Baltimore: Johns Hopkins Press, 1933). Adams was apparently not exaggerating the point for rhetorical effect. He had privately described the search right as "more formidable to human liberty than the slave trade itself," and other American officials made the same analogy. Adams diary, Apr. 29, 1819, *MJQA*, 4:353–55; Richard Rush to Adams, June 26, 1818, *ASPFR*, 4:373–74.

In truth, the British proposal for mutual search rights was largely in good faith. British abolitionist William Wilberforce had floated the idea to Thomas Jefferson as early as 1808, and, after Napoleon's surrender, Britain secured similar agreements with several nations, which included the creation of bilateral tribunals that would adjudicate cases of alleged slave trading by vessels of the signatory nations. Betty Fladeland, *Men and Brothers: Anglo-American Antislavery Cooperation* (Urbana: University of Illinois Press, 1972), 107–13; Martinez, *Slave Trade.*

95. Monroe to Daniel Brent, Sep. 15, 1821, Sep. 17, 1821, Sep. 24, 1821, *WJM*, 6:193–203.
96. Adams diary, Nov. 3, 1821, Nov. 7, 1821, Nov. 8, 1821, *MJQA*, 5:380–82, 389, 389–92; Restoration of Africans Recaptured from Pirates, 1 U.S. Op. Atty. Gen. 534 (1822); Restoration of a Danish Slave, 1 U.S. Op. Atty. Gen. 566 (1822).
97. Adams diary, Nov. 8, 1821, *MJQA*, 5:389–92; United States v. Peters, *DHSC*, 6:719–27; The Schooner Exchange v. McFaddon, 11 U.S. 116 (1812).
98. Joseph Story, "A Charge Delivered to the Grand Jury of the Circuit Court of the United States, at its First Session in Portland for the Judicial District of Maine," *MWJS*, 1:122–47; Joseph Story, *A Charge Delivered to the Grand Juries of the Circuit Court at October Term, 1819, in Boston, and at November Term, 1819, in Providence* (Boston, 1819); Paul Finkelman, *Supreme Injustice: Slavery in the Nation's Highest Court* (Cambridge: Harvard University Press, 2018), 119–30.
99. Adams diary, Nov. 1, 1821, Nov. 15, 1821, *MJQA*, 5:376–80, 395–400; Jean Guillaume Hyde de Neuville, *Memoirs of Baron Hyde de Neuville: Outlaw, Exile, Ambassador* (London: Sands & Co., 1913), 2:111.
100. United States v. La Jeune Eugenie, 26 F. Cas. 832, 840 (C.C.D. Mass. 1822).
101. La Jeune Eugenie, 26 F. Cas. at 845, 851; The Plattsburgh, 23 U.S. 133, 142 (1825).
102. La Jeune Eugenie, 26 F. Cas. at 849–50. On France's post-Napoleonic efforts against the slave trade, see Alan Forrest, *The Death of the French Atlantic: Trade, War, and Slavery in the Age of Revolution* (Oxford: Oxford University Press, 2020), 233–69.
103. Le Louis, 165 Eng. Rep. 1464 (1817); La Jeune Eugenie, 26 F. Cas. at 846. Story later admitted to a friend that it was "hard to have Sir William Scott and the Court of King's Bench upon my back." Story to Simon Greenleaf, May 28, 1822, *LLJS*, 1:357. On Story's natural law reasoning in *La Jeune Eugenie*, see Fehrenbacher, *Slaveholding Republic*, 192–93; Gerald T. Dunne, *Justice Joseph Story and the Rise of the Supreme Court* (New York: Simon & Schuster, 1970), 243; R. Kent Newmyer, *Supreme Court Justice Joseph Story: Statesman of*

the Old Republic (Chapel Hill: University of North Carolina Press, 1985), 333–37.

Tellingly, Story supported his argument that legal principles could be widely rejected and still form part of the law of nations by citing the positions that the United States and Great Britain had recently taken on belligerent rights in wartime (which, as we saw in Chapter 5, Story himself was significantly responsible for advancing). Story admitted those doctrines were of "recent origin," and had met the "decided hostility" of some European nations, but the approbation of time and other sovereigns was unnecessary. According to Story, any legal principle deducible "by correct reasoning" could be "enforced by a court of justice." La Jeune Eugenie, 26 F. Cas. at 846.

104. La Jeune Eugenie, 26 F. Cas. at 850–51; Story to Lord Stowell, Jan. 2, 1822, *LLJS*, 1:357–58.

105. Noonan, *Antelope*, 31–50. However callous and negligent, the Supreme Court's delay may have simply been circumstantial. It's docket was perpetually overcrowded, and delays were common. But while evidence is thin that the Monroe administration actively discouraged the Court from hearing the case, there is also no indication that it pushed for a quicker decision. Ibid., 74–92.

106. Hollander, "Sea of Troubles," 502–24; Martinez, *Slave Trade*, 60–66; Soulsby, *Right of Search*, 27–38.

107. Elkison v. Deliesseline, 8 F. Cas. 493 (C.C.D.S.C. 1823); Marshall to Story, Sep. 26, 1823, *PJM*, 9:338–39; Rugemer, *Problem of Emancipation*, 57–67, 78–91; Edlie L. Wong, *Neither Fugitive nor Free: Atlantic Slavery, Freedom Suits, and the Legal Culture of Travel* (New York: New York University Press, 2009), 184–240. On the legal restrictions black mariners faced in the period, see Michael A. Schoeppner, *Moral Contagion: Black Atlantic Sailors, Citizenship, and Diplomacy in Antebellum America* (Cambridge: Cambridge University Press, 2019), 31–63.

108. The Antelope, 23 U.S. 66, 120–23 (1825). In 1842, Story told a friend that he thought he was right in *La Jeune Eugenie*, "and continue[d] to think so." Story to Ezekiel Bacon, Nov. 19, 1842, *LLJS*, 2:431.

109. The Antelope, 23 U.S. at 126–32; Noonan, *Antelope*, 112–32.

110. Marbury v. Madison, 5 U.S. 137 (1803).

111. Adams to Hyde de Neuville, Feb. 22, 1822, *WJQA*, 7:210–12. Adams struck this line from the final version of the letter. Ibid., 212 n. 1.

112. In 1822, Monroe pardoned two convicted slave ship captains on account of their youth and willingness to admit fault. Hollander, "Sea of Troubles," 188–226. John Smith, the *Antelope*'s captain, was tried for piracy but acquitted by a jury. Noonan, *Antelope*, 51–53. In 1862, the government executed a slave ship captain named Nathaniel Gordon. Ron Soodalter, *Hanging Captain Gordon: The Life and Trial of an American Slave Trader* (New York: Washington Square Press, 2006).

113. Robert M. Cover, *Justice Accused: Antislavery and the Judicial Process* (New Haven: Yale University Press, 1975), 238–43; David F. Ericson, "John Quincy Adams: Apostle of Union," in David Waldstreicher, ed., *A Companion to John Adams and John Quincy Adams* (Newark: John Wiley & Sons, 2013), 367–82; Paul Finkelman, "Story Telling on the Supreme Court: *Prigg v. Pennsylvania* and Justice Joseph Story's Judicial Nationalism," *Supreme Court Review* (1994): 247–94; Finkelman, *Supreme Injustice*, 26–75; Newmyer, *Statesman*, 351–79; Daniel Preston, "James Monroe and the Practicalities of Emancipation and Colonization," in Beverly C. Tomek and Matthew J. Hetrick, eds., *New Directions in the Study of African American Recolonization* (Gainesville: University Press of Florida, 2017), 129–45.

114. United States v. La Jeune Eugenie, 26 F. Cas. 832, 850–51 (C.C.D. Mass. 1822); The Antelope, 23 U.S. 66, 88 (1825); Noonan, *Antelope*, 113–14. Story's justification for his disposition of *La Jeune Eugenie* was remarkably unclear. The French owners could not have the ship, he said, because they had violated international and French law. He also seemed to suggest that the naval captain had no right to the vessel because he had not proven it was American-owned (even though Story devoted several pages of his opinion to doubting the truth of French ownership). Marshall's justification for denying the Portuguese claim in the *Antelope* was even more dubious. The question of how many captives should be restored to the Spanish and Portuguese claimants had not even been appealed, and the Supreme Court had recently confirmed what three decades of practice had already established: Foreign consuls could represent their constituents in any court where "the vicissitudes of human affairs may force them." The Bello Corrunes, 19 U.S. 152, 168 (1821).

Epilogue

1. Adams diary, May 11, 1819, *MJQA*, 4:362–63; Adams diary, July 10, 1835, *MJQA*, 9:243–44; Mark A. Graber, "Federalist or Friends of Adams: The Marshall Court and Party Politics," *Studies in American Political Development* 12 (1998): 229–66; Paul C. Nagel, *John Quincy Adams: A Public Life, a Private Life* (New York: Knopf, 1997), 309, 332.

2. John Quincy Adams, First Annual Message, Dec. 6, 1825, in James D. Richardson, ed., *Compilation of the Messages and Papers of the Presidents, 1789–1897* (Washington: Government Printing Office, 1896), 2:299–317; "An Act authorizing an additional naval force for the suppression of piracy," 3 Stat. 720 (1822); "An Act to authorize the building of ten sloops of war," 4 Stat. 131 (1825); Barry Gough and Charles Borras, *The War Against the Pirates: British and American Suppression of Caribbean Piracy in the Early Nineteenth Century* (London: Palgrave Macmillan, 2018), 105–48.

3. *LLJS*, 1:293–303. The 1825 act was especially precise regarding crimes at sea. It detailed both the variety of shipboard assaults that were criminally punishable ("striking, stabbing, wounding, poisoning, or shooting") and the various places to which federal jurisdiction extended ("the high seas, or in any arm of the sea, or in any river, haven, creek, basin, or bay"). "An Act more effectually to provide for the punishment of certain crimes against the United States," § 4, 4 Stat. 115, 115 (1825).
4. United States v. Kessler, 26 F. Cas. 766, 771–74 (C.C.D. Pa. 1829).
5. United States v. The Brig Malek Adhel, 43 U.S. 210 (1844); United States v. Schooner Amistad, 40 U.S. 518 (1841); The Prize Cases, 67 U.S. 635 (1863); John F. Witt, *Lincoln's Code: The Laws of War in American History* (New York: Simon & Schuster, 2012), 141–51.
6. Stuart L. Bernath, *Squall Across the Atlantic: American Civil War Prize Cases and Diplomacy* (Berkeley: University of California Press, 1970).
7. *Prize Cases*, 67 U.S. at 670; Andrew Kent, "The Constitution and the Laws of War During the Civil War," *Notre Dame Law Review* 85 (2010): 1839–1930; Witt, *Lincoln's Code*, 141–51.
8. Johnson v. M'Intosh, 21 U.S. 543, 589 (1823); United States v. Rogers, 45 U.S. 567, 572 (1846); Sarah Cleveland, "Powers Inherent in Sovereignty: Indians, Aliens, Territories, and the Nineteenth Century Origins of Plenary Power over Foreign Affairs," *Texas Law Review* 81 (2002): 1–284. In *Dred Scott*, Taney ruled that the Missouri Compromise of 1820 was unconstitutional. Dred Scott v. Sandford, 60 U.S. 393 (1857). In *Ex parte Merryman*, Taney ruled that President Lincoln did not have the power to suspend the writ of habeas corpus. *Ex parte Merryman*, 17 F. Cas. 144 (C.C.D. Md. 1861).
9. Ping v. United States, 130 U.S. 581, 606 (1889); Ekiu v. United States, 142 U.S. 651, 659 (1892); United States v. Lee, 106 U.S. 196, 209 (1882); Cleveland, "Powers Inherent," 81–163; G. Edward White, "The Transformation of the Constitutional Regime of Foreign Relations," *Virginia Law Review* 85 (1999): 1–150.
10. Cleveland, "Powers Inherent," 273–77; White, "Constitutional Regime of Foreign Relations," 46–146.
11. United States v. Curtiss-Wright Exp. Corp., 299 U.S. 304, 319–20 (1936). For discussions of judicial competency in foreign affairs, see Jack L. Goldsmith, "The New Formalism in United States Foreign Relations Law," *University of Colorado Law Review* 70 (1999): 1395–438; Joel R. Paul, "The Geopolitical Constitution: Executive Expediency and Executive Agreements," *California Law Review* 86 (1998): 671–773; Ganesh Sitaraman and Ingrid Wuerth, "The Normalization of Foreign Relations Law," *Harvard Law Review* 128 (2015): 1897–979.
12. *Curtiss-Wright*, 299 U.S. at 319; Korematsu v. United States, 323 U.S. 214, 220 (1944); Johnson v. Eisentrager, 339 U.S. 763 (1950); Ex parte Quirin, 317 U.S. 1 (1942); Louis Fisher, "Judicial Review of the War

Power," *Presidential Studies Quarterly* 35 (2005): 466–95. The Court's deference was not absolute. In 1952, it ruled that President Eisenhower did not have the authority to seize domestic steel mills in support of the Korean War effort. Youngstown Sheet & Tube Co. v. Sawyer, 343 U.S. 579 (1952).

13. Oetjen v. Central Leather Co., 246 U.S. 297, 302 (1918); Japan Whaling Ass'n v. American Cetacean Society, 478 U.S. 221, 230 (1986). Some commentators question how much force the political question doctrine retains as a general matter, but they concede that it still has an impact in foreign affairs disputes, especially in the lower federal courts. Rachel E. Barkow, "More Supreme than Court? The Fall of the Political Question Doctrine and the Rise of Judicial Supremacy," *Columbia Law Review* 102 (2002): 237–336; Curtis A. Bradley and Eric A. Posner, "The Real Political Question Doctrine," *Stanford Law Review* 75 (2023): 1031–90; Michael E. Tigar, "Judicial Power, the Political Question Doctrine, and Foreign Relations," *UCLA Law Review* 17 (1970): 1135–79.

14. Curtis A. Bradley, "Chevron Deference and Foreign Affairs," *Virginia Law Review* 86 (2000): 649–726; Martin S. Flaherty, *Restoring the Global Judiciary: Why the Supreme Court Should Rule in U.S. Foreign Affairs* (Princeton: Princeton University Press, 2019), 3; Louis Henkin, *Foreign Affairs and the United States Constitution* (New York: Oxford University Press, 1996), 132. On whether judicial deference is waning, compare Sitaraman and Wuerth, "Normalization of Foreign Relations Law," 1924–35; Deborah N. Pearlstein, "After Deference: Formalizing the Judicial Power for Foreign Relations Law," *University of Pennsylvania Law Review* 159 (2011): 783–852, with Carlos M. Vázquez, "The Abiding Exceptionalism of Foreign Relations Doctrine," *Harvard Law Review Forum* 128 (2015): 305–21; Stephen I. Vladeck, "The Exceptionalism of Foreign Relations Normalization," *Harvard Law Review Forum* 128 (2015): 322–30.

15. Martin v. Hunter's Lessee, 14 U.S. 304 (1816); Dartmouth College v. Woodward, 17 U.S. 518 (1819); McCulloch v. Maryland, 17 U.S. 316 (1819); Cohens v. Virginia 19 U.S. 264 (1821); Gibbons v. Ogden, 22 U.S. 1 (1824); Charles F. Hobson, "Defining the Office: John Marshall as Chief Justice," *University of Pennsylvania Law Review* 154 (2006): 1421–61; Robert G. McCloskey, *The American Supreme Court* (Chicago: University of Chicago Press, 2016), 35–52; R. Kent Newmyer, *John Marshall and the Heroic Age of the Supreme Court* (Baton Rouge: Louisiana State University Press, 2001), 267–72; Jean Edward Smith, *John Marshall: Definer of a Nation* (New York: H. Holt & Co., 1998), 417–81.

16. Albert J. Beveridge, *The Life of John Marshall: The Building of the Nation* (Boston: Houghton Mifflin Co., 1919), 4:429–30; Woodrow Wilson, *Constitutional Government in the United States* (New York: Columbia

University Press, 1908), 168; Joel Richard Paul, *Without Precedent: Chief Justice John Marshall and His Times* (New York: Riverhead Books, 2017), 1; James Bradley Thayer, *John Marshall* (Boston: Houghton, Mifflin, 1901), 90; William H. Rehnquist, "John Marshall," *William and Mary Law Review* 43 (2002): 1549–56. For discussions of how Marshall has been characterized over time, see Michael J. Gerhardt, "The Lives of John Marshall," *William and Mary Law Review* 43 (2002): 1399–452; R. Kent Newmyer, "A Judge for All Seasons," *William and Mary Law Review* 43 (2002): 1463–94.

17. *Annals*, 41:1306–8 (Randolph); newspaper quoted in Charles Warren, *The Supreme Court in United States History* (Boston: Little, Brown and Co., 1922), 1:552; Marshall to Story, Sep. 18, 1821, *PJM*, 9:183–85; Marshall to Story, Dec. 30, 1827, *PJM*, 11:64–66; Mark A. Graber, "Federalist or Friends of Adams: The Marshall Court and Party Politics," *Studies in American Political Development* 12 (1998): 229–66; Michael J. Klarman, "How Great Were the Great Marshall Court Decisions?," *Virginia Law Review* 87 (2001): 1111–84; R. Kent Newmyer, "John Marshall, *McCulloch v. Maryland*, and the Southern States' Rights Tradition," *John Marshall Law Review* 33 (2000): 875–934. It is questionable whether Marshall thought the Court's rulings could extend to the abolition of slavery, and he almost certainly did not want them to. He was a slaveholder himself, and a consistent defender of the institution in his judicial rulings. Paul Finkelman, *Supreme Injustice: Slavery in the Nation's Highest Court* (Cambridge: Harvard University Press, 2018), 26–75; John Mikhail, "McCulloch v. Maryland, Slavery, the Preamble, and the Sweeping Clause," *Constitutional Commentary* 36 (2021): 131–47.
18. Bray Hammond, *Banks and Politics in America: From the Revolution to the Civil War* (Princeton: Princeton University Press, 1957), 233–34; Klarman, "How Great," 1126–44; Newmyer, "Southern States' Rights Tradition," 924–26; David S. Schwartz, *The Spirit of the Constitution: John Marshall and the 200-Year Odyssey of McCulloch v. Maryland* (New York: Oxford University Press, 2019), 87–110.
19. Worcester v. Georgia, 31 U.S. 515 (1832); Dred Scott v. Sanford, 60 U.S. 393 (1857); Stuart Banner, *How the Indians Lost Their Land: Law and Power on the Frontier* (Cambridge: Harvard University Press, 2007), 191–227; Don E. Fehrenbacher, *Slavery, Law, and Politics: The Dred Scott Case in Historical Perspective* (New York: Oxford University Press, 1981), 72–120; Alison L. LaCroix, *The Interbellum Constitution Union, Commerce, and Slavery in the Age of Federalisms* (New Haven: Yale University Press, 2024), 285–335.
20. Gerhardt, "Lives of John Marshall," 1408–29; Newmyer, "Judge for All Seasons," 1471–87; Schwartz, *Spirit of the Constitution*, 87–236.
21. Kenneth Cmiel, "The Emergence of Human Rights Politics in the United States," *Journal of American History* 86 (1999): 1231–50; Beth Stephens,

"The Curious History of the Alien Tort Statute," *Notre Dame Law Review* 89 (2014): 1467–543. On the postwar development of human rights globally, see Samuel Moyn, *Not Enough: Human Rights in an Unequal World* (Cambridge: Harvard University Press, 2018).

22. Key works in this voluminous literature include Curtis A. Bradley and Martin S. Flaherty, "Executive Power Essentialism and Foreign Affairs," *Michigan Law Review* 102 (2004): 545–688; Thomas M. Franck, *Political Questions/Judicial Answers: Does the Rule of Law Apply to Foreign Affairs?* (Princeton: Princeton University Press, 1992); Goldsmith, "New Formalism"; Derek Jinks and Neal Kumar Katyal, "Disregarding Foreign Relations Law," *Yale Law Journal* 116 (2007): 1230–83; Saikrishna B. Prakash and Michael D. Ramsey, "The Executive Power over Foreign Affairs," *Yale Law Journal* 111 (2001): 231–356. For brief overviews, see Kevin Arlyck, "The Courts and Foreign Affairs at the Founding," *BYU Law Review* (2017): 1–64; Flaherty, *Global Judiciary*, 3–4.

23. David J. Barron and Martin S. Lederman, "The Commander in Chief at the Lowest Ebb – A Constitutional History," *Harvard Law Review* 121 (2008): 941–1112; Curtis A. Bradley and Jack L. Goldsmith, "Presidential Control over International Law," *Harvard Law Review* 131 (2018): 1201–97; Michael J. Glennon, "Two Views of Presidential Foreign Affairs Power: Little v. Barreme or Curtiss-Wright," *Yale Journal of International Law* 13 (1988): 5–20; Jane Manners, "Executive Power and the Rule of Law in the Marshall Court: A Rereading of *Little v. Barreme* and *Murray v. Schooner Charming Betsy*," *Fordham Law Review* 89 (2021): 1941–74; H. Jefferson Powell, "The Founders and the President's Authority over Foreign Affairs," *William and Mary Law Review* 40 (1999): 1471–537; J. Gregory Sidak, "The Quasi War Cases – and Their Relevance to Whether 'Letters of Marque and Reprisal' Constrain Presidential War Powers," *Harvard Journal of Law & Public Policy* 27 (2005): 465–99; John Yoo, "The Continuation of Politics by Other Means: The Original Understanding of War Powers," *California Law Review* 84 (1996): 167–305.

There are a handful of scholars who have explored the courts' role in the Neutrality Crisis of the 1790s. Arlyck, "Courts and Foreign Affairs," 14–54; William R. Casto, *Foreign Affairs and the Constitution in the Age of Fighting Sail* (Columbia: University of South Carolina Press, 2006); David Sloss, "Judicial Foreign Policy: Lessons from the 1790s," *Saint Louis University Law Journal* 53 (2008): 145–96.

24. Eugene Kontorovich, "A Guantánamo on the Sea: The Difficulty of Prosecuting Pirates and Terrorists," *California Law Review* 98 (2010): 243–75; Gary Williams, "Indefinite Detention and Extraordinary Rendition," *Los Angeles Lawyer* (Sep. 2006): 44–49. On the possibility of applying prize law to modern conflicts in cyberspace and outer space, see Timothy Steigelman, "The Promise and Perils of Prize Law," *World History Connected* 19 (2022): 1–23.

25. Flaherty, *Restoring the Global Judiciary*; Boumediene v. Bush, 553 U.S. 723, 797 (2008); Bradley, "Deference and Foreign Affairs"; Robert M. Chesney, "Disaggregating Deference: The Judicial Power and Executive Treaty Interpretations," *Iowa Law Review* 92 (2007): 1723–74; Pearlstein, "After Deference"; Eric A. Posner and Cass R. Sunstein, "Chevronizing Foreign Relations Law," *Yale Law Journal* 116 (2007): 1170–228.
26. Arlyck, "Courts and Foreign Affairs," 59–60; Jamal Greene, "Giving the Constitution to the Courts," *Yale Law Journal* 117 (2008): 886–919. On whether the FSIA actually serves the goals the State Department had in mind, see Adam S. Chilton and Christopher A. Whytock, "Foreign Sovereign Immunity and Comparative Institutional Competence," *University of Pennsylvania Law Review* 163 (2015): 411–86.
27. Anne-Marie Burley, "The Alien Tort Statute and the Judiciary Act of 1789: A Badge of Honor," *American Journal of International Law* 83 (1989): 461–93; Robert Knowles, "A Realist Defense of the Alien Tort Statute," *Washington University Law Review* 88 (2011): 1117–76; Beth Stephens, "Upsetting Checks and Balances: The Bush Administration's Efforts to Limit Human Rights Litigation," *Harvard Human Rights Journal* 17 (2004): 169–205; Ted Piccone, "The Compounding Rule of Law Crisis," *Brookings* (Nov. 10, 2023), www.brookings.edu/articles/the-compounding-rule-of-law-crisis/.
28. "The Guantanamo Docket," *New York Times* (Feb. 3, 2024), www.nytimes.com/interactive/2021/us/guantanamo-bay-detainees.html; Ashley S. Deeks, "The Observer Effect: National Security Litigation, Executive Policy Changes, and Judicial Deference," *Fordham Law Review* 82 (2013): 827–98; Christopher Ewell, Oona A. Hathaway, and Ellen Nohle, "Has the Alien Tort Statute Made a Difference?: A Historical, Empirical, and Normative Assessment," *Cornell Law Review* 107 (2022): 1205–301; Stephen I. Vladeck, "The D.C. Circuit after Boumediene," *Seton Hall Law Review* 41 (2011): 1451–90; Stephen I. Vladeck, "The Passive-Aggressive Virtues," *Columbia Law Review Sidebar* 111 (2011): 122–40.
29. *John Marshall Bicentennial Celebration, 1955: Final Report* (Washington, DC: Government Printing Office, 1956), 76–83; Gerhardt, "Lives of John Marshall," 1430–35.
30. *Marshall Bicentennial Report*, 76–83; Brown v. Board of Educ. of Topeka, 347 U.S. 483 (1954); Brown v. Bd. of Educ. of Topeka, 349 U.S. 294, 301 (1955); Dwight D. Eisenhower, "Radio and Television Address to the American People on the Situation in Little Rock," Sep. 24, 1957, in *Public Papers of the Presidents of the United States: Dwight D. Eisenhower, 1957* (Washington, DC: Government Printing Office, 1958), 689–94; Mary L. Dudziak, *Cold War Civil Rights: Race and the Image of American Democracy* (Princeton University Press, 2000), 115–51.

31. *Marshall Bicentennial Report*, 83; Erwin Chemerinsky, "The Segregation and Resegregation of American Public Education: The Court's Role," *North Carolina Law Review* 81 (2003): 1597–622; Jonathan Kozol, *The Shame of the Nation: The Restoration of Apartheid Schooling in America* (New York: Crown Publishers, 2005); Gary Orfield and Susan E. Eaton, *Dismantling Desegregation: The Quiet Reversal of Brown v. Board of Education* (New York: New Press, 1996).

Index

Page number in *italics* refers to figure.

STUDIES IN LEGAL HISTORY

(continued from page ii)

Ada Maria Kuskowski, *Vernacular Law: Writing and the Reinvention of Customary Law in Medieval France*

E. Claire Cage, *The Science of Proof: Forensic Medicine in Modern France*

Kristin A. Olbertson, *The Dreadful Word: Speech Crime and Polite Gentlemen in Massachusetts, 1690–1776*

Edgardo Pérez Morales, *Unraveling Abolition: Legal Culture and Slave Emancipation in Colombia*

Lyndsay Campbell, *Truth and Privilege: Libel Law in Massachusetts and Nova Scotia, 1820–1840*

Sara M. Butler, *Pain, Penance, and Protest: Peine Forte et Dure in Medieval England*

Michael Lobban, *Imperial Incarceration: Detention without Trial in the Making of British Colonial Africa*

Stefan Jurasinski and Lisi Oliver, *The Laws of Alfred: The Domboc and the Making of Anglo-Saxon Law*

Sascha Auerbach, *Armed with Sword and Scales: Law, Culture, and Local Courtrooms in London, 1860–1913*

Alejandro de La Fuente and Ariela J. Gross, *Becoming Free, Becoming Black: Race, Freedom, and the Law in Cuba, Virginia, and Louisiana*

Elizabeth Papp Kamali, *Felony and the Guilty Mind in Medieval England*

Jessica K. Lowe, *Murder in the Shenandoah: Making Law Sovereign in Revolutionary Virginia*

Michael A. Schoeppner, *Moral Contagion: Black Atlantic Sailors, Citizenship, and Diplomacy in Antebellum America*

Sam Erman, *Almost Citizens: Puerto Rico, the U.S. Constitution, and Empire*

Martha S. Jones, *Birthright Citizens: A History of Race and Rights in Antebellum America*

Julia Moses, *The First Modern Risk: Workplace Accidents and the Origins of European Social States*

Cynthia Nicoletti, *Secession on Trial: The Treason Prosecution of Jefferson Davis*

Edward James Kolla, *Sovereignty, International Law, and the French Revolution*

Assaf Likhovski, *Tax Law and Social Norms in Mandatory Palestine and Israel*

Robert W. Gordon, *Taming the Past: Essays on Law and History and History in Law*

Paul Garfinkel, *Criminal Law in Liberal and Fascist Italy*

Michelle A. McKinley, *Fractional Freedoms: Slavery, Intimacy, and Legal Mobilization in Colonial Lima, 1600–1700*

Karen M. Tani, *States of Dependency: Welfare, Rights, and American Governance, 1935–1972*

Stefan Jurasinski, *The Old English Penitentials and Anglo-Saxon Law*

Felice Batlan, *Women and Justice for the Poor: A History of Legal Aid, 1863–1945*

Sophia Z. Lee, *The Workplace Constitution from the New Deal to the New Right*

Mitra Sharafi, *Law and Identity in Colonial South Asia: Parsi Legal Culture, 1772–1947*

Michael A. Livingston, *The Fascists and the Jews of Italy: Mussolini's Race Laws, 1938–1943*

For EU product safety concerns, contact us at Calle de José Abascal, 56–1°,
28003 Madrid, Spain or eugpsr@cambridge.org.

www.ingramcontent.com/pod-product-compliance
Lightning Source LLC
LaVergne TN
LVHW091523200926
848483LV00002B/286

* 9 7 8 1 0 0 9 3 9 3 0 6 5 *